The Scientific Basis of Educational Productivity

a volume in
Research in Educational Productivity

Series Editor:
Herbert J. Walberg, *Stanford University Hoover Institution*

Research in Educational Productivity

Herbert J. Walberg, Series Editor

Optimizing Student Success in School With the Other Three Rs: Reasoning, Resilience, and Responsibility (2005)
edited by Robert J. Sternberg and Rena F. Subotnik

Can Unlike Students Learn Together? Grade Retention, Tracking, and Grouping (2004)
edited by Herbert J. Walberg, Arthur J. Reynolds, and Margaret C. Wang

Advancing Educational Productivity: Policy Implications for National Databases (2004)
edited by Susan J. Paik

Successful Reading Instruction (2002)
edited by Michael L. Kamil, JoAnn B. Manning, and Herbert J. Walberg

School Reform Proposals: The Research Evidence (2002)
edited by Alex Molnar

Efficiency, Accountability, and Equity Issues in Title I Schoolwide Program Implementation (2002)
edited by Kenneth Wong and Margaret C. Wang

Improving Educational Productivity (2001)
edited by David H. Monk, Margaret C. Wang, and Herbert J. Walberg

The Scientific Basis of Educational Productivity

edited by

Rena F. Subotnik
American Psychological Association Center for Psychology in Schools and Education

and

Herbert J. Walberg
Stanford University Hoover Institution

Greenwich, Connecticut
www.infoagepub.com

Published in cooperation with

Library of Congress Cataloging-in-Publication Data

The scientific basis of educational productivity / edited by Rena F. Subotnik and Herbert J. Walberg
p. cm. -- (Research in educational productivity)
Includes bibliographical references.
ISBN 1-59311-449-4 (paperback) -- ISBN 1-59311-450-8 (hardcover)
1. Educational productivity--United States--Congresses. 2. Education--Research--United States--Congresses. 3. Education--United States--Evaluation--Congresses. I. Subotnik, Rena Faye. II. Walberg, Herbert J., 1937- III. Series.
LB2806.24.S35 2005
370.7'2--dc22

2005025936

Printed in the United States of America

The Mid-Atlantic Regional Educational Laboratory, the Laboratory for Student Success (LSS), is one of 10 regional educational laboratories funded by the Institute of Education Sciences (IES) of the U.S. Department of Education. LSS seeks to significantly improve the capacity of the region—including Delaware, Maryland, New Jersey, Pennsylvania, and Washington, DC—and the nation to enact and sustain systemic educational reform. LSS aims to transform research-based knowledge into useful tools that can be readily integrated into the educational reform process.

CONTENTS

PREFACE

Herbert J. Walberg

American citizens, including parents, educators, and policymakers, have increasingly realized that our schools need to be more productive if we are to give our children the best chances for themselves and for our nation's continued prosperity, democracy, health, and values and ideals we dearly hold. Students need to learn more. Among other things, they need to read well; calculate; compute; understand science; know U.S. history, civics, and geography; understand world history; and appreciate art and music.

This volume, however, is not primarily concerned with what students should learn, nor even how they should learn. Rather it concerns how we can discover the best means and conditions for teaching them in school, at home, and in society. Expressed more explicitly, we seek to find out how students can learn efficiently or productively as much as possible within a given amount of time and resources. As in agriculture, medicine, public health, and modern industries, we can turn to rigorous science as one of the best sources for informing ourselves.

Thus, the purpose of this book was to present a variety of views of first-class authorities who could help in such efforts. The intended audiences are not only scholars in a variety of academic disciplines but also research consumers, including educators, policymakers, parents, and citizens who seek principles to critically separate valid from invalid claims for the efficacy and efficiency of education products, personnel, and policies.

Initial versions of the chapters were discussed at a national invitational conference sponsored by the Laboratory for Student Success (LSS), the mid-Atlantic regional educational laboratory, at Temple University Center for Research in Human Development and Education. LSS operates under a contract with the U.S. Department of Education's Institute of Education Sciences.

The conference was cosponsored by the American Psychological Association (APA). Rena Subotnik, Director of the APA's Center for Psychology in Schools and Education, provided much of the scholarly leadership for the conference and this book. Two former APA presidents participated in the conference and wrote chapters for this book.

At the conference, the chapter authors benefited from discussions with one another, other scholars, policymakers, educators, and parents. The consensual recommendations of the conference participants are reported in the last chapter.

C. Kent McGuire, Dean of the College of Education at Temple University, and Marilyn Murphy, Co-director of LSS, inspired, supported, and participated in the conference. Julia St. George and Robin Neal helped plan and coordinate the conference to ensure it was well managed and productive. Stephen Page, together with Danielle Shaw and Robert Sullivan, provided skilled copy editing of the papers.

As a long-time coordinator of the book–conference series, I express my gratitude to the chapter authors and the others who contributed their special talents to the preparation of this book.

Herbert J. Walberg
June 2005

CHAPTER 1

INTRODUCTION AND OVERVIEW

Rena F. Subotnik and Herbert J. Walberg

This volume, titled *The Scientific Basis of Educational Productivity*, emerged from a conference sponsored by the Laboratory for Student Success and the American Psychological Association. The book and its companion conference were founded on the idea that education research can, and must, be rigorous to contribute substantially to education reform and the improvement of American students' achievement. Although a variety of scientific approaches to research are represented, the book emphasizes the special credibility of multiple methods and multiple studies converging on policy- and practice-relevant results.

As evidenced by the federal No Child Left Behind Act and more stringent testing and accountability systems in the states, rigorous methods to assess the effectiveness of educational interventions are particularly needed for K–12 school reform. Educators need definitive findings about what effectively and efficiently raises achievement and contributes to success of their students.

The Scientific Basis of Educational Productivity, 1–8

ASSESSING THE ADVANTAGES OF VARIOUS RESEARCH DESIGNS

Experiments are not foolproof in determining causality: students in an experimental group may not have been given the treatment with complete fidelity, the outcome measures may be insensitive, or a "Hawthorne effect" of being in a special group may elicit greater motivation among experimental students. In well-designed experiments, however, such threats to experimental validity can be enumerated, explicated, and taken into consideration.

Randomized control-group experimentation is one of several ways to seek causal confidence. Single-subject studies, for example, obtain many observations over time while employing random, on-again, off-again treatment and control conditions to a single subject.

In some cases, however, randomization may not be feasible. Two of the most controversial policies in education—school choice and accountability for results—are of keen interest to policymakers. Yet neither can easily be randomly assigned to schools or school districts. Detailed descriptive methods can illuminate how causality may work or not work in various contexts. Confidence in all such methods and their results grows when many studies yield converging evidence suggesting the same policies and practical implications.

MODELS IN EDUCATIONAL PRODUCTIVITY

Since models should also serve as both the source and product of high-quality research, this book includes three models relevant to improving the academic and life skills of students in our schools. Each has been tested extensively, and each was derived from previous studies that neglected to explain sufficiently how to maximize student potential.

A disadvantage of working with a model or theoretical framework is that, when it is applied to school contexts, the central concepts may be misinterpreted or may be poorly implemented. Thoughtful theoreticians and model builders testing their work in schools ensure fidelity through multiple forms of implementation and through searches through the literature for confirmation of similar outcomes from a variety of different sources.

APPLYING SCIENTIFIC EVIDENCE TO PROFESSIONAL PRACTICE

Once an effective program has been devised, tested, implemented, and evaluated, policymakers must approve its use in professional settings. Even so, practitioners may not welcome the intervention if it is not introduced appropriately. Too often, evidence-based practices are ignored while less effective but cheaper, easier, or more popular interventions are widespread, particularly in K–12 classrooms. The goal of this book is to promote scientifically based practice designed to ensure academic and life success for students in our schools.

CHAPTER OVERVIEW

The Scientific Basis for Educational Productivity is divided into four parts: The first part reviews selected methods of research, the second explores the development of models and theories that focus on educational productivity, and the third section describes actual and prospective applications of scientific methods to real problems in education. The final chapter includes recommendations for policy and practice derived from the chapter contributions and the face-to-face deliberations conducted at the conference that preceded the publication of the book.

Methodology

The first section on methodology begins with a chapter by Susan J. Paik, of Clarmount Graduate University. Her paper provides readers with an overview of the key elements of experimental research design as well as the reasons rigorous research is so important to the success of school reform. Although she presents a rank ordering of research design quality, Paik notes that design choices are dependent on the problem being addressed. For the purposes of policymaking, however, randomized control-group studies may provide the best evidence for the effectiveness of interventions. In light of feasibility and practicality, Paik also discusses the alternative of rigorous quasi-experimental research designs.

Paik outlines criteria for analyzing the quality of research designs and discusses threats to internal and external validity illustrated through school-based examples. Readers will find invaluable a list of important questions to ask when reviewing or conducting research. These questions help assess, on a case-by-case basis, whether a design is suited to the question or problem at hand. Although the highest quality designs are often the most difficult to conduct, Paik urges us to put forth our most rigorous efforts at solving pressing academic problems.

Joe Layng and his Headsprout colleagues, Greg Stikeleather and Janet Twyman, bring to bear their expertise on the contributions of single-subject design to the scientific generation and prediction of educational productivity. In establishing the framework for their chapter, they draw our attention to the fact that some interventions have been designed based on evidence and can be called research based. Some interventions might not be research based but have been subjected to scientific evaluation. Such interventions might be called "research filtered."

The chapter explains the role of single-subject control analysis in assessing the effectiveness of an intervention. The Headsprout group offers a powerful analogy comparing the preparation of an aircraft to fly to teaching a child to read. Manufacturers do not test one plane against another. Instead, they test the planes, make revisions, and then retest the planes. This form of formative or "research-guided" evaluation is offered as a reliable method for ensuring program success, and the three-by-three matrix at the end of the chapter provides an elegant summary of the authors' argument.

Reading competency is crucial for student success. Elizabeth Pang and Michael Kamil, of the Singapore Ministry of Education and Stanford University, respectively, summarize and analyze the reading strategies taught to preservice and inservice teachers. Although policymakers might seek to know the effect of teacher education and professional development on student reading achievement, the research reviewed by the authors yields consistent results based on a relatively small number of studies.

Of the 306 studies reviewed by Pang and Kamil, 267 were categorized as nonexperimental and 39 as experimental or quasi-experimental studies. Only 4% of preservice preparation studies used experimental or quasi-experimental designs, precluding insights into the effectiveness of preservice interventions. Research on inservice professional development used experimental methods more frequently (36% of the studies), but the number of studies, 28, was small. Although Pang and Kamil cite the important contributions of nonexperimental studies to understanding reflective teaching and teacher decision making, they promote a future for educational research that carefully delineates the assumptions behind published research, uses mixed methods, and reflects greater familiarity on the part of scholars with a range of research paradigms.

Models and Theories

Diane Halpern, past president of the American Psychological Association and psychology professor at Claremont McKenna College, challenges us to consider critical thinking as a key factor contributing to educational productivity. Halpern has devoted much of her scholarly career to demonstrating scientific support for enhancing students' thinking skills, especially their abilities to think critically. She argues that teaching for transfer of critical thinking skills to classroom settings and beyond is the only acceptable outcome of educational interventions in this arena.

To address the "messiness" of real-life contexts, her investigations employ an instrument titled "The Critical Thinking Assessment About Everyday Events," which elicits responses to innovative scenarios. Halpern proposes that, although controlled experimental studies help us to know whether an intervention really worked, an insufficient number of such studies have been conducted. Therefore, "a large effect size summarized over a large number of diverse studies from many different participants and contexts also provides good evidence, even if it is not strictly causal." Halpern concludes by suggesting that, because of the importance of critical thinking to educational productivity, financial and intellectual investment must be made to promote further experimental studies of critical thinking intervention studies.

Herbert Walberg, emeritus professor of education and psychology at the University of Illinois at Chicago and now Distinguished Visiting Fellow at the Stanford University Hoover Institution, exemplifies the goals of the conference and book project by providing readers with a comprehensive analysis of substantive research associated with educational productivity. The purpose of his analysis is to provide policymakers and educators with the information they need to make policy, improve the preparation of teachers, and base school reform on scientific evidence. As a basis for Walberg's conceptions of educational productivity, he has conducted wide-ranging syntheses of research literature, with a particular emphasis on meta-analyses and econometric analyses of large-scale surveys.

Walberg compares the productivity of schools with the rest of the American economy. In general, schools are not efficient in increasing the intellectual capacity of children. The comparison is of concern because the future of the country's economic productivity is related to the success of schools in developing informed, responsible, thoughtful citizens. Walberg's analysis provides readers with factors that enhance and impede student learning according to their proportional learning influences. With Walberg's conceptualization, policymakers have a superb tool for assessing the efficacy and efficiency of various interventions in relationship to available time, money, and expertise.

Robert Sternberg, dean of arts and sciences at Tufts University, and a former president of the American Psychological Association, guides readers through the development of his theory of intelligence from its beginnings as a concept to testing instructional materials based on the theory. Sternberg views successful intelligence as a useful goal for schooling, more so than traditional notions of achievement. At each stage of his argument, Sternberg demonstrates the rigorous thinking required to introduce change in schools that will promote both increased achievement and the acquisition of important life skills.

The chapter describes the efforts made by Sternberg and his team to ensure internal and external validation of the theory. The descriptions of their efforts provide readers with a model for applying other theories to the rigors of testing. Notably, the devotion of time, money, and talent to theory development and testing needs to be conducted on ideas and models that can reasonably be expected to make a difference in educational productivity and quality of life.

Applications to Education Professions and Problems

Lisa Towne of the National Research Council (NRC) provides readers with a comprehensive view of the central role played by the NRC in helping to shape discussions surrounding definitions of high-quality education research. The debate she describes is an old one, but the heat of the arguments has not diminished. The work conducted by the NRC provides a platform for reasoned discussion of the contributions of science to the messy realm of education policy and practice.

For 50 years, the NRC has addressed questions associated with the quality, organization, and use of education research. In the past 5 years, through a series of books, forums, and dialogues, the NRC has debunked myths related to the nature of methodology and the progression of scientific understanding in education. Towne challenges us to embrace scientifically based educational research and to integrate its concepts throughout the educational system, with a focus on teacher preparation and professional development.

Kathleen Madigan, former president of the American Board for Certification of Teaching Excellence (ABCTE), applies econometric, psychometric, and experimental studies to addressing the shortage of teachers prepared to improve the academic achievement of children and youth. A panel of experts worked with ABCTE to identify the research-based teaching skills and content knowledge essential to success as a beginning teacher. ABCTE's staff and expert panelists categorized the professional knowledge literature that met criteria of rigor into five key areas: organizing, planning, and designing instruction for student success; effective instructional strategies; classroom management and organization; monitoring students and working with parents; and assessment.

Panelists translated identified skills and concepts into test items, many of which used innovative interactive technologies. After the test items had been created and reviewed, the next task involved field-testing with more than 2,000 individuals who met specific demographic characteristics. The results of field-testing generated data about the performance of each item and informed the process for determining test score cutoffs that reflect levels of candidate competence. This chapter provides readers with an example of applying standards of science to the process of assessing professional preparation for K–12 classrooms, and it complements the work conducted by the other authors of this section.

Thomas Kratochwill's chapter offers a comprehensive view of the efforts made by school psychologists to document, organize, and implement their evidence-based practices. Although we would hope that every profession aspired to a scientific foundation for its activities, many health and education disciplines rely heavily on professional judgment free of empirical support. This work models how a group of scholar–practitioners can reflect on the science behind all aspects of their profession including education, testing, evaluation, and clinical practice.

School psychologists serve at the interface of mental health and education sciences, and their work is central to providing a holistic picture of educational productivity. Educators tend to underutilize school psychologists' expertise, especially in areas of prevention and intervention programs for mental health. The research literature in school psychology, moreover, is underused in educational planning and productivity. This chapter should help to bridge these gaps.

The What Works Clearinghouse (WWC) was designed to evaluate and catalogue the knowledge base for education science. Robert Boruch from the University of Pennsylvania and Rebecca Herman from Johns Hopkins University provide readers with a guided tour of the WWC, including its history, its long- and short-term goals, and how it processes and reviews studies.

The WWC began as an initiative of the Institute of Education Sciences in 2001. Its first priority was to delineate the standards for judging the effectiveness of an intervention. Most of the work evaluated by the WWC relies on well-designed randomized trials. Topics and interventions are selected based on the centrality of the problem to policy and practice. After multiple studies on the same intervention are collected and analyzed, the WWC publishes a Topic Area Report. The WWC's challenge is staggering, yet it has already provided educators and scholars with invaluable tools for policy, practice, and research.

Thus, Part One explicates and illustrates fundamental scientific methods for educational research, policy, and practice. Part Two concentrates on models and theories associated with educational productivity. Part Three focuses on single projects—several in conjunction with qualitative research methods—that exemplify outstanding uses of these methods. Part Four includes our recommendations for policy and practice.

CONCLUSIONS

The authors of this volume represent a variety of scientific approaches. They submitted chapter drafts for discussion at our cosponsored conference. The main work of the conference took place in smaller groups, each representing important stakeholders in the education community. With a chair and recorder for each group, the task of each group—based on the conference papers, discussion, and members' own experience—was to develop consensus around next steps for applying scientific methods to questions of educational policy and practice, and in deriving valid implications from extant and future research. Reported briefly and orally at the end of the conference, the synthesized recommendations serve as the basis for the last chapter in this book.

CHAPTER 2

EVIDENCE-BASED REFORM

Experimental and Quasi-Experimental Research Considered

Susan J. Paik

What constitutes good research? Considered one of the most important topics by educators and policymakers today, this question continues to be asked. Justifiably so. For decades, poorly designed studies have yielded insufficient information for improving student achievement. The United States not only continues to rank close to last in international achievement surveys, but progress remains stagnant as confirmed by the National Assessment of Educational Progress (NAEP) that shows nearly flat achievement results during the past three decades. Consequently, rigorous research is of high priority and evidence is the key to educational reform at all levels.

In 2001, the No Child Left Behind (NCLB) Act stated that educational research should be rigorous, using "scientifically based research." Critics have long remarked that educational research is too "soft" and should return to the gold standard of research: experiments employing random assignment and control groups. Rigorous research standards including experiments have returned to education under the influence of other

The Scientific Basis of Educational Productivity, 9–28

fields such as medicine, agriculture, and technology. Economists have also increasingly explored and utilized experimentation to establish fundamental economic principles that involve benefit, cost, and risk.

Increasingly, educational policy and reform are based on programs and practices that actually work. Driven by evidence-based reform, this new era of educational research has substantial implications for improving achievement, attitudes, behavior, and other outcomes. Experiments may not be the only solution to what makes good educational research, but they have proven themselves in the development of effective drugs, building better crops, and improving technology. Though there are several means of valid research, well-executed experiments are generally superior in ascertaining causality, which is a key question in formulating policy and practice.

In the field of education, some reforms have been effective, but unfortunately many are ineffective. Too often, interpretations are made from biased reports rather than evidence-based data. For many policymakers, researchers, and educators, concerns have grown, especially about academic achievement, since the dismal results of the well-known report *A Nation at Risk* (National Commission on Excellence in Education, 1983). In a country driven by performance-based results where achievement scores lag behind international competitors, how can we know if programs affect such achievement and other outcomes?

This chapter is divided into three parts and draws from the classic work of Campbell and Stanley (1963), the comprehensive analysis of Cook and Campbell (1979), and the most recent work by Shaddish, Cook, and Campbell (2002). Following a brief description of the history of experimentation, Part I introduces three kinds of research designs: pre-experimental, quasi-experimental, and experimental designs. This section also presents the hallmarks of good research and provides a basic outline and important questions in evaluating experiments.

Part II presents examples of the most common research designs. This section illustrates the advantages of using experimental research along with its disadvantages. While experiments provide more confident causal conclusions, there may be real-world constraints. In the ideal world, experiments might be the best solution to what makes good research, but essential resources such as time, money, and even ethics can raise issues of feasibility and practicality. As alternatives, quasi-experimental designs may provide indications of cause and effect, especially when considering naturally formed groups, such as families, classrooms, and schools. Randomly controlling participants who fall into these groups may not be as easily manipulated in natural settings. And finally, Part II presents pre-experimental designs as pitfalls to effective research as they are the least rigorous design. These designs should be considered the last option or as preliminary pilot studies for future work.

Part III discusses the threats to the validity of research. Although Campbell and Stanley (1963) and Cook and Campbell (1979) originally presented four types of validity (statistical conclusion,[1] internal, external, and construct validity[2]), this chapter focuses on the two most common threats as found in most references: internal and external validity (Krathwohl, 1998; Patten, 2002). Clear examples of rival explanations are presented to illustrate possible threats. This section concludes with a brief discussion on analytic threats that may be additional threats to studies.

The chapter ends with recommendations for good research. The terminology in this chapter draws mostly from the original work of Campbell and Stanley (1963). For an exhaustive list and description of experimental and quasi-experimental designs, readers can consult Shaddish, Cook, and Campbell (2002).

BACKGROUND

In the 1960s, the short golden age of education research may have started with Donald Campbell and Julian Stanley (1963) through their chapter in the *Handbook of Research on Teaching*. Campbell and Stanley showed how true experiments usually produced more confident causal conclusions than quasi-experiments on programs, curricula, and teaching effects when students were randomly assigned to experimental and control groups. Although quasi-experiments make use of statistical controls for preexisting differences among groups in an effort to equate them, random assignment minimizes the chance of differences, thereby reducing threats to the validity of studies. Cook and Campbell (1979) refined and elaborated these original ideas and also recorded the various threats to the validity of experimental research, incorporating Bracht and Glass's (1968) threats to external validity.

Following the short age of experimental research, case studies and other forms of qualitative research became increasingly popular. Consequently, experiments were used less often in mainstream educational research. Psychologists continued with experiments, though they often focused on phenomena that educators viewed with questionable relevance to problems and decisions they faced.

Recently, the National Reading Panel (NRP) emphasized the importance of rigorous research. Established by Congressional mandate to summarize research-based knowledge and commissioned by the National Institute of Child Health and Human Development (2000), the NRP reviewed the enormous body of existing research on the teaching of reading. The Panel uncovered 1,962 articles on phonemic awareness ("PA"), of which only 52 articles were scientifically rigorous. The rigorous studies showed one of the largest effects (.86) ever uncovered in the field of educational research, which would place the average student instructed in PA at the 80th percentile of control groups using other methods.

In 2002, the National Research Council of the National Academy of Sciences noted the benefits of experiments: the relevance of research to theory and practice, the importance of statistical controls, and the compliance with rigorous research standards. In 2003, the new Institute of Education Sciences (IES) released "Identifying and Implementing Educational Practices Supported by Rigorous Evidence: A User Friendly Guide" (2003) to promote scientifically based research as noted in NCLB. IES seems unlikely to fund research that fails to meet such criteria.

The new research standards allow us to determine the scientific rigor or validity of any given evaluation or study. More rigorous designs employed allow greater confidence in the conclusions of educational research. Similarly, fields such as agriculture, medicine, and technology scientifically established a foundation for large productivity gains. Understanding what contributes to effective research is a step towards improving educational reform and productivity in the United States.

PART I: RESEARCH DESIGNS AND HALLMARKS OF GOOD RESEARCH

This section begins with the introduction of three designs: pre-experiments, quasi-experiments, and true experiments. To provide a basic understanding of well-designed experimental studies, this section highlights the hallmarks to making good research and provides an outline of important questions to ask when designing or evaluating an experiment.

Types of Experimental Designs

Experimental designs have at least one independent variable and one dependent variable. At least one group receives treatment (the experimental group), but may not have a control group (a group that receives no treatment). The treatment (e.g., teaching methods and program effectiveness) is the independent variable since it can physically manipulate other variables. The dependent variable is the outcome (e.g., achievement and attitude). The purpose of experimental designs is to determine if the independent variables cause any changes in the dependent variables.

As an example, Mrs. Warden wants to know if the new math book is helping her sixth-grade students to develop math skills. She decides to give them a pretest before using the book. The experimental group receiving treatment is Mrs. Warden's students. The hypothesized independent variable (the stimulus or the possible "cause") is the new math book. The dependent variable (what is being observed or the "effect") is learning. Learning can be "operationalized" or operationally defined as math test scores. After 4 weeks, Mrs. Warden gives them a posttest and compares both scores. Because their scores are higher, she concludes that the new math book has worked.

The goal of experimental designs is to determine a cause-and-effect relationship. Did the new math book really cause scores to increase? How can Mrs. Warden be sure that increased scores are attributable to the book? Such possible "cause-and-effect" relationships can be assessed through three main designs:

Pre-experimental designs.[3] Pre-experiments focus on a single treated group and have no control group. Posttest only and pretest–posttest designs without control groups are usually uninformative. Unfortunately, evaluators often confront situations in which a control group is lacking. Using the earlier example, Mrs. Warden used a pretest–posttest design without a control group. Determining the effectiveness of the new math book from the scores of a single group may not be credible without a comparable group even if pretest and posttest scores are compared. The students, for example, may have learned much of the math content in a physics class or perhaps Mrs. Warden's excellent teaching caused the gains. Mrs. Warden still does not have any valid evidence to establish a cause-and-effect relationship with this design since it is hard to rule out alternative explanations.

Quasi-experimental designs. Quasi-experiments are characterized by nonrandomly assigned participants to experimental and control groups that may have initially differed. If Mrs. Warden decided to compare two groups, but she did not randomly assign students to a control and experimental group, superiority of the new math book may still be attributable to their physics instruction or other uncontrolled factors. Alternative explanations still exist. Students may have even remembered what was on the test after taking it a second time. Remembering test items would certainly raise scores the second time. Although better than a pre-experimental design, quasi-experiments have validity issues since students were not randomly assigned.

Experimental designs. True experiments are characterized by research's gold standard: random assignment to experimental and control groups. Compared to the previous designs, experiments can better assess a cause-and-effect relationship. For example, let's say that Mrs. Warden decided to use randomly assigned control and experimental groups. She picked names out of a hat and placed students in the control group and experimental group. The experimental group used the new book. The control group used a regular book. After comparing pretest and posttest scores, she found that students actually did better using the new book. This finding is more credible than the other two designs because there is no reason to think the groups initially differed.

Of the thousands of educational studies, however, many do not have this feature because it is difficult to assign students, teachers, and schools in this way. Unless carefully designed, we may only find out about how students perform in artificially contrived conditions rather than in everyday circumstances.

Compared to pre-experiments and quasi-experiments, true experiments have fewer threats to internal validity, which is further discussed in Part III. Experiments have the strongest internal validity, because causal efficacy can be attributed to either the treatment or random differences. With other designs, there are possible alternative explanations. The following section discusses ways to strengthen the internal validity of studies.

Hallmarks of Good Research

The features described below are hallmarks of effective research since they increase the internal validity of a study by reducing threats to studies and systematically controlling for variables. Although not an exhaustive list, this section describes the most common factors of rigorous research.

The **Gold** *Standard*

Random Assignment and Control Groups. Randomly assigning students means that each participant has an equal chance of being in control or experimental groups. For example, by flipping a coin, two equally distributed groups might be presumed the same on all variables except for possible random differences. Since inferential statistics can assess random errors, we can tolerate random variations in their effects. Both groups of students randomly selected are considered "equal" in all respects except for the treatment. The cause in differences could be explained by either the treatment or random errors. Although randomization is the gold standard, it may be difficult and expensive to achieve as naturally formed groups, such as families, classes, and schools must be sampled.

Statistical Power and Significance

Matching. If random assignment is not possible, matching characteristics of participants or schools may provide some confidence in results only if the experimental and control groups are similar. For example, in a matched study, students in a class receiving treatment are matched with those in a control group by test scores, ability, socioeconomic status, age, gender, etc. The goal is to make treatment and control groups "equal" with the same characteristics from the matching variables. Though often more feasible and more commonly used, matching is still inferior to random assignment, since any causal inferences assume that the students are matched on all relevant factors. It still bears risks of some incomparability, especially if participants drop out of the study.

Statistical Controls. By using statistical controls for initial status and conditions of the groups, experiments and quasi-experiments may be strengthened substantially. For example, the best statistical controls are pretest achievement scores, since learning over time is of chief interest. Pretest scores are used to compare gains from pretest to posttest scores, but are not always easy to obtain since students move and classroom groups do not remain intact. Statistical controls usually increase the power of a design to detect effects, but may not control for all initial variations among groups.

Increase Sample Size. The larger the sample size, the more power to detect effects. How many is enough? The answer to this question is not a simple one, but common sense tells us that the more, the better. For example, investigating one public school in the city of Chicago might not be as telling as studying 10 public schools. By increasing the sample size, the schools might be more representative of schools in general in most urban cities. The key, however, is to make sure the pool is unbiased and representative of the population. Researchers can also use a power analysis to identify the most appropriate sample size for groups.

Effect Sizes. Evaluators and other researchers are interested in knowing whether experimental groups score significantly higher or lower than control groups on outcome measures. Effect sizes are helpful because they inform us on *how* much better (or worse) the experimental groups performed. The formula for calculating effect sizes is to divide the difference between program and control group means by the standard deviation of the control group. Underlying scores are usually raw scores, normal curve equivalents, or other equal interval expressions. In short, effect sizes enable rough comparisons of effects despite use of different tests in more than one study.

Valid and Reliable Measures

Nationally Standardized Tests. Valid and reliable measures are essential to avoid bias. In the past, program developers designed their own achievement tests and other assessments to measure the degree to which they have accomplished their particular objectives. But these tests do not answer the consumer question of how well the students do on more broadly acknowledged criteria. To answer their question, the Stanford, Iowa, and Metropolitan tests can be cited as examples of widely used tests to assess students, schools, districts, and programs. As with most measures in psychology and the social sciences, their published materials are far from perfect, though do provide technical information on their scope, validity, and reliability. The publishers provide results based on national random samples in terms of percentiles or grade equivalents.

Calibrated Developer Tests. What happens if scores on nationally standardized tests are unavailable? In such cases, we may have to rely on developer tests alone. It will be highly desirable to show that the developer tests correlate substantially with nationally standardized tests. The tests could also be calibrated as scores expressed on national scales such as grade equivalents. Comparing scores from national standardized tests with developer tests can be difficult and controversial.

Value-Added Gains. When using standardized tests to compare measures, value-added gains are better than status scores in measuring learning. Value-added scores are the gains from one test administration to another. For example, if we wanted to know if Mrs. Warden's students did better in sixth grade than in fifth grade, we would take the difference of the scores, rather than just the sixth-grade scores. Thus, schools serving disadvantaged children may have made excellent value-added progress even though their sixth-grade achievement scores are low. Similarly, achievement scores in affluent neighborhoods may be misleading in suggesting school effectiveness. Achievement scores may have been largely determined by their social advantages. In summary, value-added analysis takes into consideration how much students have learned rather than where they stand at the end of an experiment or quasi-experiment. Many evaluations and studies are currently using gains, rather than scores, as their indicators.

Designing an Experiment

When conducting an experiment, it is helpful to keep in mind that experimental designs follow a similar format. Although true experiments are more promising than pre- and quasi-experimental designs, the hallmarks of good research as mentioned above depend upon many variables. Randomly assigning participants to control groups and controlling for any environmental influences, such as properly administering treatment to experimental groups, are only some of the elements that contribute to an effective study. The questions outlined below in Table 2.1 may be helpful in designing and determining the validity of an experimental study.[4]

Table 2.1. Important Questions to Ask

A. Research Hypotheses:
   1. What is the specific research question?
   2. What kind of design is most appropriate?

B. Variables:
   1. What is/are the independent variable(s)?
   2. What is/are the dependent variable(s)?

C. Population:
   1. Who are the participants?
   2. How will they be selected? Will group membership be determined by random selection?
   3. Is the population sample size large enough?

D. Methods & Procedures:
   1. What kinds of materials will be involved?
   2. How will treatment be administered?
   3. How will you protect the participants?
   4. How can you control for rival explanations?

E. Instrumentation:
   1. What kinds of measures will be used?
   2. Are they reliable and valid?
   3. How will they be administered?

F. Data Analysis:
   1. How will the data be analyzed?
   2. How will they be reported?
   3. Who is the audience?

G. Conclusion & Recommendations
   1. What did you gain from this study?
   2. What kinds of recommendations can you make?

PART II: TECHNICAL DESIGNS AND EXAMPLES

This section presents the most widely used research designs and explores their merits and practicality.

Pre-Experimental Designs

As mentioned earlier, pre-experimental designs are weak and susceptible to many threats. The first of three common but flawed one-group designs is the *one-shot case study*. Treatment is administered to one group and then measured. This design measures results without regard to other groups. For example, if we wanted to understand if computerized instruction increased learning, the study could be followed with a test. Although scores might be high, it is almost impossible to tell whether using computers promoted a desired effect, or whether achievement scores were caused by other factors (e.g., motivated students and good teachers). Since many factors could account for the scores, this design tells us very little about what might be causing the effect and how well students might be performing without a control group. Unfortunately, according to Campbell and Stanley (1963), "such studies have such a total absence of control as to be of almost no scientific value" (p. 6).

The *one-group pretest–posttest design*, although widely used and better than the one-shot case study, is flawed because changes may be attributed to factors other than the treatment. For example, pretest scores and posttest scores are compared after computerized instruction. If students scored higher on the posttest than the pretest, one might conclude that computerized instruction influenced the scores. Unfortunately, other explanations could also explain a change in scores, and the study yields no information on the cause of higher scores. High scores might result from an easier posttest. Low initial scores may have resulted from a distraction in the classroom. Overall, this type of study is not scientifically rigorous, because there are many confounding variables with alternative explanations.

The third pre-experimental design is the *static-group comparison or posttest only design with nonequivalent groups*. The experimental group is compared to a comparable group and tested after the treatment. Subjects are not randomly assigned. The two groups formed from previously existing groups are intact. While this may seem more credible than the other designs, there is no way to ensure that the two groups started at the same level. Using the example of computerized instruction, let's say Class A is a required class that all students take during school hours. Class B is an elective class after school for those who want to learn more. This class might attract students who are more motivated and intelligent, and thus attain higher achievement scores. Although better than the first two designs, the static group comparison is still susceptible to many threats.

Quasi-Experimental Designs

Quasi-experiments may be the best option when true experiments are not possible, and are therefore widely employed. Quasi-experiments are very similar to true experiments, except participants are not randomly assigned to control groups and treatment groups. For example, students in one school are a control group and those in another are the experimental group. Since students were not assigned to schools at random, the two groups may have been initially different. Even so, quasi-experimental designs can be worthwhile if we can assume rival causes have been statistically controlled.

Single-group experimental designs. A *time series design* or *single-group interrupted time series design* involves a series of periodic observations or measurements. Measures of a single group are recorded before and after the treatment. An example might be an 8-week reading class to increase learning. The researcher would make daily or weekly classroom observations to establish a benchmark. While subjects receive treatment (e.g., new instructional technique), periodic observations after 4 weeks could be made after the treatment. A large achievement jump with the introduction of the treatment may indicate a caused effect. This design also lacks control over influences outside the classroom. A national crisis or even simply the weather, for example, could explain changes in the subjects as readily as the treatment.

The *equivalent time-samples design* is for use with a single subject or group. In this case, control and experimental participants are the same individuals. The equivalent time-samples design is a recurrent approach, which alternates the treatment on and off at various intervals. Results are compared between episodes when the treatment is present to when the treatment is absent. This design works well with treatment effects that are short-lived or easily reversible. A classic example is the effect of music while working. Music on a widget assembly line is turned on for an hour and then turned off. The number of produced widgets is compared with music and without. To reduce rival explanations (e.g., the beginning of the workday, the end of the workday, before and after lunch), music should be turned on randomly at different times.

A weakness in this design is whether the treatment, music, is causing the desired effect of more widgets produced per hour. The test itself or the employees knowing they are being watched may be a possible explanation. In addition, we need to take into account that higher productivity does not mean leaving the music on all the time. This design helps us to understand the recurrent effect of turning treatment, music, on and off. This design might be used in the classroom if a teacher wants to study the effects of students' participation during the presence or absence of parent volunteers or more teachers.

Multiple group experimental designs. A widely used multiple group design is the *nonequivalent control-group design*. This design uses pretests and posttests for both control and experimental groups. Treatment, however, is not randomly assigned. A classic example is giving a new drug to an experimental group, while the control group receives a placebo drug. Both groups are tested after treatment. Another example might be Class A receives group-oriented instruction, while Class B receives traditional instruction. Both groups are compared. If it can be assumed that the pretest controls for the group differences, except the treatment, this design comes close to the rigor of true experimentation. Although this design lacks random assignment, it may be one of the most feasible designs in natural settings.

The *multiple time series design* or *control group interrupted time series design* is another common design. This design is similar to the single group time series experiment; however, two groups participate in the study. A series of observations or measurements are made between the two groups, and treatment is randomly applied to one of the groups, followed by post measurements. Again, there is no random assignment. Although similar to the nonequivalent control group design, this design is more powerful since the effect is compared with the pre-treatment observations of its own series and against a control group. For example, if we wanted to monitor attendance rates, we could find two similar schools and collect weekly attendance results for several weeks, then randomly introduce, say, a family–school partnership program at one of the schools. We could continue to collect weekly attendance records. This design is also feasible for use in schools.

True Experimental Designs

Ideally, we would assign students randomly to treatment and control groups. The strengths of true experiments are found in randomly assigning subjects to determine cause and effect. Random assignment allows two groups (control and treatment) of subjects to be equal except for random differences. Random assignment allows equal chance of being in either group. Mosteller, Light, and Sachs (1996) randomized experiments and showed, for example, that small classes of 15 students on average actually did better than 60% of the students in regular-sized classes (23 students).

In the *pretest–posttest control-group design*, students are randomly assigned to a treatment or control group. Both groups are pretested, and the treatment is given to the treatment group, while the control group receives no treatment or the usual treatment. Both groups are tested afterwards and the scores are compared. Random assignment of subjects to control and treatment groups increases the probability that both groups start on a level playing field; the pretest serves to equate them further.

As an example, students' names are selected by lottery to attend a new charter school or their present school. Both groups are tested before and after the treatment period. Although this solves most of the problems raised so far, it also raises some concerns. For example, it might be difficult to find parents that would accept the random assignment of their children to different schools, and for practical reasons, difficulties may arise if the schools were geographically distant (e.g., why should Johnny go 15 miles to school A, when he lives across the street from school B?).

The *posttest-only control group design* is another commonly used experiment. Subjects are randomly assigned to two groups. Neither group is pretested. After the treatment is given to one group, control and experimental groups are measured on the posttest. Although the exclusion of pretests may seem counterintuitive, random assignment alone is powerful enough to reduce possible differences between groups. Pretests, however, help determine whether randomization worked. Pretests also enable investigators to learn about the sensitivity of the evaluation to learning gains made during the study, increasing the study's power to detect group differences. For example, students might be randomly assigned to different schools and then tested at the end of the school year.

The *Solomon four-group design*, while not as common, improves the generalizability of its results. Similar to the pretest–posttest control-group design, subjects are randomly assigned not to two, but to four groups. Two groups receive pretests and two do not. Only one of the two pretested groups receives treatment, and only one of the two groups that did not receive the pretest receives treatment. All groups receive a posttest. The strength of this design may be the reduction or elimination of the pretest effect on the outcome. The findings may be more generalizable to other settings. For example, everything else being equal, the generalization that charter schools outperform other schools from this design would carry more weight than the previous designs.

True experiments are difficult in education; yet it may be argued that they are difficult in most fields. For example, medical experiments may increase mortality and morbidity with a flip of a coin. Ethics and moral obligation obviously need to be taken into consideration. It may be unethical to administer treatments of unknown worth in medicine or education. For this reason, modern medicine depends heavily on scientifically based research from true experiments. For the same reason, improving educational productivity requires evidence-based confidence.

In conclusion, random assignment undoubtedly provides more confident causal conclusions. Without such randomization, much uncertainty arises about the causes of achievement differences between groups. Preferable, but difficult to implement, randomization also has its complications. Findings from artificially contrived circumstances may not be as generalizable to other everyday settings. For these reasons, quasi-experiments have been more commonly used in natural settings.

In summary, three types of designs are used in educational research: pre-experiments, quasi-experiments, and true experiments. Pre-experiments are the easiest to implement, but are the weakest and provide no defensible causal explanation. Quasi-experiments do not incorporate random assignment, but provide some causal confidence and are generally more feasible. And finally, true experiments are the most rigorous, but they are rare and difficult to implement. Designs, however, should be assessed on a case-by-case basis to determine which is most suited for a given situation. And what is essential to any study is the validity of the design discussed in the next section.

PART III: INTERNAL AND EXTERNAL VALIDITY

This section describes the threats to the internal and external validity of research studies. It ends with a brief discussion on the threats to analytic validity.

Internal Validity

According to Cook and Campbell (1979), "internal validity refers to the approximate validity with which we infer that a relationship between two variables is causal or that the absence of a relationship implies the absence of cause" (p. 37). In other words, does the research design rule out any rival explanations? Does the research design allow the researcher to claim that the effects found in the study are due to the treatment or independent variable? The procedures, treatments, or any experiences may threaten the validity of drawing causal inferences from the results.

Below are examples of common rival explanations that threaten the internal validity of research designs:

Consider this scenario: Ms. Alexis teaches an academic enrichment class that consists of 20 pre-kindergarten students in the inner city of Chicago. She wants to know if her research-based curriculum on language development is effective for her students. She has already given them a test at the beginning of the school year. At the end of the school year, she gives them another test. Results show that students' achievement scores are higher than the pretests. She is pleased and decides to use the curriculum again.

First, let's identify this example. This is a pre-experimental *one-group pretest–posttest design*. There is only one group of 20 students. They are given a pretest and a posttest to measure their performance.

Second, what are the independent and dependent variable? The independent variable is language curriculum. Since this curriculum is being taught to every student, this is also the treatment. The dependent variable is the achievement scores. We want to know what effect the curriculum had on the scores of the pre-K students. Apparently, students scored higher, but did the curriculum really cause the higher scores?

Threats to Internal Validity

Ms. Alexis's study is a weak design, because there are many threats to this study. Among the threats to the validity of this study are the following:

History. Did any event occur before the pretest or posttest that might influence the group's performance? History is associated with any unanticipated events involving the participants after the pretest. For example, perhaps Ms. Alexis's students scored higher on the posttests because her teaching assistant reviewed several lesson plans that were similar to test items before the actual test. Another rival explanation could be a parents' program was formed the same year where parents were encouraged to talk more with their children to build their language skills. If scores were lower, students might have been distracted during the test and, thus, performed poorly. Perhaps an emergency at the school caused the students to do badly on the pretest.

Maturation. Were there any natural changes such as getting older and more adept at language, even bored, fatigued, or hungry? Maturation includes "all those biological and psychological processes which systematically vary with the passage of time independent of specific external events" (Campbell & Stanley, 1963, p. 177–178). If there were any changes between the pretest and posttest, this might be a rival explanation. Over a period of a year, students might increase their vocabulary and language skills even if they weren't in school.

Instrumentation or *Instrument Decay*. Were there any changes or inconsistent use in measuring the dependent variables? Instrumentation refers to the changes in measurement or observation processes. This may include changes in standards of classroom observers or test scorers over time. For example, test administrators who made pretest observations may have been more or less experienced in testing students than those who made posttest observations.

Testing. Did retesting affect scores? Retesting may affect the scores of a second test despite treatment. Testing is the effect of the pretest on the dependent variable, which is the posttest. In the example of Ms. Alexis or even in Mrs. Warden's case, the mere fact of pretesting may sensitize students to learn the content of the special curriculum that is being implemented, thus giving them an advantage.

Statistical Regression. Did extremely high or low scores "regress" toward the mean? Initially poor scoring groups may increase and high scoring groups may decrease. For example, let's say a large group of students were tested for Ms. Alexis's class, and those in the lowest 25% were selected for treatment. Students who score low, on average, may do better on retesting, and those who are very high may decline in rank. Both kinds of scores regress closer to the mean.

Mortality or Attrition. Did any participants drop out of the study? Mortality is the differential loss of subjects that may influence a group mean. If the 10 weakest of 20 students enrolled in Ms. Alexis's class dropped out of the study, it would lead to an overestimate of posttest performance.

Selection. Did group membership determine the outcome of the treatment? When subjects are not randomly assigned to groups, there is an effect on the dependent variable caused by nonequivalent groups. Selection bias can occur when comparisons are made between groups with preexisting differences such as abilities, motivation, age, and interest. For example, selection bias already exists from Ms. Alexis's class, because those pre-K students attending the program might have parents who are more aware and motivated about their children's education, thus influencing their performance in school. The mere fact that their parents enrolled them in the special program may already set them apart from those not attending the program. Selection from these groups may bias results from the start.

Treatment Interactions. Was the treatment affected by another treatment, situation, or participants? For example, *selection-maturation interaction* occurs when maturation is not consistent across groups due to some selection bias. Perhaps some pre-kindergarten students were actually older than most of the population. If the ages range from 3 to 5, developmental differences are incremental in these formative years and may influence ability and scores. Another example is *instrument decay by treatment interaction*. Observers in a study are affected positively or negatively by what they are seeing and judgements may be more lenient or tougher, thereby biasing results.

In conclusion, there are many kinds of threats or rival explanations to internal validity. Well-designed studies can control for these threats by random assignment and other thoughtfully design features.

External Validity

Are the sample results generalizable to the population in question? Can the same findings be expected with other people, settings, and times? (Bracht & Glass, 1968; Cook & Campbell, 1979). More broadly,

Shaddish, Cook, and Campbell (2002) describe external validity "in terms of interactions of the causal relationship (including mediators of that relationship) with (1) units, (2) outcomes, (3) measures, and (4) settings" (p. 86). External validity concerns whether studies employing different students, intended effects and their measures, and in other places would yield the same results. For example, do findings about Appalachian children extend to school children living in affluent Lake Forest, Illinois? There are several kinds of threats to external validity; some are described in the next section.[5]

Threats to External Validity

Obtrusiveness and Reactivity. When treatment, observations, or measures are "obtrusive," participants naturally "react" when being observed. Participants become aware that they are subjects, which can affect the results. One threat is the well-known *Hawthorne Effect* suggesting "I'm special." Subjects may improve their performance as they think they are receiving special attention. *Hypothesis Guessing* occurs when participants respond as expected in the study. An example might be that participants respond positively to most questions because they think it would be helpful. *Compensatory Rivalry* may occur in educational research when control teachers work harder to make up for any loss of benefit for their students. The *Novelty Effect* occurs when the new curriculum is new and interesting. Often met with enthusiasm, the students may be very responsive and then eventually lose their zeal, in which case the treatment may lose its effect.

Researcher Expectancy Effect or *Pygmalion Effect*. Researchers may inadvertently tip the scales toward a desired effect—for example, encouraging subjects verbally or smiling when subjects get the right answers. Researcher expectancy effects also occur when researchers know exactly who is receiving the treatment or intended effect. One way to minimize this threat is to keep observers, treatment administrators, and subjects "blind" to the design's features.

Analytic Validity

Findings may be threatened by problems of analytic validity. Although earlier works provided a foundation for discussion on external validity, discussions on external validity neglect some of these analytic threats except for power, error rate, and reliability. Although important to consider, these threats are often neglected in published educational research. These threats can be applied to both experimental and observational data. This section describes some common threats to analytic validity.[6]

Some Threats to Analytic Validity

Leveling. Leveling occurs when grouping continuous measurements into levels such as high, middle, low intelligence, thus losing the original precision of the variables. Sociologists, for example, often prefer to classify rather than to measure, seeking all-inclusive, mutually exclusive taxonomies. Regression analysis is preferable to analysis of variance since it does not require leveling. Categorizing and leveling continuous variables should generally be avoided, and while a few classifications such as male–female may be necessary, many should be reconsidered.

Outliers. Outliers, often mismeasures or otherwise mistaken data, are problematic, since they may produce interaction, reversals, curvature, and abnormal residuals. Educational research publications, however, rarely mention the detection of such aberrant data, despite the frequency of occurrence. Hoerl (1954), Kruskal (1965), Daniel and Wood (1971), and Mosteller and Tukey (1977), however, provide helpful formulas to the problems of outliers in educational research.

Colinearity. Because the independent variables are correlated or co-occur, it may be difficult to separate their effects. A new math program for children in a suburb may only appear to do well, but its apparent success may be largely attributable to affluent status of the families in the community.

CONCLUSION AND RECOMMENDATIONS

First, strengthening the internal and external validity of studies is essential to improving educational research. Well-designed studies help interpret the causes behind learning. Random assignment to experimental and control groups is the gold standard of research, but may not always be feasible in the real world. Cost, time, and ethics are real-world constraints. Quasi-experimental designs may not meet the gold standard, but may lead to valid conclusions when well-designed.

Second, the best evidence may be found in the multiplicity of results. No matter how large and well designed, a single experiment may not be definitive. Consistent results from many studies provide the best evidence. Although experiments provide the best internal validity or basis of causal inference, quasi-experiments may be less disruptive and provide a better indication of efficacy in natural settings. However, the more we have of both designs, the better and greater our confidence in conclusions.

Third, in the same vein, reviewing multiple studies might increase confidence in results. Some examples might be vote counts or meta-analytic studies. Vote counts refer to the wins, losses, and ties of existing research. Essentially, each finding or study counts as a vote. Meta-analytic studies allow overall estimates of the magnitude of effects. Using multiple well-designed experiments in meta-analytic studies is another way of providing confident causal conclusions. In conclusion, experimental and quasi-experimental designs are hardly a simple matter. There are many elements to consider in formulating a successful study as many things can go wrong with research in education, psychology, and the social sciences. In field research, difficulties multiply, yet the status of our educational reform in the United States requires our best efforts to overcome them.

NOTES

1. Shaddish, Cook, and Campbell (2002, p. 42). Statistical conclusion validity concerns "two related statistical inferences that affect the covariation component of causal inferences: (1) whether the presumed cause and effect covary and (2) how strongly they covary."
2. "Construct validity involves making inferences from the sampling particulars of a study to the higher-order constructs they represent" (Shaddish, Cook, & Campbell, 2002, p.65).
3. Shaddish, Cook, and Campbell (2002) label pre-experimental designs as "quasi-experimental designs" in their book. The term "pre-experimental design" was used to keep consistency with the original work of Campbell and Stanley (1963).
4. Creswell (2003), Krathwohl (1998), and Shaddish, Cook, and Campbell (2002) provide a comprehensive list of questions and examples for designing an experiment.
5. Krathwohl (1998) provides a helpful list and examples on external validity.
6. The reader can consult "Quantification Reconsidered" by Walberg (1984) for more threats and examples.

REFERENCES

Bracht, G. H., & Glass, G. V. (1968). The external validity of experiments. *American Educational Research Journal, 5*, 437–474.

Campbell, D. T., & Stanley, J. C. (1963). Experimental and quasi-experimental designs for research on teaching. In N. L. Gage (Ed.), *Handbook of research on teaching*. Chicago: Rand-McNally.

Cook, T. D., & Campbell, D. T. (1979). *Quasi-experimentation: Design and analysis issues for field settings*. Chicago: Rand McNally.

Creswell, J. W. (2003). *Research design: Qualitative, quantitative, and mixed methods approaches*. Thousand Oaks, CA: Sage.

Daniel, C., & Wood, F. S. (1971). *Fitting equations to data: Computer analysis of multifactor data for scientists and engineers.* New York: Wiley-Interscience.

Hoerl, A. E. (1954). Fitting curves to data. In J. H. Perry (Ed.), *Chemical business handbook*. New York: McGraw-Hill.

Institute of Education Sciences (2003). *Identifying and implementing educational practices supported by rigorous evidence: A user friendly guide*. Washington DC: U.S. Department of Education.

Krathwohl, D. R. (1998). *Methods of educational and social science research. An integrated approach* (2nd ed.). New York: Addison-Wesley.

Kruskal, J. B. (1965). Analysis of factorial experiments by estimating monotone transformations of the data. *Journal of the Royal Statistical Society, 27*, 251–263.

Mosteller, F., Light, R. J., Sachs, J. A. (1996). Sustained inquiry in education: Lessons from skill grouping and class size. *Harvard Education Review, 66*(4), 797–842.

Mosteller, F., & Tukey, J. W. (1977). *Data analysis and regression*. Reading, MA: Addison-Wesley.

National Commission on Excellence in Education (1983). *A nation at risk*. Washington, DC: U.S. Department of Education.

National Institute of Child Health and Human Development (2000). *Report of the National Reading Panel. An evidence-based assessment of the scientific research literature on reading and its implications on reading instruction* (NIH Publication No. 00-4769). Washington, DC: U.S. Government Printing Office.

Patten, M. (2002). *Understanding research methods: An overview of the essentials* (3rd ed.). Los Angeles: Pryczak.

Shaddish, W. R., Cook, T. D., & Campbell, D. T. (2002). *Experimental and quasi-experimental designs for generalized causal inference*. Boston: Houghton Mifflin.

Walberg, H. J. (1984). Quantification reconsidered. In *Review of research in education*. Washington, DC: American Educational Research Association.

CHAPTER 3

SCIENTIFIC FORMATIVE EVALUATION

The Role of Individual Learners in Generating and Predicting Successful Educational Outcomes

T. V. Joe Layng, Greg Stikeleather, and Janet S. Twyman

The effort to bring scientific verification to the development and testing of educational products and practices has begun in earnest (see, for example, No Child Left Behind Act of 2001). The first products targeted for improvement are those whose primary goal is the teaching of reading (U.S. Department of Education, n.d.). Other products and practices are sure to follow, particularly if the initial effort is successful in having a major impact on children's reading performance. But what does it mean to take a scientific approach to instructional productivity? This chapter hopes to contribute to that discussion by examining the role scientific assessment can play in enhancing educational productivity through the application of a thorough scientific evaluation *during* the development of

The Scientific Basis of Educational Productivity, 29–44

instructional programs as well as in their post-development validation. Since reading is the current focus, we shall begin there.

For a beginning reading program to be successful, the National Reading Panel (National Institute of Child Health and Human Development, 2000), among others, has identified critical program constituents that scientific investigation has determined as essential to that success. These constituents include: phonemic awareness, phonics, vocabulary, fluency, and comprehension. Further, it may be argued that the instructional program itself, rather than just its constituents, be research-based. But what does it mean to be research-based?

RESEARCH-BASED: SOME DEFINITIONS

Current uses of the term "research-based" as applied to early reading programs range from claims that (1) programs contain elements that research suggests are effective (see, for example, Simmons & Kame'enui, 2003), or (2) pretest vs. posttest or simple comparison studies have provided some evidence of effectiveness for an instructional program, or (3) the program has undergone some form of scientifically controlled study, often involving randomized control groups (Coalition for Evidence-Based Policy, 2003). All of these uses, however, fail to distinguish between the *scientific development* of a program and the *scientific evaluation of outcomes* after a program has been developed.

This latter use of "research-based" might more properly be considered "research-filtered." That is, a program, regardless of how it was designed, is measured against an alternative form of instruction or, at times, no instruction at all. This use of the term "research-based" would find in its referent an emphasis on *summative* evaluation (Bloom, Hastings, & Madhaus, 1971). In the research-filtered approach, there is no requirement that the program itself must be scientifically designed or based on research.

Yet another use of the term "research-based" might be more properly considered as "research-guided." By that, we are referring to a program of instruction that has been scientifically designed and tested during its development, or at least its design is guided by previous research results. This use of the term "research-based" would find in its referent an emphasis on *formative* evaluation (Bloom et al., 1971; Scriven, 1974). In the research-guided approach, formative evaluation is intertwined into the instructional design protocols and, at its most thorough. influences program development through iterations of testing, revising, and testing again.

LEVELS OF VERIFICATION

Both formative and summative evaluation may comprise varying degrees of verification and commitment to a scientific approach. In the more thorough forms of formative evaluation (also referred to as developmental testing; see Markle, 1967), data are continuously collected and analyzed as the program is developed in order to provide an ongoing *experimentally controlled* research base for ensuring program effectiveness with individual learners (cf. Sidman & Stoddard, 1966; Stikeleather & Sidman, 1990). In the more thorough forms of summative evaluation, data from randomized, or matched, experimental and control groups are collected and analyzed to provide a *statistically controlled* research base for determining program effectiveness with groups of learners (Habicht, Victora, & Vaughan, 1999).

In the least thorough forms of formative and summative evaluation, philosophy, point of view, and anecdotal evidence comprise the approach. Little attention is paid to direct measurement of instructional effect, or to the determination of functional relations among variables. Of course, both forms of evaluation also have middle grounds where there is an attempt to use some form of empirical evidence, to influence program development in the case of formative evaluation, and to make judgments about outcomes in the case of summative evaluation.

Table 3.1 provides a 3 X 2 matrix which describes critical features of formative and summative evaluation across three levels of analysis, with each level representing a scale of verification from least to most thorough: experiential evaluation, evidence-based evaluation, and scientific evaluation. Table 3.2 provides a 3 X 3 matrix depicting the relations between each level of verification as they intersect with one another. The rows denote formative evaluation; the columns denote summative evaluation. The outcome of each interaction across rows and columns is described in the cell for each intersection. The level of verification for formative evaluation is indicated numerically, with 1 representing the least thorough, and 3 indicating the most. The level of verification for summative evaluation is indicated alphabetically, with A representing the least thorough, and C indicating the most.

Social validity, which is important for both formative and summative evaluation, is not indicated in the 3 X 3 matrix presented in Table 3.2. For entries falling in column C, the critical question is: Do the measurement instruments chosen for the evaluation reflect what the community considers important? For entries falling in Row 3, the critical question is: Do the mastery criteria, which each individual performance must meet, reflect what the community considers important? The discussion of these questions, although of considerable importance, falls beyond the scope of this chapter.

Table 3.1. A 3 X 2 Matrix Depicting Three Corresponding Levels of Verification for Formative and Summative Evaluation as They Relate to Claims of Effectiveness

	Formative Evaluation: Basis for Program Revision	*Summative Evaluation: Basis for Outcomes Assessment*
Experiential Derived from philosophy or personal experience	Consensus of best practices, experience, point of view. Little or no testing during developmental process itself. Design revisions based on consistency of content with prevailing point of view. May employ limited tryouts that result in some program revisions. Clarity of communication typically the issue.	Correspondence to a point of view—philosophy or personal experience. Evaluation based on anecdotal evidence, look & feel, personal satisfaction, testimonials
Evidence Based Derived from scientific principles or Comparative measures	Consensus of best practices, experience, point of view, but design largely based on previous research, which may come from a variety of disciplines, may be on elements found in program content and not program itself. Design revisions often based on consistency of content with prevailing point of view, may employ checks for adherence to research. May employ limited tryouts that result in some program revisions. Clarity of communication typically the issue.	Pretest-vs.-posttest measures, meta-analysis, simple comparison studies—not employing random assignment or other controls
Scientific Application of scientific methods	Consensus of best practices, experience, point of view, design may or may not be initially based on previous research, may come from a variety of disciplines. All elements of program tested for effectiveness, if fails criteria, alternative built and tested, processes iterates until criteria met. Performance is always measured against a set of criteria. Sequence of program steps and the relation of behavior to the sequence are explicitly identified, thereby generating new knowledge. Process continues and is aggregated as the "chunks" of the program units change in size (e.g., a segment of a lesson, a lesson, groups of lessons, the program). Research based on, and systematically replicated with, individuals— thereby, can generalize to individuals (Neuman & McCormick, 2002; Sidman, 1960).	Randomized controlled group studies, measured against other programs, standard, or placebo. (See Paik, this volume, for a detailed discussion of outcomes assessment.)

Table 3.2. A 3 X 3 Matrix Describing the Relation Between Formative and Summative Evaluation in Program Design and Outcomes Assessment

Approaches to Formative Evaluation: Basis for Program Revision	*Approaches to Summative Evaluation: Basis for Outcomes Assessment*		
	A. Experiential—Assessment	*B. Evidence Based—Assessment*	*C. Scientific-Controlled Group Research & Assessment*
1. Experiential—Program Development	Cannot predict group or individual performance. Works or not with groups or individuals purely subjective; a matter of opinion; argued on point of view—a matter of social agreement	Provides some indication that the program may be effective with a group; but Cannot confidently predict group or individual performance.	Can confidently predict group performance, but Cannot predict individual's performance (Sidman, 1960). If works or not, not clear what program elements, alone or together, are responsible.
2. Evidence Based—Program Development	If limited tryouts, may indicate that the program might work with those tested; but Cannot confidently predict group or individual performance. Still primarily a matter of social agreement, but has some validity by relation to past research and perhaps limited tryouts.	Provides some indication that the program may be effective with a group; but Cannot confidently predict group or individual performance. If works, not really clear why; if it does not work, can lead to reevaluation of principles or the way they were applied. Not clear where the problem is.	Can confidently predict group performance; but Cannot confidently predict individual's performance. If works or not, not clear what program elements, alone or together, are responsible, but can lead to reconsideration of principles or the way they were applied.

(Table continues on next page)

FORMATIVE EVALUATION: IMPLICATIONS FOR RESEARCH-BASED INSTRUCTION

As noted in the 3 X 3 matrix, programs that evolve from a thorough formative evaluation process can predict *individual* learner outcomes across all summative evaluation levels of verification, just as programs tested under the most thorough form of summative evaluation can predict *group*

Table 3.2. (Continued)

Approaches to Formative Evaluation: Basis for Program Revision	*Approaches to Summative Evaluation: Basis for Outcomes Assessment*		
	A. Experiential—Assessment	*B. Evidence Based—Assessment*	*C. Scientific—Controlled Group Research & Assessment*
3. Scientific—Program Development	Able to predict group performance based on individual performance; and Can confidently predict individual's performance. Since program able to predict individual's performance, some prediction of group performance implied; may have some validity by relation to past research.	Able to predict group performance based on individual performance; and Can confidently predict individual's performance. If doesn't work, issues are in transfer—able to identify and isolate variables to change and revise for retest. Individual data not lost and can be analyzed in relation to outcome.	Can confidently predict group performance; and Can confidently predict individual's performance. If doesn't work, issues are in differences in formative criteria & summative measurement instruments—able to identify and isolate variables to change and revise criteria & program for retest, or to revise summative measurement instruments. Individual data not lost and can be analyzed in relation to outcome.

The level of verification for each type of evaluation is indicated by the numbers 1–3 for formative evaluation, with Row 3 representing the most thorough; the letters A–C indicate the level of verification for each type of summative evaluation, with Column C representing the most thorough. Cell 3C represents the intersection of greatest verification for formative & summative evaluation.

outcomes across all formative evaluation levels. Both should be considered to have equal predictive power: formative evaluation for individual learners, and summative evaluation for groups of learners. Both formative evaluation (*research-guided* instruction) and summative evaluation (*research-filtered* instruction) are important, and may be combined to provide useful information on individual performance and group averages. Cell 3C of the 3 X 3 matrix represents the ideal intersection between scientific formative evaluation and scientific summative evaluation.

At its most thorough, formative evaluation requires a careful control analysis design to ensure that each constituent part of the program is working alone, or together with other constituent parts, to produce a reliable and predictable outcome (Goldiamond & Thompson, [1967] 2004).

Accordingly, such formative evaluation lends itself most readily to single-subject research designs (Bernard, 1865/1927; Neuman & McCormick, 1995, 2002; Sidman, 1960) in which participants respond over long periods of time while variables are experimentally changed and controlled. In these designs, variance is controlled through direct procedural or experimental intervention during the course of the experiment.

Whereas group designs, typically the basis for summative evaluation, are readily known and accepted as providing scientific evidence for program effectiveness (see Paik, this volume), single-subject designs, which are typically the basis for formative evaluation, are not so well known. While both group and single-subject designs are descended from highly successful scientific traditions and both may provide equally thorough and informative results, single-subject designs are relatively less understood. Both do, however, differ in the questions asked; one asks about the behavior of groups, the other asks about the behavior of individuals.

SINGLE-SUBJECT CONTROL-ANALYSIS RESEARCH AND EVALUATION

Single-subject designs are most valuable when the questions addressed concern how program components working alone or together affect an individual's performance. These designs provide predictions on how *individuals* using the program will perform compared to a *standard*; group designs provide predictions on how one *group* will perform as compared to another *group*. Single-subject and group designs may also differ in the way variance is typically controlled. In the case of group experimental designs, statistical control and analysis is the primary method of controlling variance, often employing randomized or matched control groups. On the other hand, in single-subject experimental designs, procedural change is the preferred method of analyzing and controlling variance.

Although sharing the goal of predicting program outcomes with summative evaluation, the procedural control-analysis designs, which typify formative evaluation, differ from that of summative evaluation and statistical control designs in another important aspect. Within a procedural control-analysis framework, the "*concern is not merely with specifying the conditions under which behavior is appropriate, but with being able to develop such appropriateness, to develop corrective procedures where the existent functional repertoire is inappropriate, and to maintain appropriate functional repertoires once they are developed*" (Goldiamond & Thompson, 1967/2004, Chapter 8, Part 1, p. 18, emphasis added).

Stated differently, in single-subject research designs important to formative evaluation, the essential question is whether experimental control is maintained over the learner's behavior as response criteria are systematically changed (Layng, 1995; also see for example, Layng, Twyman, & Stikeleather, 2003; Layng, Twyman, & Stikeleather, 2004a; Twyman, Layng, Stikeleather, & Hobbins, 2004). Further, once such control can be demonstrated for an individual, the question is raised as to whether that control can be replicated for other individuals across a range of settings. In such systematic replication (Sidman, 1960), the occurrence of increased variance in responding, both within a learner's individual performance and between the performance of different learners, is an occasion for the examination of the program elements and sequence in which the variance occurred, and the modification of, or the design of new, procedures so as to reduce or control the variance found in meeting the mastery criteria.

Systematic replication with new individuals provides increased confidence that the same procedures will provide similar outcomes for other individuals. Each new learner can be considered an experimental replication—that is, one can predict that future learners will show similar results. There are many single-subject designs that can be used to address different experimental questions. Regrettably, a detailed discussion of single-subject design is beyond the scope of this chapter. Interested readers are referred to many fine texts on this topic (e.g., Bernard, [1865] 1927; Johnston & Pennypacker, 1993; Neuman & McCormick, 1995, 2002; Sidman, 1960).

WHY FORMATIVE EVALUATION AND ITS EMPHASIS ON THE INDIVIDUAL IS SO IMPORTANT

Scientists and engineers whose responsibility it is to design and build working complex systems, such as airplanes, rely on thorough formative evaluation to produce a vehicle that will fly the very first time it is tested. In the case of an airplane, careful wind tunnel and other experiments test how the bolts applied stand up to stress, how the materials used perform, how much lift is provided by the wings, and how the overall aerodynamics are implemented. Each revision based on the testing is itself retested until the component meets a quality standard. Only after thorough testing of the components, both separately and together, is the final question asked, "Does it fly?"

Each flight is considered a replication; the more conditions encountered, the more systematic the replication. Design modifications that come from test flights serve to improve stability and reliability even more. Aircraft are not constructed and then compared to other aircraft to determine, on average, if one group stays aloft longer than differently built aircraft comprising a control group. Comparative tests between only one or two competing aircraft typically provide enough data for the intended customer to make a buying decision.

Similarly, thorough formative evaluation may have the same effect on teaching reading and other instructional program development (see for example Markle & Tiemann, 1967; Twyman et al., 2004). By ensuring that each component meets a specified quality standard, which in the case of instruction would be a high mastery standard achieved by the learners tested, we should be able to design and build instructional programs that have the same high likelihood of success as does building modern aircraft. Rigorous "single-subject" iterative cycles (test–revise–test) provide great confidence that all aircraft built in accord with the design and development process will fly—without the need for tests comparing groups of aircraft. A similar approach to educational program development may provide comparable confidence.

When thorough formative evaluation is not possible, the only recourse is summative evaluation. Here statistical, rather than direct experimental investigation, must be used to evaluate the efficacy of the procedures or treatment being developed. For example, the pharmaceutical industry is faced with developing new drugs with only limited guidance from formative evaluation—Row 2 of the 3 X 3 matrix. Accordingly, a research-filtered methodology featuring a thorough summative evaluation is the approach of choice for assessing pharmaceutical effectiveness. Although effectiveness information is obtained, often little is learned about precisely how a drug does or does not work (Valenstein, 1998), leaving the conclusions described in Cell 2C of the 3 X 3 matrix. Accordingly, when assessing instructional programs, exclusively relying on FDA-like summative evaluation protocols may not necessarily be the most informative approach.

A thorough research-guided formative evaluation applied to designing and building instructional programs tells us more than that the "mean" experimental child performs better than the "mean" control group child. It tells us *how* the program components work separately and together, and whether or not it is effective with each individual. By setting formative evaluation criteria high, we may be able to ensure that nearly all children who use a program so developed succeed. This is quite a different statement than saying the experimental group performed significantly better (statistically) than did the control group. We are all aware that, with a large enough "N," small absolute differences between groups can produce highly significant results.

We would not board an aircraft based on a design that demonstrated that, "on average," time aloft for one group of aircraft was greater than for another "control group" of aircraft. Should we be satisfied using a reading or other instructional program that works only on average better than another instructional program, even if that outcome has been "scientifically" determined? We argue that it may be a better scientific—or social—goal to produce educational programs that are the product of a thorough formative evaluation, and therefore must "fly" with each individual learner, one learner at a time. The important contribution that can be made by rigorous formative evaluation to predicting program outcomes, especially for individual learners, should not be overlooked.

SOME ESSENTIAL FEATURES OF A SCIENTIFIC FORMATIVE EVALUATION

In a different paper (Twyman et al., 2004), we described the scientific formative evaluation approach employed by Headsprout as applied to the development of a beginning reading program. We distinguished scientific formative evaluation (Row 3 of the 3 X 3 matrix) from other types of formative evaluation (Rows 1 and 2 of the 3 X 3 matrix), as illustrated in the following edited excerpt:

> One typical approach to instructional design is to apply a top-down process. The goal is identified, broken down into smaller steps, and checked for "social agreement"—do experts, or at least those with some familiarity, think it's reasonable? [Row 1 or possibly 2 of the 3 X 3 matrix]; the program is then written in its entirety and tested with students. At times, designers will take data, note if their students fail, and redo some portion of the program [Row 2 of the 3 X 3 matrix]. This often occurs in the context of field-testing with groups of learners. If the overall group tends to meet the goal [often judged by consensus and learner emotional reaction], then the product is considered finished. Many designers and curriculum publishers fail to perform the last two steps of minimal test and revision [staying firmly in Row 1 of the 3 X 3 matrix]. Such a program may purport to present content that is derived from scientific principles, but the program itself does not meet the criteria for a scientifically developed program. The program may even provide a better outcome than some alternative approach against which it is compared, but still, the program cannot be considered scientifically developed.
>
> Markle and Tiemann (1967) described a different instructional programming process. They noted that the entire instructional design process determines whether an instructional product will fulfill its vision. Markle and Tiemann took the position that a rigorous scientific control-analysis system is necessary for successful instructional design. Nevertheless, that recommendation has seldom been followed (Cook, 1983; Markle, 1969, 1990). One reason may be that there are few examples of its application on a large scale that can serve as a guide to others who are interested in producing

quality instructional materials. Another, perhaps greater, obstacle is the time and expertise required to fully implement all elements of a scientific instructional design process. Markle and Tiemann's program development process can be slightly updated and summarized as follows:

1. Perform a content analysis. Content is examined and classified as to the type of learning involved (e.g., strategy, principle, concept, verbal repertoire, sequence or algorithm, multiple discrimination, paired associate, kinesthetic repertoire, chain or motor response [after Tiemann & Markle, 1991]).
2. State the objectives. Clear, measurable objectives are developed that reflect the content analysis and the overall goal of the program.
3. Determine the criterion tests. Tests are constructed against a standard that often involves both accuracy and frequency criteria (see Lindsley, 1997). The tests are developed for each teaching activity or routine within a lesson segment, for each lesson, for blocks of lessons, and finally for the program.
4. Establish the required entry repertoire. Given what is to be learned, determine the skills needed to progress through the program. Entry repertoires are the specific prerequisite skills needed for success, not simply prerequisite experiences (such as taking a "prerequisite" course without actually acquiring the behaviors identified in the course).
5. Build the instructional sequence. The content analysis and the criterion tests are used as a guide to produce instruction that will result in learner behavior that meets specified criteria.
6. Use performance data to continually adjust the instructional sequence (5) until it meets the objectives (2), as measured by the criterion tests (3), which reflect the content analysis (1).
7. Build in maintaining consequences. Plan for the different types of motivation that will be required, both program extrinsic and intrinsic (after Goldiamond, 1974). Use performance data, including affective data, to test and revise the motivational variables.

The learner begins at 4 (Entry Repertoire), goes to 5 (Instructional Sequence), and is evaluated at 3 (Criterion Tests) to determine if 2 (Instructional Objectives) has been reached. As is evident, the student does not progress through a sequence in the same way as the program was built. Nor is the program written in its entirety before it is tested. In this approach, the learner's behavior shapes the program until nearly all learners meet the specified criteria. (p. 58)

That is, the performance data (6) are used to continually adjust the program until nearly all learners meet the mastery criteria. To continue:

All elements of the program are tested for effectiveness, and if the criteria are not met, alternative strategies are built and tested. The process iterates until all criteria are met, with performance always measured against a set of standards. The sequencing of program steps and their relation to the

> learner's behavior is explicitly identified, thereby generating new knowledge: about both the program and about learner behavior. This process continues and becomes aggregated as the "chunks" of the program units change in size (e.g., for Headsprout, a segment of a lesson, a lesson, groups of lessons, and the entire program). The research is based on individuals, and therefore can be generalized to individuals (Goldiamond & Thompson, [1967] 2004; Sidman, 1960).
>
> It is the job of the learning scientists and instructional designers to consider these factors when designing instruction, testing program segments, revising sequences, and interpreting learner data. It is important, therefore, to carefully control and vary how stimuli are presented, their sequence of presentation, the salience of the stimuli, the learner's history of responding to the alternatives, how the response request to the learner is made, and the consequences of responding to all alternatives (see Markle, 1990; Ray, 1969; Ray & Sidman, 1970; Stikeleather & Sidman, 1990). (p. 63)

This careful control analysis characterized by a scientific formative evaluation as represented by Row 3 in the 3 X 3 matrix not only provides the predictive confidence educators need to make important decisions regarding the curriculum they select, but may also provide answers as to why a particular curriculum is effective. For example, in the online beginning reading program Headsprout Early Reading™, a single learner makes about 200 meaningful responses per 20-minute lesson, about 10 per minute. That means approximately 16,000 responses are individually collected and analyzed during the course of the program. As of this writing, across all learners, well over 100 million instructional interactions or "learn units" (after Greer, 2002) have been collected and regularly examined in an effort to understand how learners interact with the program and to continually improve it. This latter point should not be overlooked. For within the context of a thorough formative evaluation, experimental control and analysis of learner behavior can lead to new behavioral insights. Indeed, work from Headsprout's laboratory has experimentally replicated and extended procedures that can ensure successful discovery learning in the context of online educational programs (Layng, Twyman, & Stikeleather, 2004b).

LARGER SCALE FORMATIVE EVALUATION

There is yet another way a more scientific formative evaluation can play an important role in improving educational productivity—that is, on the district and school level. Though uncommon, some school districts (see for example Johnson, 2003) are working diligently to put in place sophisticated data gathering instruments and frequent assessment so that educational practices at the classroom level can be tested, revised, and tested again until the practices are successful as measured against a standard. As a result, entire school districts have begun to make progress in closing the achievement gap between majority and minority students (Mozingo, 2003; Muffet & Wimberley, 2003), often with both achieving at much higher levels when careful formative evaluation practices have been used over time. (See also Farris, Carnine, and Silbert's [1993] description of formative evaluation being applied by the Mattawan, Michigan school district to produce considerable districtwide progress and a very high level of student achievement.)

CONCLUSION

Today, examples of commercial instructional programs built through a scientific process of thorough formative evaluation are rare (but see Layng et al., 2003, 2004a; Twyman et al., 2004). Currently, a more common practice is to design and write materials that correspond in some identifiable way with previous research or authoritative consensus. Once written, the materials are perhaps tested with simple comparative or pretest-vs.-posttest studies in an attempt to provide at least some evidence that the materials may be effective, Cell 2B in the 3 X 3 matrix. Consequently, as the movement toward more scientific practices continues, and given that most current reading and other instructional programs have not been scientifically developed, thorough summative evaluation, Column C in the 3 X 3 matrix, will remain as the scientific method of choice for determining relative success for most programs. However, it should not go unappreciated that a rigorous control-analysis formative evaluation, Row 3 in the 3 X 3 matrix, offers an equally scientific and arguably more reliable method of not only measuring, but of ensuring, program success.

Indeed, in an important recognition of the importance of a thorough formative evaluation, Wilbur Wright, when describing the use of the first wind tunnel to test wing designs, questioned whether powered flight would ever have been achieved without it:

> It is difficult to underestimate the value of that very laborious work we did over that homemade wind tunnel. It was, in fact, the first wind tunnel in which small models of wings were tested and their lifting properties accurately noted. From all the data that Orville and I accumulated into tables, an accurate and reliable wing could finally be built...In fact, the accurate wind tunnel data we developed was so important, it is doubtful if anyone would have ever developed a flyable wing without first developing this data...
>
> In any case, as famous as we became for our "Flyer" and its system of control, it all would never have happened if we had not developed our own wind tunnel and derived our own correct aerodynamic data.
>
> —Wilbur Wright (1903)

Similarly, instructional programs whose designs have evolved from "educational wind tunnels" may provide not only a new "gold standard" for the application of scientific methods in the design and evaluation of instructional practices, but products not possible without it. Accordingly, scientific formative evaluation not only deserves the support of all those interested in the intersection of rigorous science with educational practices, but perhaps offers an even surer route to leaving no child behind.

REFERENCES

Bernard, C. (1927). *An introduction to the study of experimental medicine* (H. C. Greene, Trans.). New York: Macmillan. (Original work published 1865)

Bloom, B. S., Hastings, J. T., & Madhaus, G.E. (1971). *Handbook on the formative and summative evaluation of student learning*. New York: McGraw-Hill.

Cook, D. A. (1983). CBT's feet of clay: Questioning the informational transmission model. *Data Training, 3*(12), 12–17.

Coalition for Evidence-Based Policy (2003). *Identifying and implementing educational practices supported by rigorous evidence: A user friendly guide*. Retrieved March 14, 2004, from http://www.ed.gov/rschstat/research/pubs/rigorousevid/index.html

Farris, H., Carnine, D., & Silbert, J. (1993). Learning is our business. *The American School Board Journal, 186*(12), 31–33.

Goldiamond, I. (1974). Toward a constructional approach to social problems: Ethical and constitutional issues raised by applied behavior analysis. *Behaviorism, 2*, 1–84.

Goldiamond, I., & Thompson, D. (2004). *The Blue Books: Goldiamond & Thompson's The functional analysis of behavior.* Edited and revised by P. T. Andronis. Cambridge, MA: Cambridge Center for Behavioral Studies. (Original work published 1967)

Greer, R. D. (2002). *Designing teaching strategies: An applied behavior analysis systems approach.* San Diego, CA: Academic Press.

Habicht, J. P., Victora, C. G., & Vaughan, J. P. (1999). Evaluation designs for adequacy, plausibility, and probability of public health programme performance and impact. *International Journal of Epidemiology, 28*(1), 10–18.

Johnson, A. (2003, October). Building the information foundation. Paper presented at the Council on Great City Schools 47th Annual Fall Conference, Chicago, IL.

Johnston, J. M., & Pennypacker, H. S. (1993). *Strategies and tactics of behavioral research* (2nd ed.) Hillsdale, NJ: Erlbaum.

Layng, T. V. J. (1995). Causation and complexity: Old lessons, new crusades. *Journal of Behavior Therapy & Experimental Psychiatry, 26*(3), 249–258.

Layng, T. V. J., Twyman, J. S., & Stikeleather, G. (2003). Headsprout Early Reading: Reliably teaching children to read. *Behavioral Technology Today*, 3, 7–20.

Layng, T. V. J., Twyman, J. S., & Stikeleather, G. (2004a). Selected for success: How *Headsprout Reading Basics*™ teaches children to read. In D. J. Moran & R. W.

Malott (Eds.), *Evidence based education methods* (pp. 171–200). St. Louis, MO: Elsevier/Academic Press.

Layng, T. V. J., Twyman, J. S., & Stikeleather, G. (2004b). Engineering discovery learning: The contingency adduction of some precursors of textual responding in a beginning reading program. *The Analysis of Verbal Behavior, 20,* 99–109.

Lindsley, O. R. (1997). Precise instructional design: Guidelines from Precision Teaching. In C. R. Dills & A. J. Romiszowski (Eds.), *Instructional development paradigms* (pp. 537–554). Englewood Cliffs, NJ: Educational Technology Publications.

Markle, S. M. (1967). Empirical testing of programs. In P. C. Lange (Ed.), *Programmed instruction: Sixty-sixth yearbook of the National Society for the Study of Education: 2* (pp. 104–138). Chicago: University of Chicago Press.

Markle, S. M. (1969). *Good frames and bad: A grammar of frame writing* (2nd ed.). New York: Wiley.

Markle, S. M. (1990). *Designs for instructional designers*. Champaign, IL: Stipes.

Markle, S. M., & Tiemann, P. W. (1967). *Programming is a process*: Slide/tape interactive program. Chicago: University of Illinois at Chicago.

Mozingo, T. (2003, October). Project acceleration: The advanced academic story. Paper presented at the Council on Great City Schools 47th Annual Fall Conference, Chicago, IL.

Muffet, G., & Wimberley, L. (2003, October). Decreasing the achievement gap: What works now? Paper presented at the Council on Great City Schools 47th Annual Fall Conference, Chicago, IL.

National Institute of Child Health and Human Development (2000). *Report of the National Reading Panel. Teaching children to read: an evidence-based assessment of the scientific research literature on reading and its implications for reading instruction: Reports of the subgroups* (NIH Publication No. 00–4754). Washington, DC: U.S. Government Printing Office.

Neuman, S. B., & McCormick, S. (1995). *Single-subject experimental research: Applications for literacy.* Newark, DE: International Reading Association.

Neuman, S. B., & McCormick, S. (2002). A case for single-subject experiments in literacy research. In M. L. Kamil, P. B. Mosenthal, P. D. Pearson, & R. Barr (Eds.), *Methods of literacy research* (pp. 105–118). Mahwah, NJ: Erlbaum.

No Child Left Behind Act of 2001 (2002). Pub. L. No 107–110, 115 Stat. 1425, Section 1201. Retrieved March 14, 2004, from http://www.ed.gov/policy/elsec/leg/esea02/pg4.html

Paik, S. J. (2005). Evidence-based reform: Experimental and quasi-experimental research considered. In R. F. Subotnik & H. J. Walberg (Eds.), *The scientific basis of educational productivity* (pp. 9–28). Greenwich, CT: Information Age.

Ray, B. A. (1969). Selective attention: The effects of combining stimuli which control incompatible behavior. *Journal of the Experimental Analysis of Behavior,* 12, 539–550.

Ray, B. A., &, Sidman, M. (1970). Reinforcement schedules and stimulus control. In W. N. Schoenfeld (Ed.), *The theory of reinforcement schedules* (pp. 187–214). New York: Appleton-Century-Crofts.

Scriven, M. (1974). Evaluation perspectives and procedures. In James W. Popham (Ed.), *Evaluation in education: Current application* (pp. 68–84). Berkeley, CA: McCutchan.

Sidman, M. (1960). *Tactics of scientific research: Evaluating experimental data in psychology*. Boston, MA: Authors Cooperative.

Sidman, M. & Stoddard, L. T. (1966). Programming perception and learning for retarded children. In N. R. Ellis (Ed.), *International review of research in mental retardation* (Vol. 2, pp. 151–208). New York: Academic Press.

Simmons, D. C., & Kame'enui, E. J. (2003). *A consumer's guide to evaluating a core reading program Grades k–3: A critical elements analysis*. Eugene: OR: Institute for the Development of Institutional Development, University of Oregon College of Education.

Stikeleather, G., & Sidman, M. (1990). An instance of spurious equivalence relations. *The Analysis of Verbal Behavior*, 8, 1–12.

Tiemann, P. W., & Markle, S. M. (1991). *Analyzing instructional content*. Champaign, IL: Stipes.

Twyman, J., Layng, T. V. J., Stikeleather, G., & Hobbins, K. A. (2004). A non-linear approach to curriculum design: The role of behavior analysis in building an effective reading program. In W. L. Heward et al. (Eds.), *Focus on behavior analysis in education*, Vol. 3 (pp. 55–68). Upper Saddle River, NJ: Merrill/Prentice Hall.

U.S. Department of Education. (n.d.). *Proven methods*. Retrieved March 14, 2004, from http://www.ed.gov/nclb/methods/index.html?src=ov

Valenstein, E. S. (1998). *Blaming the brain: The real truth about drugs and mental health*. New York: The Free Press.

Wright, W. (1903). Retrieved May 5, 2005, from http://www.wrightflyer.org/WindTunnel/testing1.html

CHAPTER 4

BLENDING EXPERIMENTAL AND DESCRIPTIVE RESEARCH

The Case of Educating Reading Teachers

Elizabeth S. Pang and Michael L. Kamil

It is a bedrock principle of research that the questions that are being posed by researchers should determine methodology and design decisions (Shavelson & Towne, 2002). However, few research reports explicitly describe the relationship between research questions and choices of methodology. Readers of research reports are left on their own to infer the reasons for the choice of methodology. This paper analyzes the differences between research studies on teacher education and professional development for literacy instruction, attempting to relate the problems being studied to issues of methodology and design.

For purposes of synthesis, this type of analysis is critical because studies using different methodologies are not all relevant to the same issues. The following is a case study of the body of research on teacher preparation and professional development for reading instruction. We have chosen to analyze this body of research because of its relevance to current policy issues and because it illustrates the difficulties of synthesizing research

---

The Scientific Basis of Educational Productivity, 45–84

across paradigms. It also provides an opportunity to show the potential benefits that may result from combining methodologies in research.

The importance of teacher preparation and professional development in educational research has generated considerable public interest as a result of various school reform efforts, such as the standards-based movement, that are predicated on having highly qualified and committed teachers. More recently, teacher preparation and teacher quality have come under close scrutiny as a result of the U.S. Department of Education's (2002) report calling for new standards in teacher education programs. According to the report, "There is little evidence that education school coursework leads to improved student achievement." The No Child Left Behind Act also emphasizes the need for professional development. There is clearly a need to reexamine the state of research in literacy teacher education to address these concerns.

The research on teacher education and professional development is also split along methodological lines. This is an important consideration because many of the criticisms of large-scale syntheses (Coles, 2000; Garan, 2001; Yatvin, 2002) have revolved around issues of the choices of methodologies.

TEACHER EDUCATION FOR READING

A key question for many policymakers and educators is whether teacher education programs are effective in bringing about change in teachers' knowledge and practices. A further question is whether the knowledge imparted in teacher education programs has a positive effect on students' learning. Related to this larger question are narrower questions regarding the specific characteristics of effective programs for reading teachers.

This chapter seeks to answer these questions by drawing on both experimental and descriptive research. Multiple layers of complexity are involved in teacher education research, encompassing teacher educators, the relationships between teachers and student teachers, methods, students, materials, and instructional settings. Nested within each of these layers are other variables that affect both teacher and student performance, such as attitudes, beliefs, experience, and motivation, to name a few. Typically, researchers focus on a few processes and issues at a time, usually using a specific method to answer their research question. But to synthesize the findings and make recommendations for implementing effective programs and improving existing ones, we need to critically examine research studies and their methodologies. This critical analysis will form a coherent picture of what works and why, and will point the direction for needed changes in the conduct of research. The field of reading teacher education is particularly suited to this kind of analysis because so much research has been undertaken yet so little has been agreed upon.

Correlational data suggest that certain aspects of teacher quality characteristics such as certification status and degree in the field to be taught are significantly and positively correlated with student outcomes (Darling-Hammond, 2000). This is very suggestive of the relationship between teacher quality and student outcomes, but it does not tell us if providing appropriate certification and degree programs to teachers ultimately leads to better student achievement. Teachers in more affluent schools tend to remain longer in their jobs and may reach higher levels of education.

In an attempt to determine whether causal relationships among teacher education efforts, teacher change, and student achievement exist, the National Reading Panel (NRP) undertook a review (National Institute of Child Health and Human Development, 2000) of the experimental research on teacher education and reading instruction. Nonexperimental research studies were not included in the original NRP analysis. This chapter reports on updates to the NRP review with more recent research studies. It also includes an analysis of the studies that use correlational, descriptive, or other methodologies that were not in the original database. Also included are studies of special education teachers and teachers of English-language learners that were previously not included in the NRP analysis.

THE DATABASE

In all, we identified 306 studies published between 1961 and 2001 (see Appendix A). The resultant studies from the electronic and hand searches were initially divided into two broad categories: experimental or quasi-experimental and nonexperimental. The experimental studies made use of control and treatment groups to which teachers were randomly assigned. In the quasi-experimental studies, the participants were not randomly assigned, even though comparison groups were included. The experimental and quasi-experimental category contained 39 studies. The nonexperimental studies used a wide range of approaches and methodologies, including quantitative methods; pre- and posttest designs without comparison groups; descriptions of programs; postcourse questionnaires; surveys by mail; course evaluations; social constructivist studies examining participants' dialogic conversations; studies examining teachers' reflections, journals, and portfolios; pilot studies; case studies; and qualitative studies using triangulation, inductive data analysis, and constant comparison procedures. A total of 267 studies were included in this second category.

Research on instructional variables generally examines the interactions between teachers and students in particular learning contexts. Research on literacy teacher education has an additional dimension: the role played by teacher educators. It is important to make this distinction because researchers often adopt different perspectives and research agendas with regard to the roles played by each of these three key variables. For instance, some studies examine literacy teacher education from the perspective of the teacher educator in order to improve programs, courses, and instruction at schools of education. Others emphasize the specific learning processes, attitudes, or perceptions of pre- or inservice teachers, and still others examine the relationships between pre- or inservice teachers and students. These studies provide insights into the processes of teacher change, and they suggest that teacher change results from the teacher education program or course.

METHODOLOGY

In order to have some basis for comparing all 306 studies in the database, we coded them according to the following descriptors: preservice, inservice, or both; number of teachers and, where applicable, number of students; instructional level (i.e., elementary, secondary, or specific grade level); duration of program or course; primary research question; data sources; methodology; and main findings.

The studies were divided into three general categories: (a) preservice, (b) inservice, and (c) both pre- and inservice. In general, we found that researchers do make a distinction between programs or courses for prospective teachers and those for practicing teachers. A few studies focused on both prospective and practicing teachers, such as studies on mentoring and field placements, as well as studies comparing prospective and experienced teachers.

After the studies were coded, we analyzed the data in terms of overall trends. Then we examined in greater detail particular themes and issues that emerged from groups of studies. Finally, we compared the findings of the two groups of research to derive principles and practices that promote both teacher learning and student achievement. We also noted gaps and unanswered questions in the research and the methodologies used.

EXPERIMENTAL VS. NONEXPERIMENTAL STUDIES

Table 4.1 shows the numbers of studies tabulated by methodology and topic. The number of nonexperimental studies (n = 267) far exceeded that of experimental and quasi-experimental studies (n = 39). There were

Table 4.1. Summary of Literacy Teacher Education and Professional Development Studies by Methodology

Preservice		*Inservice*		*Both*		*NA**		*Total*	
197		78		27		4		306	
Exp	Non-exp	Exp	Non-exp	Exp	Non-exp	Exp	Non-exp	Exp	Non-exp
7	190	28	50	2	25	2	2	39	267

*Not applicable: In two studies, teaching assistants and child-care workers received training and delivered the instructional intervention. Two other studies involved surveys of superintendents and professors of education.

also far more studies of preservice teachers than of inservice teachers. Among the preservice studies, only 4% used experimental designs compared with 36% of the inservice studies.

Both types of studies are important in building a strong foundation for research-based educational reform, including teacher education. The experimental studies provide causal evidence of teacher improvement and, in some cases, of concurrent student achievement (National Institute of Child Health and Human Development, 2000). The nonexperimental studies use a wide variety of approaches and methodologies, and in doing so, they provide multiple perspectives and rich contextual descriptions of teacher learning. Each type of research needs to be interpreted in the light of the other.

FINDINGS OF EXPERIMENTAL RESEARCH

The NRP report identified 32 studies that met the criteria for experimental or quasi-experimental research, of which 11 were preservice studies and 21 were inservice. The report highlighted the need to measure both teacher change and student outcomes in order to demonstrate the effectiveness of teacher education. That is, in order to attribute causality to the teacher education or professional development intervention, a change in teacher behaviors must have taken place. In addition, a change in student behaviors also must have occurred for the intervention to be deemed successful.

However, these conditions are often difficult to achieve for preservice education. In order to conduct experimental research on preservice education, a longitudinal study would have to be conducted that follows preservice teachers upon completion of their formal preparation to their first year of teaching and beyond. Given the differences between sites where teachers from the same programs eventually teach, the power of such a study would be a recurrent problem. Consequently, few, if any, efforts in literacy have conducted this type of study. The NRP analysis examined found no experimental studies of preservice education that measured both teacher change and student outcomes.

The problems are not quite so severe when it comes to the study of inservice education, given that professional development sites are readily identifiable and accessible. However, the NRP analysis found that many inservice studies did not report both teacher change and student outcomes.

Eleven of the 21 inservice experimental studies examined reported *both* teacher and student outcomes. Significantly, these studies showed corresponding changes in teachers' instructional practice and students' performance as a result of professional development efforts. In other words, in studies in which teacher knowledge or practice improved, student learning increased; in those in which teachers failed to implement the intervention, student outcomes did not improve.

The majority (10 of 11) of the preservice studies reported improvements in teacher knowledge. These improvements suggest that preservice teachers benefited from their courses, but it remains to be seen whether such learning impacts actual classroom practice and improves student learning. Among the inservice studies that measured *either* teacher or student outcomes, the majority of the studies showed significant or modest improvements in either teacher knowledge (15 of 17 studies) or student achievement (13 of 15 studies).

Although the experimental research base is small, it is highly consistent. It strongly suggests that inservice teacher education does bring about changes in teacher instructional behavior and consequent changes in student achievement. Whether this conclusion can be extended to include preservice education is less certain. We will reexamine this issue in the light of both the experimental and nonexperimental research. In particular, studies that use a longitudinal design would be helpful in determining the relationship between preservice education and its impact on student achievement.

TRENDS IN NONEXPERIMENTAL RESEARCH

In addition to the growing emphasis on teacher quality and standards, a noticeable shift has taken place toward reflective practice in the professional preparation and continuing education of literacy teachers. With the publication of Schon's (1983; 1987) highly influential books on reflective practitioners, a whole generation of research on reflection was initiated, both in the field of general teacher education as well as that of literacy teacher education (see Roskos, Vukelich, & Risko, 2001 for a review). Furthermore, the emphasis in teacher education has changed from competency-based "training" to "teaching" models (Hoffman & Pearson, 2000). Duffy (1990; 2004) also makes a compelling case for empowering teachers by investing in the minds of teachers instead of "training" them to follow theories, programs, and procedures. Although certain elements of training will remain in teacher education programs, these programs have a growing emphasis on reflective, discursive, and dialogic strategies (Hoffman & Pearson, 2000). Reflective teachers are a particularly popular topic in the nonexperimental research literature.

Another important trend is the impact of new technologies on literacy and teacher education. Technology has impacted the way we conceive of both literacy and learning through such advancements as multimedia (i.e., combinations of text and audiovisual material) and computer-mediated communication (e.g., e-mail, chat rooms, video conferencing). From the late 1980s onward, the number of studies of literacy teacher education using computer-based technology (see Pang & Kamil [2004] for an analysis of the research) has steadily increased. The U.S. Department of Education is also seeking to bring about a shift to "technology-infused teaching" within schools of education through the Preparing Tomorrow's Teachers to Use Technology (PT3) (2005) initiative.

FINDINGS OF NONEXPERIMENTAL RESEARCH

Preservice Literacy Teacher Education

The reason for the predominant use of nonexperimental designs for preservice studies lies in the nature of the questions asked by many researchers of preservice literacy education. As noted in the NRP analysis, many preservice studies focus on general methods courses. Researchers are interested in describing teachers' learning processes, both individually and collectively, in prescribed coursework, field experience, or combinations of these. In general, these studies affirm the importance of providing field-based experiences (e.g., internships and tutoring opportunities) in conjunction with coursework in order to help teachers connect theory with practice (e.g., Britton, 1973; Frazier, Mencer, & Duchein, 1997; Linek et al., 1999).

Reflection

Many preservice studies in literacy teacher education cluster around the concept of reflection. These researchers tend to emphasize the process of change, particularly in terms of prospective teachers' beliefs, perceptions, and attitudes in relation to a host of instructional issues, ranging from whole language to self-efficacy and general perceptions of teaching. All 18 literacy studies in the review of reflection studies by Roskos et al. (2001) were studies of preservice teachers. In addition to these studies, we found others that used "reflective journals" (Maimon, 1997), "reflective portfolios" (Oropallo & Gomez, 1996), "reflective essays" (Fazio, 2000), "reflective assessment" (Sampson, Linek, Raine, & Westergaard, 1997), "reflective teaching" (Myers, 1993), and "collaborative reflection" (Anderson & Reid, 1994).

Similar to Roskos et al. (2001), we found great variation in the way reflection was conceptualized in preservice education. Some studies described reflection as one of the tools, processes, or outcomes within a larger framework of examining changes in teachers' philosophies about reading and reading instruction (e.g., Lefever-Davis & Helfeldt, 1994; Wile, 1995). In others, the term "reflection" is largely synonymous with the extensive practice of writing journal entries and compiling teaching portfolios.

Technology and Diversity

Two topics of current importance in teacher education relate to technology and issues of diversity. These areas are where nonexperimental research is setting promising new directions for future research. In technology, whereas the experimental research primarily examined video technology in teacher education, the nonexperimental research has been instrumental in exploring new technologies such as multimedia, hypermedia, and computer-mediated communication (Pang & Kamil, 2004). This topic of research does seem to be growing in popularity as teacher educators adopt technological solutions for instructional methods.

The issue of teaching reading to culturally diverse learners, including dialect speakers and English-language learners, is not at all well researched in literacy teacher education. Only two experimental studies reported on English-language learners (Stallings & Krasavage, 1986; Stallings, Robbins, Presbrey, & Scott, 1986). The nonexperimental studies are instrumental in highlighting the importance of this issue because more of these studies have appeared in mainstream reading journals in recent years (e.g., Kidd, Sanchez, & Thorp, 2000; Mathis, 2000; Ross, 1994; Sanacore, 2000; Worthy & Patterson, 2001; Xu, 2000). This is an encouraging trend.

Similar to the experimental studies, the majority of the nonexperimental studies of preservice teachers report favorably on teacher change. An important difference between the experimental and nonexperimental research is that the latter provides descriptions of teacher learning, as well as descriptions of less-than-optimal learning conditions, such as cognitive dissonance experienced by preservice teachers in field settings (Hollingsworth, 1989; Linek et al, 1999; Sampson & Linek, 1994). In contrast, the experimental research provides specific information about whether teacher change led to improved student learning.

From Preservice Education to the Initial Years of Teaching

Whether preservice teachers later apply what they have learned in actual classroom settings is not certain. Still more uncertain is the effect of teacher knowledge on student learning. A relatively small number of researchers (Bayles, 1997; Grossman et al., 2000; Keehn, Harris, Hedrick, Martinez, & Perez, 2001) are beginning to examine this issue in studies that follow preservice teachers through to their first year of teaching and beyond. No experimental studies have followed preservice teachers through to their first and subsequent years of teaching with literacy measures of student achievement.

In the nonexperimental studies, researchers found clear influence of university preparation on the teachers during their first years of teaching (Bayles, 1997; Grossman et al., 2000). Grossman et al. found that the pedagogical tools introduced during teacher education became more evident in the teachers' second year of teaching. They cautioned against making conclusions about the effectiveness of preservice education based on data from only the first professional year. They concluded that conceptual tools buttressed with practical strategies proved to be the most influential. Bayles (1997) found that conferencing between student teachers and supervisors and between beginning teachers and mentors is especially important.

Inservice Literacy Teacher Education

The NRP analysis found that the inservice studies focused on more specific instructional methods and issues than the preservice studies. This holds true for the nonexperimental studies as well. For example, a number of inservice studies focused on different aspects of comprehension instruction, such as strategy instruction (Duffy, 1993), direct instruction (Hartman & Nielsen, 1989); reading strategies (Nichols, Rupley, & Mergen, 1998), and transactional strategies instruction (El-Dinary, Pressley, & Schuder, 1992). Others reported on content area reading approaches and writing instruction. Whole-language principles and holistic literacy instruction also appear to be a popular topic in inservice courses (e.g., Nelson, Pryor, & Church, 1990; Rickelman, Henk, & Helfeldt, 1994; Shepperson, & Nistler, 1991; Wuthrick, 1995).

The NRP report highlights the importance of adequate teacher support in order to sustain teacher change and student achievement. The nonexperimental studies report favorably on peer coaching and mentoring in supporting teacher professional development (Haid, MacBee, & Riley, 2000; Padak, Rasinski, & Ackerman, 1996; Swafford, Maltsberger, Button, & Furgerson, 1997). Studies that examine the relationship between preservice and inservice teachers learning together also show the importance of peer support and collaboration (Hughes, & Zeek, 1997; Lenski, 1998; Sampson, Walker, & Fazio, 1999). These strategies, along with administrative and resource support, should go some way to ensure the sustainability of teacher change.

KEY PRINCIPLES AND PRACTICES

The main purpose of conducting this analysis is to derive general principles and practices that can be used to improve literacy teacher education. From a consideration of the evidence from both experimental and descriptive research, we can formulate a more holistic picture of what effective teacher education looks like. First of all, clear evidence from experimental research suggests that inservice teachers do learn from professional development programs and that students thus benefit from improved teaching. These programs focus on specific types of reading instruction (e.g., Directed Reading–Thinking Activity [DRTA]) as well as more holistic curricular changes that require extensive funding support.

In preservice teacher education, very little or no direct evidence of causal links exists between university coursework and improvements in teaching. However, a great deal of information from the descriptive studies attests to the changes that teachers undergo as a result of attending courses and participating in internships, tutoring, and other educational experiences. Experimental studies that measure the changes that preservice teachers undergo further bolster this finding. In one or two studies, it has also been shown that implementation of what has been taught becomes more evident in the second year of teaching. This suggests that new teachers need a period of adjustment before they integrate what they have learned in the context of their own teaching.

Regarding the content of effective pre- and inservice programs, research-based methods and theories of literacy have been widely investigated. On the whole, the findings are positive, but they do not converge on any single method or approach to literacy. It appears that a range of instructional methods and theories are effective in teacher education programs. What seems to matter is that teachers relate the theories and methods to the specific contexts of instruction. Although no causal evidence is available for us to draw on, it appears that, among teacher educators, consensual agreement exists that a combination of coursework and field experiences is important. This body of research also suggests that both prospective and experienced teachers need to be reflective in their teaching and learning.

FUTURE DIRECTIONS FOR READING TEACHER EDUCATION RESEARCH

A central dilemma confronts us in literacy teacher education: for teacher education to be effective, it must have positive effects on both teachers and students. The experimental research can and does provide evidence of teacher change and its effect on student achievement. A small group of carefully designed experiments report corresponding changes in teacher and student outcomes as a result of the intervention. However, outcomes alone do not fully reflect the complex nature of teaching and learning. We need to understand more deeply the attitudes, beliefs, and conceptualizations of literacy that teachers have and the changes they undergo in conjunction with the study of teacher practices (e.g., how a teacher implements a new instructional strategy) and performance outcomes (e.g., student achievement data).

In one study (Sparks, 1988), correlational analyses indicated that teachers' philosophical acceptance predicted the teachers' subsequent use of the instructional methods. In the same study, qualitative analyses revealed differences between improving teachers and non-improving teachers in terms of self-efficacy and willingness to experiment. It is not easy to study the internal process of change that teachers undergo. To be able to connect those changes with student achievement is even more challenging. To date, many studies of reflection and of teacher change have been conducted, but a lack of organized information on how these processes lead to actual improvement in instruction and student learning still exists.

The nonexperimental studies ask very different questions from the experimental studies by focusing on the processes of change and reflection. In the nonexperimental studies that measured teacher change, the findings do not contradict those of the experimental research. However, given the large number (87%) of studies we examined that used descriptive methodologies, it is unfortunate that only some of them were carefully designed and reported in such a way that other researchers may conduct parallel or follow-up studies.

Another problem is that the vast majority of preservice studies are constrained by university coursework structure. The duration of these studies is typically one semester, yet teacher change happens gradually over time. Teacher change cannot be captured adequately by survey questionnaires asking teachers to report whether they used a particular method after a course is over. We found only three studies that directly examined the effect of preservice education on teachers' instructional practice. These studies take place over 1 to 3 years and follow preservice teachers through to their initial years of teaching. To answer the question of whether university teacher preparation programs benefit preservice teachers, more research of this nature is needed. Although many preservice studies use reflective, discursive, and dialogical strategies, the short durations of these studies and the inconsistent way in which concepts such as reflection and dialogism are defined and investigated do not reflect the spirit of true "teaching" models. A more principled and systematic approach is needed.

Finally, teacher education studies investigating issues of diversity should be rigorously pursued. We have known for some time that mainstream teachers need to be informed about reading in a second language and of culturally responsive teaching, but an extensive research base in the area of teacher preparation and professional development has not yet been developed.

WHAT DOES THIS ANALYSIS REVEAL ABOUT RESEARCH?

One of the strong assumptions held about teacher education and professional development is that, if it is effective, it should produce "better" instruction on the part of teachers and "better" reading by students (Anders, Hoffman, & Duffy, 2000; National Institute of Child Health and Human Development, 2000). Although this seems like an intuitive assumption, we found that it did not drive a large portion of the research, regardless of methodology.

We found dramatic differences between the experimental and nonexperimental research studies in our analysis. A major difference is simply the presence of comparison groups in the experimental studies. The use of comparison groups is a prerequisite to establishing the causal connection between the interventions and the subsequent performance of teachers and students.

However, another significant difference was the use of reading outcome measures. Proportionately, far more of the experimental studies involved outcome measures of reading and reading achievement. Providing outcome measures is a necessity in establishing the connection between interventions and student performance. It is also important for much policy work—for example, in establishing the relative costs of raising reading achievement through the use of professional development. Given the small number of studies that fulfilled *all* the requirements of establishing causal connections, it is currently not possible to do these studies. However, improvements in research conceptualization and design would allow such analyses to be conducted.

It is difficult to account for the extreme imbalances between experimental and nonexperimental work and between preservice and inservice studies. Some of the imbalance can be accounted for by the questions that were being asked. Some can be accounted for by assuming that researchers chose a methodology and decided to find a problem in the general domain of teacher education or professional development that could be studied.

What is needed is a concerted effort to have authors make their theoretical, methodological, and epistemological assumptions more explicit when they report studies. Journal editors could certainly help by requiring explicit statements of the relationships among questions, methodology, and data. Current national research policy has adopted a "gold standard" of experimental research. For some problems, this is a solid choice. For other problems, other methodologies are more important. Mosenthal and Kamil (1991) suggest that different methodologies are appropriate at different stages of development of knowledge in a field. The literature on teacher education and professional development may not have reached a stage at which experimental work is routinely used to verify hypotheses.

Additionally, researchers rarely cite relevant research from paradigms other than their own (Kamil, 1995). Consequently, researchers often do not present the richest theoretical descriptions of their work in relation to the research of other researchers and to the questions being asked. The blending of research findings from different methodologies requires acknowledgement of those "other" methodologies. The current analysis suggests much can be gained by having authors broaden their views to include research from different methodologies.

Patterns of research priorities and funding affect the nature and conduct of research. Much of the work in this area has been funded on a relatively small scale. In order to do the kind of work that would be necessary to experimentally study preservice programs, larger and more dependable funding programs are required. This is clearly a place where national research priorities can affect the accumulation of knowledge about the effects of teacher education programs.

Finally, the blending of data from research conducted using different methodologies has the potential for enriching the knowledge base. In the case of reading education, knowing about the beliefs and attitudes of teachers (from the nonexperimental literature) is important because it indexes a source of teacher behaviors. However, standard outcome measures of reading (included in many experimental studies) are also important and need to be included in research that will allow inferences about the efficacy of student learning.

We hope for a future in which research makes explicit the assumptions that guided the choices in the design and data collection. We also hope that future research will combine methodologies when appropriate. Most important, we hope that future researchers account for the data from other research studies, even those that use different methodologies.

APPENDIX: REFERENCES REVIEWED

The following is a list of the studies that were selected for review in this chapter. They are grouped as experimental and quasi-experimental articles and nonexperimental studies.

Experimental and Quasi-Experimental Articles

Anderson, L. M., Evertson, C. M., & Brophy, J. E. (1979). An experimental study of effective teaching in first-grade reading groups. *Elementary School Journal*, *79*, 193–223.

Anderson, V. (1992). A teacher development project in transactional strategy instruction for teachers of severely reading-disabled adolescents. *Teaching and Teacher Education*, *8*, 391–403.

Andrews, N. C., Moss, R. K., & Stansell, J. C. (1985). Reading (aloud, that is) to undergraduate reading methods classes. *Journal of Reading*, *28*, 315–320.

Baker, J. E. (1977). Application of the in-service training/classroom consultation model to reading instruction. *Ontario Psychologist*, *9*, 57–62.

Baker, S., & Smith, S. (1999). Starting off on the right foot: The influence of four principles of professional development in improving literacy instruction in two kindergarten programs. *Learning Disabilities Research and Practice*, *14*, 239–253.

Bean, R. M., Eichelberger, R. T., Swan, A., & Tucker, R. (1999). Professional development to promote early literacy achievement. In J. R. Dugan, P. E. Linder, W. M. Linek, & E. G. Sturtevant (Eds.), *Advancing the world of literacy: Moving into the 21st century* (pp. 94–106). Carrollton, GA: College Reading Association.

Block, C. C. (1993). Strategy instruction in a literature-based reading program. *Elementary School Journal*, *94*, 139–151.

Book, C. L., Duffy, G. G., Roehler, L. R., Meloth, M. S., & Vavrus, L. G. (1985). A study of the relationship between teacher explanation and student metacognitive awareness during reading instruction. *Communication Education, 34*, 29–36.

Bos, C. S., Mather, N., Narr, R. F., & Babur, N. (1999). Interactive, collaborative professional development in early literacy instruction: Supporting the balancing act. *Learning Disabilities Research and Practice, 14*, 227–238.

Brown, R., Pressley, M., Van Meter, P., & Schuder, T. (1996). A quasi-experimental validation of transactional strategies instruction with low-achieving second-grade readers. *Journal of Educational Psychology, 88*, 18–37.

Coladarci, T., & Gage, N. L. (1984). Effects of a minimal intervention on teacher behavior and student achievement. *American Educational Research Journal, 21*, 539–555.

Conley, M. M. W. (1983). Increasing students' reading achievement via teacher inservice education. *Reading Teacher, 36*, 804–808.

Duffy, G. G., Roehler, L. R., Meloth, M. S., Vavrus, L. G., Wesselman, R., Putnam, J., et al. (1986). The relationship between explicit verbal explanations during reading skill instruction and student awareness and achievement: A study of reading teacher effects. *Reading Research Quarterly, 21*, 237–252.

Duffy, G. G., Roehler, L. R., Sivan, E., Rackliffe, G., Book, C., Meloth, M. S., et al. (1987). Effects of explaining the reasoning associated with using reading strategies. *Reading Research Quarterly, 22*, 347–368.

Dupuis, M. M., Askov, E. N., & Lee, J. W. (1979). Changing attitudes toward content area reading: The content area reading project. *Journal of Educational Research, 73*, 65–74.

Fayne, H. R., & Gettinger, M. (1981). Narrowing the gap between research and practice in sight word reading instruction. *Psychology in the Schools, 18*, 240–245.

Fifield, M., & Farmer, L. (1976). Teacher aides provide direct instruction. *Journal of American Indian Education, 16*, 13–18.

Foegen, A., Espin, C. A., Allinder, R. M., & Markell, M. A. (2001). Translating research into practice: Preservice teachers' beliefs about curriculum-based measurement. *Journal of Special Education, 34*, 226–236.

Greenberg, K. H., Woodside, M. R., & Brasil, L. (1994). Differences in the degree of mediated learning and classroom interaction structure for trained and untrained teachers. *Journal of Classroom Interaction, 29*, 1–9.

Klesius, J. P., Searls, E. F., & Zielonka, P. (1990). A comparison of two methods of direct instruction of preservice teachers. *Journal of Teacher Education, 41*, 34–44.

Kraus, C. D. (1992). Changes in primary teachers' instructional practices after 1 year of a collaborative whole language project. In N. D. Padak, T. V. Rasinski, & J. Logan (Eds.), *Literacy research and practice: Foundations for the year 2000* (pp. 79–86). Pittsburg, KS: College Reading Association.

Levin, B. B. (1995). Using the case method in teacher education: The role of discussion and experience in teachers' thinking about cases. *Teaching and Teacher Education, 11*, 63–79.

McCutchen, D., & Berninger, V. W. (1999). Those who know, teach well: Helping teachers master literacy-related subject-matter knowledge. *Learning Disabilities Research and Practice, 14*, 215–226.

Miller, J. W., & Ellsworth, R. (1985). The evaluation of a two-year program to improve teacher effectiveness in reading instruction. *Elementary School Journal, 85*, 485–496.

Morrison, C., Harris, A. J., & Auerbach, I. T. (1969). Staff after-effects of participation in a reading research project: A follow-up study of the CRAFT project. *Reading Research Quarterly, 4*, 366–395.

O'Connor, G., & Glynn, T. (1987). Contexts for remedial reading: Practice reading and Pause, Prompt and Praise tutoring. *Educational Psychology, 7*, 207–223.

O'Connor, R. E. (1999). Teachers learning Ladders to Literacy. *Learning Disabilities Research and Practice, 14*, 203–214.

Olson, M. W., & Gillis, M. (1983). Teaching reading study skills and course content to preservice teachers. *Reading World, 23*, 124–133.

Reid, E. R. (1997). Exemplary Center for Reading Instruction (ECRI). *Behavior & Social Issues, 7*, 19–24.

Shepard, L. A., Flexer, R. J., Hiebert, E. H., Marion, S. F., Mayfield, V., & Weston, T. J. (1996). Effects of introducing classroom performance assessments on student learning. *Educational Measurement: Issues and Practice, 15*, 7–18.

Simmonds, E. P. M. (1992). The effects of teacher training and implementation of two methods for improving the comprehension skills of students with learning disabilities. *Learning Disabilities Research & Practice, 7*, 194–198.

Streeter, B. B. (1986). The effects of training experienced teachers in enthusiasm on students' attitudes toward reading. *Reading Psychology, 7*, 249–259.

Talmage, H., Pascarella, E. T., & Ford, S. (1984). The influence of cooperative learning strategies on teacher practices, student perceptions of the learning environment, and academic achievement. *American Educational Research Journal, 21*, 163–179.

Tyre, B. B., & Knight, D. W. (1972). Teaching word recognition skills to preservice teachers: An analysis of three procedures. *Southern Journal of Educational Research, 6*, 113–122.

Wedman, J. M., Hughes, J. A., & Robinson, R. R. (1993). The effect of using systematic cooperative learning approach to help preservice teachers learn informal reading inventory procedures. *Innovative Higher Education, 17*, 231–241.

Wedman, J. M., & Moutray, C. (1991). The effect of training on the questions preservice teachers ask during literature discussions. *Reading Research and Instruction, 30*, 62–70.

Westermark, T. I., & Crichlow, K. A. (1983). The effect of theoretical and situational knowledge of reading on teachers' estimates of readability. *Reading Psychology, 4*, 129–139.

Nonexperimental Studies

Afflerbach, P., Bass, L., Hoo, D., Smith, S., Weiss, L., & Williams, L. (1988). Preservice teachers use think-aloud protocols to study writing. *Language Arts, 65*, 693–701.

Allen, V. G., Freeman, E. B., & Lehman, B. A. (1989). A literacy education model for preservice teachers: Translating observation and reflection into exemplary practice. In S. McCormick & J. Zutell (Eds.), *Cognitive and social perspectives for literacy research and instruction. 38th yearbook of the National Reading Conference* (pp. 473–480). Chicago: National Reading Conference.

Altieri, E. (1998). Using literacy activities to construct new understandings of disability. In T. Shanahan & F. V. Rodriguez-Brown (Eds.), *47th yearbook of the National Reading Conference* (pp. 529–541). Chicago: National Reading Conference.

Anderson, J., & Lee, A. (1995). Literacy teachers learning a new literacy: A study of the use of electronic mail in a reading education class. *Reading Research and Instruction, 34*, 222–238.

Anderson, N. A., Caswell, I. J., & Hayes, M. E. (1994). Using peer coaching to provide additional feedback to preservice teachers of reading in an early field experience. In E. G. Sturtevant & W. M. Linek (Eds.), *Pathways for literacy* (pp. 211–222). Pittsburg, KS: College Reading Association.

Anderson, R. S., & Reid, S. (1994). A collaborative conversation about learning: Using dialogue journals for professional development. In C. K. Kinzer & D. J. Leu (Eds.), *Multidimensional aspects of literacy research, theory, and practice. 43rd yearbook of the National Reading Conference* (pp. 361–369). Chicago: National Reading Conference.

Askov, E., Dupuis, M., & Lee, J. (1978). An effective inservice model for content area reading in the secondary schools. In D. Pearson & J. Hansen (Eds.), *Reading: Disciplined inquiry in process and practice. 27th yearbook of the National Reading Conference* (pp. 6–12). Clemson, SC: National Reading Conference.

Asselin, M. (2000). Confronting assumptions: Preservice teachers' beliefs about reading and literature. *Reading Psychology, 21*, 31–55.

Bahr, C., Kinzer, C. K., & Rieth, H. (1991). An analysis of the effects of teacher training and student grouping on reading comprehension skills among mildly handicapped high school students using computer-assisted instruction. *Journal of Special Education Technology, 11*, 136–154.

Baker, E. A., & Wedman, J. M. (2000). Lessons learned while using case-based instruction with preservice literacy teachers. In T. Shanahan & F. V. Rodriguez-Brown (Eds.), *49th yearbook of the National Reading Conference* (pp. 122–136). Chicago: National Reading Conference.

Balajthy, E. (1988). Evaluation of a preservice training module in microcomputer applications for the teaching of reading. *Computers in the Schools, 5*, 113–128.

Balajthy, E. (1996). Changing themes for preparing teachers to use computers and multimedia for literacy learning. In E. G. Sturtevant & W. M. Linek (Eds.), *Growing literacy* (pp. 247–255). Harrisonburg, VA: College Reading Association.

Bean, T. W. (1994). A constructivist view of preservice teachers' attitudes toward reading through case study analysis of autobiographies. In C. K. Kinzer & D. J. Leu (Eds.), *Multidimensional aspects of literacy research, theory, and practice. 43rd yearbook of the National Reading Conference* (pp. 370–379). Chicago: National Reading Conference.

Bean, T. W., & Readence, J. E. (1995). A comparative study of content area literacy students' attitudes toward reading through autobiographical analysis. In K. Hinchman, D. J. Leu, & C. K. Kinzer (Eds.), *Perspectives on literacy research and practice. 44th yearbook of the National Reading Conference* (pp. 325–333). Chicago: National Reading Conference.

Bean, T. W., & Zulich, J. (1989). Using dialogue journals to foster reflective practice with preservice content-area teachers. *Teacher Education Quarterly, 16,* 33–40.

Bean, T. W., & Zulich, J. (1990). Teaching students to learn from text: Preservice content teachers' changing view of their role through the window of their student–professor dialogue journals. In J. Zutell & S. McCormick (Eds.), *Literacy theory and research: Analyses from multiple paradigms. 39th yearbook of the National Reading Conference* (pp. 171–178). Chicago: National Reading Conference.

Bean, T. W., & Zulich, J. (1992). A case study of three preservice teachers' beliefs about content area reading through the window of student–professor dialogue journals. In C. K. Kinzer & D. J. Leu (Eds.), *Literacy research, theory, and practice: Views from many perspectives. 41st yearbook of the National Reading Conference* (pp. 463–474). Chicago: National Reading Conference.

Bean, T. W., & Zulich, J. (1993). The other half: A case study of asymmetrical communication in content-area reading student–professor dialogue journals. In D. J. Leu & C. K. Kinzer (Eds.), *Examining central issues in literacy research, theory, and practice. 42nd yearbook of the National Reading Conference* (pp. 289–296). Chicago: National Reading Conference.

Blachowicz, C. L. Z., & Wimett, C. A. (1995). Reconstructing our pasts: Urban preservice teachers' definitions of literacy and literacy instruction. In K. Hinchman, D. J. Leu, & C. K. Kinzer (Eds.), *Perspectives on literacy research and practice. 44th yearbook of the National Reading Conference* (pp. 334-341). Chicago: National Reading Conference.

Blair, T. R., & Jones, D. L. (1990). Teacher expectations: Modifying one's teaching through the self-monitoring process. In N. D. Padak, T. V. Rasinski, & J. Logan (Eds.), *Challenges in reading* (pp. 11–16). Provo, UT: College Reading Association.

Blanton, W. E., & Moorman, G. B. (1993). A diary as a tool for mediating reading teacher activity. *Reading Research and Instruction, 32,* 76–89.

Bloem, P., Peck, J., Newton, E., Williams, A. L., & Duling, V. P. (1998). When teachers change alone: Case studies of literacy teachers in a non-supportive school environment. In B. Sturtevant, J. Dugan, P. Linder, & W. M. Linek (Eds.), *Literacy and community* (pp. 231–242). Carrollton, GA: College Reading Association.

Borko, H. (1985). Student teachers' planning and evaluations of reading lessons. In J. A. Niles & R. V. Lalik (Eds.), *Issues in literacy: A research perspective. 34th yearbook of the National Reading Conference* (pp. 263–271). Rochester, NY: National Reading Conference.

Botel, M., Ripley, P. M., & Barnes, L. A. (1993). A case study of an implementation of the "new literacy" paradigm. *Journal of Research in Reading, 16,* 112–127.

Bowling, N., Muia, J., & Shaffer, G. (1978). Preservice teachers' perceptions of reading instruction. In D. Pearson & J. Hansen (Eds.), *Reading: Disciplined inquiry in process and practice. 27th yearbook of the National Reading Conference* (pp. 1–5). Clemson, SC: National Reading Conference.

Bowman, C., & Edenfield, R. (2000). Becoming better together through collaboration and technology. *English Journal, 90*, 112–119.

Brann, B., & Hattie, J. (1995). Spelling instruction in primary schools. *New Zealand Journal of Educational Studies, 30*, 39–49.

Briggs, C., & Stieffer, T. K. (1995). Literature infusion: A shot in the arm for elementary methods courses. In W. M. Linek & E. G. Sturtevant (Eds.), *Generations of literacy* (pp. 199–208). Harrisonburg, VA: College Reading Association.

Broaddus, K. (2000). From peacemaker to advocate: A preservice teacher's case study of an emergent reader. *Journal of Literacy Research, 32*, 571–597.

Broaddus, K., & Bloodgood, J. W. (1999). "We're supposed to already know how to teach reading": Teacher change to support struggling readers. *Reading Research Quarterly, 34*, 426–451.

Bullion-Mears, A. (1994). Developing collaboration and teacher reflection in a college curriculum class. In C. K. Kinzer & D. J. Leu (Eds.), *Multidimensional aspects of literacy research, theory, and practice. 43rd yearbook of the National Reading Conference* (pp. 380–386). Chicago: National Reading Conference.

Button, K. (1992). Factors that enhance effective instruction: A single subject case study of changes in the knowledge base and practice of a kindergarten teacher. In C. K. Kinzer & D. J. Leu (Eds.), *Literacy research, theory, and practice: Views from many perspectives. 41st yearbook of the National Reading Conference* (pp. 483–490). Chicago: National Reading Conference.

Christensen, L., & Walker, B. J. (1992). Researching one's own teaching in a reading education course. In N. D. Padak, T. V. Rasinski, & J. Logan (Eds.), *Literacy research and practice: Foundations for the year 2000.* (pp. 57–64). Pittsburg, KS: College Reading Association.

Commeyras, M., Reinking, D., Heubach, K. M., & Pagnucco, J. (1993). Looking within: A study of an undergraduate reading methods course. In D. J. Leu & C. K. Kinzer (Eds.), *Examining central issues in literacy research, theory, and practice. 42nd yearbook of the National Reading Conference* (pp. 297–304). Chicago: National Reading Conference.

Copeland, W. D., & Decker, D. L. (1996). Video cases and the development of meaning making in preservice teachers. *Teaching and Teacher Education, 12*, 467–481.

Costello, M. S., & Stahl, N. A. (1997). Promoting diversity: A learning community project for college reading programs and teacher education programs. In W. M. Linek & E. G. Sturtevant (Eds.), *Exploring literacy* (pp. 220–228). Platteville, WI: College Reading Association.

Cox, B. E., Fang, Z., Carriveau, R., Dillon, D., Hopkins, C., & Nierstheimer, S. (1998). Preservice teachers' construction of professional knowledge: Teacher learning about literacy education. In T. Shanahan & F. V. Rodriguez-Brown (Eds.), *47th yearbook of the National Reading Conference* (pp. 508–516). Chicago: National Reading Conference.

Craig, M., Allen, D., & Shepperson, G. (1994). Literature-based instruction in preservice teacher education. In E. G. Sturtevant & W. M. Linek (Eds.), *Pathways for literacy* (pp. 195–202). Pittsburg, KS: College Reading Association.

Craig, M. T., & Leavell, A. G. (1995). Preservice teachers' perceptions of portfolio assessment in reading/language arts coursework. In W. M. Linek & E. G. Sturtevant (Eds.), *Generations of literacy* (pp. 83–95). Harrisonburg, VA: College Reading Association.

Daisey, P. (2000). The construction of "how-to" books in a secondary content area literacy course: The promise and barriers of writing-to-learn strategies. In P. Linder, W. M. Linek, E. G. Sturtevant, & J. R. Dugan (Eds.), *Literacy at a new horizon* (pp. 147–158). Readyville, TN: College Reading Association.

Daisey, P., & Shroyer, M. G. (1993). Perceptions and attitudes of content and methods instructors toward a required reading course. *Journal of Reading, 36*, 624–629.

Daly, P. M., & Cooper, J. O. (1993). Persuading student teachers and inservice teachers to use precision teaching after the course is over. *Education and Treatment of Children, 16*, 316–325.

Danielson, K. (1989). The autobiography as language reflection. *Reading Horizons, 29*, 257–261.

Deal, D. (1998). Portfolios, learning logs, and eulogies: Using expressive writing in a science methods class. In B. Sturtevant, J. Dugan, P. Linder, & W. M. Linek (Eds.), *Literacy and community* (pp. 243–255). Carrollton, GA: College Reading Association.

Deegan, D. H. (1995). Taking it up/taking it seriously: Critical literacy in preservice teacher education. In K. Hinchman, D. J. Leu, & C. K. Kinzer (Eds.), *Perspectives on literacy research and practice. 44th yearbook of the National Reading Conference* (pp. 342–348). Chicago: National Reading Conference.

Dickson, S. V., & Bursuck, W. D. (1999). Implementing a model for preventing reading failure: A report from the field. *Learning Disabilities Research and Practice, 14*, 191–202.

Dillingofski, M., & Dulin, K. (1980). Changes in reading-related attitudes during a one-semester preservice course in secondary reading methods. In M. L. Kamil & A. J. Moe (Eds.), *Perspectives on reading research and instruction. 29th yearbook of the National Reading Conference* (pp. 223–225). Washington, DC: National Reading Conference.

Dodson, M. M. (2000). Monologic and dialogic conversations: How preservice teachers socially construct knowledge through oral and computer-mediated classroom discourse. In T. Shanahan & F. V. Rodriguez-Brown (Eds.), *49th yearbook of the National Reading Conference* (pp. 137–152). Chicago: National Reading Conference.

Donovan, C. A. (1999). Learning to teach reading/language arts: Considering the impact of experiences on understanding. In T. Shanahan & F. V. Rodriguez-Brown (Eds.), *48th yearbook of the National Reading Conference* (pp. 451–465). Chicago: National Reading Conference.

Doyle, C. (1988). Creative applications of computer assisted reading and writing instruction. *Journal of Reading, 32*, 236–239.

Drecktrah, M. E., & Chiang, B. (1997). Instructional strategies used by general educators and teachers of students with learning disabilities: A survey. *Remedial and Special Education, 18*, 174–181.

Dressman, M., Graves, C., & Webster, J. P. (1999). Learning to read the research: How preservice teachers come to terms with cognitive versus holistic models of reading. In T. Shanahan & F. V. Rodriguez-Brown (Eds.), *48th yearbook of the*

National Reading Conference (pp. 437–450). Chicago: National Reading Conference.

Duchein, M. A., Frazier, D. W., & Willis, E. L. (1996). The bibliotherapeutic effects of ludic reading. In E. G. Sturtevant & W. M. Linek (Eds.), *Growing literacy* (pp. 139–146). Harrisonburg, VA: College Reading Association.

Duckworth, S., & Taylor, R. (1995). Creating and assessing literacy in at-risk students through hypermedia portfolios. *Reading Improvement, 32*, 26–31.

Duffy, G. G. (1993). Teachers' progress toward becoming expert strategy teachers. *Elementary School Journal, 94*, 109–120.

Duffy, G. G., Roehler, L. R., Meloth, M. S., & Vavrus, L. G. (1986). Conceptualizing instructional explanation. *Teaching and Teacher Education, 2*, 197–214.

Dugan, J. R. (1999). Learning from experience: Preservice teachers' perceptions of literature discussions. In J. R. Dugan, P. E. Linder, W. M. Linek, & E. G. Sturtevant (Eds.), *Advancing the world of literacy: Moving into the 21st century* (pp. 183–200). Carrollton, GA: College Reading Association.

Dupuis, M., & Askov, E. N. (1979). Combining university and school-based inservice education in content area reading. In M. L. Kamil & A. J. Moe (Eds.), *Reading research: Studies and applications. 28th yearbook of the National Reading Conference* (pp. 223–227). Clemson, SC: National Reading Conference.

Dynak, J., & Smith, M. J. (1994). Summarization: Preservice teachers' abilities and instructional views. In C. K. Kinzer & D. J. Leu (Eds.), *Multidimensional aspects of literacy research, theory, and practice. 43rd yearbook of the National Reading Conference* (pp. 387–393). Chicago: National Reading Conference.

Elliot, J., & Illig, B. (1994). Classroom research in cooperative learning: Assessing methodology in teaching of a reading course. In E. G. Sturtevant & W. M. Linek (Eds.), *Pathways for literacy* (pp. 203–210). Pittsburg, KS: College Reading Association.

Elliot, J. B., & Illig-Aviles, B. (1997). Building bridges: Designing project portfolios to accommodate the needs of beginners. In W. M. Linek & E. G. Sturtevant (Eds.), *Exploring literacy* (pp. 256–266). Platteville, WI: College Reading Association.

Evans, K. S. (1994). Group dialogue journals as a means of exploring preservice teachers' beliefs about content-area literacy. In C. K. Kinzer & D. J. Leu (Eds.), *Multidimensional aspects of literacy research, theory, and practice. 43rd yearbook of the National Reading Conference* (pp. 112–119). Chicago: National Reading Conference.

Farrell, R. T., & Cirrincione, J. M. (1986). The introductory developmental reading course for content area teachers: A state of the art survey. *Journal of Reading, 29*, 717–723.

Fecho, B., Commeyras, M., Bauer, E. B., & Font, G. (2000). In rehearsal: Complicating authority in undergraduate critical-inquiry classrooms. *Journal of Literacy Research, 32*, 471–504.

Feiman-Nemser, S., & Buchmann, M. (1986). The first year of teacher preparation: Transition to pedagogical thinking? *Journal of Curriculum Studies, 18*, 239–256.

Fey, M. H. (1997). Literate behavior in a cross-age computer-mediated discussion: A question of empowerment. In C. K. Kinzer, K. A. Hinchman, & D. J. Leu

(Eds.), *Inquiries in literacy theory and practice. 46th yearbook of the National Reading Conference* (pp. 507–518). Chicago: National Reading Conference.

Florio-Ruane, S., Raphael, T. E., Glazier, J., McVee, M., & Wallace, S. (1997). Discovering culture in discussion of autobiographical literature: Transforming the education of literacy teachers. In C. K. Kinzer, K. A. Hinchman, & D. J. Leu (Eds.), *Inquiries in literacy theory and practice. 46th yearbook of the National Reading Conference* (pp. 452–464). Chicago: National Reading Conference.

Foote, M. M., & Linder, P. E. (2000). What they know and believe about family literacy: Preservice and mentor teachers respond and reflect. In P. Linder, W. M. Linek, E. G. Sturtevant, & J. R. Dugan (Eds.), *Literacy at a new horizon* (pp. 159–176). Readyville, TN: College Reading Association.

Ford, M. P. (1993). The process and promise of portfolio assessment in teacher education programs: Impact on students' knowledge, beliefs, and practices. In T. V. Rasinski & N. D. Padak (Eds.), *Inquiries in literacy learning and instruction* (pp. 145–152). Pittsburg, KS: College Reading Association.

Ford, M. P., Anderson, R. S., Bruneau, B. J., & Scanlan, P. A. (1996). Student portfolios in four literacy education contexts: Challenging decisions about evaluation and grading. In D. J. Leu, C. K. Kinzer, & K. A. Hinchman (Eds.), *Literacies for the 21st century: Research and practice. 45th yearbook of the National Reading Conference* (pp. 398–407). Chicago: National Reading Conference.

Fox, D. L. (1994). What is literature? Two preservice teachers' conceptions of literature and of the teaching of literature. In C. K. Kinzer & D. J. Leu (Eds.), *Multidimensional aspects of literacy research, theory, and practice. 43rd yearbook of the National Reading Conference* (pp. 394–406). Chicago: National Reading Conference.

Frager, A. M. (1993). First steps in teaching reading: A descriptive study. In T. V. Rasinski & N. D. Padak (Eds.), *Inquiries in literacy learning and instruction.* (pp. 191–198). Pittsburg, KS: College Reading Association.

Frazier, D. W., Palmer, P. S., Duchein, M. A., & Armato, C. (1993). Preservice elementary teachers' evolving perceptions of portfolio assessment. In D. J. Leu & C. K. Kinzer (Eds.), *Examining central issues in literacy research, theory, and practice. 42nd yearbook of the National Reading Conference* (pp. 305–314). Chicago: National Reading Conference.

Gillespie, C., & Clements, N. (1991). Attitudes toward teaching reading in the content areas: A correlational study. In T. V. Rasinski, N. D. Padak, & J. Logan (Eds.), *Reading is knowledge* (pp. 161–166). Pittsburg, KS: College Reading Association.

Goetze, S. K., Walker, B. J., & Yellin, D. (2000). Preservice teachers' conceptual development using computer mediated communication in language arts classes. In P. Linder, W. M. Linek, E. G. Sturtevant, & J. R. Dugan (Eds.), *Literacy at a new horizon* (pp. 298–310). Readyville, TN: College Reading Association.

Gordon, C. J., & Hunsberger, M. (1991). Preservice teachers' conceptions of content area literacy instruction. In J. Zutell & S. McCormick (Eds.), *Learner factors/teacher factors: Issues in literacy research and instruction. 40th yearbook of the National Reading Conference* (pp. 399–408). Chicago: National Reading Conference.

Gray-Schlegel, M. A., & Matanzo, J. B. (1993). Action research: Classroom teachers' perceptions of its impact on the teaching of reading. In T. V. Rasinski & N. D. Padak (Eds.), *Inquiries in literacy learning and instruction* (pp. 135–142). Pittsburg, KS: College Reading Association.

Grisham, D. L. (1997). Electronic literacy learning: Teachers' on-line dialogue journals. In C. K. Kinzer, K. A. Hinchman, & D. J. Leu (Eds.), *Inquiries in literacy theory and practice. 46th yearbook of the National Reading Conference* (pp. 465–473). Chicago: National Reading Conference.

Hao, R. N., & Hartley-Forsyth, P. (1993). Reading and writing across the preservice curriculum. *Kamehameha Journal of Education, 4*, 97–104.

Harlin, R. P. (1999). Developing future professionals: Influences of literacy coursework and field experiences. *Reading Research and Instruction, 38*, 351–370.

Harlin, R. P. (2000). Breaking the mold: Preservice and inservice teachers learning together. *Journal of Reading Education, 25*, 1–11.

Harmon, J., Hedrick, W., Martinez, M., Perez, B., Keehn, S., Fine, J. C., et al. (2001). Features of excellence of reading teacher preparation programs. In J. V. Hoffman, D. L. Schallert, C. M. Fairbanks, J. Worthy, & B. Maloch (Eds.), *50th yearbook of the National Reading Conference* (pp. 262–274). Chicago: National Reading Conference.

Hedrick, W. B., McGee, P., & Mittag, K. (2000). Pre-service teacher learning through one-on-one tutoring: Reporting perceptions through e-mail. *Teaching and Teacher Education, 16*, 47–63.

Herrmann, B. A. (1988). An exploratory study of preservice teachers' evolving knowledge structures. In J. E. Readence & R. S. Baldwin (Eds.), *Dialogues in literacy research. 37th yearbook of the National Reading Conference* (pp. 347–354). Chicago: National Reading Conference.

Herrmann, B. A. (1989). The evolution of preservice teachers' knowledge structures. In S. McCormick & J. Zutell (Eds.), *Cognitive and social perspectives for literacy research and instruction. 38th yearbook of the National Reading Conference* (pp. 511–519). Chicago: National Reading Conference.

Herrmann, B. A. (1990). A longitudinal study of preservice teachers' knowledge structures. In J. Zutell & S. McCormick (Eds.), *Literacy theory and research: Analyses from multiple paradigms. 39th yearbook of the National Reading Conference* (pp. 145–152). Chicago: National Reading Conference.

Herrmann, B. A., & Sarracino, J. (1992). Effects of an alternative approach for teaching preservice teachers how to teach strategic reasoning: Two illustrative cases. In C. K. Kinzer & D. J. Leu (Eds.), *Literacy research, theory, and practice: Views from many perspectives. 41st yearbook of the National Reading Conference* (pp. 331–339). Chicago: National Reading Conference.

Herrmann, B. A., & Sarracino, J. (1993). Restructuring preservice literacy methods course: Dilemmas and lessons learned. *Journal of Teacher Education, 44*, 96–106.

Hill, S. (1986). Language education and field experiences. *Journal of Teacher Education, 37*, 56–59.

Hollingsworth, P. M., & Burnett, P. (1993). An undergraduate reading laboratory for at-risk children: An ethnographic evaluation. *Journal of Instructional Psychology, 20*, 111–118.

Hoover, N. L., & Carroll, R. G. (1987). Self-assessment of classroom instruction: An effective approach to inservice education. *Teaching and Teacher Education, 3*, 179–191.

Hopkins, C. J., Schmitt, M. C., Niersthheimer, S. L., Dixey, B. P., & Younts, T. (1995). Infusing features of the Reading Recovery Professional Development Model into the experiences of preservice teachers. In K. Hinchman, D. J. Leu, & C. K. Kinzer (Eds.), *Perspectives on literacy research and practice. 44th yearbook of the National Reading Conference* (pp. 349–357). Chicago: National Reading Conference.

Hughes, J. E., Packard, B. W.-L., & Pearson, P. D. (1997). Reading classroom explorer: Visiting classrooms via hypermedia. In C. K. Kinzer, K. A. Hinchman, & D. J. Leu (Eds.), *Inquiries in literacy theory and practice. 46th yearbook of the National Reading Conference* (pp. 494–506). Chicago: National Reading Conference.

Hughes, J. E., Packard, B. W.-L., & Pearson, P. D. (2000). Preservice teachers' perceptions of using hypermedia and video to examine the nature of literacy instruction. *Journal of Literacy Research, 32*, 599–629.

Hughes, J. E., Packard, B. W.-L., & Pearson, P. D. (2000). The role of hypermedia cases on preservice teachers' views of reading instruction. *Action in Teacher Education, 22*, 24–38.

Hughes, M. T., Cash, M. M., Klingner, J., & Ahwee, S. (2001). Professional development programs in reading: A national survey of district directors. In J. V. Hoffman, D. L. Schallert, C. M. Fairbanks, J. Worthy, & B. Maloch (Eds.), *50th yearbook of the National Reading Conference* (pp. 275–286). Chicago: National Reading Conference.

Jackson, J. B., & Paratore, J. R. (1999). An early intervention supporting the literacy learning of children experiencing substantial difficulty. *Learning Disabilities Research and Practice, 14*, 254–267.

Johns, J. L., & Davis, S. J. (1991). Perceptions of preservice and inservice teachers regarding test-taking procedures and test-wiseness programs. In T. V. Rasinski, N. D. Padak, & J. Logan (Eds.), *Reading is knowledge* (pp. 121–128). Pittsburg, KS: College Reading Association.

Johns, J. L., & VanLeirsburg, P. (1993). The impact of coursework in tests and measurements on assessment literacy. In T. V. Rasinski & N. D. Padak (Eds.), *Inquiries in literacy learning and instruction* (pp. 199–205). Pittsburg, KS: College Reading Association.

Johnson, C. S., & Evans, A. D. (1992). Improving teacher questioning: A study of a training program. In N. D. Padak, T. V. Rasinski, & J. Logan (Eds.), *Literacy research and practice: Foundations for the year 2000* (pp. 65–70). Pittsburg, KS: College Reading Association.

Johnson, D. (1996). "We're helping them to be good teachers": Using electronic dialoguing to connect theory and practice in preservice teacher education. *Journal of Computing in Childhood Education, 7*, 3–11.

Johnson, D. (1997). Extending the educational community: Using electronic dialoguing to connect theory and practice in preservice teacher education. *Journal of Technology and Teacher Education, 5*, 163–170.

Johnson, J. (1988). The relationship between preservice teachers' instruction of reading and their emerging conceptions of reading. In J. E. Readence & R. S. Baldwin (Eds.), *Dialogues in literacy research. 37th yearbook of the National Reading Conference* (pp. 355–362). Chicago: National Reading Conference.

Johnson, R., & Hoffman, N. E. (1994). Analyzing preservice teachers' efficacy beliefs and conceptions of literacy development. In E. G. Sturtevant & W. M. Linek (Eds.), *Pathways for literacy* (pp. 73–84). Pittsburg, KS: College Reading Association.

Johnson, R. S., & Rinehart, S. D. (1995). Field experience components in secondary content reading courses: A national survey. In W. M. Linek & E. G. Sturtevant (Eds.), *Generations of literacy* (pp. 188–198). Harrisonburg, VA: College Reading Association.

Johnstone, J. R. (1990). A comparison of ratings of student performance by supervising teachers, reading specialists, and preservice teachers. In N. D. Padak, T. V. Rasinski, & J. Logan (Eds.), *Challenges in reading* (pp. 37–42). Provo, UT: College Reading Association.

Kaplan, D. S. (2001). Preservice reading teachers' self-awareness of past learning and development as motivation for continued learning. In J. V. Hoffman, D. L. Schallert, C. M. Fairbanks, J. Worthy, & B. Maloch (Eds.), *50th yearbook of the National Reading Conference* (pp. 300–310). Chicago: National Reading Conference.

Kaste, J. A. (2001). Examining two preservice teachers' practices for promoting culturally responsive literacy in the middle grades. In J. V. Hoffman, D. L. Schallert, C. M. Fairbanks, J. Worthy, & B. Maloch (Eds.), *50th yearbook of the National Reading Conference* (pp. 311–322). Chicago: National Reading Conference.

Kasten, C. K., & Padak, N. D. (1997). Nurturing preservice teachers' reflection on literacy. In C. K. Kinzer, K. A. Hinchman, & D. J. Leu (Eds.), *Inquiries in literacy theory and practices. 46th yearbook of the National Reading Conference* (pp. 335–346). Chicago: National Reading Conference.

Kinzer, C. K. (1989). Mental models and beliefs about classrooms and reading instruction: A comparison between preservice teachers, inservice teachers and professors of education. In S. McCormick & J. Zutell (Eds.), *Cognitive and social perspectives for literacy research and instruction. 38th yearbook of the National Reading Conference* (pp. 489–500). Chicago: National Reading Conference.

Kucan, L. (2001). Transcript Analysis Project (TAP): An opportunity for student teachers to engage in practical inquiry into classroom discussion. In J. V. Hoffman, D. L. Schallert, C. M. Fairbanks, J. Worthy, & B. Maloch (Eds.), *50th yearbook of the National Reading Conference* (pp. 346–355). Chicago: National Reading Conference.

Lapp, D., & Flood, J. (1985). The impact of writing instruction on teachers' attitudes and practices. In J. A. Niles & R. V. Lalik (Eds.), *Issues in literacy: A research perspective. 34th yearbook of the National Reading Conference* (pp. 375–380). Rochester, NY: National Reading Conference.

Laster, B. P. (1996). From white elephant to cutting edge: The transformation of the reading clinic? In D. J. Leu, C. K. Kinzer, & K. A. Hinchman (Eds.), *Literacies for the 21st century: Research and practice. 45th yearbook of the National Reading Conference* (pp. 408–419). Chicago: National Reading Conference.

Lazar, A. (2001). Preparing White preservice teachers for urban classrooms: Growth in a Philadelphia-based literacy practicum. In J. V. Hoffman, D. L. Schallert, C. M. Fairbanks, J. Worthy, & B. Maloch (Eds.), *50th yearbook of the National Reading Conference* (pp. 367–381). Chicago: National Reading Conference.

Leland, C. H., Harste, J. C., Jackson, C. A., & Youssef, O. (2001). Making teacher education critical. In J. V. Hoffman, D. L. Schallert, C. M. Fairbanks, J. Worthy, & B. Maloch (Eds.), *50th yearbook of the National Reading Conference* (pp. 382–393). Chicago: National Reading Conference.

Leland, C. H., Harste, J. C., & Youssef, O. (1997). Teacher education and critical literacy. In C. K. Kinzer, K. A. Hinchman, & D. J. Leu (Eds.), *Inquiries in literacy theory and practices. 46th yearbook of the National Reading Conference* (pp. 385–396). Chicago: National Reading Conference.

Lenski, S. D., & Pardieck, S. (1999). Improving preservice teachers' attitudes toward writing. In J. R. Dugan, P. E. Linder, W. M. Linek, & E. G. Sturtevant (Eds.), *Advancing the world of literacy: Moving into the 21st century* (pp. 269–281). Carrollton, GA: College Reading Association.

Liu, P. (1996). Limited English proficient children's literacy acquisition and parental involvement: A tutoring/family literacy model. *Reading Horizons, 37*, 60–74.

Lonberger, R. B. (1992). The belief systems and instructional choices of preservice teachers. In N. D. Padak, T. V. Rasinski, & J. Logan (Eds.), *Literacy research and practice: Foundations for the year 2000* (pp. 71–78). Pittsburg, KS: College Reading Association.

Lyons, C. A. (1991). A comparative study of the teaching effectiveness of teachers participating in a year-long or 2-week inservice program. In J. Zutell & S. McCormick (Eds.), *Learner factors/teacher factors: Issues in literacy research and instruction. 40th yearbook of the National Reading Conference* (pp. 367–376). Chicago: National Reading Conference.

Lyons, N. (1998). Reflection in teaching: Can it be developmental? A portfolio perspective. *Teacher Education Quarterly, 25*, 115–127.

Magliaro, S., & Borko, H. (1985). The reading instruction of student teachers and experienced teachers: A social organizational perspective. In J. A. Niles & R. V. Lalik (Eds.), *Issues in literacy: A research perspective. 34th yearbook of the National Reading Conference* (pp. 272–279). Rochester, NY: National Reading Conference.

Mahurt, S. R. (1998). Writing instruction: University learning to first-year teaching. In T. Shanahan & F. V. Rodriguez-Brown (Eds.), *47th yearbook of the National Reading Conference* (pp. 542–554). Chicago: National Reading Conference.

Mallette, M. H., & Readence, J. E. (1999). A beginning teacher's thoughts about reading: Influences from within and without. In T. Shanahan & F. V. Rodriguez-Brown (Eds.), *48th yearbook of the National Reading Conference* (pp. 500–509). Chicago: National Reading Conference.

Many, J. E., Howard, F. M., & Hoge, P. (1998). Personal literacy and literature-based instruction: Exploring preservice teachers' views of themselves as readers. In T. Shanahan & F. V. Rodriguez-Brown (Eds.), *47th yearbook of the National Reading Conference* (pp. 496–507). Chicago: National Reading Conference.

Martin, M. A., Martin, S. H., & Martin, C. E. (1999). Preservice teachers constructing their meanings of literacy in a field-based program. In J. R. Dugan, P. E. Linder, W. M. Linek, & E. G. Sturtevant (Eds.), *Advancing the world of literacy: Moving into the 21st century* (pp. 55–66). Carrollton, GA: College Reading Association.

Matanzo, J. B., & Doan Holbein, M. F. (1997). A collaborative model for developing a children's literature pathway into preservice methods courses. In W. M. Linek & E. G. Sturtevant (Eds.), *Exploring literacy* (pp. 295–308). Platteville, WI: College Reading Association.

Matanzo, J. B., & Harris, D. L. (1999). Encouraging metacognitive awareness in preservice literacy courses. In J. R. Dugan, P. E. Linder, W. M. Linek, & E. G. Sturtevant (Eds.), *Advancing the world of literacy: Moving into the 21st century* (pp. 201–225). Carrollton, GA: College Reading Association.

Mather, N., Bos, C., & Babur, N. (2001). Perceptions and knowledge of preservice and inservice teachers about early literacy instruction. *Journal of Learning Disabilities, 34*, 472–482.

Mathis, J. B. (1999). Preservice teachers constructing personal understandings about culture. In J. R. Dugan, P. E. Linder, W. M. Linek, & E. G. Sturtevant (Eds.), *Advancing the world of literacy: Moving into the 21st century* (pp. 226–236). Carrollton, GA: College Reading Association.

McGinnis, D. J. (1961). The preparation and responsibility of secondary teachers in the field of reading. *Reading Teacher, 14*, 92–98.

McMahon, S. I. (1997). Using documented written and oral dialogue to understand and challenge preservice teachers' reflections. *Teaching and Teacher Education, 13*, 199–213.

Meyers, R., & Ringler, L. (1980). Teacher interns' conceptualization of reading theory and practice. In M. L. Kamil & A. J. Moe (Eds.), *Perspectives on reading research and instruction. 29th yearbook of the National Reading Conference* (pp. 238–242). Washington, DC: National Reading Conference.

Meyerson, M. J. (1993). Exploring reading instructional decisions through a reflective activity: A first step in the change process. *Journal of Educational & Psychological Consultation, 4*, 153–168.

Moats, L. C. (1995). The missing foundation in teacher education. *American Federation of Teachers, 9*, 42–51.

Moore, R. A. (2000). Preservice teachers explore their conceptions of the writing process with young pen pals. *Reading Research and Instruction, 40*, 17–33.

Moore, S. A. (1986). A comparison of reading education students' instructional beliefs and instructional practices. In J. A. Niles & R. V. Lalik (Eds.), *Solving problems in literacy: Learners, teachers, and researchers. 35th yearbook of the National*

Reading Conference (pp. 143–146). Rochester, NY: National Reading Conference.

Moore, S. J., & Lalik, R. V. (1992). Circles within circles: The uses of storytelling within a seminar for preservice reading teachers. In C. K. Kinzer & D. J. Leu (Eds.), *Literacy research, theory, and practice: Views from many perspectives. 41st yearbook of the National Reading Conference* (pp. 323–330). Chicago: National Reading Conference.

Morris, A. (1989). Preparation of Australian primary teachers in the teaching of reading: 1976–1986. *Australian Journal of Education, 33*, 164–172.

Morris, J. M. (1985). The need for linguistics-informed teachers. *Early Child Development & Care, 23*, 41–52.

Mosenthal, J. (1994). Constructing knowledge and expertise in literacy teaching: Portfolios in undergraduate teacher education. In C. K. Kinzer & D. J. Leu (Eds.), *Multidimensional aspects of literacy research, theory, and practice. 43rd yearbook of the National Reading Conference* (pp. 407–417). Chicago: National Reading Conference.

Mosenthal, J. (1995). A practice-oriented approach to methods coursework in literacy teaching. In K. Hinchman, D. J. Leu, & C. K. Kinzer (Eds.), *Perspectives on literacy research and practice. 44th yearbook of the National Reading Conference* (pp. 358–366). Chicago: National Reading Conference.

Mosenthal, J. H. (1995). Change in two teachers' conceptions of math or writing instruction after in-service training. *Elementary School Journal, 95*, 263–277.

Mosenthal, J., Daniels, P., & Mekkelsen, J. (1993). The portfolio-as-text: Literacy portfolios in preservice, undergraduate teacher education. In D. J. Leu & C. K. Kinzer (Eds.), *Examining central issues in literacy research, theory, and practice. 42nd yearbook of the National Reading Conference* (pp. 315–324). Chicago: National Reading Conference.

Mosenthal, J. H., Schwartz, R. M., & MacIsaac, D. (1992). Comprehension instruction and teacher training: More than mentioning. *Journal of Reading, 36*, 198–207.

Moss, B. (1992). Preservice teachers' reminiscences of positive and negative reading experiences: A qualitative study. In N. D. Padak, T. V. Rasinski, & J. Logan (Eds.), *Literacy research and practice: Foundations for the year 2000* (pp. 29–26). Pittsburg, KS: College Reading Association.

Newton, E. V. (1997). Learning to teach in the "real world": Reflections on field-based reading instruction. In W. M. Linek & E. G. Sturtevant (Eds.), *Exploring literacy* (pp. 207–219). Platteville, WI: College Reading Association.

Nierstheimer, S. L., Hopkins, C. J., Dillon, D. R., & Schmitt, M. C. (2000). Preservice teachers' shifting beliefs about struggling literacy learners. *Reading Research and Instruction, 40*, 1–16.

Noell, G. H., Witt, J. C., LaFleur, L. H., Mortenson, B. P., Ranier, D. D., & LeVelle, J. (2000). Increasing intervention implementation in general education following consultation: A comparison of two follow-up strategies. *Journal of Applied Behavior Analysis, 33*, 271–284.

O'Brien, D. G. (1988). Secondary preservice teachers' resistance to content reading instruction: A proposal for a broader rationale. In J. E. Readence & R. S.

Baldwin (Eds.), *Dialogues in literacy research. 37th yearbook of the National Reading Conference* (pp. 237–244). Chicago: National Reading Conference.

Olson, M. W., & Gillis, M. K. (1990). Preparing teacher/researchers. In N. D. Padak, T. V. Rasinski, & J. Logan (Eds.), *Challenges in reading* (pp. 17–24). Provo, UT: College Reading Association.

Oropallo, K., King, J., Draper, M., Radencich, M. C., & Barksdale-Ladd, M. A. (1997). Prospective teacher authorship of teaching case narratives. In C. K. Kinzer, K. A. Hinchman, & D. J. Leu (Eds.), *Inquiries in literacy theory and practice. 46th yearbook of the National Reading Conference* (pp. 405–415). Chicago: National Reading Conference.

Packman, L. A. (1991). Do as I say, not as I do—Teacher education. In T. V. Rasinski, N. D. Padak, & J. Logan (Eds.), *Reading is knowledge* (pp. 105–110). Pittsburg, KS: College Reading Association.

Padak, N. D., & Nelson, O. G. (1990). Becoming a teacher of literacy: Novice whole language teachers in conventional instructional environments. In J. Zutell & S. McCormick (Eds.), *Literacy theory and research: Analyses from multiple paradigms. 39th yearbook of the National Reading Conference* (pp. 99–108). Chicago: National Reading Conference.

Pailliotet, A. W. (1997). Personal stories or "plastic sheets": Preservice teachers' perspectives of journals and portfolios. In C. K. Kinzer, K. A. Hinchman, & D. J. Leu (Eds.), *Inquiries in literacy theory and practice. 46th yearbook of the National Reading Conference* (pp. 347–359). Chicago: National Reading Conference.

Peck, J. K. (1997). Redefining reflective practice: Thinking forward about conditions that support literacy learning. In W. M. Linek & E. G. Sturtevant (Eds.), *Exploring literacy* (pp. 245–255). Platteville, WI: College Reading Association.

Perez, B. (1993). The bilingual teacher (Spanish/English) and literacy instruction. *Teacher Education Quarterly, 20*, 43–52.

Pinnell, G. S. (1987). Helping teachers see how readers read: Staff development through observation. *Theory into Practice, 26*, 51–58.

Porter, T., & Foster, S. K. (1998). From a distance: Training teachers with technology. *T.H.E. Journal, 26*, 69–72.

Pottorff, D. (1997). The unheard voices of students in school reform: A collaborative study with content reading preservice teachers. In W. M. Linek & E. G. Sturtevant (Eds.), *Exploring literacy* (pp. 282–294). Platteville, WI: College Reading Association.

Potts, A., Moore, S., Frye, S., Kile, M., Wojtera, C., & Criswell, D. (2000). Evolving partnerships: A framework for creating cultures of teacher learning. In T. Shanahan & F. V. Rodriguez-Brown (Eds.), *49th yearbook of the National Reading Conference* (pp. 165–177). Chicago: National Reading Conference.

Ray, K. J., Lee, S. C., & Stansell, J. C. (1986). New methods, old theories, and teacher education: Some observations of writing in a third-grade classroom. In J. A. Niles & R. V. Lalik (Eds.), *Solving problems in literacy: Learners, teachers, and researchers. 35th yearbook of the National Reading Conference* (pp. 152–159). Rochester, NY: National Reading Conference.

Reinking, D., Pagnucco, J., & Heubach, K. (1993). Activities for restructuring reading education courses for preservice teachers. In T. V. Rasinski & N. D.

Padak (Eds.), *Inquiries in literacy learning and instruction* (pp. 153–160). Pittsburg, KS: College Reading Association.

Richards, J. (2001). "I did not plan ahead": Preservice teachers' concerns integrating print-based literacy lessons with computer technology. In J. V. Hoffman, D. L. Schallert, C. M. Fairbanks, J. Worthy, & B. Maloch (Eds.), *50th yearbook of the National Reading Conference* (pp. 507–518). Chicago: National Reading Conference.

Ridgeway, V. G., Reinking, D., & Mealey, D. (1991). A model for teaching content area reading strategies to preservice teachers. In T. V. Rasinski, N. D. Padak, & J. Logan (Eds.), *Reading is Knowledge* (pp. 153–160). Pittsburg, KS: College Reading Association.

Ringler, L. H., Smith-Burke, T. M., & Meyers, R. S. (1979). Interactive model of teacher education. In M. L. Kamil & A. J. Moe (Eds.), *Reading research: Studies and applications. 28th yearbook of the National Reading Conference* (pp. 228–235). Clemson, SC: National Reading Conference.

Risko, V., Camperell, K., Degler, L., Eanet, M., & Richards, J. (1998). Multiple views of case teaching: Teacher educators reflect on their teaching practices. In B. Sturtevant, J. Dugan, P. Linder, & W. M. Linek (Eds.), *Literacy and community* (pp. 214–230). Carrollton, GA: College Reading Association.

Risko, V. J. (1995). Using videodisc-based cases to promote preservice teachers' problem solving and mental model building. In W. M. Linek & E. G. Sturtevant (Eds.), *Generations of literacy* (pp. 173–187). Harrisonburg, VA: College Reading Association.

Risko, V. J., McAllister, D., & Bigenho, F. (1993). Value-added benefits for reforming a remedial reading methodology course with videodisc and hypercard technology. In T. V. Rasinski & N. D. Padak (Eds.), *Inquiries in literacy learning and instruction* (pp. 179–190). Pittsburg, KS: College Reading Association.

Risko, V. J., McAllister, D., Peter, J., & Bigenho, F. (1994). Using technology in support of preservice teachers' generative learning. In E. G. Sturtevant & W. M. Linek (Eds.), *Pathways for literacy* (pp. 155–168). Pittsburg, KS: College Reading Association.

Risko, V. J., Peter, J. A., & McAllister, D. (1996). Conceptual changes: Preservice teachers' pathways to providing literacy instruction. In E. G. Sturtevant & W. M. Linek (Eds.), *Growing literacy* (pp. 104–119). Harrisonburg, VA: College Reading Association.

Risko, V. J., Roskos, K., & Vukelich, C. (1999). Making connections: Preservice teachers' reflection processes and strategies. In T. Shanahan & F. V. Rodriguez-Brown (Eds.), *48th yearbook of the National Reading Conference* (pp. 412–422). Chicago: National Reading Conference.

Risko, V. J., Yount, D., & McAllister, D. (1992). Preparing preservice teachers for remedial instruction: Teaching problem solving and use of content and pedagogical knowledge. In N. D. Padak, T. V. Rasinski, & J. Logan (Eds.), *Literacy research and practice: Foundations for the year 2000* (pp. 37–50). Pittsburg, KS: College Reading Association.

Risko, V. J., Yount, D., & Towell, J. (1991). Video-based CASE analysis to enhance teacher preparation. In T. V. Rasinski, N. D. Padak, & J. Logan (Eds.), *Reading is knowledge* (pp. 87–96). Pittsburg, KS: College Reading Association.

Robbins, M. E., & Patterson, L. (1994). Authentic contexts for learning to teach: Approximation and feedback in field-based preservice literacy courses. In E. G. Sturtevant & W. M. Linek (Eds.), *Pathways for literacy* (pp. 169–182). Pittsburg, KS: College Reading Association.

Roberts, E., Doheny, C., & Harkins, D. (2000). Literacy on-line: Learning about authentic assessments via the web. In P. Linder, W. M. Linek, E. G. Sturtevant, & J. R. Dugan (Eds.), *Literacy at a new horizon* (pp. 286–297). Readyville, TN: College Reading Association.

Roberts, S. K., & Hsu, Y.-S. (2000). The tools of teacher education: Preservice teachers' use of technology to create instructional materials. *Journal of Technology and Teacher Education, 8,* 133–152.

Roskos, K., Boehlen, S., & Walker, B. J. (2000). Learning the art of instructional conversation: The influence of self-assessment on teachers' instructional discourse in a reading clinic. *Elementary School Journal, 100,* 229–252.

Roskos, K., Risko, V., & Vukelich, C. (2000). Preparing reflective teachers of reading: A critical review of reflection studies in literacy pedagogy. In T. Shanahan & F. V. Rodriguez-Brown (Eds.), *49th yearbook of the National Reading Conference* (pp. 109–121). Chicago: National Reading Conference.

Roskos, K., & Walker, B. (1993). Preservice teachers' epistemology in the teaching of problem readers. In D. J. Leu & C. K. Kinzer (Eds.), *Examining central issues in literacy research, theory, and practice. 42nd yearbook of the National Reading Conference* (pp. 325–334). Chicago: National Reading Conference.

Roskos, K., & Walker, B. (1994). An analysis of preservice teachers' pedagogical concepts in the teaching of problem readers. In C. K. Kinzer & D. J. Leu (Eds.), *Multidimensional aspects of literacy research, theory, and practice. 43rd yearbook of the National Reading Conference* (pp. 418–428). Chicago: National Reading Conference.

Roskos, K., & Walker, B. (1997). Analytic categories for practitioners' assessment of instructional discourse in literacy teaching: Observation in the reading clinic setting. In W. M. Linek & E. G. Sturtevant (Eds.), *Exploring literacy* (pp. 143–159). Platteville, WI: College Reading Association.

Rutherford, W. L., & Weaver, S. W. (1974). Preferences of elementary teachers for preservice and in-service training in the teaching of reading. *Journal of Educational Research, 67,* 271–275.

Sampson, M. B., Raine, I. L., & Harkins, D. M. (2000). Field based or traditional: Examining preservice teachers' rationales for selecting a teacher preparation program. In P. Linder, W. M. Linek, E. G. Sturtevant, & J. R. Dugan (Eds.), *Literacy at a new horizon* (pp. 191–206). Readyville, TN: College Reading Association.

Scharer, P. L. (1996). "Are we supposed to be asking questions?" Moving from teacher-directed to student-directed book discussions. In D. J. Leu, C. K. Kinzer, & K. A. Hinchman (Eds.), *Literacies for the 21st century: Research and practice. 45th yearbook of the National Reading Conference* (pp. 420–429). Chicago: National Reading Conference.

Scheffler, A. J., Richmond, M., & Kazelskis, R. (1993). Examining shifts in teachers' theoretical orientation to reading. *Reading Psychology, 14,* 1–13.

Scott, J. M., & Ballard, K. D. (1983). Training parents and teachers in remedial reading procedures for children with learning difficulties. *Educational Psychology, 3*, 15–30.

Seaborg, M. B., Mohr, K., & Fowler, T. J. (1994). Preservice teachers' learning process: A descriptive analysis of the impact of varied experiences with portfolios. In C. K. Kinzer & D. J. Leu (Eds.), *Multidimensional aspects of literacy research, theory, and practice. 43rd yearbook of the National Reading Conference* (pp. 440–447). Chicago: National Reading Conference.

Shearer, B. A., & Lundeberg, M. A. (1996). Do models of expert reading strategies facilitate graduate students' reading of research? In D. J. Leu, C. K. Kinzer, & K. A. Hinchman (Eds.), *Literacies for the 21st century: Research and practice. 45th yearbook of the National Reading Conference* (pp. 430–436). Chicago: National Reading Conference.

Sibbett, J., Wade, S., & Johnson, L. (1998). Preservice teachers' reflective thinking during a case discussion. In D. J. McIntyre & D. M. Byrd (Eds.), *Strategies for career-long teacher education. Teacher education yearbook VI*. Reston, VA: Association of Teacher Educators.

Smith, L., & Hill, M. (1999). A shift in stance: Teacher-centered to student-centered teaching in reading clinics. In T. Shanahan & F. V. Rodriguez-Brown (Eds.), *48th yearbook of the National Reading Conference* (pp. 466–478). Chicago: National Reading Conference.

Smith, L. C., Thomas, D. G., & Nicholas, C. P. (1993). Utilizing literature as a vehicle for teaching about multicultural education in a reading methods course. In T. V. Rasinski & N. D. Padak (Eds.), *Inquiries in literacy learning and instruction* (pp. 161–170). Pittsburg, KS: College Reading Association.

Smith, W. E. (1991). Developing a meaningful early field experience for reading methods courses. In T. V. Rasinski, N. D. Padak, & J. Logan (Eds.), *Reading is knowledge*. Pittsburg, KS: College Reading Association.

Spanjer, R. A., & Layne, B. H. (1983). Teacher attitudes toward language: Effects of training in a process approach to writing. *Journal of Educational Research, 77*, 60–62.

Stallworth, B. J. (2001). Using email to facilitate dialogue between high school students and preservice English methods students. In J. V. Hoffman, D. L. Schallert, C. M. Fairbanks, J. Worthy, & B. Maloch (Eds.), *50th yearbook of the National Reading Conference* (pp. 572–583). Chicago: National Reading Conference.

Stansell, J. C. (1994). Reflection, resistance, and research among preservice teachers studying their literacy histories: Lessons for literacy teacher education. In C. K. Kinzer & D. J. Leu (Eds.), *Multidimensional aspects of literacy research, theory, and practice. 43rd yearbook of the National Reading Conference* (pp. 448-458). Chicago: National Reading Conference.

Stansell, J., Moss, R., & Robeck, C. (1982). The development of theoretical orientation to reading among preservice teachers: Effects of a professional training program. In J. A. Niles & L. A. Harris (Eds.), *New inquiries in reading research and instruction. 31st yearbook of the National Reading Conference* (pp. 242–250). Rochester, NY: National Reading Conference.

Stephens, L. C. (1997). How video-cases helped preservice teachers begin to situate themselves philosophically. In C. K. Kinzer, K. A. Hinchman, & D. J. Leu (Eds.), *Inquiries in literacy theory and practice. 46th yearbook of the National Reading Conference* (pp. 483–493). Chicago: National Reading Conference.

Strode, S. L. (1996). The annotation exchange system: A way for schools and universities to connect using children's literature. In E. G. Sturtevant & W. M. Linek (Eds.), *Growing literacy* (pp. 133–138). Harrisonburg, VA: College Reading Association.

Stuart, D., Pershey, M. G., & Hayes, L. D. (1998). The multicultural fair: A celebration of diversity. An innovative approach to teacher education. In B. Sturtevant, J. Dugan, P. Linder, & W. M. Linek (Eds.), *Literacy and community* (pp. 256–267). Carrollton, GA: College Reading Association.

Sturtevant, E. G., Dunlap, K. L., & White, C. S. (2000). Learning to teach literacy in a high-stakes testing environment: Perceptions of interns and clinical faculty in professional development schools. In T. Shanahan & F. V. Rodriguez-Brown (Eds.), *49th yearbook of the National Reading Conference* (pp. 153–164). Chicago: National Reading Conference.

Sturtevant, E. G., & Spor, M. W. (1990). Student teacher use of content reading strategies. In N. D. Padak, T. V. Rasinski, & J. Logan (Eds.), *Challenges in reading* (pp. 25–30). Provo, UT: College Reading Association.

Swafford, J., Chapman, V., Rhodes, R., & Kallus, M. (1996). A literature analysis of trends in literacy education. In D. J. Leu, C. K. Kinzer, & K. A. Hinchman (Eds.), *Literacies for the 21st century: Research and practice. 45th yearbook of the National Reading Conference* (pp. 437–466). Chicago: National Reading Conference.

Swafford, J., Peters, T., & Lee, S. (1998). Understanding preservice teachers' beliefs through autobiographical analysis. In T. Shanahan & F. V. Rodriguez-Brown (Eds.), *47th yearbook of the National Reading Conference* (pp. 517–528). Chicago: National Reading Conference.

Thomas, K. F., & Rinehart, S. D. (1990). Content area reading practices: Relationships of teacher usage and ability. In N. D. Padak, T. V. Rasinski, & J. Logan (Eds.), *Challenges in reading* (pp. 63–72). Provo, UT: College Reading Association.

Tidwell, D. L. (1995). Practical argument as instruction: Developing an inner voice. In K. Hinchman, D. J. Leu, & C. K. Kinzer (Eds.), *Perspectives on literacy research and practice. 44th yearbook of the National Reading Conference* (pp. 368–373). Chicago: National Reading Conference.

Trathen, W., & Moorman, G. (2001). Using email to create pedagogical dialogue in teacher education. *Reading Research and Instruction, 40*, 203–224.

Traw, R. (1994). School/university collaboration via email: A unique approach to teaching reading and language arts. *TechTrends, 39*, 28–31.

Truscott, D. M., & Walker, B. J. (1998). The influence of portfolio selection on reflective thinking. In E. G. Sturtevant, J. Dugan, P. Linder, & W. M. Linek (Eds.), *Literacy and community*. Carrollton, GA: College Reading Association.

Vacca, R. T., & Johns, J. L. (1980). How preservice teachers perceive traditional and competency-based reading education. *Reading Horizons, 21*, 28–33.

Van Valkenburgh, N., & Sirpa, G. (2000). Mentoring in the information age: A study of telementor functions between preservice teachers and middle school students. In P. Linder, W. M. Linek, E. G. Sturtevant, & J. R. Dugan (Eds.), *Literacy at a new horizon* (pp. 271–285). Readyville, TN: College Reading Association.

Walker, B. J. (1990). A model for diagnostic narratives in teacher education. In N. D. Padak, T. V. Rasinski, & J. Logan (Eds.), *Challenges in reading* (pp. 1–10). Provo, UT: College Reading Association.

Walker, B. J. (1991). A descriptive study of the reflective statements of preservice teachers. In T. V. Rasinski, N. D. Padak, & J. Logan (Eds.), *Reading is knowledge* (pp. 97–104). Pittsburg, KS: College Reading Association.

Walker, B. J., & Ramseth, C. (1993). Reflective practice confronts the complexities of teaching reading. In T. V. Rasinski, N. D. Padak, & J. Logan (Eds.), *Inquiries in literacy learning and instruction* (pp. 171–177). Pittsburg, KS: College Reading Association.

Walker, B. J., & Roskos, K. (1994). Preservice teachers' epistemology of diagnostic reading instruction: Observations of shifts during coursework experience. In E. G. Sturtevant & W. M. Linek (Eds.), *Pathways for literacy* (pp. 59–72). Pittsburg, KS: College Reading Association.

Wedman, J. M., & Robinson, R. (1988). Effects of a decision-making model on preservice teachers' decision-making practices and materials use. *Reading Improvement, 25*, 110–116.

Welch, M. (2000). Descriptive analysis of team teaching in two elementary classrooms: A formative experimental approach. *Remedial and Special Education, 21*, 366–376.

Wells, D. (1990). Literature study groups in a university methods class. In N. D. Padak, T. V. Rasinski, & J. Logan (Eds.), *Challenges in reading* (pp. 31–36). Provo, UT: College Reading Association.

Wesson, C., Deno, S., Mirkin, P., Maruyama, G., Skiba, R., King, R., & Sevcik, B. (1988). A causal analysis of the relationships among ongoing curriculum-based measurement and evaluation, the structure of instruction, and student achievement. *Journal of Special Education, 22*, 330–343.

Wham, M. A. (1993). The relationship between undergraduate coursework and beliefs about reading instruction. *Journal of Research and Development in Education, 27*, 9–17.

Williams, A. L. (1997). Preparing preservice elementary teachers for professional collaboration with special education literacy teachers. In W. M. Linek & E. G. Sturtevant (Eds.), *Exploring literacy* (pp. 168–183). Platteville, WI: College Reading Association.

Wilson, E. K., Konopak, B. C., & Readence, J. E. (1993). A case study of a preservice secondary social studies teacher's beliefs and practices about content-area reading. In D. J. Leu & C. K. Kinzer (Eds.), *Examining central issues in literacy research, theory, and practice. 42nd yearbook of the National Reading Conference* (pp. 335–343). Chicago: National Reading Conference.

Wimett, C. A., & Blachowicz, C. (1997). In their own words: Urban preservice teachers' elaborated constructs of literacy and literacy instruction. In C. K. Kinzer, K. A. Hinchman, & D. J. Leu (Eds.), *Inquiries in literacy theory and prac-*

tice. 46th yearbook of the National Reading Conference (pp. 319–334). Chicago: National Reading Conference.

Wiseman, D. L. (1999). The impact of school–university partnerships on reading teacher educators: Important conversations we must have. In J. R. Dugan, P. E. Linder, W. M. Linek, & E. G. Sturtevant (Eds.), *Advancing the world of literacy: Moving into the 21st century* (pp. 81–93). Carrollton, GA: College Reading Association.

Wolf, S. A., Ballentine, D., & Hill, L. A. (2000). "Only Connect!": Cross-cultural connections in the reading lives of preservice teachers and children. *Journal of Literacy Research, 32*, 533-569.

Wolf, S. A., Carey, A. A., & Mieras, E. L. (1996). The art of literary interpretation: Preservice teachers learning about the arts in language arts. In D. J. Leu, C. K. Kinzer, & K. A. Hinchman (Eds.), *Literacies for the 21st century: Research and practice. 45th yearbook of the National Reading Conference* (pp. 447–460). Chicago: National Reading Conference.

Wolf, S. A., Carey, A. A., & Mieras, E. L. (1996). "What is this literachurch stuff anyway?": Preservice teachers' growth in understanding children's literary response. *Reading Research Quarterly, 31*, 130–157.

Wolf, S. A., Hill, L., & Ballentine, D. (1999). Teaching on fissured ground: Preparing preservice teachers for culturally conscious pedagogy. In T. Shanahan & F. V. Rodriguez-Brown (Eds.), *48th yearbook of the National Reading Conference* (pp. 423–436). Chicago: National Reading Conference.

Worthy, J., & Prater, S. (1998). Learning on the job: Preservice teachers' perceptions of participating in a literacy tutorial program. In T. Shanahan & F. V. Rodriguez-Brown (Eds.), *47th yearbook of the National Reading Conference* (pp. 485–495). Chicago: National Reading Conference.

Young, S. A., & Romeo, L. (1999). University and urban school district collaboration: Preschoolers and preservice teachers gain literacy skills. *Reading Research and Instruction, 38*, 101–114.

Zeek, C., Walker, C., & Fleener, C. (1997). Connecting and reflecting: Changing beliefs about literacy instruction by integrating methods courses. In C. K. Kinzer, K. A. Hinchman, & D. J. Leu (Eds.), *Inquiries in literacy theory and practice. 46th yearbook of the National Reading Conference* (pp. 308–318). Chicago: National Reading Conference.

Zeek, C., & Wickstrom, C. (1999). The making of a teacher: The influence of personal literacy development on preservice teachers' current teaching practices. In T. Shanahan & F. V. Rodriguez-Brown (Eds.), *48th yearbook of the National Reading Conference* (pp. 479–490). Chicago: National Reading Conference.

Zulich, J., Bean, T. W., & Herrick, J. (1992). Charting stages of preservice teacher development and reflection in a multicultural community through dialogue journal analysis. *Teaching and Teacher Education, 8*, 345–360.

REFERENCES

Anders, P., Hoffman, J., & Duffy, G. G. (2000). Teaching teachers to teach reading: Paradigm shifts, persistent problems, and challenges. In M. L. Kamil, P.

Mosenthal, P. D. Pearson, & R. Barr (Eds.), *Handbook of reading research* (Vol. III, pp. 721–744). Mahwah, NJ: Lawrence Erlbaum Associates.

Anderson, R. S., & Reid, S. (1994). A collaborative conversation about learning: Using dialogue journals for professional development. In C. K. Kinzer & D. J. Leu (Eds.), *Multidimensional aspects of literacy research, theory, and practice. 43rd yearbook of the National Reading Conference* (pp. 361–369). Chicago: National Reading Conference.

Bayles, D. L. (1997). "I'm just an emergent teacher": A longitudinal exploration of dialogic patterns in learning to teach the language arts. In C. K. Kinzer, K. A. Hinchman, & D. J. Leu (Eds.), *Inquiries in literacy theory and practice. 46th yearbook of the National Reading Conference* (pp. 438–451). Chicago: National Reading Conference.

Britton, G. E. (1973). Preservice reading methods instruction: Large group/onsite/individualized. *Reading Improvement, 10*(1), 29–32.

Coles, G. (2000). Direct, explicit, and systematic—bad reading science. *Language Arts*, 77(6), 543–545.

Darling-Hammond, L. (2000). Teacher quality and student achievement: A review of state policy evidence. *Education Policy Analysis Archives* [online]. *8(1)*, Retrieved April 5, 2005, from http://epaa.asu.edu/epaa/v8n1

Duffy, G. G. (1990). What counts in teacher education? Dilemmas in educating empowered teachers. In J. Zutell & S. McCormick (Eds.), *Literacy theory and research: Analyses from multiple paradigms. 39th yearbook of the National Reading Conference* (pp. 1–18). Chicago: National Reading Conference.

Duffy, G. G. (1993). Teachers' progress toward becoming expert strategy teachers. *Elementary School Journal, 94*(2), 109–120.

Duffy, G. G. (2004). Professional development. In D. Strickland & M. Kamil (Eds.). *Professional development for teaching reading* (pp. 3–22). Norwood, MA: Christopher-Gordon.

El-Dinary, P. B., Pressley, M., & Schuder, T. (1992). Teachers learning transactional strategies instruction. In C. K. Kinzer & D. J. Leu (Eds.), *Literacy research, theory, and practice: Views from many perspectives. 41st yearbook of the National Reading Conference* (pp. 453–462). Chicago: National Reading Conference.

Fazio, M. (2000). Constructive comprehension and metacognitive strategy instruction in a field-based teacher education program. In P. Linder, W. M. Linek, E. G. Sturtevant, & J. R. Dugan (Eds.), *Literacy at a new horizon* (pp. 177–190). Readyville, TN: College Reading Association.

Frazier, D. W., Mencer, T. H., & Duchein, M. A. (1997). The field experience triad: Influences of the college instructor and cooperating teacher on the preservice teacher's beliefs, practices, and intentions concerning literacy instruction. In W. M. Linek & E. G. Sturtevant (Eds.), *Exploring literacy* (pp. 229–244). Platteville, WI: College Reading Association.

Garan, E. M. (2001). Beyond the smoke and mirrors: A critique of the National Reading Panel report on phonics. *Phi Delta Kappan, 82*(7), 500–506.

Grossman, P. L., Valencia, S. W., Evans, K., Thompson, C., Martin, S., & Place, N. (2000). Transitions into teaching: Learning to teach writing in teacher education and beyond. *Journal of Literacy Research, 32*(4), 631–662.

Haid, L. K., MacBee, J. S., & Riley, S. (2000). A new view of staff development: The role of peer coaching in effecting change in the primary literacy classroom. In P. Linder, W. M. Linek, E. G. Sturtevant, & J. R. Dugan (Eds.), *Literacy at a new horizon* (pp. 330–347). Readyville, TN: College Reading Association.

Hartman, J. H., & Nielsen, L. A. (1989). Reading comprehension instruction assessment system. *Journal of Classroom Interaction, 24*(2), 23–30.

Hoffman, J., & Pearson, P. D. (2000). Reading teacher education in the next millennium: What your grandmother's teacher didn't know that your granddaughter's teacher should. *Reading Research Quarterly, 35*(1), 28–40.

Hollingsworth, S. (1989). Prior beliefs and cognitive change in learning to teach. *American Educational Research Journal, 26*(2), 160–189.

Hughes, L., & Zeek, C. (1997). Instructional teams in a university clinic. In W. M. Linek & E. G. Sturtevant (Eds.), *Exploring literacy* (pp. 160–167). Platteville, WI: College Reading Association.

Kamil, M. L. (1995). Some alternatives to paradigm wars. *Journal of Reading Behavior, 27*, 243–261.

Keehn, S., Harris, L. A., Hedrick, W., Martinez, M., & Perez, B. (2001). A study of the impact of a reading specialization program on first-year teachers. In J. V. Hoffman, D. L. Schallert, C. M. Fairbanks, J. Worthy, & B. Maloch (Eds.), *50th yearbook of the National Reading Conference* (pp. 323–332). Chicago: National Reading Conference.

Kidd, J. K., Sanchez, S. Y., & Thorp, E. K. (2000). Integrating language and literacy through projects: An applied internship experience. In P. Linder, W. M. Linek, E. G. Sturtevant, & J. R. Dugan (Eds.), *Literacy at a new horizon* (pp. 207–225). Readyville, TN: College Reading Association.

Lefever-Davis, S., & Helfeldt, J. P. (1994). The efficacy of a site-based literacy methods course. In E. G. Sturtevant & W. M. Linek (Eds.), *Pathways for Literacy* (pp. 183–194). Pittsburg, KS: College Reading Association.

Lenski, S. D. (1998). Mentoring teachers in professional development school learn from student interns. In B. Sturtevant, J. Dugan, P. Linder, & W. M. Linek (Eds.), *Literacy and community* (pp. 177–187). Carrollton, GA: College Reading Association.

Linek, W. M., Nelson, O. G., Sampson, M. B., Zeek, C. K., Mohr, K. A. J., & Hughes, L. (1999). Developing beliefs about literacy instruction: A cross-case analysis of preservice teachers in traditional and field-based settings. *Reading Research and Instruction, 38*(4), 371–386.

Maimon, L. F. (1997). Reducing resistance to content area literacy courses. In W. M. Linek & E. G. Sturtevant (Eds.), *Exploring literacy* (pp. 267–281). Platteville, WI: College Reading Association.

Mathis, J. B. (2000). Preservice teachers explore culturally responsive instruction: Affirmation and resistance. In P. Linder, W. M. Linek, E. G. Sturtevant, & J. R. Dugan (Eds.), *Literacy at a new horizon* (pp. 226–239). Readyville, TN: College Reading Association.

Mosenthal, P., & Kamil, M. L. (1991). Research in reading and writing: A model of progress. In R. Barr, M. Kamil, P. Mosenthal, & P. D. Pearson, (Eds.), *Handbook of reading research* (Vol. 2, pp. 1013–1046). New York: Longman, Inc.

Myers, S. S. (1993). Reflective teaching in a reading instruction teacher training program. *Journal of Reading Education, 18*(2), 38–49.

National Institute of Child Health and Human Development. (2000). *Report of the National Reading Panel. Teaching children to read: An evidence-based assessment of the scientific research literature on reading and its implications for reading instruction: Reports of the subgroups* (NIH Publication No. 00-4769). Washington, DC: U.S. Government Printing Office.

Nelson, O., Pryor, E., & Church, B. (1990). Process of change in teachers' beliefs, attitudes, and concerns during a series of whole language reading and writing workshops. In N. D. Padak, T. V. Rasinski, & J. Logan (Eds.), *Challenges in reading* (pp. 53–62). Provo, UT: College Reading Association.

Nichols, W. D., Rupley, W. H., & Mergen, S. L. (1998). Improving elementary teachers' ability to implement reading strategies in their teaching of science content. In B. Sturtevant, J. Dugan, P. Linder, & W. M. Linek (Eds.), *Literacy and community* (pp. 188–213). Carrollton, GA: College Reading Association.

Oropallo, K., & Gomez, S. (1996). Using reflective portfolios in preservice teacher education programs. In E. G. Sturtevant & W. M. Linek (Eds.), *Growing literacy* (pp. 120–132). Harrisonburg, VA: College Reading Association.

Padak, N. D., Rasinski, T. V., & Ackerman, C. S. (1996). Teachers helping teachers: Ohio's Even Start Peer Assistance Team Project. In E. G. Sturtevant & W. M. Linek (Eds.), *Growing literacy* (pp. 269–283). Harrisonburg, VA: College Reading Association.

Pang, E., & Kamil, M. (2004). Professional development and the uses of technology. In D. Strickland & M. Kamil (Eds.), *Professional development for teaching reading* (pp. 149–168). Norwood, MA: Christopher-Gordon.

Preparing Tomorrow's Teachers to Use Technology (PT3). (2005). Washington, DC: U.S. Department of Education, Office of Postsecondary Education. Retrieved April 5, 2005, from http://www.ed.gov/programs/teachtech/index.html

Rickelman, R. J., Henk, W. A., & Helfeldt, J. P. (1994). The cohesiveness of preservice and inservice teachers' whole language perceptions and the information sources contributing to this knowledge. In E. G. Sturtevant & W. M. Linek (Eds.), *Pathways for literacy* (pp. 37–46). Pittsburg, KS: College Reading Association.

Roskos, K., Vukelich, C., & Risko, V. (2001). Reflection and learning to teach reading: A critical review of literacy and general teacher education studies. *Journal of Literacy Research, 33*(4), 595–635.

Ross, P. (1994). Preparing teacher educators and prospective teachers to meet the challenge of diversity. In C. K. Kinzer & D. J. Leu (Eds.), *Multidimensional aspects of literacy research, theory, and practice. 43rd yearbook of the National Reading Conference* (pp. 429–439). Chicago: National Reading Conference.

Sampson, M. B., & Linek, W. M. (1994). Change as process: A view of an instructor and her students. In E. G. Sturtevant & W. M. Linek (Eds.), *Pathways for literacy* (pp. 47–58). Pittsburg, KS: College Reading Association.

Sampson, M. B., Linek, W. M., Raine, L., & Westergaard, P. (1997). The evolution of a professional development center: Collaboration, reflective assessment and refinement. In W. M. Linek & E. G. Sturtevant (Eds.), *Exploring literacy* (pp. 184–206). Platteville, WI: College Reading Association.

Sampson, M. B., Walker, C., & Fazio, M. (1999). Collaborative research, reflection and refinement: The evolution of literacy coursework in a professional development center. In J. R. Dugan, P. E. Linder, W. M. Linek, & E. G. Sturtevant (Eds.), *Advancing the world of literacy: Moving into the 21st century* (pp. 67–80). Carrollton, GA: College Reading Association.

Sanacore, J. (2000). Promoting effective literacy learning in minority students by focusing on teacher workshops and reflective practice: A comprehensive project supported by the Annenberg Foundation. *Reading Psychology, 21*(3), 233–255.

Schon, D. (1983). *The reflective practitioner: How professionals think in action*. New York: Basic Books.

Schon, D. (1987). *Educating the reflective practitioner*. San Francisco: Jossey-Bass.

Shavelson, R. J., & Towne, L. (Eds.). (2002). *Scientific research in education*. Washington, DC: National Academy of Sciences, National Research Council.

Shepperson, G. M., & Nistler, R. J. (1991). Whole language collaboration project: Three case studies to represent change. In T. V. Rasinski, N. D. Padak, & J. Logan (Eds.), *Reading is knowledge* (pp. 129–137). Pittsburg, KS: College Reading Association.

Sparks, G. M. (1988). Teachers' attitudes toward change and subsequent improvements in classroom teaching. *Journal of Educational Psychology, 80*(1), 111–117.

Stallings, J., & Krasavage, E. M. (1986). Program implementation and student achievement in a four-year Madeline Hunter follow-through project. *Elementary School Journal, 87*(2), 117–138.

Stallings, J., Robbins, P., Presbrey, L., & Scott, J. (1986). Effects of instruction based on the Madeline Hunter model on students' achievement: Findings from a follow-through project. *Elementary School Journal, 86*(5), 571–587.

Swafford, J., Maltsberger, A., Button, K., & Furgerson, P. (1997). Peer coaching for facilitating effective literacy instruction. In C. K. Kinzer, K. A. Hinchman, & D. J. Leu (Eds.), *Inquiries in literacy theory and practice. 46th yearbook of the National Reading Conference* (pp. 416–426). Chicago: National Reading Conference.

U.S. Department of Education (2002). *Meeting the highly qualified teachers challenge: The Secretary's annual report on teacher quality*. Retrieved April 5, 2005, from http://www.ed.gov/offices/OPE/News/teacherprep/AnnualReport.pdf

Wile, J. M. (1995). Using portfolios to enable undergraduate preservice teachers to construct personal theories of literacy. In W. M. Linek & E. G. Sturtevant (Eds.), *Generations of literacy* (pp. 209–219). Harrisonburg, VA: College Reading Association.

Worthy, J., & Patterson, E. (2001). "I can't wait to see Carlos!": Preservice teachers, situated learning, and personal relationships with students. *Journal of Literacy Research, 33*(2), 303–344.

Wuthrick, M. A. (1995). Case studies of teacher change from conventional to holistic literacy instruction. In W. M. Linek & E. G. Sturtevant (Eds.), *Generations of literacy* (pp. 69–82). Harrisonburg, VA: College Reading Association.

Xu, S. H. (2000). Preservice teachers in a literacy methods course consider issues of diversity. *Journal of Literacy Research*, *32*(4), 505–531.

Yatvin, J. (2002). Babes in the woods: The wanderings of the National Reading Panel. *Phi Delta Kappan*, *83*(5), 364–369.

CHAPTER 5

THE ENHANCEMENT OF CRITICAL THINKING

With Decades of Converging Evidence, Meta-Analyses With Large Effect Sizes, and Societal Need, Would You Allow Your Child to Be Assigned to a "Control" Group?

Diane F. Halpern

Educators concerned with public policies approached the year 2000 with excitement and optimism as various pundits inside and outside the U.S. Department of Education envisioned the education that citizens in the new millennium would need for the expected challenges in the early decades of the 21st century. The Educate America Act was passed with fanfare, and six broad goals that Americans would achieve by the year 2000 were announced as part of a plan that would keep the United States competitive (and, some would add, cooperative) as we moved into the year 2000 and beyond. Children would start school "ready to learn," the United States would lead the world in science and math, high-school graduation rates would be 90% or higher, schools would be free of drugs

The Scientific Basis of Educational Productivity, 85–102

and violence, and for higher education (Objective 5, Goal 5), "the proportion of college graduates who demonstrate an advanced ability to think critically, communicate effectively, and solve problems will increase substantially" (National Education Goals Panel, 1991, p. 237).

To those who believed that the enhancement of critical thinking was an obtainable outcome from education, the fact that the United States government was making a public national commitment to enhancing critical thinking in college students and set a date by which it expected to see results—the year 2000—was a long overdue recognition of the need to teach for thinking. Unfortunately, and despite bipartisan support for the Goals 2000 Educate America Act—including both George Bush, the senior, when he was president, and Bill Clinton when he was governor of Arkansas—the goal that pertained to critical thinking was never funded and, thus, it was never implemented on the same national scale as the other goals. Despite the lack of federal funding, many colleges and universities voluntarily instituted requirements for coursework, sometimes for separate courses, in critical thinking. Others created optional courses, and critical-thinking courses have moved into secondary schools, with a variety of programs to enhance teaching at all levels of K–12. Programs to enhance critical thinking in K–12 have a variety of different names (e.g., The Productive Thinking Program, which is one of the oldest, established in 1974, and Philosophy for Children) and thus are often not identified as critical-thinking programs per se, but they share the general goal of improving the process and outcome of student thinking.

CRITICAL THINKING: A PROTOTYPICAL DEFINITION

Despite the fact that academics are trained to critique arguments and criticize each other, especially across disciplinary domains—a trait we have developed into an art form—the academic community has (mostly) agreed on a definition of critical thinking. Similar to most definitions, the boundaries for critical thinking are fuzzy, but there is considerable agreement among most of the writers in this field about its defining central features. In an extensive review, Fischer and Spiker (2000) found that most definitions for the term "critical thinking" include reasoning or logic, judgment, metacognition, reflection, questioning, and mental processes. Jones and his colleagues (Jones, Hoffman, Moore, Ratcliff, Tibbetts, & Click, 1997) obtained consensus from among 500 policymakers, employers, and educators, who agree that critical thinking is a broad term that describes reasoning in an open-ended manner and with an unlimited number of solutions. It involves constructing a situation and supporting the reasoning that went into a conclusion.

Here is a definition that I have used in multiple formats and probably two dozen different publications:

> Critical thinking is the use of those cognitive skills or strategies that increase the probability of a desirable outcome. It is used to describe thinking that is purposeful, reasoned, and goal directed—the kind of thinking involved in solving problems, formulating inferences, calculating likelihoods, and making decisions, when the thinker is using skills that are thoughtful and effective for the particular context and type of thinking task. (Halpern, 2003a, p. 6)

The use of the word "critical" in "critical thinking" is used in the sense of evaluation or judgment. When someone is thinking critically, that person is evaluating the quality of the thinking process as well as the outcome of the thinking process. Not all thinking is critical thinking. Far too much of what is learned in school and other places is rote learning or closer to rote learning than it is to learning with understanding or learning in ways that promote or allow critical thinking. Consider, for example, a lesson in developmental psychology, a topic that I often use for examples because it is well know to teachers from their own coursework. After a lesson about Piaget's stages of cognitive development, students can expect to be asked test questions in which they list the ages for each stage of cognitive development, name the stages, and provide an example of a cognitive task that is accomplished at each stage. The examples students provide are almost always the same ones that are presented in the textbook and in class, thus making this test question a test of rote memory. When students repeat the same examples they were given in class or in a text, they are not learning how to use the information in an applied setting or to theorize in ways that builds connections to other related theories and concepts.

A Skills Approach

Moseley, Miller, and Higgins (2003) worked with multiple teams of educators from all sectors in education in England to classify thinking-skills programs. They were charged with answering an important question on behalf of the Learning and Skills Development Agency (LSDA) in England. Based on their extensive review, would they recommend that all their post-16 schools (which are similar to the community colleges in the United States) require critical-thinking coursework? They conducted an extensive classification and evaluation of all critical-thinking programs they could locate and produced several hundred pages of categorized reviews, including empirical evidence of effectiveness. After a careful review of the critical-thinking literature, they concluded that approaches that were skill based are especially useful because such approaches have specific educational objectives, making them easier to assess and communicate to students and other stakeholders in education. Skill-based critical-thinking approaches are also easier for the practice of teaching because teachers can keep the framework in mind as a guide during lessons and unexpected questions. In the team review conducted by Moseley and other educators from all levels of education in England, they concluded (in carefully worded language) that "using thinking skills frameworks, we need to develop new authentic, dynamic and ecologically relevant forms of assessment and evaluation." They also stated that "strategic thinking and reflection should form part of all education and training" and "teacher training courses should include a more solid grounding in theories of thinking and learning than they do at present" (p. 4). After decades of work in critical-thinking instruction in higher education, I fully agree with Mosley et al.'s conclusions.

Thinking Skills

Critical-thinking instruction is predicated on two assumptions: (a) that there are clearly identifiable and definable thinking skills which students can be taught to recognize and apply appropriately, and (b) if recognized and applied, the students will be more effective thinkers. Here are some examples of what is meant by the term "thinking skills." A general list of skills that would be applicable in almost any class and in many different situations outside of class includes understanding how cause is determined, recognizing and criticizing assumptions, analyzing means–goals relationships, giving reasons to support a conclusion, assessing degrees of likelihood and uncertainty, incorporating isolated data into a wider framework, and using analogies to solve problems. These are general thinking skills that should be applicable across a wide variety of subjects and contexts. Thinking skills can be grouped or categorized into skills that serve specific tasks, such as those used in understanding the conclusion of an argument or deciding if the conclusion is well supported (good reasons, strong evidence) or not, or the likelihood of a particular outcome. (It is interesting to note that the theme of this series of papers is the strength of evidence in support of an educational claim of effectiveness.) Some categories of thinking skills are presented in Table 5.1.

CAN CRITICAL THINKING BE IMPROVED WITH INSTRUCTION?

The question is not whether students can be taught to think with instruction, but whether they can be taught to think better—the research question is about improving thinking skills. Of course, the use of the word

Table 5.1. A Sampler of Critical-Thinking Skills

- The Relationship Between Thought and Language
  - ◊ How to understand and use questioning and listening strategies
  - ◊ How to recognize and defend against the use of inappropriate, emotional language
  - ◊ How to choose and use graphic organizers
- Reasoning: Drawing Deductively Valid Conclusions
  - ◊ How to discriminate between deductive and inductive reasoning
  - ◊ How to understand the differences between truth and validity
  - ◊ How to use quantifiers in reasoning
- Analyzing Arguments
  - ◊ How to diagram the structure of an argument
  - ◊ How to examine the credibility of an information source
  - ◊ How to judge arguments
- Thinking As Hypothesis Testing
  - ◊ How to understand the limits of correlational reasoning
  - ◊ How to isolate and control variables in order to make strong causal claims
  - ◊ How to know when causal claims can and cannot be made
- Likelihood and Uncertainty: Understanding Probabilities
  - ◊ How to use probability judgments to improve decision making
  - ◊ How to compute expected values in situations with known probabilities
  - ◊ How to avoid overconfidence in uncertain situations
- Decision Making
  - ◊ How to reframe decisions to consider alternatives
  - ◊ How to prepare a decision-making worksheet
  - ◊ How to understand the distinction between the quality of a decision and its outcome
- Development of Problem-Solving Skills
  - ◊ How to plan and monitor a strategy for finding a solution
  - ◊ How to use graphs, diagrams, hierarchical trees, matrices, and models as solution aids
  - ◊ How to select appropriate problem-solving strategies
- Creative Thinking
  - ◊ How to visualize a problem
  - ◊ How to brainstorm productively and create alternatives
  - ◊ How to gather additional information

"better" brings its own complications, including "better than what?" and "who gets to decide what is better thinking?" However, these are not really difficult questions. Most people, if asked, will respond that they think quite well, and although many people will freely admit to memory problems, they will not admit to "thinking problems." There is a great deal of literature showing that people are poor judges of their ability to comprehend complex passages and whether they guessed on multiple-choice examination questions or actually knew the answers. Therefore, it should not be surprising that most people generally believe they are thinking well because they cannot think of any reasons why they are not thinking well, and rarely have the outcome from a choice they did not select to compare with the option they did select to check how well they are thinking. Thus, self-reports about the effectiveness of learning outcomes are not objective data.

Transcontextual Transfer

There is no reason why thinking skills could *not* be learned in a way they will be used in a context other than the one in which they were originally learned. Other basic skill areas are taught with the belief that generalized skills will be learned and transferred to a wide range of topics. *Transfer* is spontaneous use of a skill in a context that is different from that one in which it was learned. The sole reason why we have schools that are formal settings designed for learning is that we expect that learning will transfer. Sometimes information learned in one context will transfer to a different context and sometimes it will not. If we want transfer to occur, teachers need to teach in ways that encourage this process.

Transfer is the goal of critical-thinking instruction because it is of no use to provide critical-thinking instruction if students do not use the skills in out-of-classroom settings and in other classes. Of course, transfer is critical for all levels of instruction. Writing skills, for example, are taught in writing classes and presumably strengthened and somewhat specialized in different disciplinary courses such as business and creative writing. Similarly, oral communication and mathematics are taught as basic skills that are used in multiple courses. Often these skills are not learned well, and often they do not transfer to disciplinary courses, so that writing skills taught in an English literature class need to be retaught for an accounting class. But the failure to transfer is often attributable to the way the skills are taught—often with little or no attention paid to the problem of transfer, so it is not surprising that transfer is difficult to obtain or only occurs when it is cued. Transfer of skills and knowledge can vary across very different contexts and knowledge domains and across periods of time and geographic place. An example should help to make this important point:

Consider the basic thinking skill of correlation, which is taught in every standard statistics course and social science course (e.g., social studies). Most students can learn to solve for a correlation coefficient in their statistics course and can learn to define the term "correlation" and differentiate between correlation and cause in a social science course, but the same students often do not recognize a correlation when they encounter it in everyday settings. For example, many do not recognize that correlational data are being used as a causal argument when they hear that juvenile crime has increased at the same rate as the divorce rate (a false statistic that almost no students stop to question—another critical-thinking skill). Given these false facts, even top students are ready to conclude that divorce is the cause of juvenile crime. This is an example of the failure of transfer of a critical-thinking skill, but when the skills are taught *for* transfer—with multiple examples across different domains of knowledge, uncued (i.e., students are not told to think about correlation) with feedback, then these skills can and do transfer. Just as with most teaching and learning, success depends on spaced practice, informational feedback, cognitive pedagogy, and effortful learning (Halpern & Hakel, 2003).

In Walberg's (2005) review in this book of the extant research on what works in education, he clearly states that direct instruction with review, teacher modeling, guided practice with corrective feedback, and application in which the student performs independently is the preferred method for learning. Although some critical-thinking advocates (e.g., Brookfield, 2003) believe that critical-thinking instruction is somehow exempt from this general principle and should only be taught when infused in specific subject matter courses, such an approach would not promote across-discipline transfer because the examples used for each thinking skill would come from within a single domain of knowledge and students would not be required to transfer thinking skills beyond the domain boundaries.

ASSESSMENT AS AN OPERATIONAL DEFINITION

Central to the question of whether and when critical thinking is improved with instruction is the notion of what it is measuring. Readers who are sophisticated in issues of research design have probably anticipated the knotty problems of assessing (i.e., measuring) critical thinking. As soon as the question becomes whether students have become better thinkers because of some intervention—in this case, an instructional program—the question of assessment is almost as important as the intervention. Although I say "almost," in fact, many times, education "battlefields" are bloodied over assessment or measurement issues as all sides lose sight of the fact that they have stopped fighting over the issue they started out caring about. We cannot know if anyone improved in the ability to think critically if critical thinking is not measured with enough accuracy to "pick up" a change that was caused by the intervention.

Assessment is inextricably tied with issues of definition, research design, and essential debates over whether it is possible to improve thinking, so this is a central topic in education. The teaching–learning–assessing cycle is incomplete without any of these elements. Assessment is integral in education and learning—it is not an "add on." The measurement issues in critical thinking are not insurmountable, but few people care enough or perhaps know enough about psychometrics to attempt to mount them. Some "off-the-shelf" critical-thinking tests are available for purchase but, unfortunately, these tests rarely match what is taught in critical-thinking courses, and many of them have very poor psychometric properties. For example, the most widely used test, the Watson-Glaser Critical Thinking Appraisal Exam, was reviewed by Fawkes et al. (2002), who concluded that the "exam is defective in a number of areas. Of the 5 'tests' totaling 80 questions, the authors cannot recommend test 1, test 2, test 4, and test 5.... [T]he exam creates confusion and makes basic errors in critical thinking" (p. 31). The National Nursing League took a bold step several years ago by requiring that nursing education include critical-thinking instruction. However, because most nursing faculty members are not well versed in psychometrics, they decided to assess critical thinking with the Watson-Glaser Test, the "granddaddy" of critical-thinking tests. This is a disturbing move because the test is essentially a test of reading. Despite great effort, students were not showing the gains on the Watson-Glaser test that the faculty had hoped to see, so they concluded that they were not teaching their students to become better thinkers. In fact, there was a large mismatch between what they were teaching (e.g., how to read a research article, look for a control group, make credibility judgments, when to estimate probabilities, and so on) and what was being tested on the Watson-Glaser test. The problem was that their assessment did not match their instruction, so they could not determine if they were successfully improving the critical-thinking skills of their students.

Another popular off-the-shelf critical-thinking test suffers a similar criticism. The California Critical Thinking Skills Test was evaluated by psychometricians, who concluded that "the data indicate low internal consistency reliability estimates, a lack of comparability, and poor construct validity" (Jacobs, 1999, p. 211). The last criticism is particularly damning because it means that the test is *not* measuring critical thinking, at least as the term is being conceptualized. It seems that even those who are working in the field are not thinking critically about measurement issues. When the measurement is bad, as it apparently is with these two popular off-the-shelf measures, it is easy to see why we have not gotten strong results with critical-thinking instruction. A more extensive review of measurement issues can be found in Halpern (2003b).

A Better Measure

The need for providing information about the status of critical-thinking skills is relatively noncontroversial. There is currently little or no information to inform the decision makers in the workplace, higher education, the military, or any other setting that is concerned with the improvement of thinking skills. The controversies arise over questions of whether the information can be provided in a way that is meaningful, valid, useful, used, fair, and cost effective. A high-quality assessment can provide many benefits, but if the assessment is not well done, the results will be costly. Public confidence and trust are the *sine qua non* for an undertaking of this significance.

The type of measure of critical thinking that I am advocating is based on clearly defined skills that are assessed in realistic scenarios that could apply to a wide range of racial, ethnic, and socioeconomic groups. The United States is one of the most culturally diverse countries in the world, and as the globe shrinks in response to advances in technology, diversity of experiences and backgrounds needs to be considered in test designs for all countries. To provide a fair estimate of the ability of people from all cultures, the skills selected must be those that are used and needed in most cultural settings. A culture-free test is not possible (or even desirable), but fairness for various groups can be improved with careful preparation.

The Sequential Question

The Critical Thinking Assessment About Everyday Events uses believable examples with an open-ended response format, followed by specific questions that probe for the reasoning behind an answer. If, for example, the thinking skill of understanding and recognizing the distinction between correlation and cause were being assessed, it would be tested with examples taken from medical research (e.g., coffee drinkers reported more headaches), social policy analysis (e.g., welfare mothers who received job training were more likely to be employed after 1 year than welfare mothers who did not receive job training), and numerous other believable scenarios, thus testing for cross-domain use of the skill. Such materials are ecologically valid because they are representative of the many examples that could be found in newspapers and everyday discussions. The open-ended portion of the question allows test takers to demonstrate whether they spontaneously use the skill. Do the test takers recognize the fact these are correlational designs that do not permit causal statements when there are no obvious hints to consider the issue of design?

Specific probes in the form of alternatives for the forced-choice questions follow the open-ended responses. These probes allow test takers to demonstrate their understanding of the concepts, such as whether they are able to recognize the problem of determining cause when they are provided with hints (e.g., in understanding these results, is it important to know if the participants were assigned randomly to the different conditions?). These additional probes show if test takers are able to use the skill when they are told that it is needed in a specific situation, even if the participant did not spontaneously recognize that the skill was needed.

A good critical-thinking question with several sequential parts allows for different types of information about the test taker with a minimal number of questions. The open-ended constructed portion of the question could be graded simply as "recognized the need for the particular thinking skill" or "did not recognize the need for a particular thinking skill." The open-ended or constructed response portion is a test of the type of remembering that cognitive psychologists call "free recall" because there are few restraints on the type of response that the test taker can generate. (It is a type of recall that is free from restraints.) The multiple-choice or multiple-rating portion shows if the respondent was able to recognize the appropriate skill when it was presented in a list of alternatives. This sort of response is a measure of "recognition memory." Cognitive psychologists distinguish between recall and recognition paradigms in the assessment of memory. It is believed that these two types of recall use different cognitive processes and that students prepare differently for tests that require free recall (e.g., essay tests) than those that require recognition (e.g., multiple-choice tests). In general, lower scores are expected on free recall tests than recognition tests because free recall requires a search through memory plus some sort of verification that the answer retrieved is correct; recognition requires only the verification stage and provides a less stringent measure of memory.

There is good evidence that multiple-choice questions and open-ended essays are measuring somewhat separable constructs. In a study of the Advanced Placement tests, which are taken by college-bound high-school seniors, a significantly greater proportion of young women than young men obtained scores that were high on the essay questions and low on the multiple-choice questions. Young men showed an opposite pattern of results, with a significantly greater proportion obtaining high scores on the multiple-choice questions and low scores on the essay questions than the young women. Thus, a mix of the two types of questions would also help to ensure equity for boys and girls in these tests.

The multipart nature of the questions makes it possible to assess both the dispositional aspect of critical thinking and the ability to use a skill when a prompt is provided. Constructed responses have been limited in length to a maximum of two to four sentences so that scoring costs can be contained and good answers can be readily identified. Questions and responses are presented on a computer so that presentation times and scoring can be controlled and automated, and the time needed for administering and scoring is greatly reduced. A computer-administered assessment can also provide reaction-time data, a major dependent measure in cognitive psychological studies. Reaction times are sometimes used as measures of intelligence and, although it is not an appropriate use in this assessment, reaction times can help psychologists understand a great deal about the microcomponents of the underlying cognitive processes. They permit a much more fine-grained analysis of mental events than other commonly used dependent measures such as percentage of questions answered correctly. Reaction-time data could be made available to cognitive psychologists for secondary analyses. These data would not be provided to respondents or reported to the public because it is difficult to convince the general public that a difference of a few hundred milliseconds relates to any practical notion of intelligence. No one can answer the philosophical question of whether differences of a few hundred milliseconds add up over the course of a day, so that "fast thinkers" have an extra hour or so every day that "slow thinkers" lose, or whether these fractions of a second "get lost" in the ebb and flow of everyday events. Table 5.2 shows an example of a constructed response scenario followed by a forced-choice response with the same scenario.

To ensure that thinking skills transfer across different disciplinary domains (e.g., history and physics) and over time (a thinking skill that is learned will be used spontaneously after graduation) and in different physical contexts (away from school), teachers need to use examples drawn from a wide variety of domains, with the skill use spaced over time, and the need for the skill being uncued. For example, if the skill being taught were the "law of large numbers" or, loosely speaking, the fact that better estimates can be made with large samples than with small ones, newspaper articles could be used each week, thus varying the topic and making the rule less overtly obvious (i.e., uncued). Or, for example, students could be asked to comment on their thinking about a political candidate who is late for a rally. Are they ready to generalize from one late appointment? Surprisingly, many are! These can continue, and comment about one superb meal at a restaurant—what would they expect on a return trip—naturally leads to a discussion of regression to the mean, and so on.

The field of cognitive psychology can now provide sufficient knowledge of how people think, learn, and remember to provide a sound pedagogy. We know that people retain information best when they generate information from memory, space practice over increasing time intervals, remain active, receive informational and useful feedback, use visuospatial and verbal formats, and so on (Halpern, 1998; Hakel & Halpern, 2004).

Table 5.2. An Example of a Critical-Thinking Scenario with Constructed Response and Forced-choice Responses

Question 1

A recent report in a magazine for parents and teachers showed that adolescents who smoke cigarettes also tend to get low grades in school. As the number of cigarettes smoked each day increased, grade-point averages decreased. One suggestion made in this report was that we could improve school achievement by preventing adolescents from smoking.

Based on this information, would you support this idea as a way of improving the school achievement of adolescents who smoke? Type "yes" or "no" and explain why or why not.

Question 2

A recent report in a magazine for parents and teachers showed that adolescents who smoke cigarettes also tend to get low grades in school. As the number of cigarettes smoked each day increased, grade-point averages decreased. One suggestion made in this report was that we could improve school achievement by preventing adolescents from smoking.

Based on this information, which is the best answer? (Choose one.)

1. School grades will probably improve if we prevent adolescents from smoking because the researchers found that when smoking increases, grades go down.
2. School grades might improve if we prevent adolescents from smoking but we cannot be certain because we only know that grades go down when smoking increases, not what happens when smoking decreases.
3. There is no way to know if school grades will improve if we prevent adolescents from smoking because we only know that smoking and grades are related, not whether smoking causes grades to change.
4. There will probably be no effect on grades if we prevent adolescents from smoking because the magazine is written for parents and teachers, so it is probably biased against adolescent smoking.

Scoring for this question is 0 points for all options except #3, which is 1 point (correct answer).

EMPIRICAL EVIDENCE THAT CRITICAL THINKING CAN BE ENHANCED WITH SKILLS-BASED INSTRUCTION

A huge amount of research literature exists on programs to teach critical thinking. The work I am most familiar with is at the postsecondary level, but there are also many programs at pre-K–12. Numerous empirical reviews have been conducted, each focusing on a subset of programs, and each somewhat idiosyncratic. Starting again with the conclusion, each of the reviews is positive: critical thinking can be taught and learned.

Numerous qualitatively different forms of outcome evaluations are available for thinking courses that provide substantial evidence for the conclusion that it is possible to use formal education to improve the ability to think critically, especially when instruction is specifically designed to encourage the transfer of these skills to different situations and different domains of knowledge.

Meta-Analyses and Thorny Conceptual Issues

The literature on teaching thinking skills is huge but difficult to summarize statistically because of the multiple differences among the studies, including differences in the "technique" used to enhance thinking that run the gamut from team teaching, learning hierarchies, tutoring, questioning, and concept mapping, to name just a few (Hattie, 1992). The need for random-assignment field trials in education is usually made with an analogy between education and medicine, but we do not improve thinking the same way we prevent polio. There are some similarities, but there are also important differences. There is little variability in the way polio vaccinations are injected by competent medical professionals, but there are large differences in the way educational programs are delivered. Dose size is determined as a function of the weight of the patient; "dose" and rate for educational programs are far more art than science. The presence and absence of polio is fairly unambiguous; by contrast, good and poor thinking can vary in multiple ways, and judgments can vary among judges. The imperfect analogies point out imperfections in the conclusion that what is good for medicine is good medicine for education.

Over the past decade, there have been many outspoken critics of null hypothesis testing. This kind of testing is predicated on the underlying belief that researchers are rejecting a null hypothesis of no difference between intervention and control groups (or any groups of interest), and researchers can only conclude that the intervention "worked" if the difference between group means would happen by chance less than five times in 100 hypothetical replications of the experiment. The many concerns that were raised cannot be "fixed" by randomly assigning participants to conditions. One opinion that gained considerable voice during the controversy is the belief that the most critical need in research is for more synthesis of research findings that allows for information across studies to be considered along with a single estimate of the size of their effect. Others argued for structural equation models that promote complex "pictures" of multiple variables acting in concert along with variables that cannot be assigned at random—such as levels of poverty, being raised in a single-parent home, or being raised with highly intelligent, high-achieving parents and siblings—and the way these variables would work along with the intervention.

In the real world, how should multiple studies, with large effect sizes, with a matched control group be weighed against a single experiment with random assignment of subjects and a smaller effect size? Which intervention is the stronger one? In real life, how would teachers or parents choose if they had these two sets of data (and the sophistication to understand these distinctions)? This is not a hypothetical question. Consider a review of the research on instruction by Marzano (1998). In his review of thinking-skills programs (mostly high school, but some primary school) he found that those programs that taught student "heuristics" (i.e., thinking skills) had an overall effect size of d = 1.17! Marzano computed this value from 45 separate effect sizes. This is an effect size that is so large that Cohen, the statistician who popularized the use of effect size statistics, claimed that effects this large do not need statistical tests. Effect sizes over one standard deviation are so large, we can "see" them, which is why they are sometimes analyzed with the colloquial bifocal test. With an effect this large across many studies with a diverse range of subjects and many different types of classroom settings, do we need to "wait" for large random-assignment field trials before we can decide that these interventions "work" to improve thinking skills?

Given the large effect size from Marzano's (1998) and others' reviews (e.g., Halpern, 2003a, 2003b) of critical-thinking instruction, would informed parents really agree to allow their children to participate in a random-assignment study of the efficacy of thinking-skills programs? Would you, as an informed reader, really allow your own child to be in the control or no-treatment group? Of course, the "correct" response to this question is that, without random assignment, it is not possible to know if an intervention actually worked. Any experimental psychologist recognizes this is true, but it is also true that a large effect size summarized over a large number of diverse studies from many different participants and contexts also provides good evidence, even if it is not strictly causal.

An Apt Metaphor: The Women's Health Initiative as a Biased Rush to Judgment

The strongest cases for randomized field trials are often made by reference to the Women's Health Initiative, a large-scale study in which the commonly acknowledged positive effects of hormone replacement therapy (HRT) on heart disease in women were "disproved" when a large-scale study was conducted using random assignment of women to placebo and hormone therapy conditions. The results were so dramatic that the study was stopped early because of the negative effects of the HRT. But despite random assignment, the results are not as clear cut as the media reported.

First, HRT is not a single treatment. There are many types of hormones that act differently depending on their concentrations, other hormones active at the same time, stage in the women's life span (e.g., perimenopause, with its natural hormone spikes, is very different from postmenopause, when hormone levels are very low and stable), and so on.

Only one combination and dose was used in the Women's Health Initiative and, for a variety of reasons, many researchers in this area now believe that using this one combination and dose was a poor choice. In addition, the question of interest was whether estrogen (a general class of one type of hormone) could prevent some health problems, notably heart disease, if administered in a window of opportunity during early perimenopause. But more than two thirds of the women in the study were postmenopausal at the start of the study, too old to test the main hypothesis. There were numerous other complications because the complexity of life has numerous messy variables, which makes the careful manipulation of any single variable an unrealistic research design for generalization no matter how large scale the study and carefully the random assignment of subjects to conditions is achieved. Random assignment of subjects is a high-quality research design that permits causal analyses, but it also has many problems, as seen in the poster child for random assignment, the Women's Health Initiative. (The background data on flaws and misunderstanding and media bias in the Women's Health Initiative were provided at a symposium by investigators from the National Institutes of Health; Schmidt & Rubinow, 2004).

The point of this criticism is that every design is flawed in its own way. Large-scale, random-assignment studies are *absolutely needed*, but we need to be mindful of their limitations and not blindly accept conclusions from such studies as "proof" or "the answer" to important questions. Educational research needs large-scale, random-assignment studies that pay careful attention to program fidelity and measurement, but these studies are expensive, and they are not error free. We can also use meta-analyses that indicate effect sizes and other types of converging evidence. The multiple complexities of real children in real learning environments do not easily lend themselves to the manipulation of single variables under controlled conditions, but these sorts of studies need to be funded and encouraged or they will not happen because of the necessary expenses and need for replication, fidelity, and collaboration.

Strong Causal Evidence: Random-Assignment, Double-Blind Studies

Fortunately, strong causal evidence suggests that thinking skills can be taught in ways that transfer to novel topics. At least one large-scale, random-assignment experiment of a thinking-skills intervention provided excellent results. A formal evaluation of a nationwide thinking-skills program in Venezuela showed that students who had participated in classes designed for instruction in thinking skills showed greater gains in orally presented arguments and in answering open-ended essay questions than a comparable control group (Herrnstein, Nickerson, de Sanchez, & Swets, 1986). This study is particularly notable because the researchers used an experimental design that allowed them to conclude that it was the instruction and not some extraneous factor that caused students in the experimental group to improve in their ability to think critically. Students were randomly assigned to receive either the thinking-skills instruction or some other "control" instruction. Additionally, the oral arguments and writing samples were graded blindly (i.e., the graders did not know if the students they were assessing had received the thinking-skills instruction or were in the control group). The results showed that the targeted thinking skills were transferred and used appropriately with novel topics. Students who received the thinking-skills instruction showed greater gains than the control-group students on tests of general aptitude (sometimes called intelligence tests), problem solving, decision making, reasoning, creative thinking, and language. This experiment provides strong support for the conclusion that improvements in thinking are possible when instruction is designed for this purpose. Unfortunately, because of a change in government support for this program, no long-term follow-up data from the Venezuela project are available, but at least in the short term, it does seem that better thinking can be learned.

Large-scale studies of this sort are expensive and need government or other large corporate support so that results could be replicated across sites, random assignment could be used, quality materials could be developed, and all the necessary controls could be put in place to determine the effect sizes for gains in thinking skills. Conclusions from studies with poor controls suggest that the greatest gains are made by low-achieving students, perhaps because they have a greater possible latitude for additional cognitive gains. However, it is impossible to determine if the lowest achieving students would benefit the most from critical-thinking instruction without conducting the experiments to find out. There are solid reasons to support large-scale studies, including large studies from other countries, but we fall short of the best data from the United States.

CONCLUSIONS

We have converging data from multiple sources: Students can think better as a result of instruction, but we lack the strongest causal data with longitudinal follow-up. Of course, many examples of failed programs exist, but some studies do show the differences between successful and unsuccessful programs. (Although not the focus of this paper, successful programs generally teach generalizable thinking skills and metacognition; unsuccessful programs are divorced from real-world thinking, teaching, for example, abstract syllogisms.) Limited data are available from large-scale, random-assignment field studies (in Venezuela, Herrnstein et al., 1998), meta-analyses, and multiple overviews of the data and the field. The U.S. government called for critical thinking as a goal for the year 2000 and then backed down from paying for this goal, yet the need is greater than ever.

If the hesitancy to embark on a large-scale critical-thinking project, at least on the same scale as projects done on reading and mathematics, is because few randomized field trials have been conducted thus far, then it is time to call for more such studies. These studies are expensive and difficult to coordinate, but they are worth the investment. More than ever, educated adults need to be able to judge the credibility of information, recognize and defend against propaganda, reason effectively, use evidence in decision-making processes, and identify problems and find ways to solve them, if they are to benefit from the wealth of information available. It may be the best return on investment we make as a nation.

REFERENCES

Brookfield, S. (2003). Critical thinking in adulthood. In D. Fasko, Jr. (Ed.), *Critical thinking and reasoning: Current research, theory, and practice* (pp. 143–163). Cresskill, NJ: Hampton Press.

Fawkes, D., Adajian, T., Flage, D., Hoeltzel, S., Knorpp, B., O'Meara, B., & Weber, D. (2002). Examining the exam: A critical look at the Watson-Glaser critical thinking appraisal exam. *Inquiry: Critical Thinking Across the Disciplines, 21*, 31–46.

Fischer, S. C., & Spiker, V. A. (2000). *Application of a theory of critical thinking to army command and control*. Arlington, VA: U.S. Army Research Institute for the Behavioral and Social Sciences.

Hakel, M., & Halpern, D. F. (2004). How far can transfer go? Making transfer happen across physical, temporal, and conceptual space. In J. Mestre (Ed.), *Transfer of learning: Research and perspectives*. Greenwich, CT: Information Age.

Halpern, D. F. (1998). Teaching critical thinking for transfer across domains: Dispositions, skills, structure training, and metacognitive monitoring. *American Psychologist, 53*, 449–455.

Halpern, D. F. (2003a). *Thought and knowledge: An Introduction to critical thinking* (4th ed.). Mahwah, NJ: Erlbaum.

Halpern, D. F. (2003b). The "how" and "why" of critical thinking assessment. In D. Fasko, Jr. (Ed.), *Critical thinking and reasoning: Current research, theory, and practice* (pp. 355–366). Cresskill, NJ: Hampton Press.

Halpern, D. F., & Hakel, M. D. (2003). Applying the science of learning to the university and beyond: teaching for long-term retention and transfer. *Change, 35*(4), 37–41.

Hattie, J. A. (1992). Measuring the effects of schooling. *Australian Journal of Education, 36*, 5–13.

Herrnstein, R. J., Nickerson, R. S., de Sanchez, M., & Swets, J. A. (1986). Teaching thinking skills. *American Psychologist, 41*, 1279–1289.

Jacobs, S. S. (1999). The equivalence of Forms A and B of the California Critical Thinking Skills Test. *Measurement & Evaluation in Counseling & Development, 31*, 211–222.

Jones, E. A., Hoffman, S., Moore, L. M., Ratcliff, G., Tibbetts, S., & Click, B. A. (1997). *National assessment of college student learning: Identifying college graduates' essential skills in writing, speech and listening, and critical thinking*. (NCES 95-001). Washington, DC: U.S. Government Printing Office.

Marzano, R. J. (1998). *A theory-based meta-analysis of research on instruction*. Aurora, CO: Mid-continent Research for Education and Learning.

Moseley, D., Miller, J., & Higgins, S. (2003, November). *Thinking skills frameworks for use in education and training*. Paper prepared for the Knowledge and Skills for Learning to Learn Seminar, London, England.

National Education Goals Panel. (1991). *The national education goals report: Building a nation of learners*. Washington, DC: Author.

Schmidt, P. J., & Rubinow, D. R. (2004, March). *The effects of hormones on mood and cognition during midlife and the perimenopause*. Symposium presented at the 2nd World Congress on Women's Mental Health, Washington, DC.

Walberg, H. J. (2005). Improving educational productivity: As assessment of extant research. In H. J. Walberg & R. F. Subotnik (Eds.), *The scientific basis of educational productivity*. Greenwich, CT: Information Age.

CHAPTER 6

IMPROVING EDUCATIONAL PRODUCTIVITY

An Assessment of Extant Research[1]

Herbert J. Walberg

The founding of the Institute of Education Sciences and the National Board for Education Sciences may foreshadow a golden age of scientific research on education. Randomized experimentation and other rigorous research methods including the education analogs of econometric analysis and controlled epidemiological surveys in medicine hold much promise. Even so, it may take a decade or two to establish trustworthy findings to serve as a basis of education practices and policies. For this reason, this chapter is an effort to assess extant research that bears upon educational policy and school- and classroom-level decision-making. This chapter draws chiefly on previous meta-analyses (statistical analyses of the results of many control-group studies) and econometric analyses of large-scale surveys, both of which suggest or even reveal the likely causes of academic achievement.

During the past quarter century, scholarship grew rapidly on the question of what makes a difference in students' learning. The 1966 Coleman Report, the largest U.S. education survey ever undertaken, precipitated

The Scientific Basis of Educational Productivity, 103–159

such scholarship since James Coleman and his colleagues' report to Congress (Coleman et al., 1966) found little or no effect of school resources such as per-student spending and class size on how much students learned. Reanalysis of the Coleman Report and additional studies led the eminent economist and former president of the American Association for the Advancement of Science, Kenneth E. Boulding, to write a paper in 1972 titled "The Schooling Industry as a Possibly Pathological Section of the American Economy" (Boulding, 1972). He noted that schools doubled their share of the American economy from about 3% to 6% in real prices from 1930 to 1970 and were "notoriously unprogressive when it comes to productivity" (p. 135).

A few years before the Coleman Report, Benjamin Bloom (1963) published perhaps the first synthesis of many psychological studies of the stability of human characteristics including learning. He estimated that adult academic ability is fairly predictable by the age of 4 and largely predictable by the age of 8, which suggested the importance of early parental and other extramural influences rather than subsequent schooling in determining achievement.

Policymakers, however, increasingly believe that K–12 educators should be held accountable during the school years; or they should at least be responsible for the "value added" that they uniquely contribute to the "human capital" of knowledge and skills that largely determines individual and national prosperity and well-being. Though this view is traceable to Smith's 1776 *Wealth of Nations*, the widely influential report, *A Nation at Risk* (National Commission for Excellence in Education, 1983), gave it late-twentieth-century prominence.

THE PRODUCTIVITY PREDICAMENT

The learning productivity problem is better known and even more acute today: Vastly increased spending and many school reforms resulted in stagnant achievement during the past quarter century, even though children's measured intelligence or capacity for learning increased steadily (Walberg, 1998b). Unlike most sectors of the American economy that steadily increase their productivity over time, schools become less rather than more efficient, a serious matter given the size of the education sector and the central and increasing importance of learning in the American economy and society. School productivity or the relation of achievement to costs was 65% higher in 1970–71 than in 1998–99 (Hoxby, 2001).[2] Federal expenditures of more than $120 billion failed to diminish the "poverty gap" between poor and middle-class students.

American schools, moreover, have higher dropout rates than commonly reported. An 86% graduation rate is often reported notwithstanding that 74% of U.S. students actually graduate. The discrepancy is accounted for by the federal government counting dropouts passing General Educational Development (GED) tests as graduates, even though economists find that young people with GEDs do no better on the job market than dropouts. Minorities drop out, moreover, in large percentages: Only 56% of Blacks and 54% of Hispanics finish high school, in contrast to 80% of Whites who graduate (Greene, 2002a).

Internationally, the productivity problem is also obvious: Among two dozen affluent countries, the U.S. is near the top in per-student spending, but American students fall further behind others the longer they are in school (Organisation for Economic Co-Operation and Development, 1995–2001). Moreover, unlike a quarter century ago, today smaller percentages of U.S. students than those in other countries remain in school during the late teen years. Thus, American schools compare unfavorably in both quality and quantity, despite high costs.

Ironically, though research identified the learning problem, policymakers and educators ignored early and subsequent research pointing to productive solutions. They followed fad after fad, many of which were implausible and expensive, and none of which had the evidentiary basis required in such fields as agronomy, medicine, public health, and psychology. An additional irony is that much of the older research on what makes a difference was more rigorous but less acceptable to education theorists, perhaps because it suggests traditional, commonsense educational methods.[3]

PURPOSE AND SCOPE

My purpose is to synthesize (a) meta-analyses (statistical analyses of results of many studies) of control-group research and (b) large-scale surveys that reveal the causes of achievement. These two kinds of research complement one another. Psychologists prefer control-group experiments, particularly those that randomly assign students to educational methods and conditions, and measure achievement before and after to assess progress. Such experiments have causal creditability, because differences in learning are attributable only to treatments and the luck of the draw, just as in the case of medical experiments that randomly assign patients to alternative regimens.

Experiments may be weak in generalizability, however, since they typically use small and possibly atypical samples of students, such as those in a given urban or suburban site. The statistical analysis of many control-group studies, however, can compensate for the weakness of any single study, since the pervasiveness of an effect can be ascertained by statistically analyzing a variety (usually all) of samples. Such analyses can show whether an educational method works as well for boys as for girls and for urban, suburban, and rural students at various grade levels and in various school subjects.

Analyses of state, national, and international surveys can also reveal the generalizability of findings. Epidemiologists, economists, political scientists, and sociologists conduct such research, which usually encompasses whole populations or random samples. These analyses, however, yield somewhat less certain causal inferences, since they are intended to "control" for alternative causes. In achievement research, these usually include prior achievement, socioeconomic status, or poverty, which may be poorly specified and measured. Such analyses of large-scale surveys may also omit plausible causes, since measures of them were left out of the surveys originally designed for purposes other than the analyst's.

In the last decade, however, such data sets and analyses improved remarkably, particularly in measuring learning rather than achievement—that is, in assessing "value-added" learning over, say, the year from one year's test to the next. Analyzing achievement at a single point in time may be misleading, since achievement may be attributable to prior causes, such as infant poverty or prior good or bad teaching, rather than to current conditions or methods.[4]

Though economic, sociological, and political factors affect learning, their influence is indirect. Learning is fundamentally a psychological process; student motivation, instruction, and other psychological factors are the well-established, consistent, and proximal causes of learning. Thus, this report starts with psychological factors before analyzing the social conditions that affect learning less directly.

PSYCHOLOGICAL CAUSES OF LEARNING

The scarce resources in learning are opportunity and concentration rather than the amount of information available or the processing capacity of the mind. Herbert Simon, the Nobel economist and psychologist, combined these fields to synthesize what might be called "the micro-economics of cognitive learning." Summarized in this section, his synthesis sets the stage for understanding what helps students learn.

If a lifetime were devoted to acquisition of information, according to Simon's estimates, about 200 million items could be stored. "Hence, the problem for humans is to allocate their very limited processing capacity among several functions of noticing, storing, and indexing on the input side, and retrieving, reorganizing, and controlling his [sic] effectors [actions] on the output side" (Simon, 1981, p. 167).

Psychological Processing of Information

Aside from external incentives and opportunities, the major constraints on the acquisition of knowledge are the few items of information, perhaps 2 to 9, that can be held in short-term memory, and the time required, 5 to 10 seconds, to store an item in long-term memory. In chess, mathematics, science, writing, and other fields that have been studied, experts differ from novices not only in having more information in permanent memory but also in processing it more efficiently. Among experts, for example, items of information are thoroughly indexed and can be rapidly brought to conscious memory.

Among experts, items are also elaborately linked with one another, which confers two advantages: the ability to recover information by alternative links, even when memory loses parts of the direct indexing, and the capacity for extensive means–ends or trial-and-error searches. Such processes come into play in problem solving, from the elementary insights of novices through the advanced discoveries of eminent experts.

The expert's greatest advantage over novices is "chunking," the representation of related items of verbal, numerical, spatial, and other information as a single condensed symbol. A few seconds of study, for example, enable amateur chess players to remember the positions of only a few pieces, but masters may take in a whole board by readily perceiving variations of a few standard chunked patterns of individual pieces.

The sizes of chunks of information assimilated from the environment enlarge with experience and practice, because expertise confers knowledge about what information to acquire and how to code it efficiently. Experience and education (or guided experience) enable learners to assimilate ever-larger parts of the environment. For example, nearly a century ago, Edmund Huey (1908) showed that brief pauses in reading (called "fixations") do not vary in duration among novice and skilled readers. Instead, readers improve their rates by assimilating increasingly larger chunks of text ranging from parts of letters to words and phrases.

Time for Processing

Simon estimates that 50,000 chunks, about the same number as the recognition vocabulary of college-educated readers, may be required for expert mastery of a special field. The highest achievements in various disciplines, however, may require a memory store of 1 million chunks, which may take 70 hours a week for roughly a decade to acquire, notwithstanding such 7- to 9-year exceptions as Mozart and the chess master Bobby Fischer.

Speed may also be traded for accuracy in assimilation and processing. In accelerated reading or skimming, for example, chunks are sampled, and intervening meanings may be assumed—perhaps mistakenly. The fastest readers may presume to grasp paragraphs and pages with instantaneous fixations, although those who read *War and Peace* in an hour may recall only that it was about old Russia or, worse, World War II.

Assimilation also depends on the correspondence of meanings in the material and the person's memory. Psychological experiments, for example, show that, with randomly placed chess pieces in "unchunked" patterns, masters have little advantage over novices in reproducing the board. Unchunked nonsense words of randomly generated letters, similarly, put both slow and fast readers at a vast disadvantage in recalling sentences.

Language mastery, the fundamental and pervasive skill necessary for achievement in school, is determined more by experience than by psychometric intelligence. Most bright American adults, for example, would be reduced to the level of infancy or feeblemindedness in comprehending Swahili or Tamil. In principle, nonetheless, a dictionary, a coach, and unlimited time might overcome their limitation. For children, "total immersion" in their mother tongue is almost universally generally effective for listening and speaking. Immersion, moreover, in a noncognate language for as little as a year appears sufficient to bring children and adults to near-native fluency (though pronunciations are difficult for adults). Decisive is the amount and intensity of the experience rather than age or psychometric intelligence (Walberg, Hase, & Rasher, 1978).

Thus, meaning that conforms to expectation and experience promotes speed of mental processing. Parents and teachers can foster learning by presenting logical, readily understood explanations suitable to learners as well as the time, opportunity, and incentives for them to learn. These simple, commonsense principles set the stage for understanding research on the psychological causes within and outside school that foster learning.

Nine Psychological Causes of Learning

Practice makes perfect, says an old adage. An analysis of time effects on learning suggests the obvious: 88% of 376 study estimates revealed the positive effects of various aspects of study time such as preschool participation, school attendance, amount of attention to lessons, amount of homework, and length of the school year (Walberg, 1998b). The positive effect of time is perhaps most consistent of all causes of learning.

The widely read 1983 report, *A Nation at Risk*, called attention to the American school year as the shortest among economically advanced countries. U.S. students still spend about half as much time in total study hours as students in Asian countries that top the achievement charts. Until recently with the advent of summer and after-school programs, time remained neglected among school reforms.[5]

In addition to time, intensity also rules: Illogical or unsuitable instruction or student inattentiveness may mean that little is accomplished, notwithstanding much study time. Other psychological conditions also have a causal bearing on learning. The most consistent, powerful, and direct productivity factors or psychological causes of learning are defined in Table 6.1.

This taxonomy of three sets of nine factors derives from an early synthesis of 2,575 study comparisons (Walberg, 1984) that suggested that these factors are the chief psychological causes of academic achievement (and, more broadly, school-related cognitive, affective, and behavioral learning).[6] Subsequent syntheses have shown results consistent with the

Table 6.1. Nine Educational Productivity Factors

Factor	*Proportional Learning Influence*
A. Student Aptitude	
1. Ability or preferably prior achievement	.92
2. Development as indexed by chronological age or stage of maturation	.51
3. Motivation or self-concept as indicated by personality tests or the student's willingness to persevere intensively on learning tasks	.18
B. Instruction	
4. Amount of time students engage in learning	.47
5. Quality of the instructional experience, including method (psychological) and curricular (content) aspects	.18
C. Psychological Environments	
6. Morale or student perception of classroom social group	.47
7. Home environment or "curriculum of the home"	.36
8. Peer group outside school	.20
9. Minimal leisure-time mass media exposure, particularly television	.20

Source: Fraser, Walberg, Welch, and Hattie (1987).
Note: Estimates are calculated from data reported on p. 220. The indexes in the table are on the same scale as the effect sizes in Table 3 but are not necessarily pure, one-way causal effects.

original findings. Each of the first five factors—prior achievement, development, motivation, and the quantity and quality of instruction—seems necessary for learning in school. Without at least a small amount of each, the student may learn little. Large amounts of instruction and high degrees of ability, for example, may count for little if students are unmotivated or instruction is unsuitable. Each of the first five factors appears necessary but insufficient by itself for effective learning.[7]

Instructional Time

Time is a particularly pervasive constraint, since U.S. students have the shortest school year among countries of the industrialized world[8] and generally do far less homework than students from other countries. For this reason, variations in the out-of-school time factors—home environments, peer groups, and exposure to mass media, particularly television—strongly influence learning.

Even so, time in school may be inefficiently employed. It has been wisely said that it is as useless to teach students what they already know as it is to teach them what they are as yet incapable of learning. High-quality instruction can be understood as providing information cues, correctives, and positive reinforcement or encouragement that insure the fruitfulness of engaged time. Careful diagnosis and tutoring can help make instruction suitable for students. Inspired teaching can help students to persevere. Quality of instruction, then, may be considered an efficient enhancement of study time.

Similarly, the four psychological environments indicated in Table 6.1 can expand and enhance learning time. Classroom morale is measured by obtaining student ratings of their perceptions of the classroom group. Good morale means that the class members like one another, that they have a clear idea of the classroom goals, and that the lessons are matched to their abilities and interests; in general, morale is the degree to which students are concentrating on learning rather than diverting their energies because of unconstructive social climates. Peer groups outside school and stimulating home environments can help by expanding learning time and enhancing its efficiency; students can both learn in these environments and become more able to learn in formal schooling.

The last factor, mass media, particularly television, can displace homework, leisure reading, and other academically stimulating activities; and it may dull the student's keenness for academic work. For instance, some of the average of 20–30 hours a week high-school students spend viewing television might usefully be added to the mere 4 or 5 average weekly hours of homework they report.

Three factors require close attention here—quantity and quality of instruction, because the educators can alter these factors, and the home environment, because it influences the large amounts of time students spend outside school and because it can be affected by outreach programs.

Amount of Instruction

The power of American schools to affect academic learning is limited by the surprisingly small amount of time children and youth spend in school as a percentage of all time in their lives. The calculations in Figure 6.1 show that U.S. students spend only 8.2% of their time in school during the first 18 years of life.[9]

Actually, the preschool years, when children are the responsibility of parents rather than educators, constitute about a third of the child's first

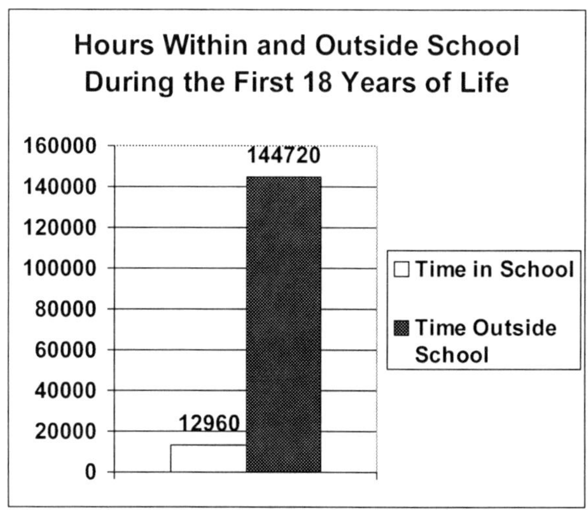

Basis of Calculating School Time in the First 18 Years of Life

Time or Activity	*Years*	*Days Per Year*	*Hours Per Day*	*Total Hours*	*Percentage of Time*
Hours, birth through age 18	18	365	24	157,680	100.0
Sleep	18	365	9	59,130	37.5
School	12	180	6	12,960	8.2

Figure 6.1.

18 years. The time in these critical years before school when children learn their mother tongue, motivations, habits, and many other things is much longer than the time spent in school in the remaining 12 years. These formative years, moreover, are crucial for children's intellectual development. As Bloom (1963) pointed out, children's adult abilities are substantially predictable before they reach school. Small preschool advantages and disadvantages often result in huge achievement gaps in the later elementary years.

With respect to time, the long American summer vacation appears particularly disadvantageous to students in poverty, because they gain less exposure to academically stimulating language and experience. Poor African American and White students in Baltimore lost achievement during the summer months (Entwisle & Alexander, 1992). One of the authors concluded, "That gap between high-SES [socioeconomic-status] students and low-SES students increases steadily over the years.... And that mostly reflects the more substantial strides upper-SES kids make during the summer months" (as cited in Viadero, 1994, p. 36). As might be expected, when poor students participated in summer school in Atlanta, they tended to make normal middle-class academic progress (Heyns, 1978).

Home Environment in Early Childhood

In addition to encouraging and supervising homework and reducing television viewing, parents can improve academic conditions in the home. What might be called "the alterable curriculum of the home" is much more predictive of academic learning than is family SES (see Walberg, 1984). This curriculum includes informed parent–child conversations about school and everyday events; encouragement and discussion of leisure reading; monitoring, discussion, and guidance of television viewing and peer activities; deferral of immediate gratification to accomplish long-term goals; expressions of affection and interest in the child's academic and other progress as a person; and perhaps, among such efforts, laughter and caprice.

In case studies of poor inner-city Chicago families, the children who succeeded in school had parents who emphasized and supported their children's academic efforts, encouraged them to read, and interceded on their behalf at school. Many statistical studies show that indexes of such parent behaviors predict children's academic achievement much better than socioeconomic status and poverty (Clark, 1983).

Cooperative efforts by parents and educators to modify alterable academically stimulating conditions in the home have had beneficial effects on learning (Walberg, 1984). In 29 controlled comparisons, 91% of the comparisons favored children in such programs over nonparticipant control groups. Although the average effect was twice that of SES, some programs had effects 10 times as large, and the programs appear to benefit older as well as younger students.

AT-RISK STUDENTS

Sizable proportions of young children, especially those in poverty, are behind in language and other skills before they begin school, and they are often placed in bilingual and special-education programs for the developmentally challenged, in which they are segregated from other children and make poor progress. The origins of their achievement problems are partly attributable to ineffective programs, but the origins can also often be traced to specific parental behaviors observed before children begin school that affect children's reading and other language skills, which are keys to achievement in academic subjects.

Sticht and James (1984) have pointed out that children first develop vocabulary and comprehension skills by listening, particularly to their parents before they begin school. As they gain experience with written language between the first and seventh grades, their reading ability gradually rises to the level of their listening ability. Highly skilled listeners in kindergarten make faster reading progress in the later grades, which leads to a growing ability gap between initially skilled and unskilled readers.

Poverty and Minority Gaps

This growing gap between good and poor readers reflects race and social class differences.[10] A chapter in the authoritative *Handbook of Reading Research* (Wigfield & Asher, 1984) concludes:

> The problems of race and socioeconomic status (SES) differences in achievement have been at center stage in educational research for nearly three decades. Research has clearly demonstrated that such differences exist; black children experience more difficulty with reading than white children, and the discrepancy increases across the school years. Similarly, children from lower SES homes perform less well than children from middle-class homes, and here too the difference increases over age. (p. 423)

These differences stem from early childhood experience, especially with respect to parent behaviors that motivate children. Studies show that middle-class parents are more likely to hold high expectations for their children's achievement and to be more often engaged with them in promoting it.

> Lower-SES mothers provide their children with poorer problem-solving strategies, and they tend to take over for their children rather than letting them do the task.... That lower-SES parents view school as a distant, rather formidable institution over which they have little control; engage in less effective teaching strategies; and lack confidence in their children's ability does not bode well for their children's school performance. (p. 429)

Home observations and interviews reveal among parents further SES differences associated with higher achievement in reading—for example "responsivity of the parent, the kinds of discipline techniques used, the organization of the physical environment, parental involvement, and provision of appropriate play materials" (pp. 431–432).

Such parent behaviors cause huge and growing gaps in preparation for school and learning to read between children in poverty and those in middle-class homes, as revealed in preschool children's vocabulary growth recorded during free play (Hart & Risley, 1995). Though vocabulary differences were miniscule at 12 to 14 months of age, by age 3, sharp differences had emerged: Welfare children had vocabularies of about 500 words, middle/lower SES children about 700, and higher SES children had vocabularies of about 1,100 words, more than twice that of welfare children.

Educative Practices of Parents

These SES differences in vocabulary were strongly associated with parent behaviors exhibited in their homes. Higher SES parents spent more minutes per hour interacting with their children and spoke to them more frequently. On average, higher SES parents spoke about 2,000 words per hour to their children; Black welfare parents, only about 500 (Hart & Risley, 1995, p. 68). According to Hart and Risley, by age 4, "an average child in a professional family would have accumulated experience with almost 45 million words, an average child in a working-class family would have accumulated experience with 26 million words, and an average child in a welfare family with 13 million words" (p. 198), as shown in Figure 6.2.

Higher SES parents, moreover, used "more different words, more multi-clause sentences, more past and future verb tenses, more declaratives, and more questions of all kinds. The professional parents also gave their children more affirmative feedback and responded to them more often each hour they were together" (Hart & Risley, 1995, pp.

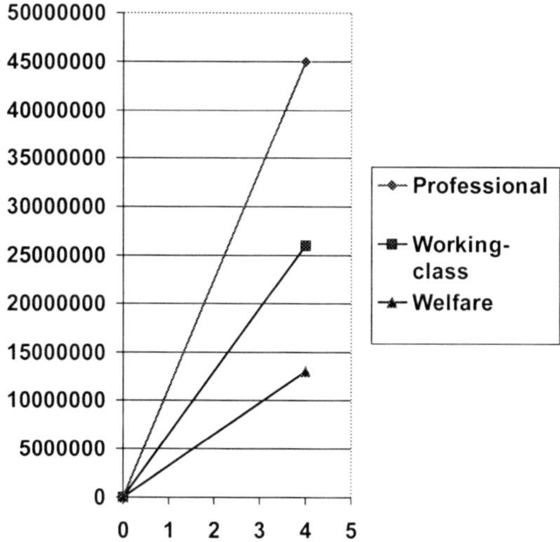

Source: Hart and Risley (1995, p. 200).

Figure 6.2

123–124). By age 4, professional parents encouraged their children with positive feedback 750,000 times, about 6 times as often as welfare parents did. The welfare parents, on the other hand, had discouraged their children with negative feedback about 275,000 times, about 2.2 times the amount employed by professional parents. Such parenting behaviors predicted about 60% of the variation in vocabulary growth and use of 3-year-olds.

As Entwisle and Alexander (1993) point out, such differences are compounded when lower SES children enter school at age 5 or 6. Not only do they lack vocabulary and other skills, but they must accommodate to a middle-class institution:

> The conventions of the school, with its achievement orientation, its expectation that children will stay on task and work independently without close monitoring, its tight schedule of moving from lesson to lesson, its use of "network" English, its insistence on punctuality, and its evaluation of children in terms of what they can do instead of who they are, all can be daunting. (p. 405)

Yet "Many minority and disadvantaged children cross the first-grade threshold lacking competencies and habits of conduct that are required by the school" (p. 405). Further,

> Lower SES children are much more often identified by their kindergarten teachers as being at risk for serious academic or adjustment problems; they are absent more in the first grade; and they receive lower teacher ratings on behaviors related to school adjustment such as interest/participation and attention span/restlessness. (p. 407)

Students who are behind at the beginning of schooling or slow to start usually learn at a slower rate; those who start ahead gain at a faster rate, which results in what has been called cumulative advantage or the "Matthew effects" of the academically rich getting richer, after the passage in the chapter of Matthew in the Bible (Walberg & Tsai, 1984). These effects are pervasive in school learning, including the development of reading comprehension and verbal literacy (Stanovich, 1986). Ironically, although improved instructional programs may benefit all students, they may confer greater advantages on those who are initially advantaged. For this reason, the first 6 years of life and the "curriculum of the home" are decisive influences on academic learning.

Success for Students in Poverty

These depressing patterns are hardly inevitable, as suggested above and in subsequent sections. Preschool programs, full-day kindergarten, and school–parent programs can help parents mitigate Matthew effects. In 47 states and the District of Columbia, moreover, effective education policies and teaching practices have enabled more than 4,500 high-poverty and high-minority schools (high meaning over 50%) to perform among the top one third of schools in their states and often to outperform predominantly White schools in advantaged communities. These schools educate about 1,280,000 low-income students, about 564,000 Black students, and about 660,000 Latino students (the groups overlap).

How do these schools do it? Their principals tend to report the following features of their schools:

- extensive use of state/local standards to design curriculum and instruction, assessment of student work, and evaluation of teachers;
- increased instruction time for reading and mathematics;

- substantial investment in professional development for teachers focused on instructional practices to help students meet academic standards;
- comprehensive systems to monitor individual student performance and to provide help to struggling students before they fall behind;
- parental involvement in efforts to get students to meet standards;
- state or district accountability systems with real consequences for adults in the school; and
- use of assessments to help guide instruction and resources, and as a healthy part of everyday teaching and learning.

These findings (Education Trust, 2001) corroborate research syntheses of control-group research and large-scale analyses of surveys discussed in subsequent sections of this report.

Because children in poverty often failed to thrive in the early grades and fell increasingly behind in the later grades, Head Start and other preschool programs have been provided for the last 3 decades. A 1985 meta-analysis of about 300 studies of these programs revealed that their moderate immediate effects on achievement and other cognitive tests faded within 2 to 3 years; that is, program students did better on achievement tests than control-group students at the end of the program, but the difference between the groups diminished to insignificance (White, 1985). Since 1985, the programs have attempted to improve by concentrating on children's academic readiness, and recent reviews have been more encouraging (Currie, 2001; Karoly et al., 1998).

The only long-term study of an academically focused school-related program showed significant long-term effects and cost-effectiveness. The Chicago Child-Parent Centers (CPC) provided academic and family-support services to children, beginning at age 3. The program emphasized the acquisition of language and premathematical experiences through teacher-directed, whole-class instruction, small-group activities, and field trips. Parental participation in the program was intensive, with coordinating activities in each centers parent resource room.

Compared with matched control-group children, the 989 CPC children in the program showed higher cognitive skills at the beginning and end of kindergarten, and they maintained greater school achievement through the later grades. As reported in the *Journal of the American Medical Association*, a study funded by the National Institutes of Health and the Department of Education showed that, by age 20, CPC graduates had substantially lower rates of special-education placement and grade retention than the control group, a 29% higher rate of school completion, and a 33% lower rate of juvenile arrest. A cost-benefit analysis showed that, at a per-child program cost of $6,730 for 18 months of part-day services, the age-21 benefits per child totaled $47,759 in increased economic well-being and reduced expenditures for remediation (Reynolds, 2000; Reynolds, Temple, Robertson, & Mann, 2001). Very few education studies have either followed children as long or calculated the costs and benefits of the programs.

Several features made for the program's effectiveness. Unlike other early childhood programs that emphasize "developmental appropriateness," self-esteem, and play,[11] the CPC program directly taught academic language and number skills. The staff coordinated preschool activities with continuing kindergarten services in neighborhood schools. Parents were intensely involved in the program and provided academically stimulating experiences for their children at home.[12]

The results extend the range of evidence for the effectiveness of three of the nine productivity factors, namely, the home environment, the quality of instruction (particularly its academic emphasis), and the amount of instruction, since the children were given the advantage of extra academic time before starting school. Even so, both the program and the evaluation are unique. Most programs lack the CPC features, and even the RAND review of recent evaluations found that about half the programs showed no significant effect on achievement.

QUALITY OF INSTRUCTION

Because the research on achievement is voluminous, scholars have synthesized it in several ways to make it more useful to policymakers and educators.[13] Rather than describing the findings of each study, they employ meta-analyses of many studies to calculate the consistency and magnitude of the effects of educational conditions and methods so that the most effective can be chosen on the broadest evidentiary basis. Other things being equal, for example, a teaching method proven superior in 90 out of 100 studies is preferable to one that excels only in 60 out of 100 studies.

The preferred calculation, featured here, is the "effect size," which reveals the size of any particular effect averaged across many studies.[14] The costs of the methods are ignored, since data about them are largely unavailable, and since most methods can be incorporated as part of normal school budgets because they simply involve different ways of teaching. Educators, moreover, presumably have had experience with many of the methods or at least should have been exposed to them in the course of professional study and experience. This chapter draws on research syntheses of the last decade or two from control-group research of the last half century (Wang, Haertel, & Walberg, 1993b).[15]

Table 6.2. Instructional Strategy Effects

Category	*Average Effect*
1. Identifying similarities and differences	1.61
2. Summarizing and note taking	1.00
3. Reinforcing effort and providing recognition	.80
4. Homework and practice	.77
5. Nonlinguistic representations (e.g., maps and other graphics)	.75
6. Cooperative learning	.73
7. Setting goals and providing feedback	.61
8. Generating and testing hypotheses	.61
9. Activating prior knowledge	.59

Note: The effects in this and other tables are generally ordered from largest to smallest as indicated by the effect sizes.
Source: Marzano (2000, p. 63).

Nine Categories of Instructional Methods

Table 6.2 shows the effects of instructional methods divided into nine categories. These can be more broadly grouped: graphic representation, especially in the form of road maps of what is to be learned; goal setting; and feedback to provide direction and redirection. Identifying similarities and differences, summarizing, and generating and testing hypotheses require students to think and express ideas in forms different from presentations. Cooperative learning provides opportunities for students to assimilate and present ideas by explaining various aspects to one another. Homework and practice are indexes of engaged study time. Reinforcement and recognition provide incentives for performance.[16]

The largest collection of estimated effect sizes, which covered 275 methods and conditions (Walberg & Lai, 1999),[17] provides further illustration. Discussed here are several of the largest effects from that collection, including those for (a) traditional methods that have large effects, (b) several newly published effect estimates, and (c) a few selected to show the range of inquiry about instructional quality (see Table 6.3).[18]

General Methods

The elements of instruction in Table 6.3 can be considered the most fundamental psychological variables in learning. Cues present what is to be learned and how to learn it. Engagement is the degree to which learn-

Table 6.3. Selected Effects of Quality of Instruction

General Methods		*Special Methods*	
Elements of Instruction		Reading Teaching	
Cues	1.25	Adaptive speed training	.95
Reinforcement	1.17	Phonemic awareness	.86
Corrective feedback	.94	Repeated oral reading	.48
Engagement	.88	Phonics	.44
Mastery Learning	.73	Writing Teaching	
Computer-Assisted Instruction		Inquiry	.57
For early elementary students	1.05	Scales	.36
For handicapped students	.66	Sentence Combining	.35
Teaching		Early Education Programs	
Direct instruction	.71	Preschool	.22–.50
Comprehension instruction	.55	Full-day vs. half-day kinder-garten	.48
Teaching Techniques		Grouping	
Homework with teacher	.83	Acceleration of gifted	
comments	.78	students	.88
Graded homework	.49	Tutoring	.40
Frequent testing	.48	Staff Development	
Pretests	.40	Feedback	.70
Adjunct questions	.40	Staff development for read-	.61
Goal setting	.28	ing teaching	.55
Assigned homework		Microteaching	
Explanatory Graphics	.75		

Source: Walberg and Lai (1999, pp. 419–453).

ers actively participate. Corrective feedback signals mistakes and furnishes redirection. Reinforcement—one of the largest general effects uncovered—provides encouragement and information that learning is correct.

Mastery learning combines the elements of instruction and requires mastery of learning units before students proceed to the next unit of instruction. In particular, it allows some students as much as 5 times more instructional time and additional cues, corrective feedback, and reinforcement. Computer-assisted instruction can provide these elements to each student individually. Though beneficial to students in general, even college students, it appears particularly effective in developing skills among handicapped students and those in the early grades.

Direct instruction can be viewed as traditional or conventional whole-group teaching done well. Specifically, it consists of phases: (a) daily review, homework check, and, if necessary, reteaching; (b) rapid presentation of new content and skills in small steps; (c) guided student practice with close monitoring by teachers; (d) corrective feedback and instructional reinforcement; (e) independent practice in seatwork and homework with high, more than 90%, success rates; and (f) weekly and monthly reviews. Comprehension instruction is similar and consists of three phases: (a) modeling, in which the teacher exhibits the desired behavior; (b) guided practice, where the students perform with help from the teachers; and (c) application, in which the student performs independently.[19]

Most of the other general methods in Table 6.3 can be broadly summarized under the rubrics of the instructional elements. Goal setting, adjunct questions, explanatory graphics, and frequent testing provide cues, reinforcement, and corrective feedback. Homework, especially with comments and grades, provides engagement.

Special Methods

Some instructional methods, though they exemplify general principles discussed in previous sections, apply only to particular skills. Consider reading, perhaps the most important skill learned before and during schooling. Phonemic awareness, repeated oral reading, and phonics provide beginning readers with mastery of sound-and-letter correspondences they may not have learned at home, in preschool, or in kindergarten (National Reading Panel, 2000).

Writing may be best taught by writing practice—that is, having students express in their own words what they have inquired about. They can also learn by applying questions and criteria such as clarity and concision to their writing and that of others and then making improvements. Combining their own sentences with those of others adds to their skill in employing appropriate sentence variety.

Grouping allows increases in instructional suitability. Accelerating gifted students allows them to learn at a faster pace without detracting from other students' learning. Tutoring tailors instructional elements to each student. Mainstreaming "handicapped" students into regular classes rather than segregating them in all-day or "pull-out" programs avoids stereotyping and stigmatizing them and helps them make normal progress. What they usually need is more and better, not special, instruction.

The last set of results in Table 6.3 shows that teachers themselves benefit from instructional elements, particularly feedback on their classroom practices, whether on new methods of teaching or on those that should be in their repertoire. New learning of difficult teaching skills may require specific practice with cues, reinforcement, corrective feedback, and engagement until they reach mastery, just as in the case of students.[20]

STUDENT EFFECTS

Although psychologists and sociologists have long studied the correlations or coincidence of student backgrounds and achievement, even substantial and consistent correlations are weak indicators of causality, since they lack experimental or statistical controls.[21] Even so, they are worth considering, just as consistent correlations of cigarette smoking and lung cancer hardly prove but do suggest consideration of causality, particularly if they corroborate other evidence, say, causality in experimental studies of mammals exposed to varying degrees of cigarette smoke. In addition, some student characteristics such as motivation can be indirectly altered by incentives, as indicated by both experimental and multivariate studies.

Prior Knowledge

Table 6.4 expresses correlations as effect sizes comparable to those in Tables 6.2 and 6.3. Students' prior knowledge has a huge predictive and possibly causal effect, perhaps since knowledgeable students can increase their learning from a bigger base (see previous discussion of chunking and Matthew effects). Previous success may also motivate students.

Motivation

Motivation itself is closely associated with how much students learn. Multivariate analysis of surveys and control-group studies of reinforcement corroborate its causal influence. Perhaps the most exciting demonstration of motivational effects is the Dallas O'Donnell Foundation

Table 6.4. Student and Family Influences

Variable	*Effect*
Prior Knowledge	1.43
Motivation	.73
Family Background	
Home Environment	1.42
Parental Income	.67
Parental Occupation	.42
Parental Education	.38

Note: The indexes in the table are on the same scale as the effect sizes in Table 3 but are not necessarily pure, one-way causal effects.
Source: Marzano (2000, pp. 69, 70, 73).

Advanced Placement Incentive Program. The foundation paid both teachers and students $100 for each Advanced Placement examination passed. In the nine participating Dallas public schools, sharply increasing numbers of boys and girls of all major ethnic groups took and passed the AP exams. The number rose more than twelvefold, from 41 the year before the program began to 521 when it ended in 1994–95. After terminating, the program continued to have carryover effects: In the 1996–97 school year, 2 years after the program ended, 442 students passed, about 11 times more than the number in the year before the program began (Walberg, 1998a).[22] This massive effect sharply contradicts the prevalent idea in education that learning must be intrinsically motivated for its own sake.

Parental Effects

The effect of the home environment can be taken very seriously for several reasons. Control-group studies corroborate many correlational findings. The home effect is far larger than apparent socioeconomic effects. Something can be done about home environments: School–parent programs can help parents academically stimulate their children by reading to them, taking them to libraries, guiding and discussing leisure television viewing, cooperating with home visitors and teachers, and similar practices.

GROUPING

Grouping students reflects common sense. If students with similar levels of knowledge and skills are grouped together, teachers can avoid teaching them what they already know and what they are yet incapable of learning; with instruction more suited to them, students should find learning more efficient and pleasant. What forms can such grouping take and what are the achievement and other effects?

Developing Prerequisites

As discussed in a previous section, a rigorous long-term study suggests that children at risk of school failure because of poverty appear to benefit from high-quality, academically focused preschools that prepare them for learning in kindergarten and subsequent grades. Closer in preparation to middle-class children, such better-prepared children may continue to benefit as late as early adulthood. Many other studies, however, show no effects or quick fade-out of early gains.

Grade Retention

By itself, retaining students in grade appears ineffective. On the other hand, "socially promoting" unqualified students may give them and their classmates little reason to study. This policy, common in big cities, probably devalues the high-school diplomas of qualified graduates in the eyes of employers and others.

As discussed below, Chicago's Summer Bridge program for failing children threatened grade retention and provided intensive academic summer school. Though some students failed, the program showed outstanding effects; it was not only effective but also highly cost-effective (Betts & Costrell, 2001). Thus, preschool and summer bridge programs tend to homogenize student achievement, that is, bring laggards up to others' achievement levels, which probably contributes to more effective learning for both groups.

Classroom Grouping

Widely used in elementary schools, homogeneous achievement grouping within classes has small, positive effects (about .25 on average). In the later elementary grades, Matthew effects (of the rich getting richer) have typically caused wide variations in student achievement; a sixth grade may have third- and ninth-grade readers. Probably for this reason, the "Joplin plan" of bringing like-ability students from different classes and grade levels into homogeneous groups has larger effects (about .35) than within-class grouping. As identified by ability or achievement tests, highly able students benefit from "enrichment" of their studies—that is, the provision of greater depth of regular grade-level content (.40). "Accelerated" homogeneous high-ability classes that allow students to study advanced-grade material benefit them greatly (.90; Kulik, in press).

Tracking

By high school, student achievement levels differ more widely, and most American high schools practice tracking; about 86% of high schools, for example, track mathematics classes. Some scholars urge "detracking" (Oakes & Lipton, in press)—that is, heterogeneously grouping all high-school classes—but surveys "show solid support for tracking among parents, teachers, and students" (Loveless, 1998, p. 1). Research on detracking is insufficiently rigorous to support the policy.

SCHOOL EFFECTS

School-level research is less rigorous than studies of individual children and classes. Why? If, in a particular school, half the teachers practiced ineffective methods and half practiced effective methods, the net result would be an average teaching effect, which would conceal important effects within the school. Many school-level studies, moreover, have inadequately measured and controlled for prior achievement and other productivity factors with strong records of affecting learning. Even so, for the sake of completeness, the possible school-level influences are worth considering, particularly those corroborated by control-group research and statistically controlled analyses of student and classroom effects.

Curriculum Alignment

Table 6.5 shows a strong influence of opportunity to learn, which refers to the extent that education goals, curriculum, instruction, and testing are "aligned." Most centrally, this means that what is tested overlaps with what is taught.[23] Aside from the Australia, Canada, Germany, and the U.S., most nations have national education systems, which allow such alignment across schools in each country. As discussed in a subsequent section, many individual states such as North Carolina and Texas are aligning their systems of education, so that if education goals are X, Y, and Z, curricula, teaching, and testing are geared not toward M, N, and O but toward X, Y, and Z.

Goal Setting

Psychological studies support the idea of setting national, state, and local achievement goals. Laboratory control-group research and field studies in a wide variety of organizations confirm the effects of setting goals on task performance. Nearly all studies showed that setting specific, challenging goals led to higher performance than setting easy goals, "do your best" goals, or no goals. "Goals," it has been concluded,

Table 6.5. School-Level Possible Influences

Variable	*Effect*
Opportunity to Learn	.88
Time	.39
Monitoring	.30
Pressure to achieve	.27
Parental involvement	.26
School climate	.22
Leadership	.10
Cooperation	.06

Note: The indexes in the table are measured on the same scale as the effect sizes in Tables 3 but are not necessarily pure, one-way causal effects.
Source: Marzano (2000, p. 56).

affect performance by directing attention, mobilizing effort, increasing persistence, and motivating strategy development. Goal setting is most likely to improve task performance when the goals are specific and sufficiently challenging ... feedback is provided ... the experimenter or manager is supportive, and assigned goals are accepted by the individual. (Lock, Shaw, Saari, & Latham, 1981, p. 125)

Other School Effects

Table 6.5 shows that school-level instructional time, student monitoring, and parental involvement influences are positive and coincide with classroom- and student-level research. The school-level effects are smaller, however, perhaps because, as noted above, they average important differences among classrooms and students within schools and because they may be unreliably reported on questionnaires rather than observed. Perhaps because they are vague and difficult to measure, school climate, administrator leadership, and staff cooperation are the weakest apparent school-level influences.

POLICY EFFECTS

Adam Smith pointed out in the *Wealth of Nations* that human capital in part determines prosperity and the quality of life of nations and individuals. The Chicago School of Economics confirmed this now commonly held view. Modern "information economies" require ever-increasing knowledge and skills; individuals who possess them are likely to thrive.

For this reason, economists have increasingly joined psychologists in asking what best promotes knowledge and skills. To find out, they have, in the last decade or two, conducted policy analyses of state, national, and multinational achievement surveys.[24]

Even more than psychologists, economists assume that people tend or try to act rationally; they seek to employ scarce means that best advance the realization of their values (which may include altruistic and unpriced values).[25] Thus, information or, more precisely, perceptions of present and future benefits and costs greatly matter. New information and changed incentives can therefore change behavior. This working assumption helps explain not only traditional economic phenomena but also many policy issues.[26]

State Reforms

A Nation at Risk and subsequent reports showed Americans the importance of achievement for national and individual prosperity and welfare. The congressionally commissioned National Assessment of Educational Progress, however, has shown little achievement change since then, which has led to increasingly substantial reforms. Some, discussed below, have shown positive learning effects. Validated by analyses of large-scale achievement surveys, economic principles help explain why some states made substantial, evidence-based reforms and large gains in achievement.

Which states developed the best achievement standards and why? A general economic answer is those states that had the greatest incentive. The specific answer is those states that had the poorest achievement. Within the last 2 decades, the National Assessment of Educational Progress began reporting the first valid state achievement comparisons (based on random samples of students within each participating state). Within the past decade, states with the poorest achievement, typically deep South states such as Alabama and Mississippi, developed clear, specific content standards and implemented assessments aligned with the standards (Betts & Costrell, 2001). Since citizens, businesspeople, and legislators in such states recognized their deficiencies as well as the dependency of economic growth and welfare on educated young people, they had the greatest incentives to develop good standards and accountability—and did so.

Student Incentives

Similarly, student incentives, particularly high standards, promote learning. The threat of grade retention, for example, can serve as an incentive for greater effort, although intensive remediation seems necessary. An example is Chicago's Summer Bridge program, which gave parents and students the choice of grade retention or passing an intensive, focused summer course. Depending on the grade level and subject, grade-equivalent increases in reading and mathematics scores over the short summer session ranged from one half to a full year. The gains were extraordinarily effective, time-efficient, and cost-effective, and they were sustained in subsequent school years. The program, moreover, most benefited the initially lowest achieving students (Betts & Costrell, 2001, pp. 31–45; see also Bishop, 1996, on external examinations discussed subsequently).

Tough grading standards and required homework also benefit learning. Requiring high-quality work for a given assigned grade generally raises achievement, particularly for high-achieving students who might not otherwise be sufficiently challenged. Corroborating control-group research, analyses of national surveys show that the effects of the amount of homework teachers require each week are

> very strong, indicating that math homework is a more important determinant of gains in achievement than any of the standard measures of school quality, such as teacher education and experience or class size. (Betts & Costrell, 2001, pp. 33–34)

A previous section (on motivation) described the Dallas O'Donnell Foundation's $100 payment of high-school teachers and students for each college-accredited Advanced Placement examination passed, which raised the numbers of passing students twelvefold. Elementary-school children can benefit from encouragement, praise, feedback about accomplishments, and other nonmonetary reinforcement. Large-scale studies show that precise measurement of accomplishments and prescription of subsequent efforts multiplies such reinforcement effects. The commercial Accelerated Reader (AR) program, for example, assumes the well-documented but often unheeded idea that the more children read, the better they read. AR developers further assume that reading material that appeals to children and that appropriately challenges them promotes their reading ability most efficiently.

The AR developers have categorized some 30,000 children's books according to their reading difficulty and children's interests, such as arts, sports, and history. Since teachers lack personal knowledge or ready objective information to guide students' reading of books commonly held in school and neighborhood libraries, the AR computer program suggests to teachers the books best suited in difficulty and genre for each student. After a student has read a chosen book, the AR computer program assesses the student's comprehension and awards points for the degree of mastery and the difficulty of the book. Over a year, teachers and students can trace progress on a point system based on the volume and difficulty of books read. Statistical analyses of as many as 600,000 student records show Accelerated Reader's excellent results in promoting reading mastery (Topping & Paul, 1999).

External Examinations

The Cornell economist John Bishop intensively studied effects of curriculum-based external examination effects on learning. He analyzed surveys of the examination effects on learning of the (U.S.) Advanced Placement program, the New York State Regents, and U.S. state and Canadian provincial systems. He also analyzed examination effects on learning in the United States in comparison with effects in Asian and European nations. The examinations have the common elements of being externally composed and geared toward agreed-upon subject matter students are to learn within a nation, state, or province. Often given at the end of related courses, they have substantial positive effects on learning (for a summary, see Bishop, 1996). Made publicly available, the examination results allow citizens, policymakers, educators, parents, and students to assess and compare achievement standings and progress.

The largest and most sophisticated international comparative analysis of national achievement yet conducted corroborates Bishop's and related findings (Woessmann, 2001).[27] Using data from 39 countries that participated in the Third International Mathematics and Science Study, a Kiel (Germany) Institute of World Economics study found that nations where students learned most employed external, curriculum-based examinations, and policymakers closely monitored the results.

How and why should such examinations yield striking effects? Though there are variations in their design, the examinations cover uniform subject matter in humanities, sciences, and other courses. Since the exams are graded by educators other than the students' own teachers, students have little incentive to challenge their teachers about course content and standards. Rather, students and teachers work together toward the common goal of meeting examination standards. Because the exams and courses are uniform, teachers can concentrate not on what to teach but how to teach, and the students' subsequent teachers can depend on what students have been taught.

Accountability

In 1989, the National Governors' Association "Education Summit," with then President George H. W. Bush and business leaders, gave impetus to business-style accountability for schools. "Systemic reform," as recommended by summiteers, meant aligning the chief parts of school systems with one another, specifically fitting state tests and curricula with state goals or standards and making exam results widely known.

Like the accountability of business boards and executives, school accountability requires simultaneous centralization and decentralization, centralization of standards at the state level and decentralization of operational responsibilities to the district or school level. State policymakers set goals and measure progress, but, unlike in the past, encourage local school districts and schools to plan and execute effective practices. State officials can set high targets for achievement or value-added learning gains and maintain more objectivity in evaluating the results than when they determine both goals and means, and without this division of labor, local districts might set easy-to-reach, unmeasurable, or obfuscated goals.

As discussed below, leading authorities on accountability contributed to a conference and book on the subject to assess the last decade's progress. As the editor pointed out, concern for achievement is bipartisan, and surveys show that the public strongly supports objective testing, higher standards, and greater specificity about what students should learn (Ravitch, 2001, p. 4). Large-scale research on school accountability shows strong public recognition of the need for accountability and corroborates the expected positive learning effect.

Need for Accountability

Reminiscent of the authors of the *Nation at Risk* report, representatives of the Business Roundtable and the National Alliance for Business have argued that standards-based reform and accountability are keys to the nation's future economic performance. Jobs requiring literacy skills, for example, will grow faster than all other occupations. More jobs also require skilled labor, particularly that involving computers.

Yet, as previously pointed out, U.S. high-school students lag behind those in other countries in essential subjects. An estimated 78% of our nation's institutions of higher learning offer remedial courses for first-year students unready for college work. It appears that about half of American firms provide training to make up for inadequate schooling, a considerable fraction of the estimated annual $55 billion budget for employee training. A U.S. Department of Labor study showed that illiteracy cost eight southern states $57.6 billion in lost productivity, substandard work, unrealized taxes, unemployment claims, and social problems (Goldberg & Traiman, 2001).

Effect of Accountability

A decade ago, few states specified what students should know and be able to do, but 49 states now do so, and the number of states with adequate academic standards has increased. The more sustained and comprehensive the accountability system, moreover, the better states' learning progress appears. A study commissioned by the National Educational Goals Panel revealed the reasons that North Carolina and Texas made the largest gains on the National Assessment of Educational Progress:

- grade-by-grade standards with aligned curricula and textbooks,
- expectations that all students would meet the standards,
- statewide assessments linked to the standards,
- accountability for results with rewards and sanctions for performance,
- deregulation and increased flexibility in ways the standards can be met, and
- computerized feedback systems and achievement data for continuous improvement.[28]

Policy analysts have begun rating the states for both standards and accountability, which to be most effective, must presumably go together. Good standards are rigorous, clear, written in plain English, communicate what is expected of students, and can be assessed. Good accountability systems are aligned with the standards and include school report cards, ratings of schools, rewards for successful schools, authority to reconstitute failing schools (for example, by replacing the staff), and the actual exercise of such legislated consequences. Only five states—Alabama, California, North Carolina, South Carolina, and Texas—have solid standards and strong accountability systems (Finn & Kanstoroom, 2001).

Employing standard economic principles, legislators and state school boards also are designing increasingly refined accountability systems and tying incentives to test results (Betts & Costrell, 2001). For example, states increasingly "disaggregate" test scores to be sure that various groups are well served. Texas, for instance, reports separate results for boys and girls, and for Whites, Blacks, and Hispanics. Similarly, the National Assessment of Educational Progress reports percentages of students that meet Advanced, Proficient, Basic, and Below Basic standards. These categories encourage improvement at all levels rather than on only a single standard that is too easy for some students, schools, and districts and too challenging for others. By a large margin, the U.S. Congress passed the No Child Left Behind legislation that extended features of the North Carolina and Texas accountability reform principles to all 50 states.

Cost of Tests and Accountability

Though some educators have protested the costs of accountability systems, their costs are surprisingly small and represent a miniscule percentage of school budgets. The payments to commercial firms for standardized testing, standard setting, and accountability in year 2000 was $234 million, which was less than a tenth of a percent of K–12 school costs and amounted to $5.81 per American student. For the 25 states with available information, the total costs per student run between $1.79 and $34.02, higher on average than commercial costs alone, since some states develop their own tests, develop their own standards, and run their own accountability systems. Even so, the total costs are tiny, despite the public's, parents', and legislators' strong interest in accountability.

These costs, moreover, will undoubtedly decline in the longer run since they were estimated in the midst of states' development of accountability systems; after development and initial revision, much of the activity can be routinized at much lower costs. Even now, raising teacher compensation by 10% would cost about 12.39% more than current accountability systems. Reducing class size by 10% (or about 2 students per class) would cost 8.81% more than current accountability in the nation (Hoxby, 2002).

Small Schools and Small Districts

In the half century through 1990, the number of U.S. school students rose from 25.4 million to 41.2 million. The number of districts, however, declined from 119,900 to 15,400, and the number of schools declined from 247,100 to 81,700. During the period, accordingly, the average number of students per school rose from an average of 103 to 504, and the number of students per district rose from 214 to 2,683. The distribution of both schools and districts is positively skewed; there are a few huge ones and many relatively smaller ones concentrated in rural areas, particularly near the Canadian border.

The massive increases in school and district size took place despite research showing that large organizations tend to become departmentalized, impersonal, bureaucratic, inefficient, and lacking in individual and institutional accountability. Their goals tend to become diffuse, and they tend to be more subject to the needs of their employees and special interests than to their clients.

Psychological Effects

Perhaps for analogous reasons, the first large-scale study showed similar inefficiency of large districts and large schools in 38 states (Walberg & Walberg, 1994). The study showed no effect of per-student spending but significant effects of each state's average district and school size. Why? Consider Montana: Usually at the top of state achievement surveys, its many districts have as few as 100 to 200 students; so school board members may be able to speak insightfully about many of the individual faculty and students in their single school. In New York City, board members might be stumped to name more than 50 of the roughly 900 schools of the 1.1 million students. If something goes wrong in a Montana school, a parent might ask a school board member at a grocery store to look into it. Can this be imagined in New York City?

Teachers in the tiny Montana district, to continue the example, would be likely to know not only the students but also their siblings and other relatives. Parents, teachers, and school board members can readily communicate. Being small, neither the district nor the school would multiply programs and courses excessively, but they would stick to fundamental subjects in a core curriculum taken by most students, such as English, mathematics and science, civics, history, and geography, foreign language, and art and music. Such a curriculum has been shown to be conducive to high achievement and elite university admission. In the 1990s, several dozen statistically controlled studies showed the achievement advantages of small schools, which tend to be concentrated in small districts (for a comprehensive review, see Lee, Bryk, & Smith, 1993).

Economic Effects

Citizens in smaller districts, moreover, are likely to be best informed about local conditions and their own desires; they are rationally motivated to avoid inefficient spending and ineffective programs for the children in their communities. Small districts confer local control conducive to achievement and other school outcomes. Such local control gives all community residents—not just parents—an incentive to monitor local public schools and ensure effectiveness and efficiency—that is, better outcomes and value for money (Borland & Howsen, 1992; Hoxby, 1994).[29] "Capitalization," rising property values to homeowners, results from better school outcomes and value, as realtors often stress and as a few dozen economic studies show (Yinger, Bloom, Borch-Supan, & Ladd, 1988; all but one of 28 studies in their detailed review showed this "capitalization" effect).

Thus, the psychological and economic advantages of small schools and small districts make them more effective and efficient. Of course, after much painful district consolidation and huge capital investments in large school buildings, the clock cannot easily be turned back. But it can be recommended that districts think twice about further consolidation and building ever-larger schools. More radically, legislators have been considering the breakup of large districts such as Los Angeles and New York into completely freestanding units with separate boards and superintendents. Citizens in parts of Los Angeles are pressuring legislators to allow secession.

Big urban districts such as Chicago and New York fostered "schools within schools" that are attempts to recover the intimacy, accountability, effectiveness, and efficiency of the smaller schools of yesteryear, though it remains to be seen if such values can be recaptured in big buildings. In any case, special forms of accountability seem necessary in large districts to insure effective, efficient schools that are satisfying to parents

CHOICE

No scholarly analyst argues that private schools or voucher programs chosen by parents deter learning. The question is whether or not schools of choice promote learning both among their own and other students in the community. Six scholarly reviews conducted at Harvard University, the RAND Corporation, the Urban Institute, and by New York scholars reach the same overall conclusion about the positive achievement effect of choice.

Private Vouchers

Firms and individuals give scholarships to poor students so that they can attend private schools of their choice. Since the achievement findings are debatable, it is worthwhile considering what the investigators and commentators actually concluded. Paul Peterson of Harvard's Kennedy School synthesized his extensive findings from (true experimental) evaluations of private voucher programs[30] in Milwaukee, Cleveland, New York, and Washington as follows:

> According to the test score results, African American students from low-income families who switch from public to a private school do considerably better after two years than students who do not receive a voucher opportunity. However, students from other ethnic backgrounds seem to learn after two years as much but no more in private schools than their public school counterparts. (Peterson, 2001, pp. 274–275)

Referring to Peterson's experiments, the RAND review concluded:

> Small-scale, experimental privately funded voucher programs targeted to low-income students suggest a possible (but as yet uncertain) modest achievement benefit for African-American students after one to two years in voucher schools (as compared with local public schools). (Gill, Timpane, Ross, & Brewer, 2001, pp. xiv–xv)[31]

The Urban Institute summarized private voucher research as follows:

> The results of this research also showed that attending a private school was beneficial, but only for African American students. On average African Americans who received vouchers scored .17 standard deviations higher on the combined test scores than African Americans in the control group. After two years they scored .33 standard deviations higher than their counterparts in the control group. (Goldhaber, 2001, p. 64)

These gains, if sustained, would be very substantial. They would eliminate the often-observed (one standard deviation) Black–White gap in 6 years.

Why should private schools apparently benefit African American students and not others? Because they favor choice more than other groups, more African American families have elected to participate. Since their numbers are greater, a given effect is statistically more likely to be significant. For reasons explained in a previous section, it is also possible that big city school systems where African Americans are concentrated treat them bureaucratically and indifferently, whereas private schools must please or lose their "customers."

General Effects of Choice

In a more comprehensive review, two political scientists have considered choice more broadly, including choice within public systems. They point out, as earlier reviews do not, that a

> combination of evidence is important in a domain in which economists, political scientists, sociologists, educational scholars, and others often read work only in their own disciplines. Moreover, while other researchers have reviewed various pieces of the choice literature, most are focused on only one aspect or type of choice. Here a broader analysis is sought. (Teske & Schneider, 2001, p. 609)

They conclude:

> While not all of these studies conclude that choice enhances performance, it is significant to note that the best ones do, and that [we] did not find any study that documents significantly lower performance in choice schools. (p. 619)

Why is choice popular and reasonable?

> Consensus results show that parents are more satisfied with choice, that they report using academic preferences to make choices, and that they tend to be

more involved with their child's education as a consequence of choice. (p. 609)

Two economists have analyzed the competitive effects of choice on education outcomes revealed by over 35 studies. Their review concerned—not charters or vouchers—but naturally occurring traditional competition within geographical areas such as cities and metropolitan areas. The studies typically analyzed the percentages of students enrolled in private schools and the degree of district monopoly—for example, the presence of many small districts as opposed to one district within a county. They conclude:

> A sizable majority of these studies report beneficial effects of competition across all outcomes, with many reporting statistically significant coefficients. The positive benefits included increased academic test scores, graduation rates, efficiency (outcomes per unit of per-student spending), teacher salaries, housing prices, and adult wages. (Belfield & Levin, 2001, p. 1)

In a large-scale study too recent to be reviewed by scholars cited above, Jay Greene has developed a *2001 Education Freedom Index* by weighing the amount of (a) charter-school choice, (b) subsidized private-school choice, (c) home-schooling choice, and (d) public-school choice, in an overall index for each state participating in the National Assessment of Educational Progress. On the index, Arizona had the greatest amount of overall choice; Hawaii, with only one school board for the whole state, the least. Greene found that, controlled for median household income, per-pupil spending, and the percentage of ethnic minorities in each state, achievement test scores and (value-added) score gains were significantly associated with the amount of total weighted choice in the state (Greene, 2002b).[32]

PRODUCTIVITY DETERRENTS

Many prevalent and incipient education policies and practices are ineffective or inefficient or both, making them unproductive. Some take time away from what works consistently and well, and some are costly, disruptive, distracting, and have unanticipated harmful consequences. Their prevalence helps explain why American students fall behind, despite high and substantially rising expenditures. For the sake of increasing educational productivity, it is worth considering and avoiding them. Discussed in this section, they range from applications of pseudoscientific psychology to categorical federal education policies. First discussed, however, are theories that underlie unproductive practices.

Slack Professional Standards and Unvalidated Theories

Some influential education theorists and educators oppose accountability, standards, testing, and the evidence-based learning principles discussed above, most of which comport with what the legislators, public, parents, and students themselves expect from schools. A Public Agenda national survey of high-school students, for example, showed that three fourths believe stiffer examinations and graduation requirements would make students pay more attention to their studies. Three fourths said schools should promote only students who master the material. Almost two thirds reported they could do much better in school if they tried. Nearly 80% said students would learn more if schools made sure they were on time and did their homework. More than 70% said schools should require after-school classes for those earning Ds and Fs (Bradley, 1997; Johnson & Farkas, 1997).

In these respects, many educators differ sharply from students and the public. Interviews with a national representative sample of elementary- and secondary-school educators and students revealed the following percentages agreeing with the degree of academic challenge in their schools (Harris Interactive, 2001):

Statement	*Principals*	*Teachers*	*Students*
School has high academic standards	71	60	38
Classes are challenging	67	48	23
Teachers have high expectations of students	56	39	25

The apparent slackness of many practicing educators may derive from views prevalent in schools of education they have attended. A 1997 Public Agenda survey of education professors showed that 64% thought schools should avoid competition. More favored giving grades for team efforts than favored grading individual accomplishments. Only 12% thought it essential for teachers to expect students to be neat, on time, and polite, compared to 88% of the public. Only about a fifth agreed with the public that teachers should stress correct spelling, grammar, and punctuation. Only 37% thought it essential for teachers to learn how to maintain an orderly classroom.

Teacher educators also differ from employers and other professions on measuring standards or even employing them at all. Employers use standardized multiple-choice examinations for hiring. So do selective colleges and graduate and professional schools for admission decisions. Such examinations are required in law, medicine, and other fields for licensing, because they are objective, efficient, and reliable. In the case of teachers, it would seem that knowledge of the subject matter is prerequisite to teaching it. Indeed, indicators of academic mastery, including objective examination results and completion of rigorous courses, appear influential on their students' achievement, at least in technical fields such as mathematics. Yet 78% of teacher educators wanted less reliance on objective examinations (Farkas & Johnson, 1997).

Nearly two thirds of teacher educators admitted that their programs often fail to prepare candidates for teaching in the real world, and only 4% reported that their programs typically dismiss students found unsuitable for teaching. Thus, even starting with their undergraduate education, many prospective educators are exposed to disparaging views of standards, incentives, and individual accomplishments. These views have often led to:

- the notion that "authentic learning" only arises from "intrinsic motivation" in which student preferences rather than curriculum and course requirements dominate the choice of what and how to learn,
- an indifference or hostility to specifying objectives and measuring results,
- a holding that children cannot learn until the "teachable moment" or until the "developmentally appropriate" time,
- a devaluing of knowledge (since "you can always look it up"),
- an insistence that students should discover or "construct" their own understanding rather than being taught, and
- the idea that comprehension must be "socially constructed" in peer groups rather than individually acquired.

These views may be characterized as "constructivism" rather than "instructivism," in which the teacher imparts knowledge and skills, and learner-centered rather than learning-centered, in which the teacher employs well-defined goals, definite subject matter, and explicit assessment of student progress.[33]

An example of how these views take form in classrooms is "discovery learning," in which students are to discover or rediscover scientific or other principles instead of being directly taught. Discovery takes precious time from comprehension and practice of principles. According to two eminent cognitive psychologists and a Nobel laureate in economics, the evidentiary basis of such discovery theory consists largely of proponents who cite one another's values and opinions. In their opposition to direct teaching, education theorists criticize the practice of knowledge and skills as

> "drill and kill," as if this pejorative slogan provided empirical evaluation.... Nothing flies more in the face of the last twenty years of research than the assertion that practice is bad. All evidence, from the laboratory and from extensive case studies of professionals, indicates that real competence only comes with extensive practice. By denying the critical role of practice, one is denying children the very thing they need to achieve competence. (Anderson, Reder, & Simon, 1998, p. 241)

Although current education theory is ill-informed about scientific findings, it often draws faddishly on "pop" psychology.

Brain-Based Learning and Other Exotic Techniques

K–12 and other education sectors have been subject to many pseudoscientific fads for which there is usually initial enthusiasm but paltry or analogous evidence. At the request of the U.S. Army, for example, the National Academy of Sciences evaluated exotic techniques and "shortcuts" for learning and enhancing performance described in "pop" psychology and claimed to be successfully employed for "super-learning." Little or no evidence, however, was found for the efficacy of learning during sleep, mental practice of motor skills, "integration" of left and right brain hemispheres, biofeedback, and such parapsychological techniques as extrasensory perception, mental telepathy, and mind-over-matter exercises. Nor could creditable evidence be found for "neurolinguistic programming," in which instructors identify students' mode of learning and mimic the students' behavior as they teach (Druckman & Swets, 1994). Even so, unvalidated "brain-based learning" is gathering momentum in education circles.

Widespread, Unsubstantiated Programs

School board members and most educators lack education and experience in accountability, evaluation, and methods of psychometrics and statistics that would enable them to choose effective, efficient programs and weed out others. Though these tasks should be central to leaders aiming to measure, evaluate, and improve learning, they are neglected. Consequently, popular programs are often chosen by fad and reputation rather than by a careful review of evidence of their results and costs. In this section, two widespread programs illustrate such choices.

Reading Recovery

Begun in 1976 in New Zealand, Reading Recovery was implemented in 40 states within 8 years. Reading Recovery was founded on the assumption that reading is essential for school success and on the value that children should be "recovered" as they begin to fail. The program also assumed that if children repeat their errors less often, they will have less to relearn and will increase their self-esteem as readers. They would presumably be less susceptible to the Matthew effects of falling further and further behind their classmates. Who would take issue with these assumptions and values? But does the program work?

Program advocates reported research that appeared to support the effectiveness of Reading Recovery. But an independent review in the leading reading research journal (Shanahan & Barr, 1995) pointed out that children who were repeatedly absent or who were not making progress and were transferred out of the program were untested. This yields a fallacious "selection effect," because the apparent program success is attributable to an unknown degree simply to purging unsuccessful learners out of the Reading Recovery program but not out of the control groups. The apparent recovery effect, moreover, diminished after first grade; this result contradicted the claim of avoiding the Matthew effects.

Further, because Reading Recovery teachers tutor a single student pulled out of regular classes for long periods, Reading Recovery students lose time in regular instruction. The annual per-student cost for the program tutoring alone, moreover, is at least three quarters that of a full program for other students in all subjects all day for the school year. As discussed in a previous section, phonics, phonological awareness, and repeated oral reading instruction have substantial effects and can be conducted cheaply, routinely, and effectively with a whole class.

Success for All

The Success for All (SFA) program also makes a big claim in its title and is aimed at teaching reading to early-grade children in poverty. Educational administrators and several scholars have praised SFA; Congress issued legislation and about $150 million of initial funding favoring its adoption; and, in school-finance litigation, a New Jersey judge ordered its use in failing schools. The number of SFA schools rapidly expanded, and the program seemed just the breakthrough needed.

Yet the first independent review of the evidence showed both obvious and subtle potential conflicts of interests among government funders, foundations, SFA program developers, and evaluators (Greenberg & Walberg, 1998). Nearly every study by SFA developers and their associates showed positive effects, but independent studies showed no effects. Contrary to SFA claims, average SFA third graders were not up to grade level in Baltimore, where the program originated; by fifth grade, they were 2.5 years behind. A later review of subsequently accumulated evidence revealed the same research flaws and program failures as well as obvious conflicts of interests among program developers and evaluators (Pogrow, 2000).

In SFA self-evaluations, the compared groups clearly differed, most obviously in that SFA schools were given substantially more funds, materials, and services than control schools. SFA, moreover, requires that 80% of the teachers vote secretly to adopt SFA. Such schools are unusual in attaining such agreement and no doubt in determination. Such schools may have inspired leaders or zealous teachers. Even so, independent evaluations showed SFA does the same or less well, even with the advantages of staff consensus and extra resources.

SFA self-evaluators also biased their research in other ways. They concentrated on reading tests to compare the SFA program, which heavily concentrates time and energy on reading, with ordinary school programs aimed at improving achievement in all the standard subjects. A more comprehensive evaluation would employ tests in all subjects to determine whether SFA sacrifices broad achievement in mathematics and other subjects for narrow reading skills. SFA self-evaluators also employed unusual tests that favor SFA and that were administered to individual children and subjectively scored by SFA's staff. A more objective evaluation would employ standard tests administered by educators entirely independent of SFA.

Federal Categorical Programs

Because the programs are aimed at particular groups, the programs require categorizing and often segregating students (a) in poverty, (b) in need of special-education services, and (c) in need of special English-language instruction. The federal government provides only about 6% of K–12 school funding, but accompanying federal dollars are rules, regulations, and program requirements, which distract school boards and educators from their primary objective of increasing learning. They also impose large costs for nonteaching staff, which amounted in the mid-1990s to 25.1% of current expenditures for primary and secondary schools in the U.S., in contrast to the 13.4% average of other advanced countries (Organisation for Economic Co-Operation and Development, 1995, p. 103).

In what has been called the "colonization of local and state agencies," federal rules require up to three quarters of state education department staff for federal compliance rather than productivity improvement. Staff preoccupation with bureaucratic means rather than educational ends frustrates state boards and superintendents aiming to improve achievement. Especially frustrated have been reform-driven superintendents in large cities where the programs are concentrated and account for a large part of their staff and budgets (Hill, 2000; see in particular pp. 25–26).

Despite burdensome costs and administrative problems, categorical programs, as discussed in this section, have done little good. Neither their principles nor operational practices appeared to contribute to the learning of needy students. Their failings may go a long way toward explaining the problems of poor and minority students in cities where they and federal programs are concentrated.

The Title I Program for Students in Poverty

The federal government has spent about $125 billion on Title I and now allocates about $8 billion annually. The program was to have reduced the gap between middle-class students, often Whites in suburbs, on the one hand, and on the other, poor students, often African Americans and Hispanics in cities and rural areas. Congressionally mandated and independent studies show that the Title I program, even after 3 decades, has not diminished, much less eliminated, the poverty gap. As Figure 6.3 indicates, even recent reforms of Title 1 have little to show: The poverty gap has remained essentially the same. Why?

A synoptic evaluation (Farkas & Hall, 2000)[34] of Title I points to the lack of evidence-based practices. Recommended for preschoolers are two of the methods in Table 6.3, phonological awareness and phonics, as well as parent programs for academically stimulating their children and skills-based summer programs between kindergarten and first grade. Recommended for 1st through 12th grade are careful, continuous assessment and remediation; schoolwide behavioral management to avoid wasting instructional time on discipline problems; and research-based teaching methods—all consonant with the idea of extending the quantity and quality of instruction as discussed in previous sections.

Special Education

The other huge federal categorical program, special education, is comparable to Title I in federal spending, ineffectiveness, and inefficiency. It includes about a tenth of American children and currently costs $7.4 billion in federal money and an (imprecisely) estimated $35 billion to $60 billion, in state and local contributions. By some estimates, 40% of the new money flowing to K–12 education in recent years went into special education, partly because of administrative complications and expense, special testing, and smaller classes, but not counting big litigation costs over placement of students in special programs (Finn, Rotherhan, &

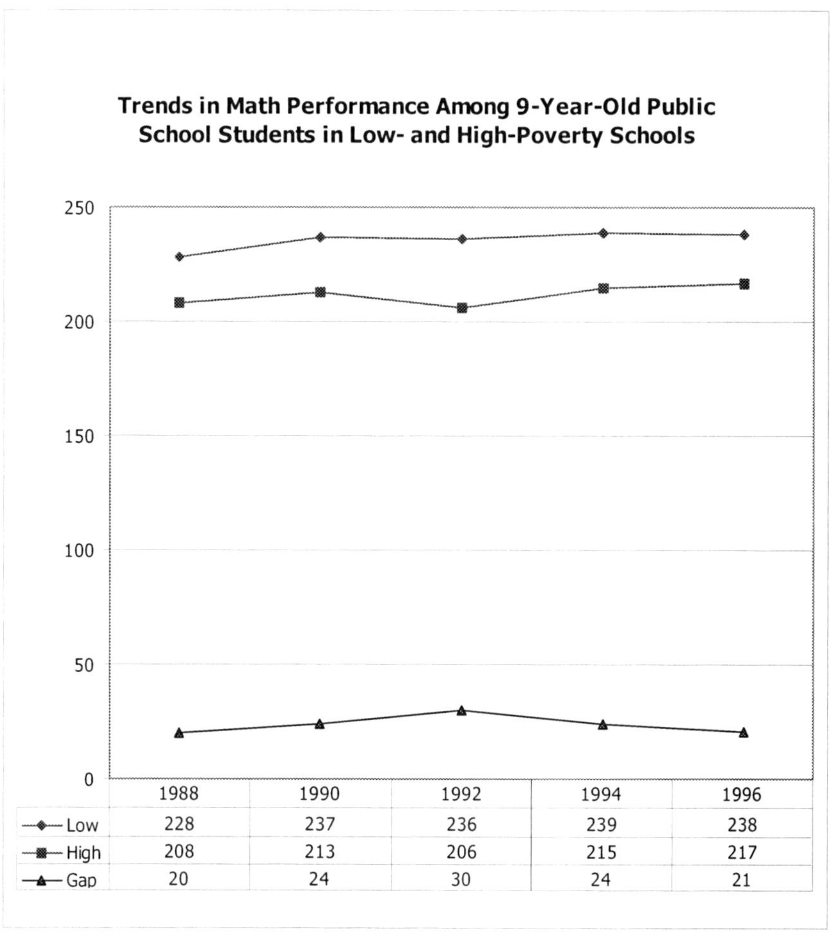

	1988	1990	1992	1994	1996
Low	228	237	236	239	238
High	208	213	206	215	217
Gap	20	24	30	24	21

Note: The scale ranges from 0 to 500; high-poverty schools had 76–100% students eligible for free lunch, low-poverty 0–25%.
Source: Puma et al. (1997, p. 6).

Figure 6.3

Hokanson, 2001, p. v; see particularly the Horn & Tynan chapter, 2001b; for effect size estimates, see the Lyon et al. chapter, 2001, especially p. 272). About 90% of special students were classified in such categories of mild disorders as "learning disabled," "language impairment," "mild retardation," "emotional disturbance," and "behavioral disorder" rather than the long-established, scientifically creditable categories of blindness and deafness, which can be reliably diagnosed.

Perhaps because it brought more funds into districts, the numbers of mildly disabled students classified, particularly "learning-disabled students,"[35] rose sharply. A National Academy of Sciences Panel (Heller, Holtzman, & Messick, 1982), however, found the classification and placement of students in special education ineffective and discriminatory against minorities. The panel recommended that students should be segregated from others only if (a) they can be reliably classified, and (b) segregated placement shows superior learning results.

Much research, however, shows that the classification systems for placing "mildly handicapped" students in special programs are deeply flawed; specialists in the field have come to little consensus about taxonomic, psychometric, and diagnostic procedures. By various classification systems, for example, as many as 80% of all American K–12 students can be classified as "learning disabled" (Reschly, 1987; Ysseldyke, 1987). Once students are placed, moreover, they are unlikely to return to regular classes without a planned and explicit exit strategy, which is rarely offered. As recommended by eminent psychologists, a better solution is to avoid psychological testing and identify children in need of assistance only by their level of achievement (Sternberg & Grigorenko, 2001). This concentrates educators' attention on what they need to know rather than on ill-founded psychological deficits. It enables children to stay with their peers and avoids psychological stigma that reduces their own and others' expectations of their potential.

Special-education programs, moreover, often lead to discrimination, unfairness, and litigation. Special educators, for example, often demeaningly classify big-city poor and minority children as "mildly retarded" and may expect less of them. But middle-class parents have learned to "game the system." Their children are more often labeled "learning disabled," a less stigmatic term. In affluent Greenwich, Connecticut, educators classify about one in three high-school students as learning disabled. Such students may get special tutors, note takers, laptop computers, and extra time on tests, including those for college admission. A national poll revealed that 65% of parents said that the extra attention paid to disabled students came at the expense of their own children (Horn & Tynan, 2001a, 2001b), a view more likely to be associated with alienation and withdrawal than with parent involvement.

Aside from classification and fairness problems, evidence shows the unproductive effects of special education. At twice the cost of regular education, special-education placement has an estimated effect of about .07, a small fraction of the effect of methods that can be routinely applied in regular classrooms, such as graded homework, which is about 10 times larger, and frequent testing, which is 7 times larger (see Table 6.3). Since reading mastery is often the core difficulty of learning-disabled and other mildly disabled students, the policies and practices recommended for children in poverty, such as early intervention and effective methods of teaching reading (see previous section), are likely to be much more effective and cost-effective than special-education placement (Lyon et al., 2001, especially pp. 272, 276–278). Syntheses of special-education research, moreover, suggest that methods that are successful in regular education like direct instruction and diagnostic-prescriptive methods are also successful with special-education students (Gersten, Schiller, & Vaughn, 2000; Kavale & Forness, 1985; Swanson, 1999). If so, why classify? Why segregate? Who benefits?

The Present Teaching Force

Maintaining certification as the criterion for employment and reemployment, and graduate credits and experience as the basis for compensation may mean that unproductive teachers are paid just as much as their colleagues who best promote learning. These policies offer no incentives for improvement. Why should even the best teachers work hard and long when their compensation will be the same as the worst performers? Why not put their energies and talents into moonlighting, travel, or their families?

A national survey of 853 public-school superintendents and 909 principals corroborates such concerns (Farkas, Johnson, Duffett, Foleno, & Foley, 2001). Large majorities of superintendents (76%) and principals (67%) said they need more autonomy to reward outstanding teachers. Almost the same percentages said they need more autonomy to remove ineffective teachers. Nearly all superintendents (96%) and principals (95%) said making it much easier to remove bad teachers—even those with tenure—would be somewhat or very effective.

Teacher Selection and Compensation

As explained in the opening section, U.S. students fall behind those in other countries the longer they are in school, despite the nearly highest per-student spending in this country. Summaries of research by economists, moreover, find little or no consistent influence of spending on learning in studies of U.S. samples (Hanushek, 1986). Though noneconomists in schools of education have disputed these findings (Greenwald, Hedges, & Laine, 1996), many policymakers might agree that what money buys is more than the total amount spent. The two main determinants of spending are teacher compensation and class sizes, both discussed here. Do they buy higher achievement?

Public-school teachers' salaries have long been chiefly determined by whether they are certified, their years of teaching experience, and their degree level, commonly a bachelor's or master's. Despite thousands of doctoral dissertations in education written each year, little solid evidence shows these salary determinants promote student learning. In fact, studies by labor economists suggest that verbal ability, knowledge of the subject matter, and graduation from a selective college are at least as important as the usual salary determinants.

To investigate the contribution of the contending measurable teacher attributes to student learning, the following equation could be estimated:

> Student achievement = Student input + teacher experience + teacher education + teacher verbal ability + teacher pedagogical knowledge + teacher subject-matter knowledge + teacher certification

In this equation, student input is indexed by previous achievement and demographic characteristics such as poverty, verbal ability is indexed by verbal tests or college selectivity or reputation, knowledge is measured by tests or course completion in the subject matter such as science, and a weight is estimated for each factor.

No study, however, comes close to this equation. The consequence of such flawed studies is misleading implications for teacher certification, hiring, retention, and compensation. For example, simply showing that the students whose teachers have a master's degree achieve better may reflect not the learning advantage of a master's but the fact that teachers who are more experienced are more likely to have master's degrees and vice versa. Similarly, failing to take previous student achievement and demographics into consideration may mean that an apparent connection between experience and achievement is attributable to teachers transferring to middle-class schools that achieve well in any case. Estimating the equation above would test these and other causal possibilities.

A limited standard of proof calls for including prior achievement and student demographics in testing the possible influences of the other factors one or two at a time. A recent search uncovered only 18 such studies, nearly all by economists. These studies suggested that college selectivity, verbal test scores, and, only for high-school students in mathematics, subject-matter knowledge contribute to student learning (Wayne & Youngs, 2001).

Examining studies that control only for student input trades a larger pool of studies for research rigor. Since teacher effects and costs are so critical, even less certain evidence is worth considering. Such research corroborates the importance of verbal facility and college selectivity, but suggests that only 3% of teachers' contribution to student learning is attributable to teacher experience and graduate degree attained. Few studies show significant positive effects of experience and education, and some studies show significant negative effects. Certified teachers apparently perform no better than those who are uncertified (Goldhaber, 2002).

Even though teaching comprises about half the total schooling costs, research provides no support for traditional and current policies of certifying, selecting, and compensating teachers. Excluding candidates on weakly predictive or nonpredictive criteria is arbitrary; in an apparently tight labor market, this longstanding policy unduly excludes large numbers of younger and older people who are as likely to teach as well as other candidates and the present labor force. In fact, Teach for America demonstrates that very recent graduates of elite colleges, knowledgeable of the subjects they teach, but with no experience and little pedagogical training, are highly regarded by their principals and that they also induce greater achievement than other teachers (Kopp, 2001; Raymond & Fletcher, 2002).

Class Size and Student/Teacher Ratio

Student–teacher ratios fell from about 27-to-1 in 1955 to 17-to-1 in 1997 (U.S. Department of Education, 1997, Table 64), which accounts for much of the substantial rise in per-student expenditures. More teachers, however, do not necessarily make for smaller classes, since they may perform administrative and special duties, especially in large cities with substantial federal programs, which may require much bureaucracy. In any case, as pointed out in the opening section, student achievement remained stagnant, despite the sizable investment in more teachers per student.

The first meta-analysis of education research on class-size effects on achievement suggested a small beneficial effect of class-size reductions. The biggest apparent effects were in reductions below class sizes of 10; classes between 15 and 35 students differed very little in achievement. Few studies had been made of classes between 8 and 15, because classes in this range were rare and prohibitive in cost. In any case, the overall effect of class-size reduction appeared to be much smaller than the use of effective teaching methods (Glass & Smith, 1979). Even a small effect was disputed. Large-scale studies, mostly by economists, showed no consistent effect of class-size reductions (Betts, 1995; Hanushek, 1999a).[36]

A much-noted Tennessee experiment seemed to show an effect of reduced class sizes (Finn & Achilles, 1990), even though a single study may not outweigh the inconsistent results of many other studies. Even at face value, moreover, the Tennessee study showed a very small effect, limited to kindergarten. Continuing exposure to smaller classes in first through third grade showed no advantage, and returning students to normal-sized classes in fourth through sixth grades showed no harm. So reduced class size apparently only benefited kindergartners, and changes in class sizes did not affect achievement in the six later grades (Hanushek, 1999b).

In addition, the apparent effect was not of class-size reduction alone but also of accompanying monetary incentives for increased student achievement. Thus, the apparent small transient effect may be attributable to smaller class sizes, monetary incentives, or a combination of these factors.

A more recent large-scale natural experiment on all Connecticut elementary schools overcomes limitations of the Tennessee research. It is perhaps the most comprehensive study ever made of the class-size question, because it measured the effects of natural changes in class sizes from 10 to 30 students over 2 decades. It showed no effects of class-size reduction overall, nor any at the upper or lower range of class-size reduction, nor in the earlier or later grades, nor for disadvantaged or middle-class students (Hoxby, 1998).

What would happen if a state concentrated resources on reducing class sizes? California policymakers did just this at a cost of about $5 billion per year from 1996 through 2001. About two thirds of California school districts took money from libraries, art, music, and maintenance to reduce class sizes in the first three grades. After 3 years, evaluators could infer no achievement effect of class-size reduction. As they concluded, "There is no clear relationship between changes in the amount of exposure to CSR [class-size reduction] and changes in the average level of achievement. Increased exposure is not associated with greater gains in achievement" (Stecher & Bohrnstedt, 2001, p. 90).[37]

In view of definitively inconsistent research and California's experience, further class-size reductions seem unpromising. Such reductions, moreover, have been exceedingly costly. They are even more costly today, since student/teacher ratios have already been cut massively in recent decades. Reducing class size, for example, by a single student from 15 to 14 incurs more than twice the teaching costs of a single-student reduction from 35 to 34, even aside from the costs of new classrooms.

CONCLUSION

Syntheses of experimental and quasi-experimental classroom studies of instructional methods and large-scale econometric studies reveal policies and practices that work well and cost relatively little. Other policies and practices, even though prevalent in American schools, are costly, but little evidence suggests their efficacy. Though more research would yield better estimates and resolve some uncertainties, the present body of knowledge about effects and costs suggests how American schools can be made more productive.

NOTES

1. This chapter is intentionally longer than the others in this collection because it represents an effort to assess preliminarily the large extant body of research on achievement effects. This research was supported in part by the Institute of Education Sciences (IES) of the U.S. Department of Education (ED) through a grant to the Mid-Atlantic Regional Educational Laboratory, the Laboratory for Student Success (LSS). The opinions expressed do not necessarily reflect the position of the supporting agencies, and no official endorsement should be inferred.
2. Professor Hoxby (2001) concludes as follows: "Consider the simplest productivity calculation, achievement per dollar, without any attempt to control for student characteristics. Such a calculation (which I describe in detail below) suggests that average public-school productivity was about 65 percent higher in 1970–71 than in 1998–99. [If we] were simply to restore school productivity to its 1970–71 level, then the average student in the United States would be scoring at an advanced level where fewer than ten percent of students now score" (p. 2).
3. These theories are discussed in a subsequent section.
4. For several reasons, economists have often led this work. They have generations of experience in inferring causality from nonexperimental data. Acutely conscious of priced and nonpriced costs and benefits, they have a long history of influence on legislators, jurists, and executives. Perhaps they may be more influential on policy since their professional incentive is to answer the policy question, what works best given a set of goals, rather than confusing goals and means or advocating values.
5. A recent synthesis of many estimates from comparative studies showed that Asian students who typically top the international achievement charts spend far more time studying than American students, since they have more school days during the year, usually attend private after-school tutoring schools, and do lots of homework for both schools. On average, Chinese students spend about double the American study time, and Korean about 73% more. Many Asian immigrant families continue extensive study, which undoubtedly accounts in part for their academic success. See Paik, Wang, and Walberg (2002). Fortunately, in recent years American educators have more often employed preschools, all-day kindergarten, extended-day schooling, and summer school, especially for students at risk of failure.
6. Subsequent larger collections of research syntheses are discussed elsewhere, including Fraser, Walberg, Welch, and Hattie (1987). The learning influences reported in Table 6.1 are correlations, which are roughly proportional to multivariate regression weights. In 23 studies of about 250,000 students in 13 countries, 89% of 341 mulitivariate regression

weights controlling for these and other factors were in the expected positive direction. See Paschal and Starhia (1989).

7. It may be useful for economists to think of these five factors as having Cobb-Douglas-like relations with achievement, namely, multiplicativity and diminishing returns. These imply that each factor is necessary, but each addition to its amount or intensity results in smaller and smaller additional amounts of learning. There may also be inflection points. Too much study, for example, may be counterproductive; too much motivation may become anxiety.
8. Despite the well-known 1983 warning of the National Commission for Excellence in Education's report, *A Nation at Risk*, the U.S. school year remains at about 180 days in contrast to 190 to 220 in most of Western Europe and up to 260 days, including Saturdays, in the Orient.
9. They spend only about 13% of their *waking* hours in school, assuming 9 hours per day of sleep, which is, of course, longer in the early years and shorter in late adolescence.
10. Though in the U.S. there are more poor Whites than poor African Americans and poor Hispanics, the rates of poverty are higher among the minority groups, which has led to increased policy research in the last few decades. Far more research, however, has been carried out on African American than on Hispanic students.
11. In contrast to such learning-centered approaches that directly teach children language and numbers are such learner-centered "Theoretical Principles of Child Development and Learning": "Children learn best when their physical needs are met and they feel psychologically safe and secure. Children construct knowledge. Children learn through social interaction with adults and other children. Children learn through play. Children's interests and 'need to know' motivate learning. Human development and learning are characterized by individual variation" (Bredekamp, Knuth, Kunesh, & Shulman, 1992, p. 1).
12. Unvalidated education theory dominates many preschool and kindergarten programs, which is probably the major reason why dozens of evaluations have shown only transient effects; see subsequent section on this subject.
13. The largest synthesis thus far drew upon three sources: (a) 134 meta-analyses of 7,827 studies of about 10 million students; (b) content analysis of 86 reviews (leading authorities' summaries of and commentaries on research), 44 research handbook chapters, 18 other chapters, 20 government and commissioned reports, and 11 journal articles containing 3,700 references; and (c) ratings of the learning effectiveness of educational conditions and methods by 34 authorities. See Wang, Haertel, and Walberg (1993a).
14. Technically but simply, an effect size or "effect" may be thought of and actually often calculated as the difference between experimental and control group means divided by the standard deviation of the control group. Its size may be estimated for various educational conditions and for student characteristics such as grade level and ethnic group, to test the consistency or robustness of the effect. For the same purpose, separate estimates may be for studies with varying degrees of experimental rigor. As might be expected, factors with big effects are usually robust.

15. Other publications for educators that contain many references and suggestions for implementing the best methods are Cawelti (2000); Maryland Department of Education (1990); and uncopyrighted booklets in the series edited by the present author on teaching, tutoring, and other topics. These booklets are distributed by the United Nations Educational, Scientific, and Cultural Organization to 189 countries and also freely downloadable and republishable gratis on the Internet at www.ibe.org.
16. The effects reported are based on research in which investigators generally insured implementation. In practice, the various methods need to be reasonably well implemented to insure similar effects. On the other hand, long-term, well-managed implementation might result in larger effects.
17. These estimates are based on control-group rather than correlational research and mostly include experimental studies that randomly assign students or classes to groups or quasi-experiments that roughly equate the groups by measuring gains from a pretest taken before enacting the method to a posttest afterwards, or by employing statistical methods—such as covariance or regression—of determining the "net effect" or "value-added learning gain" after adjusting for initial achievement and other variables.
18. To my knowledge, the effects are the best but hardly infallible estimates. They depend, for example, on the quality of the underlying research; still, many studies by many scholars in many circumstances and pointing in the same direction compel more creditability than any single study, no matter how well planned and executed. The ways of synthesizing research have improved during the past quarter century, but the newer ways usually yield similar results. So older studies are not necessarily excluded here, since they may be the only ones available.
19. An interesting variant is "reciprocal teaching," in which paired students take turns leading dialogues on pertinent features of a text. By assuming the planning and executive control ordinarily exercised by teachers, students learn planning, structuring, and self-management similarly to the way tutors learn from teaching, and they learn why it is said that if you want to learn something well, teach it. Comprehension instruction encourages students to measure independently their progress toward explicit goals—a big lesson in life.
20. If both teacher- and self-instruction are considered, perhaps these elements apply to much of human learning, including such diverse fields as sports, ballet, chess, music, foreign languages, and the professions.
21. Most creditability can be given to the nine factors in Table 6.1, because the underlying research controlled for the complete set of factors in large national and international surveys and synthesized control-group research.
22. Many education theorists deny the role of incentives and hold that true or superior learning only takes place when it is intrinsically valuable to the student. But there is little evidence that students are unaffected by long- and short-term external incentives. Even if they were unaffected, they need preparation for adult life, and most adult work, with the notable exceptions of that in bureaucracies and public schools, employs merit pay—that is, rewards results.

23. Opportunity to learn results comport with common sense. Students taught Japanese would undoubtedly obtain better reading and listening test scores than students not taught Japanese.
24. The studies typically employ huge international, national, and state samples, and estimation of learning effects statistically controlled for spending, demographics, prior achievement, and other variables.
25. If people seem irrational in overindulging in smoking, drinking, drugs, carousing, or, in the case of students, sports, watching television, and mall walking instead of studying, observers might ask if their perceptions and calculations of benefits and costs are identical to those of the people they observe.
26. In his popular economics textbook, the Harvard professor N. Gregory Mankiw lists 10 fundamental principles of economics (1998, pp. 3–16), including "people face tradeoffs," "the cost of something is what you give up to get it," and "people respond to incentives." Inspired by the Nobel laureate Gary Becker, economists have ingeniously explained and demonstrated such principles in the fields of crime, immigration, fertility, marriage, government, addictions, social influence, and public health. See Tommasi and Ierulli (1995).
27. Employing delegation of means or division of labor, highly achieving nations allowed teachers considerable discretion over instructional methods.
28. The authors also attributed the gains in the two states to the intensity and stability of business support for the reforms but not to per-pupil spending, pupil/teacher ratios, proportion of teachers with advanced degrees, and average of teacher experience. See Grissmer and Flanagan, 1998, 2001.
29. Hoxby also points out that smaller districts can often accommodate families with varying preferences. A parent's voice and vote count far more in a district with an enrollment of 200 than in one of several thousand students on issues that may be important to them. If, for example, parents dislike emphasis on soccer over football, they can raise the issue and campaign for their views with like-minded others. Since, in many cases, relatively few people vote in school board elections, a few dozen votes of a resolute minority may be decisive.
30. Private vouchers are scholarships given by wealthy individuals and firms so that students, most often poor minority students in big cities, can go to parochial and independent schools of their parents' choice. Since the programs are usually highly oversubscribed, students are admitted by lottery, which makes for a randomized experiment with a "treated" and a control group that can be compared after a time.
31. In addition, the authors point out that vouchers promoted racial integration and that charter schools generally have racial-ethnic compositions similar to local public schools.
32. This study might be faulted for using states rather than schools or students as units of analysis, but it is consistent with other evidence and covers the whole of the United States.
33. These views may be traced to the French Romanticism of Jean-Jacques Rousseau and to German Hegelianism, especially as passed on to educators by John Dewey. At an extreme today, university humanities departments' postmodernism and social constructivism promote the idea that

knowledge is socially constructed by groups, and that one group's knowledge, even that of mathematicians and scientists, is as good as another's. Taking this view seriously undermines the authority of the teacher, science, and the canon of received knowledge, since student and savage views are just as authentic and valid as the views of those who have devoted their lives to acquiring and sharing special knowledge. Though such views would seem absurd, they are common among education theorists and those responsible for educating teachers; see survey results discussed above in this section. The philosophical underpinnings of such views are described in Hirsch (1996), Ravitch (2001), and Stone (1996).

34. Other problems with Title I include (a) measuring poverty, (b) the possible conflict of interest between educators who seek additional funds and families and students who may not wish to be identified as poor, and (c) concentrating Title I services on only poor children while trying to avoid the administrative problems and possible stereotyping harms of segregating them.

35. On the basis of extensive research syntheses, in their book, two prominent University of California authorities in this field titled two chapters "Learning Disability: A Pseudo-Science" and "Learning Disability: A Victim of Its Own History." See Kavale and Forness (1985).

36. In addition, Asian classes, which have as many as 60 students, usually rank at the top of international achievement surveys.

37. In an interview, the first author, Stecher, a senior social scientist at RAND Corporation, said, "It would be nice if we could give an unequivocal answer to the achievement question. Then people could decide if the benefits were worth the costs. Unfortunately we can't" (as cited in RAND Corporation, 2002). The authors have yet to reach a final conclusion and will continue to study the initiative, but their latest finding corroborates the pervasive elusiveness of the class-size effect.

REFERENCES

Anderson, J. R., Reder, L. M., & Simon, H. A. (1998). Radical constructivism and cognitive psychology. In D. Ravitch (Ed.), *Brookings papers on education policy, 1998* (pp. 227–255). Washington, DC: Brookings Institution.

Belfield, C. R., & Levin, H. M. (2001). *The effects of competition on educational outcomes: A review of U.S. evidence.* New York: Columbia University, Teachers College, National Center for the Study of Privatization in Education.

Betts, J. R. (1995). Is there a link between school inputs and earnings? In G. Burtless (Ed.), *Does money matter? The link between schools, student achievement, and adult success* (pp. 141–191). Washington, DC: Brookings Institution.

Betts, J. R., & Costrell, R. M. (2001). Incentives and equity under standards-based reform. In D. Ravitch (Ed.), *Brookings papers on education policy, 2001* (pp. 9–74). Washington, DC: Brookings Institution.

Bishop, J. H. (1996). The impact of curriculum-based external examinations on school priorities and student learning. *International Journal of Educational Research, 23*, 653–752.

Bloom, B. S. (1963). *Change and stability in human characteristics.* New York: Wiley.

Borland, M., & Howsen, R. (1992). Student academic achievement and the degree of market concentration in education. *Economics of Education Review, 11*(1), 31–39.

Boulding, K. E. (1972). The schooling industry as a possibly pathological section of the American economy. *Review of Educational Research,* 129–143.

Bradley, A. (1997, February 12). Survey reveals teens yearn for high standards. *Education Week*, pp. 1, 38–39.

Bredekamp, S., Knuth, R. A., Kunesh, L. G., & Shulman, D. D. (1992). *What does research say about early childhood education?* Oak Brook, IL: NCREL.

Cawelti, G. (2000). What is our knowledge base for improving student achievement? *Iowa Educational Leadership, 28,* 3–8.

Clark, R. (1983). *Family life and school achievement: Why black children succeed or fail.* Chicago: University of Chicago Press.

Coleman, J. S., Campbell, E., Hobson, C., McPartland, J., Mood, A., Weinfeld, F. D., et al. (1966). *Equality of educational opportunity.* Washington, DC: U.S. Department of Health, Education, and Welfare; and U.S. Government Printing Office.

Currie, J. (2001). Early childhood programs. *Journal of Economic Perspectives 15,* 213–238.

Druckman, D., & Swets, J. A. (Eds.). (1994). *Enhancing human performance: Issues, theories, techniques.* Washington, DC: National Academy Press.

Education Trust. (2001). *Dispelling the myth revisited.* (Washington, DC: Education Trust.

Entwisle, D. R., & Alexander, K. L. (1992). Summer setback. *American Sociological Review, 57,* 72–84.

Entwisle, D. R., & Alexander, K. L. (1993). Entry into school: The beginning school transition and educational stratification in the United States. *Annual Review of Sociology, 19,* 401–423.

Farkas, G., & Hall, L. S. (2000). Can Title I attain its goal? In D. Ravitch (Ed.), *Brookings papers on education policy, 2000* (pp. 59–123). Washington, DC: Brookings Institution.

Farkas, S., & Johnson, J. (1997). *Different drummers: How teachers of teachers view public education.* New York: Public Agenda.

Farkas, S., Johnson, J., Duffett, A., Foleno, T., & Foley, P. (2001). *Trying to stay ahead of the game: Superintendents and principals talk about school leadership.* New York: Public Agenda.

Finn, C. E., & Kanstoroom, M. (2001). State academic standards. In D. Ravitch (Ed.), *Brookings papers on education policy, 2001* (pp. 131–180). Washington, DC: Brookings Institution.

Finn, C. E., Jr., Rotherham, A. J., & Hokanson, C. R., Jr. (Eds.). (2001). *Rethinking special education for a new century.* Washington, DC: Thomas B. Fordham Foundation; and Progressive Policy Institute.

Finn, J. D., & Achilles, C. M. (1990). Answers and questions about class size: A statewide experiment. *American Educational Research Journal, 27*(3), 557–577.

Fraser, B. J., Walberg, H. J., Welch, W. W., & Hattie, J. (1987). Synthesis of educational productivity research. *International Journal of Educational Research, 11,* 73–145.

Gersten, R., Schiller, E. P., & Vaughn, S. (Eds.). (2000). *Contemporary special education research: Syntheses of the knowledge base on critical instructional issues.* Mahwah, NJ: Erlbaum.

Gill, B. P., Timpane, P. M., Ross, K. E., & Brewer, D. J. (2001). *Rhetoric versus reality: What we know and what we need to know about vouchers and charter schools.* Santa Monica, CA: RAND Corporation.

Glass, G. V., & Smith, M. L. (1979). Meta-analysis of research on class size and achievement. *Educational Evaluation and Policy Analysis, 1*(1), 2–16.

Goldberg, M., & Traiman, S. L. (2001). Why business backs education standards. In D. Ravitch (Ed.), *Brookings papers on education policy, 2001* (pp. 81–90). Washington, DC: Brookings Institution.

Goldhaber, D. (2001). The interface between public and private schooling. In. D. H. Monk, H. J. Walberg, & M. C. Wang (Eds.), *Improving educational productivity* (pp. 47–76). Greenwich, CT: Information Age.

Goldhaber, D. (2002). The mystery of good teaching. *Education Next, 2*(1), 50–55.

Greenberg, R. C., & Walberg, H. J. (1998). The Diogenes effect: Why program evaluations fail. In K. Wong (Ed.), *Advances in educational policy: Perspectives on the social functions of schools* (pp. 167–178). Greenwich, CT: JAI Press.

Greene, J. P. (2002a). *High school graduation rates in the United States.* New York: Manhattan Institute.

Greene, J. P. (2002b). *2001 education freedom index.* New York: Manhattan Institute.

Greenwald, R., Hedges, L. V., & Laine, R. D. (1996). The effect of school resources on student achievement. *Review of Educational Research, 66,* 361–396.

Grissmer, D., & Flanagan, A. (1998). *Exploring rapid achievement gains in North Carolina and Texas.* Washington, DC: National Educational Goals Panel.

Grissmer, D., & Flanagan, A. (2001). Searching for indirect evidence for the effects of statewide reforms. In D. Ravitch (Ed.), *Brookings papers on education policy, 2001* (pp. 181–229). Washington, DC: Brookings Institution.

Hanushek, E. A. (1986). The economics of schooling: Production and efficiency in public schools. *Journal of Economic Literature, 24,* 557–577.

Hanushek, E. A. (1999a). The evidence on class size, In S. E. Mayer & P. Peterson (Eds.), *Earning and learning: How schools matter* (pp. 131–168). Washington, DC: Brookings Institution.

Hanushek, E. A. (1999b). Some findings from an independent investigation of the Tennessee STAR experiment and from other investigations of class size effects. *Educational Evaluation and Policy Analysis, 21,* 143–164.

Harris Interactive. (2001). *The MetLife survey of the American teacher 2001: Key elements of quality schools.* New York: Author.

Hart, B., & Risley, T. R. (1995). *Meaningful differences in the everyday experience of young American children.* Baltimore: Paul H. Brooks.

Heller, K. W., Holtzman, W., & Messick, S. (1982). *Placing children in special education: A strategy for equity.* Washington, DC: National Academy of Science Press.

Heyns, B. (1978). *Summer learning and the effects of schooling.* New York: Academic Press.

Hill, P. T. (2000). The federal role in education. In D. Ravitch (Ed.), *Brookings papers on education policy, 2000* (pp. 11–58). Washington, DC: Brookings Institution.

Hirsch, E. D. (1996). *The schools we need and why we don't have them.* New York: Doubleday.

Horn, W., & Tynan, D. (2001a). Revamping special education. *Public Interest, 144,* 36–54.

Horn, W., & Tynan, D. (2001b). Time to make special education "special" again. In C. E. Finn, Jr., A. J. Rotherham, and C. R. Hokanson, Jr. (Eds.), *Rethinking special education for a new century* (pp. 23–51). Washington, DC: Thomas B. Fordham Foundation; and Progressive Policy Institute.

Hoxby, C. M. (1994). *Does competition among public schools benefit students and taxpayers? Evidence from natural variation in school districting* (Working Paper No. 4979). Cambridge, MA: National Bureau of Economic Research.

Hoxby, C. M. (1998). *The effects of class size and composition on student achievement.* Cambridge, MA: National of Bureau Economic Research.

Hoxby, C. M. (2001). *School choice and school productivity (or could school choice be a tide that lifts all boats?).* Washington, DC: National Bureau of Economic Research Conference on the Economics of School Choice.

Hoxby, C. M. (2002). The cost of accountability. In W. M. Evers & H. J. Walberg (Eds.), *School accountability* (pp. 47–74). Stanford, CA: Hoover Institution Press.

Huey, E. B. (1908). *The psychology and pedagogy of reading.* Bristol, England: Thoemmes Press.

Johnson, J., & Farkas, S. (1997). *Getting by: What American teenagers really think about their schools.* New York: Public Agenda.

Karoly, L. A., Greenwood, P. W., Everingham, S. S., Houbé, J., Kilburn, M. R., Rydell, C. P., et al. (1998). *Investing in our children: What we know and don't know about the costs and benefits of early childhood interventions.* Santa Monica, CA: RAND Corporation.

Kavale, K. A., & Forness, S. R. (1985). *The science of learning disabilities.* Boston: Little, Brown.

Kopp, W. (2001). Ten years of teach for America. In M. C. Wang & H. J. Walberg (Eds.), *Tomorrow's teachers* (pp. 221–234). Richmond, CA: McCutchan.

Kulik, J. A. (in press). Tracking, de-tracking, and skill grouping. In A. J. Reynolds, M. C. Wang, & H. J. Walberg (Eds.), *Can unlike students learn together?*

Lee, V. E., Bryk, A., & Smith, J. B. (1993). The organization of effective secondary schools. *Review of Research in Education, 19,* 171–268.

Lock, E. A., Shaw, K. N., Saari, L. M., & Latham, G. P. (1981). Goal setting and task performance. *Psychological Bulletin, 90,* 125–152.

Loveless, T. (1998). *The tracking and ability grouping debate.* Washington, DC: The Fordham Foundation.

Lyon, G. R., Fletcher, J. M., Shaywitz, S. E., Shaywitz, B. A., Torgesen, J. K., Wood, F. B., et al. (2001). Rethinking learning disabilities. In C. E. Finn, Jr., A. J. Rotherham, & Charles R. Hokanson, Jr. (Eds.), *Rethinking special education for a new century* (pp. 259–287). Washington, DC: Thomas B. Fordham Foundation; and Progressive Policy Institute.

Mankiw, N. G. (1998). *Principles of economics.* Fort Worth, TX: Harcourt Brace Dryden.

Maryland Department of Education. (1990). *Better thinking and learning.* Baltimore, MD: Maryland Department of Education, Division of Instruction.

Marzano, R. J. (2000). *A new era of school reform: going where research takes us.* Aurora, CO: Mid-Continent Research for Education and Learning.

National Commission for Excellence in Education. (1983). *A nation at risk: The imperative for school reform.* Washington, DC: U.S. Government Printing Office.

National Reading Panel. (2000). *The national reading panel report: Teaching children to read* Washington, DC: U.S. Department of Health and Human Services, Public Health Service, National Institute of Health, National Institute of Child Health and Human Development.

Oakes, J., & Lipton, M. (in press). Can unlike children learn together? In A. J. Reynolds, M. C. Wang, & H. J. Walberg (Eds.), *Can unlike students learn together?*

Organisation for Economic Co-Operation and Development. (1995). *Education at a glance: OECD indicators.* Paris: Author.

Organisation for Economic Co-Operation and Development. (1995–2001). *Education at a glance* [Annual editions]. Paris: Author.

Paik, S., Wang, D., & Walberg, H. J. (2002). Timely learning improvements. *Educational Horizons, 80*(2), 69–71.

Paschal, R. A., & Starhia, W. E. (1989). *Educational productivity studies: A quantitative synthesis.* Paper presented at the annual meeting of the American Educational Research Association.

Peterson, P. E. (2001). Choice in American education. In T. Moe (Ed.), *A primer on America's schools* (pp. 249–284). Stanford, CA: Hoover Institution Press.

Pogrow, S. (2000). Success for All does not produce success for students. *Phi Delta Kappan, 82*(1), 67–80.

Puma, M. J., Karweit, N. Price, C., Ricciuti, A., Thompson, W., & Vaden-Kiernan, M. (1997). *Prospects: Final report on student outcomes* [prepared for the U.S. Department of Education, Office of the Undersecretary]. Cambridge, MA: Abt Associates.

RAND Corporation. (2002, February 4). *Press release.* Santa Monica, CA: RAND Corporation.

Ravitch, D. (2001). Introduction. In D. Ravitch (Ed.), *Brookings papers on education policy, 2001* (pp. 1–8). Washington, DC: Brookings Institution.

Raymond, M., & Fletcher, S. (2002). Teach for America: The first evidence on classroom performance. *Education Next, 2*(1), 62–68.

Reschly, D. J. (1987). Learning characteristics of mildly handicapped students: Implications for classification, placement, and programming. In M. C. Wang, M. C. Reynolds, & H. J. Walberg (Eds.), *Handbook of special education: Research and practice: Vol. 1. Learner characteristics and adaptive education* (pp. 35–58). Oxford, England: Pergamon Press.

Reynolds, A. J. (2000). *Success in early intervention: The Chicago Child–Parent Centers.* Lincoln, NE: University of Nebraska Press.

Reynolds, A. J., Temple, J. A., Robertson, D. L., & Mann, E. L. (2001). Long-term effects of an early childhood intervention on educational achievement and juvenile arrest: A 15-year follow-up of low-income children in public schools. *Journal of the American Medical Association, 285,* 2339–2346.

Shanahan, T., & Barr, R. (1995). Reading Recovery: An independent evaluation of the effects of an early instructional intervention for at-risk learners. *Reading Research Quarterly, 40,* 958–996.

Simon, H. A. (1981). *Sciences of the artificial.* Cambridge, MA: MIT Press.

Stanovich, K. E. (1986). Matthew effects in reading. *Reading Research Quarterly, 21,* 360–406.

Stecher, B. M., & Bohrnstedt, G. W. (2001). *Class size reduction in California: Findings from 1999–00 and 2000–01.* Sacramento, CA: California Department of Education.

Sternberg, R. J., & Grigorenko, E. L. (2001). Learning disabilities, schooling, and society. *Phi Delta Kappan, 83*(4), 335–338.

Sticht, T. G., & James, J. H. (1984). Listening and reading. In P. D. Pearson, R. Barr, M. Kamil, & P. L. Mosenthal (Eds.), *Handbook of Reading Research* (Vol. 1, pp. 293–317). New York: Longman.

Stone, J. E. (1996). Developmentalism: An obscure but pervasive restriction on educational improvement. *Education Policy Analysis Archives, 4*(8). Retrieved from http://olam.edu.
asu.edu/epaa/v4n8.html

Swanson, H. L. (1999). *Interventions for students with learning disabilities.* New York: Guilford Press.

Teske, P., & Schneider, M. (2001). What research can tell policymakers about school choice. *Journal of Policy Analysis and Management, 20,* 609–631.

Tommasi, M., & Ierulli, K. (Eds.). (1995). *The economics of human behavior* Cambridge, England: Cambridge University Press.

Topping, K. J., & Paul, T. D. (1999). Computer-assisted assessment of practice at reading: A large-scale survey using accelerated reader data [Entire issue]. *Reading and Writing Quarterly, 15*(3).

U. S. Department of Education. (1997). *Digest of education statistics* Washington, DC: Author.

Viadero, D. (1994, July 13). Focus on: Research. School's out for the summer. *Education Week*, pp. 35–37.

Walberg, H. J. (1984). Improving the productivity of America's schools. *Educational Leadership, 41*(8), 19–27.

Walberg, H. J. (1998a, November 4). Incentivized school standards work. *Education Week*, p. 48.

Walberg, H. J. (1998b). Uncompetitive American schools: Causes and cures. In D. Ravitch (Ed.), *Brookings papers on education policy, 1998* (pp. 173–206). Washington, DC: Brookings Institution.

Walberg, H. J., Hase, K., & Rasher, S. P. (1978). English mastery as a diminishing function of time. *TESOL Quarterly, 12*(4), 427–437.

Walberg, H. J., & Lai, J.-S. (1999). Meta-analytic effects for policy. In G. J. Cizek (Ed.), *Handbook of educational policy* (pp. 419–453). San Diego, CA: Academic Press.

Walberg, H. J., & Tsai, S.-L. (1984). Matthew effects in education. *American Educational Research Journal, 20,* 359–374.

Walberg, H. J., & Walberg H. J., III. (1994). Losing local control. *Educational Researcher 23*(5), 23–29.

Wang, M. C., Haertel, G. D., & Walberg, H. J. (1993a). Toward a knowledge base for school learning. *Review of Educational Research, 63,* 249–294.

Wang, M. C., Haertel, G. D., & Walberg, H. J. (1993b). What helps students learn? *Educational Leadership, 50,* 74–77.

Wayne, A. J., & Youngs, P. (2001, November). *Teacher characteristics and student achievement gains: A review.* Paper presented at the annual meeting of the Association for Public Policy Analysis and Management, Washington, DC.

White, K. R. (1985). Efficacy of early intervention. *Journal of Special Education, 19,* 401–416.

Wigfield A., & Asher, S. R. (1984). Social and motivational influences on reading. In P. D. Pearson, R. Barr, M. Kamil, & P. L. Mosenthal (Eds.), *Handbook of reading research* (Vol. 1, pp. 423–452). New York: Longman.

Woessmann, L. (2001). Why students in some countries do better: International evidence on the importance of education policy. *Education Matters, 1*(2), 67–74.

Yinger, J., Bloom, H. S., Borch-Supan, A., & Ladd, H. F. (1988). *Property taxes and housing values*. Boston: Academic Press.

Ysseldyke, J. E. (1987). Classification of handicapped students. In M. C. Wang, M. C. Reynolds, & H. H. Walberg (Eds.), *Handbook of special education: Research and practice: Vol. 1. Learner characteristics and adaptive education* (pp. 253–271). Oxford, England: Pergamon Press.

CHAPTER 7

THE SCIENTIFIC BASIS FOR THE THEORY OF SUCCESSFUL INTELLIGENCE

Robert J. Sternberg

Research in education must be based on valid ideas and measures founded in recognized academic disciplines such as psychology and economics. The development of the theory of successful intelligence discussed in this chapter drew on numerous scientifically based studies; synthesizing these studies has led to a scientifically based theory. This chapter provides an example of how a theory can be developed through the use of scientifically based methods. This chapter guides readers through the development of a theory, from its beginnings as a concept to testing instructional materials based on the theory. At each stage of his argument, the chapter demonstrates the rigorous thinking required to introduce change in schools that will promote both increased achievement and the acquisition of important life skills.

Many different definitions of intelligence have been proposed over the years (see, e.g., "Intelligence and its measurement," 1921; Sternberg & Detterman, 1986). Among psychologists, the conventional, consensual definition of intelligence is stated in terms of generalized adaptation to the environment. Some theories of intelligence extend this definition by

The Scientific Basis of Educational Productivity, 161–184

positing a general factor of intelligence, often labeled *g*, which underlies all adaptive behavior (Brand, 1996; Jensen, 1998; see essays in Sternberg & Grigorenko, 2002). In many theories, including the theories most widely accepted today (e.g., Carroll, 1993; Gustafsson, 1994; Horn, 1994), other mental abilities are hierarchically nested under this general factor at successively greater levels of specificity. For example, whereas Carroll suggests that three levels can nicely capture the hierarchy of abilities, Cattell (1971) and Vernon (1971) suggest that two levels are especially important. According to Cattell, nested under general ability are fluid abilities of the kind needed to solve abstract reasoning problems, such as figural matrices or series completions, and crystallized abilities of the kind needed to solve problems of vocabulary and general information. For Vernon, the two levels correspond to verbal–educational and practical–mechanical abilities.

Lay conceptions of intelligence are quite a bit broader than those of psychologists who believe in *g* (Berry, 1974; Sternberg & Kaufman, 1998). For example, a study of people's conceptions of intelligence (Sternberg, Conway, Ketron, & Bernstein, 1981; see also Sternberg, 1985b) found that laypersons had a three-factor view of intelligence, composed of practical problem solving, verbal, and social-competence abilities. Only the first of these abilities is measured by conventional tests. A study of Taiwanese people's conceptions of intelligence (Yang & Sternberg, 1997a, 1997b) found that, although these people included a cognitive factor, they also included factors of interpersonal competence, intrapersonal competence, intellectual self-assertion, and intellectual self-effacement. A study of Kenyans' conceptions of intelligence (Grigorenko et al., 2001) found four distinct terms constituting conceptions of intelligence among rural Kenyans—*rieko* (knowledge and skills), *luoro* (respect), *winjo* (comprehension of how to handle real-life problems), and *paro* (initiative)—with only the first directly referring to knowledge-based skills (including but not limited to academics). Even more important, perhaps, are the results of a study (Okagaki & Sternberg, 1993) of 359 ethnically diverse parents, their children's success in school, and their children's teachers. The more closely the parents' conceptions of intelligence—which differed by ethnicity—matched those of the teachers, the better the children did in school. In other words, teachers rewarded students who did well on the kinds of attributes that the teachers associated with intelligence.

Because some laypeople's conceptions of intelligence are more linked to real-world success than is the professional, conventional conception of intelligence, it may be useful to think in terms of the concept of *successful intelligence,* which deals not just with intelligence in its academic aspect but also as it pertains to all aspects of life. Such a conception calls into question the conventional theories of intelligence and others like them—

mentioned above and described in more detail elsewhere (Brody, 2000; Embretson & McCollam, 2000; Herrnstein & Murray, 1994; Sternberg, 2000). This chapter, therefore, argues that a body of scientifically based research demonstrates that factors other than intelligence, as traditionally defined, contribute to success and that attributes typically associated with intelligence are consequently too limited. The remainder of this chapter is divided into four parts. The first part defines successful intelligence, the second part describes two kinds of research focusing on internal validation of the theory, the third part describes two kinds of research that focus on external validation of the theory, and the fourth part draws conclusions.

WHAT IS SUCCESSFUL INTELLIGENCE?

To study any construct scientifically, one must first define one's terms and then justify one's definitions. The relevant term here is *successful intelligence*. What is it, and how does one justify its definition and its use?

Successful intelligence is defined in terms of the ability to achieve success in life in terms of one's personal standards within one's sociocultural context. One's ability to achieve success depends on capitalizing on one's strengths and correcting or compensating for one's weaknesses. This balancing of abilities is achieved in order to adapt to, shape, and select environments. Success is attained through a balance of the three aspects of successful intelligence: analytical, creative, and practical thinking.

Information-Processing Components Underlying Successful Intelligence

According to the theory of intelligence proposed by Sternberg (1977, 1980b, 1984, 1985a, 1990, 1997, 1999a), a universal set of processes, or components, underlies all three aspects of intelligence. For example, although the solutions to problems that are considered intelligent in one culture may be different from the solutions considered to be intelligent in another culture, the need to define problems and translate strategies to solve these problems exists in every culture. People use *metacomponents*, or executive processes, to plan what to do, monitor things as they are being done, and evaluate things after they are done. We use *performance components* to execute the instructions of the metacomponents. *Knowledge-acquisition components* are used to learn how to solve problems or simply to acquire declarative knowledge in the first place (Sternberg, 1985a).

Although the same processes are universally used for all three aspects of intelligence, these processes are applied to different kinds of tasks and situations depending on whether a given problem requires analytical, creative, or practical thinking or a combination. In particular, analytical thinking is invoked when components are applied to fairly familiar kinds of problems abstracted from everyday life; creative thinking is used when the components are applied to relatively novel kinds of tasks or situations; and practical thinking is drawn on when the components are applied to experience to adapt to, shape, and select environments.

Because the theory of successful intelligence is composed of three subtheories—a componential subtheory dealing with the components of intelligence, an experiential subtheory dealing with the importance of coping with relative novelty and of automatization of information processing, and a contextual subtheory dealing with processes of adaptation, shaping, and selection—the theory has sometimes been referred to as *triarchic*.

INTERNAL VALIDATION OF THE THEORY OF SUCCESSFUL INTELLIGENCE

An important step in developing a scientifically based theory is to ensure internal and external validation of the theory. This section describes how the theory of successful intelligence has demonstrated internal validity through componential and factor analyses.

Componential Analyses

Componential analyses involve studying the information-processing components underlying performance on cognitive tasks. These kinds of analyses have been used to study both analytical and creative thinking.

Analytical Intelligence

Analytical intelligence is involved when the components of intelligence are applied to analyze, evaluate, judge, or compare and contrast. It typically is involved when components are applied to relatively familiar kinds of problems for which the judgments to be made are of a fairly abstract nature.

Some of Sternberg's early work (Guyote & Sternberg, 1981; Sternberg, 1977, 1980b, 1983; Sternberg & Gardner, 1983; Sternberg & Turner, 1981) reveals how analytical problems, such as analogies or syllogisms, can be analyzed componentially, with response times or error rates decomposed to yield their underlying information-processing components. The goal of this research is to understand the information-processing origins of individual differences in (the analytical aspect of) human intelligence. With componential analysis, one could specify sources of individual differences underlying a factor score such as that for "inductive reasoning." For example, response times on analogies (Sternberg, 1977) and linear syllogisms (Sternberg, 1980a) were decomposed into their elementary performance components.

Research on the components of human intelligence yielded some interesting results. First, whereas execution of early components (e.g., inference and mapping) tends to exhaustively consider the attributes of the stimuli, execution of later components (e.g., application) tends to consider the attributes of the stimuli in self-terminating fashion, with only those attributes processed that are essential for reaching a solution (Sternberg, 1977). Second, in a study of the development of figural analogical reasoning, Sternberg and Rifkin (1979) found that, although children generally became quicker in information processing with age, not all components were executed more rapidly with age. The encoding component first showed a decrease in component time with age and then an increase. Apparently, older children realized that their best strategy was to spend more time encoding the terms of a problem so that they would later be able to spend less time in operating on the encodings. A related, third finding was that better reasoners tend to spend relatively more time than do poorer reasoners in global, up-front metacomponential planning when solving difficult reasoning problems. Poorer reasoners, on the other hand, tend to spend relatively more time in local planning (Sternberg, 1981). Presumably, the better reasoners recognize that it is better to invest more time up front in order to be able to process a problem more efficiently later on. Fourth, in a study of the development of verbal analogical reasoning, Sternberg and Nigro (1980) found that, as children grow older, their strategies shift so that they rely on word association less and abstract relations more.

Studies of reasoning need not use artificial formats. In a more recent study, Sternberg and Kalmar (1997) looked at predictions for everyday kinds of situations, such as when milk will spoil. The study looked at both predictions and postdictions (hypotheses about the past when information about the past is unknown) and found that postdictions take longer to make than do predictions.

Some of the componential studies concentrate on knowledge-acquisition components rather than performance components or metacomponents. For example, in one set of studies (Sternberg & Powell, 1983; Sternberg, Powell, & Kaye, 1983; see also Sternberg, 1987b), the investigators were interested in sources of individual differences in vocabulary.

The researchers were not content simply to view these as individual differences in declarative knowledge because they wanted to understand why some people acquired this declarative knowledge and others did not. They found that individual and developmental differences have multiple sources. The three main sources are in knowledge-acquisition components, use of context clues, and use of mediating variables (e.g., position of clues in a sentence).

Creative Intelligence

Intelligence tests contain a range of problems, some more novel than others. In some of the componential work, Sternberg and colleagues (e.g., Sternberg, 1981, 1982; Sternberg & Gastel, 1989a, 1989b) have shown that, when one goes beyond the range of conventionality of the conventional tests of intelligence, one starts to tap sources of individual differences measured little or not at all by the tests. According to the theory of successful intelligence, (creative) intelligence is particularly well measured by problems assessing how well an individual can cope with relative novelty. Thus, it is important to include in a battery of tests problems that are relatively novel in nature. These problems can be either convergent or divergent in nature.

In work with convergent problems, Sternberg and his colleagues presented 80 individuals with novel kinds of reasoning problems that had a single best answer (Sternberg, 1982; Tetewsky & Sternberg, 1986). The participants' task was to predict future states from past states, given incomplete information. In another set of studies, 60 people were given more conventional kinds of inductive reasoning problems, such as analogies, series completions, and classifications, and were told to solve them. But the problems had premises preceding them that were either conventional or novel. The participants had to solve the problems as though the counterfactuals were true (Sternberg & Gastel, 1989a, 1989b).

In these studies, Sternberg and his colleagues found that correlations with conventional kinds of tests depended on how novel or nonentrenched the conventional tests were. The more novel the items, the higher the correlations of the tests with scores on successively more novel conventional tests. Thus, the components isolated for relatively novel items tend to correlate more highly with more unusual tests of fluid abilities (e.g., Cattell & Cattell, 1973) than with tests of crystallized abilities. Sternberg and colleagues also found that, when response times on the relatively novel problems were componentially analyzed, some components better measured the creative aspect of intelligence than did others.

Factor Analyses

Componential analyses provide one means of internal validation of the triarchic theory. But their emphasis is on testing specific models of task performance for particular components of information processing. Factor analyses make it possible internally to validate the triarchic theory as a whole, and four such factor-analytic studies support the internal validity of the theory of successful intelligence.

In one study (Sternberg, Grigorenko, Ferrari, & Clinkenbeard, 1999), the investigators used the so-called Sternberg Triarchic Abilities Test (STAT; Sternberg, 1993) to investigate the internal validity of the theory. A total of 326 high-school students from diverse parts of the United States took the test, which consisted of items measuring analytical, creative, and practical abilities. These abilities were assessed using verbal, quantitative, and figural items. Thus, there was a total of 12 subtests (e.g., analytical–verbal, analytical–figural, practical–quantitative). The items on the test were presented in both multiple-choice and open-response formats.

Confirmatory factor analysis on the data from the 12 subtests was supportive of the triarchic theory of human intelligence, yielding separate and uncorrelated analytical, creative, and practical factors. The lack of correlation was caused by the inclusion of essay as well as multiple-choice subtests. Although the multiple-choice tests tended to correlate substantially with multiple-choice tests, their correlations with essay tests were much weaker. The multiple-choice analytical subtest loaded most highly on the analytical factor, but the essay creative and practical subtests loaded most highly on their respective factors. Thus, measurement of creative and practical abilities ideally should probably be accomplished with other kinds of testing instruments that complement multiple-choice instruments.

In a second study, conducted with 3,252 students in the United States, Finland, and Spain, the investigators (Sternberg, Castejón, Prieto, Hautamäki, & Grigorenko, 2001) used the multiple-choice section of the STAT to compare five alternative models of intelligence, again via confirmatory factor analysis. A model featuring a general factor of intelligence fit the data relatively poorly. The triarchic model, allowing for intercorrelation among the analytic, creative, and practical factors, provided the best fit to the data.

In a fourth study, Grigorenko and Sternberg (2001) tested 511 Russian school children (ranging in age from 8 to 17 years) as well as 490 mothers and 328 fathers of these children. They used entirely distinct measures of analytical, creative, and practical intelligence. In this study, exploratory principal-component analysis for both children and adults yielded similar factor structures. Both varimax and oblimin rotations yielded clear-cut analytical, creative, and practical factors for the tests. Thus, this test, with a sample of a different nationality, a different set of tests, and a different method of analysis (exploratory rather than confirmatory analysis), again supported the theory of successful intelligence.

EXTERNAL VALIDATION OF THE THEORY OF SUCCESSFUL INTELLIGENCE

External validity is another important aspect of developing a scientifically based theory. The external validity of the triarchic theory of successful intelligence has been tested with two methods: correlational studies and instructional studies.

Correlational Studies

Analytical Intelligence

In the componential-analysis work already described, correlations were computed between component scores of individuals and scores on tests of different kinds of psychometric abilities. First, the studies of inductive reasoning (Sternberg, 1977; Sternberg & Gardner, 1982, 1983) found that, although inference, mapping, application, comparison, and justification tended to correlate with such tests, the highest correlation was typically with the preparation-response component. This result was puzzling at first because this component was estimated as the regression constant in the predictive regression equation. This result gave birth to the concept of the metacomponents, or higher order processes used to plan, monitor, and evaluate task performance. Second, some studies (Sternberg, 1977; Sternberg & Gardner, 1983) found that the correlations obtained for all the components showed convergent–discriminant validation: the correlations tended to be significant with psychometric tests of reasoning but not with psychometric tests of perceptual speed. Third, significant correlations with vocabulary tended to be obtained only for encoding of verbal stimuli (Sternberg, 1977, Sternberg & Gardner, 1983). Fourth, studies of linear-syllogistic reasoning found that components of the proposed (mixed linguistic–spatial) model that were supposed to correlate with verbal ability did so and did not correlate with spatial ability; components that were supposed to correlate with spatial ability did so and did not correlate with verbal ability. In other words, it was possible to successfully validate the proposed model of linear-syllogistic reasoning not only in terms of the fit of response time or error data to the predictions of the alternative models but also in terms of the correlations of component scores with psychometric tests of verbal and spatial abilities (Sternberg, 1980b). Fifth, studies found that there were individual differences in strategies in solving linear syllogisms, whereby some people used a largely linguistic model, others a largely spatial model, and most the proposed linguistic–spatial mixed model (Sternberg, 1980a). Thus, sometimes, a less-than-perfect fit of a proposed model to group data may reflect individual differences in strategies among participants.

Creative Intelligence

In work with divergent reasoning problems having no one best answer, the investigators asked 63 people to create various kinds of products (Lubart & Sternberg, 1995; Sternberg & Lubart, 1991, 1995, 1996) in which an infinite variety of responses were possible. Individuals were asked to create products in the realms of writing, art, advertising, and science. Participants created two products in each domain.

Sternberg and Lubart found, first, that creativity comprises the components proposed by their investment model of creativity: intelligence, knowledge, thinking styles, personality, and motivation. Second, they found that creativity is relatively—although not wholly—domain specific. Correlations of ratings of the creative quality of the products across domains were moderately low, generally around the 0.4 level. Thus, some degree of relation existed across domains, at the same time that there was plenty of room for someone to be strong in one or more domains but not in others. Third, the investigators found a range of correlations of measures of creative performance with conventional tests of abilities. For example, correlations were higher with fluid than with crystallized ability tests. Furthermore, the more novel the fluid test was, the higher the correlations were.

These results indicate that tests of creative intelligence have some overlap with conventional tests (e.g., in requiring verbal skills or the ability to analyze one's own ideas; Sternberg & Lubart, 1995) but also tap skills beyond those typically measured, even by relatively novel kinds of items on the conventional tests of intelligence.

The work on creativity revealed a number of sources of individual and developmental differences and addressed the following questions: (a) To what extent was the thinking of the individual novel or nonentrenched? (b) What was the quality of the individual's thinking? (c) To what extent did the thinking of the individual meet the demands of the task?

Tests of creative intelligence go beyond tests of analytical intelligence in measuring performance on tasks that require individuals to deal with relatively novel situations. At the same time, they probably measure creativity that is, for the most part, within existing paradigms (see Sternberg, 1999c). But how about situations that are relatively familiar but in a practical rather than an academic domain? Can one measure intelligence in the practical domain, and if so, what is its relation to intelligence in more academic kinds of domains?

Practical Intelligence

Practical intelligence involves individuals applying their abilities to the kinds of problems that confront them in daily life, such as on the job or in the home. Practical intelligence involves applying the components of intelligence to experience so as to adapt to, shape, and select environments. Adaptation is involved when one changes oneself to suit the environment. Shaping is involved when one changes the environment to suit oneself. And selection is involved when one decides to seek out another environment that is a better match to one's needs, abilities, and desires. People differ in their balance of adaptation, shaping, and selection and in the competence with which they balance among the three possible courses of action.

Much of the work of Sternberg and colleagues on practical intelligence (Sternberg et al., 2000; Sternberg & Wagner, 1993; Sternberg, Wagner, & Okagaki, 1993; Sternberg, Wagner, Williams, & Horvath, 1995; Wagner, 1987; Wagner & Sternberg, 1986) has centered on the concept of tacit knowledge. They have defined this construct as what one needs to know to work effectively in an environment that one is not explicitly taught and that often is not even verbalized. Sternberg and colleagues represent tacit knowledge in the form of production systems, or sequences of "if–then" statements that describe procedures one follows in various kinds of everyday situations.

Sternberg and colleagues have typically measured tacit knowledge using work-related problems that present problems encountered on the job. They have measured tacit knowledge for both children and adults, and among adults, for people in more than two dozen occupations. In a typical tacit knowledge problem, people are asked to read a story about a problem someone faces and to rate, for each statement in a set of statements, how adequate a solution the statement represents.

In the tacit knowledge studies, Sternberg et al. (2000) have found, first, that practical intelligence as embodied in tacit knowledge increases with experience, but it is profiting from experience, rather than experience per se, that results in increases in scores. Some people can hold jobs for years and still have acquired relatively little tacit knowledge. Second, Sternberg et al. have found that subscores on tests of tacit knowledge (e.g., for managing oneself, managing others, managing tasks) correlate significantly with each other. Third, scores on various tests of tacit knowledge, such as for academics and managers, are also correlated fairly substantially (at about the 0.5 level) with each other. Thus, fourth, tests of tacit knowledge may yield a general factor across these tests. However, fifth, scores on tacit knowledge tests do not correlate with scores on conventional tests of intelligence, whether the measures used are single-score measures of multiple-ability batteries. Thus, any general factor from the tacit knowledge tests is not the same as any general factor from tests of academic abilities (suggesting that neither kind of *g* factor is truly general, but rather, general only across a limited range of measuring instruments). Sixth, despite the lack of correlation of practical intellectual with conventional measures, the scores on tacit knowledge tests predict performance on the job as well as or better than do conventional psychometric intelligence tests. In one study done at the Center for Creative Leadership, the investigators further found, seventh, that scores on tests of tacit knowledge for management were the best single predictor of performance on a managerial simulation. In a hierarchical regression, scores on conventional tests of intelligence, personality, styles, and interpersonal orientation were entered first, and scores on the test of tacit knowledge were entered last. Scores on the test of tacit knowledge were the single best predictor of managerial simulation score. Moreover, these scores also contributed significantly to the prediction, even after everything else was entered first into the equation. Eight, in recent work on military leadership, Hedlund et al. (1998) and Sternberg et al. (2000) found that, whereas the scores of 562 participants on tests of tacit knowledge for military leadership predicted ratings of leadership effectiveness, scores on a conventional test of intelligence and on a tacit knowledge test for managers did not significantly predict the ratings of effectiveness.

In a study in Kenya, Sternberg and colleagues (Sternberg & Grigorenko, 1997; Sternberg et al., 2001) devised a test of practical intelligence for adaptation to the environment and studied 85 school-age children's ability to adapt to their indigenous environment. Based on work the researchers had done elsewhere, they expected that the test scores would not correlate with scores on conventional tests of intelligence. To test this hypothesis, they also administered the Raven Coloured Progressive Matrices Test, which measures fluid or abstract reasoning-based abilities, and the Mill Hill Vocabulary Scale, which measures crystallized or formal knowledge-based abilities. In addition, they gave the children a comparable test of vocabulary in their own language, Dholuo.

The researchers found no correlation between the test of indigenous tacit knowledge and scores on the fluid ability tests. But to their surprise, they found statistically significant correlations of the tacit knowledge tests with the tests of crystallized abilities. The correlations, however, were *negative*. In other words, the higher the children scored on the test of tacit knowledge, the lower they scored, on average, on the tests of crystallized abilities!

The test of practical intelligence developed for use in Kenya, as well as some of the other practically based tests described in this chapter, may seem more like tests of achievement or of developing expertise (see Ericsson, 1996; Howe, Davidson, & Sloboda, 1998) than of intelligence. But it can be argued that intelligence is itself a form of developing expertise, that there is no clear-cut distinction between the two constructs (Sternberg, 1998a, 1999b). Indeed, all measures of intelligence measure a form of developing expertise.

An example of how tests of intelligence measure developing expertise emanates from work Sternberg, Grigorenko, and colleagues have done in Tanzania. A study done in Tanzania (see Sternberg & Grigorenko, 1997; Sternberg et al., 2002) points out the risks of giving tests, scoring them, and interpreting the results as measures of some latent intellectual ability or abilities. The investigators administered to 358 school children between the ages of 11 and 13 years near Bagamoyo, Tanzania, tests that included a form-board classification test; a linear syllogisms test; and a 20-questions test, which measure the kinds of skills required on conventional tests of intelligence. The investigators obtained scores that they could analyze and evaluate, ranking the children in terms of their supposed general or other abilities. However, they administered the tests dynamically rather than statically (Brown & Ferrara, 1985; Budoff, 1968; Day, Engelhardt, Maxwell, & Bolig, 1997; Feuerstein, 1979; Grigorenko & Sternberg, 1998; Guthke, 1993; Haywood & Tzuriel, 1992; Lidz, 1987, 1991; Tzuriel, 1995; Vygotsky, 1978). Dynamic testing is similar to conventional static testing in that individuals are tested and inferences about their abilities made. But dynamic tests differ in that children are given some kind of feedback in order to help them improve their scores.

The investigators first gave children the ability tests. The children were given a brief period of instruction in which they were able to learn skills that would potentially enable them to improve their scores. Then they were tested again. Because the instruction for each test lasted only about 5 to 10 minutes, one would not expect dramatic gains. Yet on average, the gains were statistically significant. More importantly, scores on the pretest showed only weak, although significant, correlations with scores on the posttest. These correlations, at about the 0.3 level, suggested that when tests are administered statically to children in developing countries, the tests may be rather unstable and easily subject to influences of training. The reason could be that the children are not accustomed to taking Western-style tests, so they profit quickly even from small amounts of instruction as to what is expected from them. The more important question is not whether the scores changed or even correlated with each other but rather how they correlated with other cognitive measures. In other words, which test was a better predictor of transfer to other cognitive performance, the pretest score or the posttest score? The investigators found the posttest score to be the better predictor.

Crystallized ability tests, such as tests of vocabulary and general information, measure test takers' developing and developed knowledge base. And data suggest that fluid ability tests, such as tests of abstract reasoning, measure developing and developed expertise even more strongly than do crystallized ability tests. Probably the best evidence for this claim is that fluid ability tests have shown much greater increases in scores over the past several generations than have crystallized ability tests (Flynn, 1984, 1987, 1998; Neisser, 1998). The relatively brief period of time during which these increases have occurred (about 9 points of IQ per generation) suggests an environmental rather than a genetic cause of the increases. And the substantially greater increase for fluid than for crystallized tests suggests that fluid tests, like all other tests, actually measure an expertise acquired through interactions with the environment. This is not to say that genes do not influence intelligence; almost certainly they do (Bouchard, 1997; Plomin, 1997; Scarr, 1997). Rather, the point is that the environment always mediates their influence, and tests of intelligence measure gene–environment interaction effects. The measurement of intelligence is by assessment of various forms of developing expertise.

The forms of developing expertise that are viewed as practically or otherwise intelligent may differ from one society to another or from one sector of a given society to another. For example, procedural knowledge about natural herbal medicines, on the one hand, or Western medicines, on the other, may be critical to survival in one society and irrelevant in another. Whereas what constitutes components of intelligence is universal, the content that constitutes the application of these components to adaptation to, shaping, and selection of environments is culturally and even subculturally variable.

In the Grigorenko and Sternberg (2001) study in Russia, which was already described, the investigators used analytical, creative, and practical tests to predict mental and physical health among the Russian adults. Mental health was measured by widely used paper-and-pencil tests of depression and anxiety, and physical health was measured by self-reports. The best predictor of mental and physical health was the practical intelligence measure. Analytical intelligence came second, and creative intelligence came third. All three contributed to prediction, however. Thus, the researchers again concluded that a theory of intelligence encompassing all three elements provides better prediction of success in life than does a theory comprising just the analytical element.

Instructional Studies

Improving School Achievement

In a first set of studies (Sternberg & Clinkenbeard, 1995; Sternberg, Ferrari, Clinkenbeard, & Grigorenko, 1996; Sternberg et al., 1999), researchers explored whether conventional school education systematically discriminates against children with creative and practical strengths. Motivation for this work was the belief that the systems in most schools strongly favor children with strengths in memory and analytical abilities.

The investigators used the Sternberg Triarchic Abilities Test, as already described, in some of the instructional work. The test was administered to 326 children across the United States and in some other countries who were identified by their schools as gifted by any standard whatsoever. Children were selected for a summer program in (college-level) psychology if they fell into one of five ability groupings: high analytical, high creative, high practical, high balanced (high in all three abilities), or low balanced (low in all three abilities). The students were then divided into four instructional groups. Students in all four instructional groups used the same introductory psychology textbook (a preliminary version of Sternberg [1995]) and listened to the same psychology lectures. What differed among the groups was the type of afternoon discussion section to which they were assigned. They were assigned to an instructional condition that emphasized either memory, analytical, creative, or practical instruction.

Students in all four instructional conditions were evaluated in terms of their performance on homework, a midterm examination, a final examination, and an independent project. Each type of work was evaluated for memory, analytical, creative, and practical quality. Thus, all students were evaluated in exactly the same way. The results suggested the utility of the theory of successful intelligence. This utility showed itself in several ways.

First, the investigators observed when the students first arrived at Yale that the students in the high-creative and high-practical groups were much more diverse in terms of their racial, ethnic, socioeconomic, and educational backgrounds than were the students in the high-analytical group, suggesting that correlations of measured intelligence with status variables such as these may be reduced by using a broader conception of intelligence. Thus, the kinds of students identified as strong by our augmented measures differed in terms of populations from which they were drawn in comparison with students identified as strong by conventional measures. More importantly, just by expanding the range of abilities measured, the investigators discovered intellectual strengths that might not have been apparent through a conventional test.

Second, the investigators found that all three ability tests—analytical, creative, and practical—significantly predicted course performance. When multiple-regression analysis was used, at least two of these ability measures contributed significantly to the prediction of each of the measures of achievement. Perhaps as a reflection of the difficulty of deemphasizing the analytical way of teaching, one of the significant predictors was always the analytical score. (However, in a replication of our study with low-income African American students from New York, Deborah Coates of the City University of New York found a different pattern of results. Her data indicated that the practical tests were better predictors of course performance than were the analytical measures, suggesting that what ability test predicts what criterion depends on population as well as mode of teaching.)

Third and most importantly, there was an aptitude–treatment interaction whereby students who were placed in instructional conditions that better matched their pattern of abilities outperformed students who were mismatched. In other words, when students are taught in a way that fits how they think, they do better in school. Children with creative and practical abilities, who are almost never taught or assessed in a way that matches their pattern of abilities, may be at a disadvantage in course after course, year after year.

A follow-up study (Sternberg, Torff, & Grigorenko, 1998a, 1998b) examined learning of social studies and science by third- and eighth-grade students. The 225 third graders were students in a very low-income neighborhood in Raleigh, North Carolina. The 142 eighth graders were largely middle- to upper-middle-class students in Baltimore, Maryland, and Fresno, California. Students were assigned to one of three instructional conditions. In the first condition, they were taught the course that basically they would have learned had there been no intervention. The course emphasized memory. In a second condition, students were taught in a way that emphasized critical (analytical) thinking. In the third condition, students were taught in a way that emphasized analytical, creative, and practical thinking. Each student's performance was assessed for memory learning (through multiple-choice assessments) as well as for analytical, creative, and practical learning (through performance assessments).

As expected, students in the successful intelligence (analytical, creative, practical) condition outperformed the other students in terms of the performance assessments. One could argue that this result merely reflected the way they were taught. Nevertheless, the result suggested that teaching for these kinds of thinking succeeded. More important, however, was the result that children in the successful intelligence condition outperformed the other children even on the multiple-choice memory tests. In other words, to the extent that one's goal is just to maximize children's memory for information, teaching for successful intelligence is still superior. It enables children to capitalize on their strengths and to correct or compensate for their weaknesses, and it allows children to encode material in a variety of interesting ways.

Grigorenko, Jarvin, and Sternberg (2002) have extended these results to reading curricula at the middle- and the high-school levels. In a study of 871 middle-school students and 432 high-school students, researchers taught reading either triarchically or through the regular curriculum. At the middle-school level, reading was taught explicitly. At the high-school level, reading was infused into instruction in mathematics, physical sciences, social sciences, English, history, foreign languages, and the arts. In all settings, students who were taught triarchically substantially outperformed students who were taught in standard ways.

Thus, the results of these three sets of studies suggest that the theory of successful intelligence is valid as a whole. Moreover, the results suggest that the theory can make a difference not only in laboratory tests but also in school classrooms and even the everyday life of adults.

Improving Abilities

The kinds of analytical, creative, and practical abilities discussed in this chapter are not static; rather, they are modifiable.

Analytical skills can be taught. For example, in one study, Sternberg (1987a) tested whether it is possible to teach people better to decontextualize meanings of unknown words presented in context. In this study, Sternberg gave 81 participants in five conditions a pretest on their ability to decontextualize word meanings. Then the participants were divided into five conditions, two of which were control conditions that lacked formal instruction. In one condition, participants were not given any instructional treatment and were merely asked later to take a posttest. In a second condition, participants were given practice as an instructional condition, but they were not given any formal instruction. In a third condition, participants were taught knowledge-acquisition component processes that could be used to decontextualize word meanings. In a fourth condition, participants were taught to use context cues. In a fifth condition, participants were taught to use mediating variables. Participants in all three of the theory-based formal instructional conditions outperformed participants in the two control conditions, whose performance did not differ. In other words, theory-based instruction was better than no instruction at all or just practice without formal instruction.

Creative thinking skills also can be taught, and a program has been devised for teaching them (Sternberg & Williams, 1996; see also Sternberg & Grigorenko, 2000). In some relevant work, the investigators divided 86 gifted and nongifted fourth graders into experimental and control groups. All children took pretests on insightful thinking. Then some of the children received their regular school instruction, and others received instruction on insight skills. After the instruction, all children took a posttest measuring their insight skills. The investigators found that children taught how to solve the insight problems using knowledge-acquisition components gained more from pretest to posttest than did students who were not so taught (Davidson & Sternberg, 1984).

Practical intelligence skills can also be taught. Williams, Blythe, White, Sternberg, and Gardner (1996) have developed a program for teaching practical intellectual skills to middle-school students that explicitly teaches them "practical intelligence for school" in the contexts of doing homework, taking tests, reading, and writing. Sternberg and colleagues (Gardner, Krechevsky, Sternberg, & Okagaki, 1994; Sternberg, Okagaki, & Jackson, 1990) evaluated the program in a variety of settings and found that students taught with this program outperform students in control groups who did not receive the instruction.

Individuals' use of practical intelligence can be to their own gain in addition to or instead of the gain of others. People can be practically intelligent for themselves at the expense of others; therefore, wisdom needs to be studied in its own right in addition to practical or even successful intelligence (Baltes & Staudinger, 2000; Sternberg, 1998b).

In sum, practical intelligence, like analytical intelligence, is an important antecedent of life success. Because measures of practical intelligence predict everyday behavior at about the same level (and sometimes even better) as do measures of analytical intelligence, the sophisticated use of such tests could roughly double the explained variance in various kinds of criteria of success. Using measures of creative intelligence as well might increase prediction still more. Thus, tests based on the construct of successful intelligence might take us to new and higher levels of prediction. At the same time, expansions of conventional tests that stay within the conventional framework of analytical tests based on standard psychometric models do not seem likely greatly to expand our predictive capabilities (Schmidt & Hunter, 1998). But how did psychologists get to where they are, both with respect to levels of prediction and with respect to the kinds of standard psychometric tests used to attain these levels of prediction?

CONCLUSIONS

The chapter has described the efforts made to ensure internal and external validation of the theory of successful intelligence. The descriptions of these efforts provide a model for applying other theories to the rigors of testing. There is no lack of new theories of intelligence; the difficult thing is collecting predictive empirical data that indicate whether the theories stand up to empirical scrutiny.

The time has come to move beyond conventional theories of intelligence. This chapter has provided data suggesting that conventional theories and tests of intelligence are incomplete. The general factor is an artifact of limitations in populations of individuals tested, types of materials with which they are tested, and types of methods used in testing. Indeed, our studies show that, even when one wants to predict school performance, the conventional tests are somewhat limited in their predictive validity (Sternberg & Williams, 1997). The proposed theory of successful intelligence and its development fares well in construct validations, whether one tests in the laboratory, in schools, or in the workplace. The greatest obstacle to moving on is in vested interests, both in academia and in the world of tests. Psychologists now have ways to move beyond conventional notions of intelligence; they need only the will.

Perhaps the time has come to expand people's notions of what it means to be intelligent. This change should include an expansion of the conventional conception of intelligence to include not only memory and analytical abilities but creative and practical abilities as well. Other expansions are also possible. For example, research is ongoing with regard to emotional intelligence (Davies, Stankov, & Roberts, 1998; Mayer, Salovey, & Caruso, 2000), with promising yet mixed results. Hopefully, predictive empirical research will also be forthcoming regarding the theory of multiple intelligences (Gardner, 1983, 1999). Ultimately, the answer to the question of how to expand psychological conceptions of intelligence will depend partly on the imagination of theorists, but more importantly, on the data showing construct validity, and in particular, incremental internal and external validity over the conventional notions that have dominated theory and research on intelligence to date. The memory and analytical abilities measured by these tests have mattered and likely will continue to matter for many forms of success in life. These abilities have never been—and are unlikely ever to be—the only intellectual abilities that matter for success. It is for this reason that psychologists have needed and will continue to need theories such as the theory of successful intelligence.

ACKNOWLEDGMENT

Preparation of this manuscript was supported by Grant REC-9979843 from the National Science Foundation and by a government grant under the Javits Act Program (Grant No. R206R000001) as administered by the Office of Educational Research and Improvement, U. S. Department of

Education. Grantees undertaking such projects are encouraged to express freely their professional judgment. This chapter, therefore, does not necessarily represent the positions or the policies of the U.S. government, and no official endorsement should be inferred.

REFERENCES

Baltes, P. B., & Staudinger, U. M (2000). Wisdom: A metaheuristic (pragmatic) to orchestrate mind and virtue toward excellence. *American Psychologist, 55*(1), 122–136.

Berry, J. W. (1974). Radical cultural relativism and the concept of intelligence. In J. W. Berry & P. R. Dasen (Eds.), *Culture and cognition: Readings in cross-cultural psychology* (pp. 225–229). London: Methuen.

Bouchard, T. J., Jr. (1997). IQ similarity in twins reared apart: Findings and responses to critics. In R. J. Sternberg & E. L. Grigorenko (Eds.), *Intelligence, heredity, and environment* (pp. 126–160). New York: Cambridge University Press.

Brand, C. (1996). *The g factor: General intelligence and its implications*. Chichester, England: Wiley.

Brody, N. (2000) History of theories and measurements of intelligence. In R. J. Sternberg (Ed.), *Handbook of intelligence* (pp.16–33). New York: Cambridge University Press.

Brown, A. L., & Ferrara, R. A. (1985). Diagnosing zones of proximal development. In J. V. Wertsch (Ed.), Culture, communication, and cognition: Vygotskian perspectives (pp. 273–305). New York: Cambridge University Press.

Budoff, M. (1968). Learning potential as a supplementary assessment procedure. In J. Hellmuth (Ed.), *Learning disorders* (Vol. 3, pp. 295–343). Seattle, WA: Special Child.

Carroll, J. B. (1993). *Human cognitive abilities: A survey of factor-analytic studies*. New York: Cambridge University Press.

Cattell, R. B. (1971). *Abilities: Their structure, growth and action*. Boston: Houghton Mifflin.

Cattell, R. B., & Cattell, H. E. P. (1973). *Measuring intelligence with the Culture Fair Tests*. Champaign, IL: Institute for Personality and Ability Testing.

Davidson, J. E., & Sternberg, R. J. (1984). The role of insight in intellectual giftedness. *Gifted Child Quarterly, 28*(2), 58–64.

Davies, M., Stankov, L., & Roberts, R. D. (1998). Emotional intelligence: In search of an elusive construct. *Journal of Personality and Social Psychology, 75*(4), 989–1015.

Day, J. D., Engelhardt, J. L., Maxwell, S. E., & Bolig, E. E. (1997). Comparison of static and dynamic assessment procedures and their relation to independent performance. *Journal of Educational Psychology, 89*(2), 358–368.

Embretson, S. & McCollam, K. (2000) Psychometric approaches to the understanding and measurement of intelligence. In R. J. Sternberg (Ed.), *Handbook of intelligence* (pp. 423–444). New York: Cambridge University Press.

Ericsson, K. A. (Ed.) (1996). *The road to excellence*. Mahwah, NJ: Lawrence Erlbaum Associates.

Feuerstein, R. (1979). *The dynamic assessment of retarded performers: The learning potential assessment device theory, instruments, and techniques*. Baltimore: University Park Press.

Flynn, J. R. (1984). The mean IQ of Americans: Massive gains 1932 to 1978. *Psychological Bulletin, 95*, 29–51.

Flynn, J. R. (1987). Massive IQ gains in 14 nations. *Psychological Bulletin, 101*, 171–191.

Flynn, J. R. (1998). WAIS-III and WISC-III gains in the United States from 1972 to 1995: How to compensate for obsolete norms. *Perceptual and Motor Skills, 86*, 1231–1239.

Gardner, H. (1983). *Frames of mind: The theory of multiple intelligences*. New York: Basic Books.

Gardner, H. (1999). *Intelligence reframed: Multiple intelligences for the 21st century*. New York: Basic Books.

Gardner, H., Krechevsky, M., Sternberg, R. J., & Okagaki, L. (1994). Intelligence in context: Enhancing students' practical intelligence for school. In K. McGilly (Ed.), *Classroom lessons: Integrating cognitive theory and classroom practice* (pp. 105–127). Cambridge, MA: MIT Press.

Grigorenko, E. L., Geissler, P. W., Prince, R., Okatcha, F., Nokes, C., Kenny, D. A., et al. (2001). The organization of Luo conceptions of intelligence: A study of implicit theories in a Kenyan village. *International Journal of Behavioral Development, 25*(4), 367–378.

Grigorenko, E. L., & Sternberg, R. J. (1998). Dynamic testing. *Psychological Bulletin, 124*(1), 75–111.

Grigorenko, E. L., & Sternberg, R. J. (2001). Analytical, creative, and practical intelligence as predictors of self-reported adaptive functioning: A case study in Russia. *Intelligence, 29*(1), 57–73.

Grigorenko, E. L., Jarvin, L., & Sternberg, R. J. (2002). School-based tests of the triarchic theory of intelligence: three settings, three samples, three syllabi. *Contemporary Educational Psychology, 27*(2), 167–208.

Gustafsson, J. E. (1994). Hierarchical models of intelligence and educational achievement. In A. Demetriou, & A. Efklides, (Eds.). *Intelligence, mind, and reasoning: Structure and development. Advances in psychology* (pp. 45–73). Amsterdam, Netherlands: North-Holland/Elsevier Science Publishers.

Guthke, J. (1993). Current trends in theories and assessment of intelligence. In J. H. M. Hamers, K. Sijtsma, & A. J. J. M. Ruijssenaars (Eds.) *Learning potential assessment* (pp. 13–20). Amsterdam: Swets & Zeitlinger.

Guyote, M. J., & Sternberg, R. J. (1981). A transitive-chain theory of syllogistic reasoning. *Cognitive Psychology, 13*(4), 461–525.

Haywood, H. C. &. Tzuriel, D. (Eds.) (1992). *Interactive assessment*. New York: Springer-Verlag.

Hedlund, J., Horvath, J. A., Forsythe, G. B., Snook, S., Williams, W. M., Bullis, R. C., et al. (1998). *Tacit knowledge in military leadership: Evidence of construct validity*. (Technical Report 1080). Alexandria, VA: U.S. Army Research Institute for the Behavioral and Social Sciences.

Herrnstein, R. J, & Murray, C. (1994). *The bell curve*. New York: Free Press.

Horn, J. L. (1994). Theory of fluid and crystallized intelligence. In R. J. Sternberg (Ed.), *The encyclopedia of human intelligence* (Vol. 1, pp. 443–451). New York: Macmillan.

Howe, M. J., Davidson, J. W., & Sloboda, J. A (1998). Innate talents: Reality or myth? *Behavioral and Brain Sciences, 21*(3), 399–442.

Intelligence and its measurement: A symposium. (1921). *Journal of Educational Psychology, 12*, 123–147, 195–216, 271–275.

Jensen, A. R. (1998). *The g factor: The science of mental ability*. Westport, CT: Praeger/Greenwoood.

Lidz, C. S. (Ed.) (1987). *Dynamic assessment*. New York: Guilford Press.

Lidz, C. S. (1991). *Practitioner's guide to dynamic assessment*. New York: Guilford Press.

Lubart, T. I., & Sternberg, R. J. (1995). An investment approach to creativity: Theory and data. In S. M. Smith, T. B. Ward, & R. A. Finke (Eds.), *The creative cognition approach* (pp. 269–302). Cambridge, MA: MIT Press.

Mayer, J. D. Salovey, P. Caruso, D. (2000). Emotional intelligence. In R. J. Sternberg (Ed.), *Handbook of intelligence* (pp. 396–421). New York: Cambridge University Press.

Neisser, U. (Ed.). (1998). *The rising curve*. Washington, DC: American Psychological Association.

Okagaki, L., & Sternberg, R. J. (1993). Parental beliefs and children's school performance. *Child Development, 64*(1), 36–56.

Plomin, R. (1997). Identifying genes for cognitive abilities and disabilities. In R. J. Sternberg & E. L. Grigorenko (Eds.), *Intelligence, heredity, and environment* (pp. 89–104). New York: Cambridge University Press.

Scarr, S. (1997). Behavior-genetic and socialization theories of intelligence: Truce and reconciliation. In Sternberg, R. J., & Grigorenko, E. L. (Eds.), *Intelligence, heredity and environment* (pp. 3–41). New York: Cambridge University Press.

Schmidt, F. L., & Hunter, J. E. (1998). The validity and utility of selection methods in personnel psychology: practical and theoretical implications of 85 years of research findings. *Psychological Bulletin, 124*(2), 262–274.

Sternberg, R. J. (1977). Intelligence, information processing, and analogical reasoning: The componential analysis of human abilities. Hillsdale, NJ: Lawrence Erlbaum Associates.

Sternberg, R. J. (1980a). Representation and process in linear syllogistic reasoning. *Journal of Experimental Psychology: General, 109*(2), 119–159.

Sternberg, R. J. (1980b). Sketch of a componential subtheory of human intelligence. *Behavioral and Brain Sciences, 3*, 573–584.

Sternberg, R. J. (1981). Intelligence and nonentrenchment. *Journal of Educational Psychology, 73*, 1–16.

Sternberg, R. J. (1982). Nonentrenchment in the assessment of intellectual giftedness. *Gifted Child Quarterly, 26*, 63–67.

Sternberg, R. J. (1983). Componential theory and componential analysis: Is there a "Neisser" alternative? *Cognition, 15*, 199–206.

Sternberg, R. J. (Ed.). (1984). *Mechanisms of cognitive development*. San Francisco: Freeman.

Sternberg, R. J. (1985a). *Beyond IQ: A triarchic theory of human intelligence*. New York: Cambridge University Press.
Sternberg, R. J. (1985b). Implicit theories of intelligence, creativity, and wisdom. *Journal of Personality and Social Psychology, 49*(3), 607–627.
Sternberg, R. J. (1987a). Most vocabulary is learned from context. In M. G. McKeown & M. E. Curtis (Eds.), *The nature of vocabulary acquisition* (pp. 89–105). Hillsdale, NJ: Erlbaum.
Sternberg, R. J. (1987b). The psychology of verbal comprehension. In R. Glaser (Ed.), *Advances in instructional psychology* (Vol. 3, pp. 97–151). Hillsdale, NJ: Erlbaum.
Sternberg, R. J. (1990). *Metaphors of mind: Conceptions of the nature of intelligence*. New York: Cambridge University Press.
Sternberg, R. J. (1993). *Sternberg Triarchic Abilities Test.* Unpublished test.
Sternberg, R. J. (1995). *In search of the human mind.* Orlando, FL: Harcourt Brace College Publishers.
Sternberg, R. J. (1997). *Successful intelligence.* New York: Plume.
Sternberg, R. J. (1998a). Metacognition, abilities, and developing expertise: What makes an expert student? *Instructional Science, 26*(1–2), 127–140.
Sternberg, R. J. (1998b). A balance theory of wisdom. *Review of General Psychology, 2*(4), 347–365
Sternberg, R. J. (1999a). Intelligence as developing expertise. *Contemporary Educational Psychology, 24*(4), 259–375.
Sternberg, R. J. (1999b). The theory of successful intelligence. *Review of General Psychology, 3*(4), 292–316.
Sternberg, R. J. (Ed.). (1999c). *Handbook of creativity.* New York: Cambridge University Press.
Sternberg, R. J. (Ed.). (2000). *Handbook of intelligence*. New York: Cambridge University Press.
Sternberg, R. J., Castejón, J. L., Prieto, M. D., Hautamäki, J., & Grigorenko, E. L. (2001). Confirmatory factor analysis of the Sternberg Triarchic Abilities Test (multiple-choice items) in three international samples: An empirical test of the Triarchic Theory of Intelligence. *European Journal of Psychological Assessment, 17*(1), 1–16.
Sternberg, R. J., & Clinkenbeard, P. R. (1995). A triarchic model applied to identifying, teaching, and assessing gifted children. *Roeper Review, 17*(4), 255–260.
Sternberg, R. J., Conway, B. E., Ketron, J. L., & Bernstein, M. (1981). People's conceptions of intelligence. *Journal of Personality and Social Psychology, 41*(1), 37–55.
Sternberg, R. J., & Detterman, D. K. (1986). *What is intelligence?* Norwood, N.J.: Ablex Publishing Corporation.
Sternberg, R. J., Ferrari, M., Clinkenbeard, P. R., & Grigorenko, E. L. (1996). Identification, instruction, and assessment of gifted children: A construct validation of a triarchic model. *Gifted Child Quarterly, 40*(3), 129–137.
Sternberg, R. J., Forsythe, G. B., Hedlund, J., Horvath, J., Snook, S., Williams, W. M., et al. (2000). *Practical intelligence in everyday life.* New York: Cambridge University Press.

Sternberg, R. J., & Gardner, M. K. (1982). A componential interpretation of the general factor in human intelligence. In H. J. Eysenck (Ed.), *A model for intelligence* (pp. 231–254). Berlin: Springer-Verlag.

Sternberg, R. J., & Gardner, M. K. (1983). Unities in inductive reasoning. *Journal of Experimental Psychology: General, 112*(1), 80–116.

Sternberg, R. J., & Gastel, J. (1989a). Coping with novelty in human intelligence: An empirical investigation. *Intelligence, 13*, 187–197.

Sternberg, R. J., & Gastel, J. (1989b). If dancers ate their shoes: Inductive reasoning with factual and counterfactual premises. *Memory and Cognition, 17*(1), 1–10.

Sternberg, R. J., & Grigorenko, E. L. (Eds.) (1997). *Intelligence, heredity, and environment*. New York: Cambridge University Press.

Sternberg, R. J., & Grigorenko, E. L. (2000). *Teaching for successful intelligence*. Arlington Heights, IL: Skylight Training and Publishing.

Sternberg, R.J., & Grigorenko E. L. (Eds.). (2002). *The general factor of intelligence: How general is it?* Mahwah, NJ: Erlbaum.

Sternberg, R. J., Grigorenko, E. L., Ferrari, M., & Clinkenbeard, P. (1999). A triarchic analysis of an aptitude-treatment interaction. *European Journal of Psychological Assessment, 15*(1), 1–11.

Sternberg, R. J., Grigorenko, E. L., Ngrosho, D., Tantufuye, E., Mbise, A., Nokes, C., et al. (2002). Assessing intellectual potential in rural Tanzanian school children. *Intelligence, 30*, 141–162.

Sternberg, R. J., & Kalmar D.A. (1997). When will the milk spoil? Everyday induction in human intelligence. *Intelligence, 25*(3), 185–203.

Sternberg, R. J., & Kaufman J. C. (1998). Human abilities. *Annual Review of Psychology, 49*, 479–502.

Sternberg, R. J., & Lubart, T. I. (1991). An investment theory of creativity and its development. *Human Development, 34*(1), 1–31.

Sternberg, R. J., & Lubart, T. I. (1995). Defying the crowd: Cultivating creativity in a culture of conformity. New York: Free Press.

Sternberg, R. J., & Lubart, T. I. (1996). Investing in creativity. *American Psychologist, 51*(7), 677–688.

Sternberg, R. J., & Nigro, G. (1980). Developmental patterns in the solution of verbal analogies. *Child Development, 51*, 27–38.

Sternberg, R. J., Nokes, K., Geissler, P. W., Prince, R., Okatcha, F., Bundy, D. A., et al. (2001). The relationship between academic and practical intelligence: A case study in Kenya. *Intelligence, 29*(5), 401–418.

Sternberg, R. J., Okagaki, L., & Jackson, A. (1990). Practical intelligence for success in school. *Educational Leadership, 48*(1), 35–39.

Sternberg, R. J., & Powell, J. S. (1983). Comprehending verbal comprehension. *American Psychologist, 38*(7), 878–893.

Sternberg, R. J., Powell, J. S., & Kaye, D. B. (1983). Teaching vocabulary-building skills: A contextual approach. In A. C. Wilkinson (Ed.), *Classroom computers and cognitive science* (pp. 121–143). New York: Academic Press.

Sternberg, R. J., & Rifkin, B. (1979). The development of analogical reasoning processes. *Journal of Experimental Child Psychology, 27*, 195–232.

Sternberg, R. J., Torff, B., & Grigorenko, E. L. (1998a). Teaching for successful intelligence raises school achievement. *Phi Delta Kappan, 79*(9), 667–669.

Sternberg, R. J., Torff, B., & Grigorenko, E. L. (1998b). Teaching triarchically improves school achievement. *Journal of Educational Psychology, 90*(3), 374–384.

Sternberg, R. J., & Turner, M. E. (1981). Components of syllogistic reasoning. *Acta Psychologica, 47*, 245–265.

Sternberg, R. J., & Wagner, R. K. (1993). The g-ocentric view of intelligence and job performance is wrong. *Current Directions in Psychological Science, 2*(1), 1–4.

Sternberg, R. J., Wagner, R. K., & Okagaki, L. (1993). Practical intelligence: The nature and role of tacit knowledge in work and at school. In H. Reese & J. Puckett (Eds.), *Advances in lifespan development* (pp. 205–227). Hillsdale, NJ: Lawrence Erlbaum Associates.

Sternberg, R. J., Wagner, R. K., Williams, W. M., & Horvath, J. A. (1995). Testing common sense. *American Psychologist, 50*(11), 912–927.

Sternberg, R. J., & Williams, W. M. (1996). *How to develop student creativity.* Alexandria, VA: Association for Supervision and Curriculum Development.

Sternberg, R. J., & Williams, W. M. (1997). Does the Graduate Record Examination predict meaningful success in the graduate training of psychologists? A case study. *American Psychologist, 52*(6), 630–641.

Tetewsky, S. J., & Sternberg, R. J. (1986). Conceptual and lexical determinants of nonentrenched thinking. *Journal of Memory and Language, 25*, 202–225.

Tzuriel, D. (1995). Dynamic-interactive assessment: The legacy of L. S. Vygotsky and current developments. Unpublished manuscript.

Vernon, P. E. (1971). *The structure of human abilities*. London: Methuen.

Vygotsky, L. S. (1978). Mind in society: The development of higher psychological processes. Cambridge, MA: Harvard University Press.

Wagner, R. K. (1987). Tacit knowledge in everyday intelligent behavior. *Journal of Personality and Social Psychology, 52*(6), 1236–1247.

Wagner, R. K., & Sternberg, R. J. (1986). Tacit knowledge and intelligence in the everyday world. In R. J. Sternberg & R. K. Wagner (Eds.), *Practical intelligence: Nature and origins of competence in the everyday world* (pp. 51–83). New York: Cambridge University Press.

Williams, W. M., Blythe, T., White, N., Li, J., Sternberg, R. J., & Gardner, H. I. (1996). *Practical intelligence for school: A handbook for teachers of grades 5–8*. New York: HarperCollins.

Yang, S., & Sternberg, R. J. (1997a). Conceptions of intelligence in ancient Chinese philosophy. *Journal of Theoretical and Philosophical Psychology, 17*(2), 101–119.

Yang, S., & Sternberg, R. J. (1997b). Taiwanese Chinese people's conceptions of intelligence. *Intelligence, 25*(1), 21–36.

CHAPTER 8

SCIENCE, POLITICS, AND EDUCATION REFORM

The National Academies' Role in Defining and Promoting High-Quality Scientific Education Research, 2000–2004[1]

Lisa Towne

This chapter briefly chronicles the recent role of the National Academies in promoting high-quality scientific research in education. It begins with an overview of the current policy context as background for a discussion of two phases of work in the area of education research quality that have been undertaken by the National Academies in the past 4 years. In depicting each phase, the chapter covers only a select set of issues treated by the committees of experts who led both efforts. Finally, the chapter describes future initiatives and identifies key issues that are likely to shape evidence-based education in the near term.

The Scientific Basis of Educational Productivity, 185–199

POLICY CONTEXT

High-stakes testing and accountability is the coin phrase of the modern education policy realm. The No Child Left Behind Act of 2001 (Public Law Number 107-110) cements this mainstay of school reform into a set of ambitious performance goals that call for all students to be proficient in core subjects by 2014. The immediate implication of the No Child Left Behind Act (NCLB) for states has been the dual challenge of creating systems to define and track progress as specified in the law and identifying and helping schools in need of improvement. Although these efforts continue to dominate state and local actions, the 111 references to "scientifically based research" (SBR) throughout the law have also started to garner high-level attention. These SBR provisions in NCLB, as well as similar provisions in the Education Sciences Reform Act of 2002 and parts of the pending reauthorizations of both the Higher Education Act and the Individuals with Disabilities Education Act, set standards for the use of research to guide policy and practice in education. A sample definition of SBR is shown in Table 8.1.

Key players in state and federal education posts do not agree whether the SBR provisions were intended to be or are being interpreted as strict legal requirements to adopt only programs with "scientific" backing or guidance as practicable (Viadero, 2004). However, it is clear that the current cadre of education lawmakers and administration officials intend to promote the widespread use of scientific evidence as a basis for instructional and programmatic decisions. Education research and its role in education policy and practice have been topics of discussion and the foci of reform efforts for some time. But its current prominence in federal education law and political rhetoric is unique. And it has reignited age-old controversies about the nature of education research and its applicability to day-to-day education reform.

The SBR provisions are part of a broad-based, international push for "evidence-based practice," which can be traced to the 1950s and 1960s in medicine (see, e.g., Institute of Medicine, 2001).[2] A more recent entrant in this trend, evidence-based education has additional counterparts in such areas as nursing, social work, and occupational therapy. Additionally, the tools and applications of evidence-based practice extend beyond the borders of the United States: the international Cochrane Collaboration (http://www.cochrane.org) in medicine and the Campbell Collaboration (http://www.campbellcollaboration.org) in social work, criminal justice, and education, for example, encourage the development of and house—for use by practitioners and others—systematic reviews of studies that estimate the effectiveness of social interventions. Furthermore, several models that integrate the use of a range of evidence to inform government

Table 8.1. Scientifically Based Research in the Education Sciences Reform Act of 2002

The term "scientifically based research standards" means research standards that

- Apply rigorous, systematic, and objective methodology to obtain reliable and valid knowledge relevant to education activities and programs
- Present findings and make claims that are appropriate to and supported by the methods that have been used

The term includes, appropriate to the research being conducted,

- Using systematic, empirical methods that draw on observation or experiment
- Involving data analyses that are adequate to support the general findings
- Relying on measurements or observational methods that provide reliable data
- Making claims of causal relationships only in random assignment experiments or other designs (to the extent such designs substantially eliminate plausible competing explanations for the obtained results)
- Ensuring that studies and methods are presented in sufficient detail and clarity to allow for replication or, at a minimum, to offer the opportunity to build systematically on the findings of the research
- Obtaining acceptance by a peer-reviewed journal or approval by a panel of independent experts through a comparably rigorous, objective, and scientific review
- Using research designs and methods appropriate to the research questions posed

Source: Education Sciences Reform Act (2002).

decision making are in operation in countries around the world (see, e.g., Davies, 2004 for a detailed description of evidence-based government practices in the United Kingdom).

THE RECENT ROLE OF THE NATIONAL ACADEMIES

In these rapidly changing policy and research contexts, the National Academies have continued their longstanding tradition of providing independent advice to the federal government on matters of science and technology.[3] Indeed, the National Academies have been bringing the best scientific expertise to bear on complex problems since its charter was signed by President Lincoln in 1863.

In particular, the National Research Council (NRC, the operating arm of the National Academies) has a 50-year track record of work in education research and its links to education reform. Key publications include *A Proposed Organization for Research in Education* (National Research Council, 1958); *Fundamental Research and the Process of Education* (National Research Council, 1977); *Research and Education Reform: Roles for the Office of Educational Research and Improvement* (National Research Council, 1992); *Improving Student Learning: A Strategic Plan for Education Research and Its Utilization* (National Research Council, 1999);

and *Strategic Education Research Partnership* (National Research Council, 2003).

Building on this substantial foundation, the NRC's Center for Education initiated a line of work in 2000 focused on defining and promoting the quality of scientific education research. This activity has involved two phases of work, both involving top experts in the field. The first phase resulted in the publication *Scientific Research in Education* (National Research Council, 2002); the second extended this work by convening a series of high-level public forums to consider key issues in more depth. Both are described in some detail in the sections that follow.

Phase 1: Committee on Scientific Principles in Education Research

In the summer of 2000, U.S. Representative Mike Castle (R-DE), chair of the Subcommittee on Education Reform of the House Education and Workforce Committee, introduced a bill to reauthorize the then U.S. Office of Educational Research and Improvement (OERI). In this relatively low-profile reauthorization ritual, the debates surrounding the bill were familiar, with one exception. In the list of terms and definitions that typically make up the front matter of legislation, the statute included definitions of quantitative methods and qualitative methods for education research. Although similar language had crept into federal education law starting in the mid-to-late 1990s,[4] the implications of their inclusion in this bill were different: incorporating definitions of scientific research, methodology, and related technical concepts in a bill that would authorize the activities of the primary research arm of the U.S. Department of Education, lawmakers were signaling their deep skepticism about the quality of existing education research and attempting a sweeping fix by defining what would count toward that end in the statute.

As news of the pending bill reached researchers in schools of education, many researchers were taken aback by what they viewed as a brazen attempt to dictate and constrain the contours of their profession by political forces. At that time, Kenji Hakuta, who was serving as chair of the National Educational Research Policy and Priorities Board (NERPPB), approached the NRC to initiate a study that could infuse the voice of researchers into this and similar initiatives. Thus, the NRC's Committee on Scientific Principles for Education Research was created to produce a scholarly articulation of the nature of scientific research in education and to consider the implications for the future of a federal education research agency.

As is customary for NRC panels, the committee that was convened to take on this charge was a prestigious and diverse mix of experts. The group included scholars from sociology, economics, demography, statistics, cultural anthropology, chemistry, philosophy, history, cell biology, and psychology.[5] Most of them had done research related to education in some way, but few, if any, would identify with one another as part of their core academic circle.

With the reauthorization of OERI still pending, NERPPB asked the NRC to finish its work in time to inform congressional debate on the future of the Department of Education's research activities. Richard Shavelson, education and psychology professor at Stanford University and chair of the committee, and I, the study director for the project, knew that we needed to hit the ground running if we were to have impact on these deliberations. As a result, when planning our first committee meeting, we agreed, as a way to start our deliberations, to ask each member to send us, individually, their first attempt at defining the features of scientific research in education. Given the diverse composition of the panel, we anticipated the responses with some trepidation: would the results vary as widely as the backgrounds of the members? Would we be able to reach consensus?

We were pleasantly surprised. Despite stark differences in disciplinary and epistemological orientation, many of the core principles committee members submitted for this initial exercise were duplicated. In subsequent deliberations, committee members came to agree (often to their own pleasant surprise) that these core principles transcended the scientific study of education. Thus, one of the chief conclusions of the book that would result was reached: the fundamental tenets of scientific inquiry are shared across all domains, including scientific education research. In its final report titled *Scientific Research in Education* (National Research Council, 2002), the committee articulated these commonalities by developing six guiding principles, shown in Table 8.2.

Stating common principles that guide the scientific enterprise illustrated the ways in which scientific inquiry in education are common to other fields. The committee also argued that, although scientific research in education shares these fundamental principles, conducting research in education is different than conducting research in labor economics, particle physics, or cell biology.[6] After some discussion about how to characterize these differences, the committee concluded that the ways in which the common principles of science are instantiated in practice vary by discipline and field. To illustrate this idea as it applies to scientific education research, the committee described the features that shape its systematic study (e.g., the role of values and democratic ideals in the schools; the volition and diversity of people [teachers, students, administrators]; and

Table 8.2. Guiding Principles for Scientific Inquiry in *Scientific Research in Education*

- Pose significant questions that can be investigated empirically.
- Link research to relevant theory.
- Use methods that permit direct investigation of the question.
- Provide a coherent and explicit chain of reasoning.
- Replicate and generalize across studies.
- Disclose research to encourage professional scrutiny and critique.

Source: National Research Council (2002, pp. 3–5).

the variability of curriculum, instruction, and governance across educational settings). The committee argued that these features, although not individually unique from other professional and disciplinary fields of study, are singular in their combination and require close attention to powerful contextual factors in the education research process.

In detailing the guiding principles and the features of education and education research that shape their application, the committee debunked many of the misperceptions about education research that are often implicit in policy debates. First, the committee made clear that methods are the tools of science; they are not science itself. As already described, early standards proposed in education bills defined quantitative and qualitative methodologies as if method alone was the stuff of scientific inquiry and progress. In addition to its careful treatment of methodology in the book, the committee also emphasized the crucial role of theoretical frameworks; the need to identify, consider, and rule out plausible alternative explanations for observations; and the presence of a skeptical community of investigators engaging in an ongoing, professional dialogue to consider how new theoretical and empirical findings fit into or challenge prevailing ideas in the field.

Related, the committee illustrated that methods are used to address particular questions posed in an investigation; stated another way, absent the specifics of the inquiry itself, methods in and of themselves cannot be judged as "good," "bad," or even "scientific." This conclusion was especially important given that much debate about the quality of education research seemed to turn on ill-conceived dichotomies: randomized field trials or not? Quantitative methods or qualitative methods? The committee made clear that randomized field trials are indeed an important (and underused) research tool for investigators pursuing causal questions in education but that no one methodology could possibly be adequate to model and explain the complexities of education *or any other field*. To put a point on it, medical research, to which education research is often derisively compared, also relies heavily on a range of methods, including but certainly not limited to controlled trials. The committee also argued that hackneyed debates pitting quantitative against qualitative methods were not fruitful and that both types of methods could be pursued rigorously. The issues, again, are the appropriate matching of method to question and the role that multiple methods play in strengthening the validity of conclusions by subjecting them to scrutiny from a variety of perspectives.

Finally, the committee dedicated its first substantive chapter to the idea of the accumulation of research knowledge over time. Critics of education research cite the common incidence of two studies addressing the same question and reaching seemingly opposite conclusions as evidence of failure, calling on the field to identify "proven" practices and to answer a research question "once and for all." Similar studies reaching different conclusions, however, are not only common in a range of fields, they are to be expected given the uncertain and nonlinear nature of scientific progress in general and in the highly context-dependent world of education research in particular. The real issue is how and whether these differences are explained or resolved over time. The committee emphasized the importance of understanding research as a set of interrelated lines of inquiry conducted by multiple investigators over multiple years, arguing that such sustained inquiry can reduce uncertainty over time (but rarely does it eliminate it altogether). Highlighting several examples of areas in education research that had some success in this regard, the committee made clear that the field of education would be more effective if it paid greater collective attention to the question of how studies can be integrated to be greater than the sum of their parts.

After just 6 months of committee deliberation, *Scientific Research in Education* was completed in time to inform the reauthorization of OERI, and the committee was invited to testify in front of Rep. Castle's subcommittee to present its findings (see http://edworkforce.house.gov/hearings/107th/edr/oeri22802/towne.htm for written testimony submitted to the *Congressional Record*). Compelling evidence suggests that the resultant Education Sciences Reform Act of 2002 reflected many of the conclusions outlined in the book (for an analysis, see Eisenhart and Towne, 2003). Policy officials and their staffs from both parties have reported the book to be useful in their work crafting and implementing the SBR provisions now omnipresent in federal education law.

The book has also influenced a heated dialogue among education researchers that has reemerged since the SBR provisions began to appear. Many of the issues raised as part of those conversations are treated in a 2003 feature issue of *Educational Researcher* (Vol. 32, No. 7, October 2003), a journal of the American Educational Research Association. Naturally, the vast and diverse group of scholars that make up the professional ranks of education researchers are not of one mind with respect to *Scientific Research in Education* or the broader evidence-based education movement of which it is a part. Generally, many education researchers are concerned about a stifling effect they fear will come from attempts to standardize what science is (and is not) in federal statute and that a narrowly defined mantra of science will be used to marginalize other research traditions. As for *Scientific Research in Education*, some education researchers view it as a balanced treatment of a polarized topic; others see it as complicit in the wrongheaded push to mandate definitions in law.

The committee intended *Scientific Research in Education* to be a thoughtful consensus that tackled some of the fundamental questions regarding the nature of education research. The committee presented the main issues in a report that would be accessible to multiple audiences. It was the hope and expectation that critical consideration of these and related issues would continue, as it has in many instances (for a recent example, see Maxwell, 2004). It is in the spirit of continuous reflection and dialogue that the National Academies continued their work in this important area.

Phase 2: Committee on Research in Education

Scientific Research in Education was released in late 2001. During that unique time in the early implementation of the SBR provisions and the larger evidence-based education movement, the NRC anticipated the need for ongoing, structured dialogue among researchers, policy officials, and other stakeholders to enhance their understanding of key issues and to promote change that would foster high-quality education research. To meet this need, the NRC convened a new panel (with some members from the previous committee) called the Committee on Research in Education (CORE)[7] to develop and implement a series of events focused on important topics in promoting high-quality, scientific education research.[8]

CORE held a five-part workshop series in 2003 and is issuing a set of related reports (see National Research Council, 2004a, 2004b, 2005). The five events were developed to focus on pending policy and research issues and to extend the central themes of *Scientific Research in Education*. Each topic and event is briefly described below; transcripts are available on CORE's website (http://www7.nationalacademies.org/core).

Understanding and Promoting Knowledge Accumulation in Education

Scientific Research in Education depicts research knowledge as developing in fits and starts through a complex interaction among investigators and the theoretical and empirical contributions that shape an area of inquiry. The committee argued that the development of a knowledge base in education that is cumulative—that is, investigations build on, extend, or challenge existing models and findings—is shaped by the nature of education. For example, the powerful role of contextual variables in teaching, learning, and schooling have made the identification of stable scientific generalizations elusive. That said, however, the committee also concluded that promoting a more coherent knowledge base in key areas in education was critical to the long-term success of education research.

To build on this conceptual foundation, CORE designed a workshop to consider how several elements of the research infrastructure—the tools, practices, models, and standards that support researchers and research institutions—could promote the accumulation of knowledge in education and the development of a more coherent body of related work. In this context, researchers and federal officials discussed the challenges and potential benefits of three kinds of efforts: developing common measures of key constructs that could be used across investigations (e.g., measures of socioeconomic status), making data publicly available (e.g., submitting datasets to centralized repositories that ensure confidentiality and privacy while encouraging replication and reanalysis), and emphasizing various ways of taking stock of the knowledge base (e.g., meta-analysis).

Journal Practices in Publishing Education Research

Peer-reviewed journals are key in any scholarly field. Through explicit policies and informal practices, journals influence both the quality of the scholarship in the field and the extent to which the primary output of research projects (i.e., peer-reviewed articles) systematically contribute to a core body of knowledge. Taking its cue from the broader discussion of how to build a coherent knowledge base in education, another CORE workshop focused specifically on the role of journals that publish education research.

Editors, publication committee members, and others involved in the production and use of journal articles considered ways to promote high-quality education research and contribute to the larger body of knowledge about important areas of policy and practice. Participants discussed issues such as standards for publication (including guidelines for abstracts and the development of common definitions for key terms); the roles of professional associations, universities, and individual contributors; expectations for submission of data to promote replication and secondary analysis; and how tenure and promotion policies affect publication in education research journals.

Peer Review in Federal Education Research Programs

In setting out its recommendations for a federal education research agency, the Committee on Scientific Principles in Education Research emphasized the critical role of peer-review processes in the agency and the field. Shortly after CORE was convened, the Education Sciences Reform Act of 2002 replaced OERI with IES, and required that an advisory board be assembled to oversee the new agency's system of peer review (a function similar to that of its predecessor, NERPPB). Furthermore, in the past several years, the importance of peer review as a quality control mechanism had taken on heightened importance across the many agencies in the federal government that fund education research.

To provide a venue to reconsider peer review in this context, CORE convened a workshop that focused on the purposes and practices of peer review in the federal agencies that fund education research. Federal officials and researchers considered a range of models used across the federal government to involve peers in the review of proposals for funding and discussed ways to foster high-quality scientific research. A report with the committee's conclusions and recommendations on this topic (National Research Council, 2004b) can be viewed free of charge at http://books.nap.edu/catalog/11042.html.

Random Assignment Experimentation in Education

The push to transform education into an evidence-based field has brought to the fore decades of debate about the appropriateness of randomized field trials in education. For its part, *Scientific Research in Education* contains a detailed treatment of this method and its role in scientific inquiry in education. Despite high-level debates about randomized designs in education, however, very little attention has been paid to the practical aspects of conducting such studies in educational settings. Furthermore, because very few trials have been done in education (Boruch, deMoya, & Snyder, 2002), the field as a whole has limited experience carrying them out.

As the federal government gears up to fund more trials than ever before, researchers and practitioners alike are largely unaware of the lessons learned through this limited past experience. To bring attention to common problems and successful solutions, CORE convened a workshop featuring researchers and practitioners with experience implementing random assignment studies in urban educational settings. Furthermore, experts reflected on how the current trend to fund more of these studies is influencing states, districts, and students. The committee has issued a summary of this event (National Research Council, 2004a), which can be viewed free of charge at http://books.nap.edu/catalog/10943.html.

Education Doctoral Programs for Future Leaders in Education Research

Science advances when a cadre of competent investigators, working toward the goal of improving scientific understanding, actively contributes to the knowledge base. Indeed, the crucial role of a community of researchers was the central theme of *Scientific Research in Education*. The ways that education researchers have been trained historically and should be trained in the future are not straightforward matters, however. And the advent of evidence-based education has fixed a spotlight on schools of education in particular as the pivotal institution in the training of future leaders in education research.

CORE sponsored a 1-day event focused on the professional development of education researchers, with a specific emphasis on doctoral programs in schools of education. Deans, graduate study coordinators, foundation officials, and policymakers came together to share observations and chart potential paths for progress. In light of the history and nature of education research and schools of education, participants considered how to develop curriculum and methodological training, connect with disciplinary departments, and serve an increasingly diverse talent pool and set of professional interests.

The final product of the CORE project is a report that identifies the key issues raised during these events and outlines the committee's recommendations related to these issues. It is available in PDF format free of charge at http://books.nap.edu/catalog/11112.html.

LOOKING AHEAD

The National Academies have plans to continue and to deepen their role in promoting improvements in education research and systematic connections between research and practice. Two initiatives are noteworthy in this context: the next phase of the Strategic Education Research Partnership (SERP) and the launch of a broad-based initiative across the behavioral and social sciences and education on the nature of evidence.

The Strategic Education Research Partnership is a large-scale, comprehensive plan to engage researchers and educators in a long-term partnership to improve both education research and its use. It is designed to develop the capacity and infrastructure for a sustained effort in linking education research and reform. Over the past 5 years, the NRC has been the home of several related committees that have developed a series of products outlining the rationale, design, and illustrative areas of inquiry and use that make up this proposed plan. The next phase of SERP is to implement the plan. Now established as an independent nonprofit entity,

SERP officials (including Bruce Alberts, chair of the NRC) are currently working with university, state, and school leaders to set up the organization that would form the backbone of a fully functioning partnership.

Related, the Division of Behavioral and Social Sciences and Education (DBASSE) of the NRC (of which the Center for Education is a part) is in the early stages of launching a bold new initiative aimed at continuous improvement of social and behavioral research for policy and practice. Drawing on the multidisciplinary expertise of DBASSE and its boards and committees, this initiative will consider the connections between technical issues—such as evidentiary standards, theoretical and empirical lines of inquiry, internal and external validity, and replication and generalizability—and the use of research in the policy and practical worlds.

What will the evidence-based education movement, of which these NRC initiatives will be a part, look like in the coming years? The answer is, of course, speculative and multifaceted. In a recent paper, I describe some of the issues I believe will define the contours of evidence-based education in the near term (Towne, 2005). One of those issues, of course, will continue to be defining and enforcing standards of research quality. I conclude with a brief discussion of how this issue is likely to be addressed, and suggest that a broader consideration of the relationship between research quality and its use will be critical for the long-term success of evidence-based education.

The guiding principles outlined in *Scientific Research in Education* were not developed to take the place of the current standards of SBR in law but, in general terms, they might be thought of as the scientific counterpart to the politically devised definitions. Comparing Tables 8.1 and 8.2 reveals both commonalities and differences. In practical terms, however, the magnitude of the difference between the political and scientific definitions will depend on how the U.S. Department of Education interprets and enforces the SBR provisions across the many programs it administers. The statutory language in Table 8.1 is sufficiently broad that it leaves open how to apply the provisions in practice.

The input of the research communities in these and future government initiatives will be crucial to ensuring that quality standards are upheld in ways that capitalize on the full range of methods, perspectives, and strengths in the field. Perhaps more importantly, however, will be the less visible but more powerful "self-policing" in which all research fields engage through such formal mechanisms as teaching, manuscript review, and proposal development, but also through informal communications and priority setting in academics' daily lives.

As complex as the issue of quality is as a strictly technical matter, however, the dialogue will need to go beyond it. High-quality research is an absolute necessity for the long-term viability of evidence-based education, but it is not sufficient, and it is related to questions of research use. Efforts to promote the use of evidence in education must be framed in terms of its end goal of utilization, with quality as a crucial—but nonetheless, supporting—function.[9]

Finally, efforts to focus attention on the implications of evidence-based education for the profession of educators will be needed. If evidence-based education is portrayed or understood as merely a federal mandate to implement off-the-shelf packaged programs that have been deemed "scientifically based," then this kind of education will likely be viewed as nothing more than the most recent fad. Evidence can empower teachers and administrators to bring the best of what research has to offer to bear on their practice, surely to the betterment of all. Professional development across the continuum of education careers will need to embody this idea by integrating research—and its application to the practice of education—into its core.

NOTES

1. This chapter draws heavily from work by Eisenhart and Towne (2003); Feuer, Towne, and Shavelson (2002); and Towne (2005). This chapter also summarizes the efforts and conclusions of two committees with which I have served as study director; the Committee on Scientific Principles in Education Research and the Committee on Research in Education. Although I have gained much from their wisdom and guidance, none of these coauthors or committee members is responsible for, nor do they necessarily endorese, the conclusions I draw in this chapter. All errors or omissions are mine and do not necessarily reflect the positons of the National Academics.
2. Fields such as public policy, policy analysis, and public administration have followed a roughly similar chronology (see, e.g., Radin, 2000). Although similar in their aims, for simplicity I do not focus on them here.
3. The focus of federal initiatives related to SBR and of the National Academics described here is on scientific education research. For the Committee on Scientific Principles in Education Research, the Committee on Research in Education, and this chapter, this choice of emphasis reflects a strong belief in the power of scientific inquiry to promote improvements in education. This choice of emphasis do not suggest, however, that other forms of inquiry, including those emanating from historical and philosophical traditions, are less important.
4. Specifically, references to the use of rigorous research and associated definitions first appeared in the Comprehensive School Reform Demonstration Act of 1997 and in the Reading Excellence Act of 1998.
5. Members included Richard J. Shavelson (chair), Donald I. Barfield, Robert Boruch, Jere Confrey, Rudolph Crew, Robert L. DeHaan, Margaret Eisenhart, Jack McFarlin Fletcher, Eugene E. Garcia, Norman Hackerman, Eric

Hanushek, Robert Hauser, Paul W. Holland, Ellen Condliffe Lagemann, Denis C. Phillips, and Carol H. Weiss.

6. Committee member and cell biologist Robert DeHaan conveyed this truth best when he quipped that it was a lot easier to control, and therefore to study, a Petri dish of heart cells than a classroom of third graders.
7. As of 2004, members of CORE included Laurie Wise (chair), Linda Chinnia, Kay Dickersin, Margaret Eisenhart, Karen Falkenberg, Jack McFarlin Fletcher, Robert E. Floden, Ernest M. Henley, Vinetta C. Jones, Brian W. Junker, David Klahr, Ellen Condliffe Lagemann, Barbara Schneider, and Joseph Tobin.
8. CORE is funded by the William and Flora Hewlett Foundation, the former National Educational Research Policy and Priorities Board/Institute of Education Sciences, and the Spencer Foundation.
9. Both the SERP initiative and the DBASSE initiative take up these issues explicitly.

REFERENCES

Boruch, R., DeMoya, D. & Snyder, B. (2002). The importance of randomized field trials in education and related areas. In F. Mosteller & R. Boruch (Eds.), *Evidence matters: Randomized trials in education research* (pp. 50–79). Washington, DC: Brookings Institution Press.

Davies, P. (2004, February). *Is evidence-based government possible?* Jerry Lee Lecture 2004. Paper presented at the 4th Annual Campbell Collaboration Colloquium, Washington, DC.

Education Sciences Reform Act of 2002, Pub. L. No. 107-279, 116 Stat. 1940 (2002).

Eisenhart, M., & Towne, L. (2003). Contestation and change in national policy on "scientifically based" education research. *Educational Researcher, 32*(7), 31–38.

Feuer, M. J., Towne, L., & Shavelson, R. J. (2002). Scientific culture and educational research. *Educational Researcher, 31*(8), 4–14.

Institute of Medicine. (2001). *Crossing the quality chasm: A new health system for the 21st century.* Washington, DC: National Academies Press.

Maxwell, J. (2004). Causal explanation, qualitative research, and scientific inquiry in education. *Educational Researcher, 33*(2), 3–11.

National Research Council. (1958). *A proposed organization for research in education.* Washington, DC: National Academy of Sciences.

National Research Council. (1977). *Fundamental research and the process of education.* Committee on Fundamental Research Relevant to Education. S. B. Kiesler & C. F. Turner (Eds.). Assembly of behavioral and social sciences. Washington, DC: National Academy of Sciences.

National Research Council. (1992). *Research and education reform: Roles for the Office of Educational Research and Improvement.* Committee on the Federal Role in Education Research. R. C Atkinson & G. B. Jackson (Eds.). Commission on Behavioral and Social Sciences and Education. Washington, DC: National Academy Press.

National Research Council. (1999). *Improving student learning: A strategic plan for education research and its utilization*. Committee on a Feasibility Study for a Strategic Education Research Program. Commission on Behavioral and Social Sciences and Education. Washington, DC: National Academy Press.

National Research Council. (2002). *Scientific research in education*. R. J. Shavelson & L. Towne (Eds.), Committee on Scientific Principles in Education Research. Center for Education, Division of Behavioral and Social Sciences and Education. Washington, DC: National Academies Press.

National Research Council. (2003). *Strategic education research partnership*. M. S. Donovan, A. K. Wigdor, & C. E. Snow (Eds.). Committee on a Strategic Education Research Partnership. Division of Behavioral and Social Sciences and Education. Washington, DC: National Academies Press.

National Research Council. (2004a). *Implementing randomized field trials in education: Report of a workshop*. L. Towne & M. Hilton (Eds.). Committee on Research in Education. Division of Behavioral and Social Sciences and Education. Washington, DC: National Academies Press.

National Research Council. (2004b). *Strengthening peer review in federal agencies that support education research*. L. Towne, J. M. Fletcher, & L. Wise (Eds.). Committee on Research in Education. Division of Behavioral and Social Sciences and Education. Washington, DC: National Academies Press.

National Research Council. (2005). *Advancing scientific research in education*. L. Towne, L. W. Wise, & T. M. Winters (Eds.). Committee on Research in Education. Division of Behavioral and Social Sciences and Education. Washington, DC: National Academies Press.

Radin, B. A. (2000). *Beyond Machiavelli: Policy analysis comes of age*. Washington, DC: Georgetown University Press.

Towne, L. (2005). Scientific evidence and inference in educational policy and practice: Defining and implementing "scientifically based research." In C. Dwyer (Ed.), *Measurement and research issues in a new accountability era*. Princeton, NJ: Educational Testing Service.

Viadero, D. (2004). Call for "scientifically based" programs debated. *Education Week*, *23*(28), 10.

CHAPTER 9

AMERICAN BOARD FOR CERTIFICATION OF TEACHER EXCELLENCE

Applying Research to Develop a Standards-Based Teacher Certification Program

Kathleen Madigan

The American Board for Certification of Teacher Excellence (the "American Board") represents a groundbreaking opportunity in education. American Board certification is based on a teacher's broad general knowledge and in-depth subject matter knowledge; fundamental knowledge of proven instructional, classroom management, and assessment strategies; and, for veteran teachers, measured student learning gains. There are two levels to American Board certification: *Passport to Teaching Certification* for aspiring teachers with a Bachelor's degree in any field and *Master Teacher* certification which recognizes experienced teachers for their exceptional subject-area proficiency and strong achievement gains by their students.

The Scientific Basis of Educational Productivity, 201–228

The purpose of this paper is to highlight one of the American Board certification levels—*Passport to Teaching Certification*—in order to emphasize how different types of research have helped shape this new certification process: econometric studies showing that mastery of the subject matter is predictive of teaching success, experimental studies suggesting that some teaching methods are more effective than others, and psychometric studies to develop high-stakes examinations.

THE IMPORTANCE OF TEACHER EXCELLENCE

Of the things we can do to increase student achievement in elementary and secondary education, improving the quality of teaching will have the greatest impact. We know that whatever a student's socioeconomic and family background may be, teacher quality has an effect above and beyond any societal and demographic factors (Ferguson, 1991a; Sanders & Rivers, 1996). The stakes are high. Apart from the important role that schools can play in building a sense of responsibility, duty, and good citizenship, the academic outcome of schooling remains the essential factor for children's future economic success. Research has demonstrated that reading and math test scores are strong indicators of future earnings (Ferguson, 1991b). School math scores in particular have even been shown to be a good predictor of the wages of young adults whose education ended with a high-school diploma (Murnane, Willett, & Levy, 1995).

Beginning with the Coleman Report of 1966, researchers have established that teachers' academic competence in general and subject area proficiency in particular correlate with measurable student learning gains (Ehrenberg & Brewer, 1994; Ferguson 1991a; Ferguson & Ladd, 1996). This research begins to confirm what common sense tells us: effective teachers have themselves "walked the walk" of academic excellence. Careful research on the data from the National Educational Longitudinal Study (NELS) of 1988, for example, has shown a consistent correlation between math teachers who are well trained in their subject and higher student scores on standardized math tests (Goldhaber & Brewer, 1999; Monk, 1994).

Research has also demonstrated that certain pedagogical strategies work better than others, and that the pupils of teachers who use these methods are likelier to achieve to high standards than their peers. One of the largest syntheses of research to determine effective practices completed by Margaret C. Wang, Geneva D. Haertal, and Herbert J. Walberg (1993) drew upon three sources: (1) 134 meta-analyses of 7,827 studies of about 10 million students; (2) content analysis of 86 reviews (leading authorities' summaries of and commentaries on research), 44 research handbook chapters, 18 other chapters, 20 government and commissioned reports, and 11 journal articles containing 3,700 references; and (3) ratings of the learning effectiveness of educational conditions and methods by 34 authorities. In their work, Wang, Haertal, and Walberg (1993) identified the key instructional variables which impact student achievement. For example, well-ordered classrooms and carefully structured instruction tend to produce greater learning gains, especially among disadvantaged students (Anderson, Reder, & Simon, 1998; Brophy & Good, 1986; Rosenshine & Stevens, 1986). Researchers have found, moreover, that a positive disciplinary climate is directly linked to student learning (Barton, Coley, & Weglinsky, 1998; Bryk, Lee, & Holland, 1993; Chubb & Moe, 1990).

We urgently need to get many more teachers of high quality into classrooms around the nation, particularly in challenging schools with high levels of poverty. Nearly 2 decades of experience and research show the potential of alternative certification to help fill this need. Consistently, teachers who are selected to enter teaching through rigorous alternative certification programs demonstrate higher verbal ability and subject matter knowledge than traditionally trained teachers—in other words, in those very qualities that are most highly associated with producing higher student achievement. For example, an evaluation in Connecticut reported that an overwhelming majority of supervisors found alternate-route teachers superior to teachers from traditional preparation programs (Feistritzer, 2003; Klagholz, 2000; Kwiatkowski, 1999). Studies conducted by the New Jersey Department of Education found that teachers who came through alternative routes had higher licensure exam scores and were more likely to stay in teaching beyond the second year than their colleagues who came from conventional teacher education programs (Klagholz, 2000).

Attracting highly talented individuals with the potential to be successful public-school teachers will require creativity and resourcefulness. For example, a 1998 National Research Council study pointed out that there are 20,000 well-trained scientists of an average age of 32–40 with an average of 5 years of postdoctoral research experience, most of whom are in non-tenured academic positions with few benefits, low pay, and little opportunity for tenured academic positions. Identifying similar high-potential subgroups and recruiting them for the teaching profession will likely be a critical part of any plan to address teacher quality nationwide.

HISTORY OF THE AMERICAN BOARD

In September 2001, the National Council on Teacher Quality received a $5 million 2-year grant from the United States Department of Education's Fund for the Improvement of Education, in order to create the American

Board for Certification of Teacher Excellence (the "American Board"). Less than 2 years later, the American Board was launched using a standards-based approach to teacher certification with preparation resources, online advisors, and pioneering new computer-based teacher exams with nationally recognized passing scores in elementary education (K–6), English (6–12), math (6–12), and professional teaching knowledge. Given American Board's outstanding progress, the USDOE recently awarded it a 5-year $35 million grant to implement innovative teacher recruitment strategies, expand subject area certifications, develop preparation resources, create mentoring programs using technology, and fully evaluate the effectiveness of this approach.

Cited in No Child Left Behind (P.L. 107-110) as one of the premier pathways to the teaching profession, the American Board is providing the nation with a new system to certify the quality of both its new and veteran teaching force. The American Board has been designed to identify those teacher attributes that are currently measurable and that directly correlate with a teacher's effectiveness in the classroom. By offering a practical and rigorous alternative route to certification, the promise of a qualified teacher in every classroom can be met without regard to whether a teacher approaches the profession from a traditional education-school background or by way of a different career path.

THE *PASSPORT TO TEACHING* SYSTEM FOR NEW TEACHERS

Passport to Teaching certification is a career pathway for highly motivated, self-disciplined individuals who are interested in teaching and hold a bachelor's degree or higher. *Passport to Teaching* certification recognizes subject matter expertise and the professional teaching knowledge needed for classroom effectiveness. Candidates must pass two separate 4-hour computer-based exams developed according to rigorous standards—the Professional Teaching Knowledge exam and a subject area knowledge exam—using multimedia and simulations to assess complex skill and knowledge sets. For aspiring new teachers wishing to enter the profession from other careers or with backgrounds other than education-school training, the American Board provides a *Passport to Teaching*, valid anywhere in the nation (contingent upon state acceptance), that attests to their mastery of particular subjects and their firm grasp of the professional skills needed for classroom effectiveness. Schools and districts may weigh other factors, but the American Board appraisal system can form the core of a nationwide network of teachers, certified for their competence and united by their firm command of the subject matter.

In order to ensure that teachers with *Passport to Teaching* certification are not only proficient in the subjects they will teach, but also ready to enter the classroom and be effective there, they also have to pass a test of Professional Teaching Knowledge, which assesses candidates' knowledge of effective teaching strategies, classroom management, assessment, teacher–parent communication skills, and school safety issues. The Professional Teaching Knowledge standards are based on a thorough review of the literature on effective teaching and are grounded in scientifically-based studies that meet rigorous standards regarding impact upon student learning.

In addition to multiple-choice questions that test a candidate's grasp of these basic pedagogical areas and a written essay on a school-related topic, the Professional Teaching Knowledge exam requires candidates to respond to classroom situations and challenges through a multimedia platform. Subject matter examinations also use the multimedia platform to assess candidate knowledge. For example, on the elementary education exam, an audio question captures a moment in which a second-grade student is reading to a teacher. The student makes numerous errors in decoding and the test taker is asked to identify the errors and the appropriate follow-up strategy for instruction.

DEVELOPMENT OF AMERICAN BOARD STANDARDS

The development of the American Board standards for professional competency in Subject Area and Professional Teaching Knowledge was comprehensive. These exacting standards represent a consensus of content specialists, including outstanding teachers, principals, administrators, scholars, teacher educators, researchers, psychologists, and policymakers. These individuals, each an expert in a particular area, were recruited from across the nation to ensure the broadest representation of regions, school size, teaching experience, and diversity (for a full listing of the individuals who participated in the development and a complete narrative of the standards for each area, go to www.abcte.org and look under the section labeled "standards"). To develop the standards, group facilitators and content specialists used a seven-step process:

1. Extensive review of state and national teacher certification standards, such as Interstate New Teacher Assessment and Support Consortium (INTASC), National Council for the Accreditation of Teacher Education (NCATE), and all 50 state certification requirements.
2. Thorough analysis of highly regarded state K–12 standards, including Massachusetts, California, and Virginia.

3. Literature review and analysis of scientifically based research that met rigorous requirements in demonstrating a link between effective teaching and student learning gains.
4. Synthesis and distribution of documents summarizing findings (to further educate specialists and offer a reference point).
5. Development of standards and framework over 7-month commitment.
6. Consistent review of drafts.
7. Revision and prioritization of standards during the development of the test blueprint.

OVERVIEW OF THE CONTENT STANDARDS

The Professional Teaching Knowledge Content

Beginning teachers should know a professional body of knowledge that is research-based and promotes student achievement. A highly regarded group of panelists reviewed a large body of experimental and quasi-experimental studies to determine effective teaching practices which have a connection to improving student achievement (see Appendix for a complete listing of studies selected for use in the development of the standards). The panel then synthesized the research to establish what a *beginning* teacher would need to know to be effective in the classroom. Specific standards were created and verified by educators throughout the United States. The standards are organized around five key areas: organizing, planning, and designing instruction for student success; effective instructional strategies; classroom management and organization; monitoring students and working with parents; and assessment.

The examination assesses these standards by combining short-answer questions with interactive simulations that test a candidate's readiness to enter the classroom and respond to classroom challenges. Since career-changers are more likely to need training in professional teaching skills than in subject areas, the American Board has developed extensive online resources. In addition to mastering the question-and-answer component of the exam, successful candidates also have to pass a full-length essay that measures their writing and communication skills.

Elementary Education Content

The challenges of the elementary classroom require teachers with broad competence in the core elementary-school subjects: English language arts—including reading and composition—mathematics, science, geography, and history, as well as deep understanding of language development, phonics and reading instruction in particular. The exam ensures that teachers who pass it possess the essential content knowledge and academic skills to be effective in K–6 classrooms.

Middle-School and High-School Mathematics Content

This subject-specific examination tests the mathematical knowledge and skills of prospective secondary math teachers. All of the branches of mathematics represented in the middle-school and high-school curriculum are tested: arithmetic functions, probability, statistics, algebra, geometry, trigonometry, and calculus.

Middle-School and High-School English

The English examination tests the range of knowledge and skills needed for effective teaching of English composition, critical reading, and literature. Candidates must demonstrate their firm grasp of the elements of grammar, effective writing, and editorial techniques, as well as a deep knowledge of major works and genres of literature. Candidates are required to demonstrate their literary interpretation skills directly in the essay section of the exam. Hiring authorities thus can have clear insight into a candidate's academic readiness, and also into the candidate's ability to help students meet state standards in reading and writing and to guide students in reading and comprehending sophisticated, complex works of literature.

EXAMINATION DEVELOPMENT

Once the content standards and test blueprints were created for each subject area, test items were developed. Hundreds of educators participated in developing thousands of innovative questions using multimedia, short-answer, essay, matching, sequencing, and multiple-choice formats. Each item was specifically aligned with the test blueprint and the content standards. Having well-designed test items that reliably measure the content standards is the hallmark of American Board examinations. Beta testing was conducted for every item. Over 2,000 people participated in the field-testing for the four different content areas. The data from the field-tested items were reviewed and analyzed by panelists representing each content area and outstanding items were selected to create the final examination forms.

It is essential to maintain the security and integrity of the American Board examinations. Among other things, this requires a large number of items from which to draw, so that the content of the test remains secure regardless of how often the test is administered.

Ideally, candidates are able to take the tests whenever they want to, which alleviates the current difficulties teachers face when trying to take less-frequently-administered state tests. Given the intended frequency and ready availability of the American Board tests, six forms will be used for each subject area. To further ensure the security of the test, candidates will only be able to take the test by going to an approved testing center. These centers have protocols in place to ensure the security of the test.

Not only is test security an ongoing concern, but also the quality of the individual items that are created must continue to meet our high standards. One especially powerful feature of the American Board examinations is that the test questions employ multimedia formats (e.g., dynamic graphics, video and audio recordings) to better simulate the daily dilemmas that teachers must face in the classroom.

ESTABLISHING NATIONALLY RECOGNIZED PASSING SCORES

In order to establish the passing scores, several different teams gathered throughout the year to create performance level descriptors, then analyzed the data using the highly regarded modified Angoff rating system to determine nationally recognized passing scores for all four exams. Over 100 participants from across the United States representing all aspects of education determined the national passing scores.

Candidates can either earn a proficient or distinguished score. To achieve *Passport to Teaching* certification, candidates must obtain scores in the proficient range; to achieve *Master Teacher* certification, candidates must receive scores at the distinguished level. Although each exam has its own score requirements, in general, individuals must score at least one Standard Deviation above the mean to meet Proficiency and in some cases three SDs to achieve Distinguished status. Individuals who meet either of these standards demonstrate superb subject area mastery and an outstanding grasp of the necessary professional teaching knowledge—which are predictors of effective teachers.

CERTIFICATION PREPARATION

Each candidate is assigned an advisor (usually a retired teacher) to guide them through the certification process. With the advisor, the candidate completes a diagnostic self-examination leading to the design of an individual learning plan that guides candidate preparation. The advisor remains constant throughout the candidate's preparation, suggesting and offering the candidate relevant resources in addition to providing certification information and advice. Candidates have 1 year to complete the certification process. All candidates must have a Bachelor's degree from an approved college or university, complete an FBI background records check (includes fingerprinting), and pass all of their American Board exams.

ONGOING RESEARCH

The American Board is committed to conducting a longitudinal study that will consist of three parts: (1) a descriptive analysis comparing the candidates and eventual awardees; (2) an impact analysis of their success in producing measurable student gains; (3) the duration of their employment as a teacher or in the field of education.

CONCLUSION

The American Board is an undertaking of major and enduring national significance. It establishes the first national alternative route to certification for teachers called the *Passport to Teaching*, making it both possible and practical for states to meet No Child Left Behind's explicit mandate of having a highly qualified teacher in every classroom. By tapping into the large pool of skilled professionals who have the interest and ability to be highly effective teachers but who did not go through traditional teacher preparation institutions, the American Board is creating an efficient, comprehensive system that will provide well-prepared and effective aspiring teachers with a pathway to U.S. schools and students, whose success depends so much upon teacher quality. Through innovative recruitment and assessment strategies, the American Board will identify a rich source of talented new teachers for our public schools. Using its expert National Advisory Panel and leading consultants in the targeted subject areas, it will design and validate rigorous new instruments for appraising teacher knowledge and competence. Teachers certified by the American Board will have a nationally recognized, portable credential.

Not only will the American Board certifications significantly broaden the pool of talented candidates who can be considered for a career in teaching, it will also represent a critical step in reducing outdated regulations which create barriers, not standards, to entering the teaching profession. By accepting *Passport to Teaching* certifications as another route for teacher licensure, states can focus their attention on outputs, or verifying *what* teachers know and can do, and move away from overseeing inputs, or *how* knowledge and skills are acquired.

APPENDIX: SOME SELECTED REFERENCES FOR THE AMERICAN BOARD FOR CERTIFICATION OF TEACHER EXCELLENCE PROFESSIONAL TEACHING KNOWLEDGE STANDARDS

Agne, K. J., Greenwood, G. E., & Miller, L. D. "Relationships between teacher belief systems and teacher effectiveness." *The Journal of Research and Development in Education* 27/3 (1994): 141–152.

Allen, J. D. "Classroom management: Students' perspectives, goals, and strategies." *American Educational Research Journal* 23/3 (Fall 1986): 437–459.

Anderson, L. M, Evertson, C. M., & Emmer, E. "Dimensions in classroom management derived from recent research." *Journal of Curriculum Studies* 12/4 (October–December 1980): 343–362.

Anderson, C. S. "The investigation of school climate." In *Research on exemplary schools*, edited by G. R. Austin & H. Garber, 97–126. Orlando, FL: Academic Press, 1985.

Anderson, L. W. "Learning time and educational effectiveness." *NASSP Curriculum Report* 10/2 (December 1980) (ED 210 780).

Anderson, L. W. "Policy implications of research on school time." *The School Administrator* 40/11 (December 1983): 25–28.

Anderson, L. W. "Time and timing." In *Perspectives on instructional time*, edited by C. W. Fisher and D. C. Berliner, 157–168. New York: Longman, 1985.

Armor, D., Conry-Oseguera, P., Cox, M., King, N., McDonnell, L., Pascal, A., Pauly, E., & Zellman, G. *Analysis of the School Preferred Reading Program in selected Los Angeles minority schools*. Santa Monica, CA: Rand Corporation, 1976 (ED 130 243).

Aschbacher, P. "Humanitas: A thematic curriculum." *Educational Leadership* 49/2 (October 1991): 16–19.

Atwood, V. A., & Wilen, W. W. "Wait time and effective social studies instruction: What can research in science education tell us?" *Social Education* 55/3 (March 1991): 179–181.

Ausubel, D.1968. Educational psychology: A cognitive view. New York, Holt, Rinehart & Winston

Bain, H. P., & Jacobs, R. *The case for smaller classes and better teachers*. Alexandria, VA: National Association of Elementary School Principals, 1990 (ED 322 632).

Bain, H., Lintz, N., & Word, E. *A study of first grade effective teaching practices from the Project STAR class size research. A study of fifty effective teachers whose class average gain scores ranked in the top 15% of each of four school types in Project STAR*. 1989 (ED 321 887).

Bamburg, J. D. *Raising expectations to improve student learning*. Oak Brook, IL: North Central Regional Educational Laboratory, 1994.

Bangert-Drowns, R. L., & Bankert, E. *Meta-analysis of effects of explicit instruction for critical thinking*. Paper presented at the Annual Meeting of the American Educational Research Association, Boston, MA, April 1990 (ED 328 614).

Barba, R. H., & Merchant, L. J. "The effects of embedding generative cognitive strategies in science software." *Journal of Computers in Mathematics and Science Teaching* 10/1 (Fall 1990): 59–65.

Baum, R. "Finishing touches—10 top programs." *Learning* 18/6 (February 1990): 51–55.

Becher, R. M. *Parent involvement: A review of research and principles of successful practice*. Urbana, IL: ERIC Clearinghouse on Elementary and Early Childhood Education, 1984 (ED 247 032).

Behr, G., & Bachelor, B. *Identifying effective schools—A case study involving Black racially isolated minority schools and instructional accomplishments/information systems*. Los Alamos, CA: SWRL Educational Research and Development, May 1981 (ED 252 627).

Bennett, J. P. "Effectiveness of the computer in the teaching of secondary school mathematics: Fifteen years of reviews of research." *Educational Technology* 31/8 (August 1991): 44–48.

Berliner, D. C. "Tempus Educare." In *Research in teaching*, edited by P. Peterson & H. Walberg, 120-135. Berkeley, CA: McCutchan Publishing Corp., 1979.

Berliner, D. C. "Effective classroom teaching: The necessary but not sufficient condition for developing exemplary schools." In *Research on exemplary schools*, edited by G. R. Austin and H. Garber, 127–154. Orlando, FL: Academic Press, 1985.

Bielefeldt, T. "Classroom discipline." *Research Roundup* 5/2 (February 1990) (ED 318 133).

Block, A. W. *Effective schools: A summary of research*. Research Brief. Arlington, VA: Educational Research Service, Inc., 1983 (ED 240 736).

Block, J. H., & Burns, R. B. "Mastery learning." In *Review of research in education*, Vol. 4, edited by L. S. Schulman, 3–49. Itasca, IL: F. E. Peacock, 1976.

Block, J. H., Efthim, H. E., & Burns, R. B. "How well does mastery learning work?" In *Building effective mastery learning schools*. New York: Longman, 1989.

Bloom, B. S. "Time and learning." *American Psychologist* 29/9 (September 1974): 682–688.

Bloom, B. S. *Human characteristics and school learning*. New York: McGraw-Hill, 1976.

Bossert, S. T. "Cooperative activities in the classroom." In *Review of research in education*, Vol. 15, edited by E. L. Rothkopf, 225–250. Washington, DC: American Educational Research Association, 1988a.

Bossert, S. T. "Effective elementary schools." In *Reaching for excellence: An effective schools sourcebook*, 39–53. Washington, DC: National Institute of Education, May 1985.

Bransford, J. D., Burns, M. S., Delclos, V. R., & Vye, N. J. "Teaching thinking: Evaluating evaluations and broadening the data base." *Educational Leadership* 44/2 (October 1986): 68–70.

Brookover, W. B. *School social systems and student achievement: Schools can make a difference*. New York: Praeger Publishers, 1979.

Brookover, W. B., & Lezotte, L. W. *Changes in school characteristics coincident with changes in student achievement.* East Lansing, MI: Michigan State University, College of Urban Development, 1979 (ED 181 005).

Brophy, J. E. "Teacher behavior and its effects." *Journal of Educational Psychology* 71/6 (December 1979): 733–750 (ED 181 014).

Brophy, J. E. *Teacher praise: A functional analysis.* East Lansing, MI: The Institute for Research on Teaching, 1980 (ED 181 013).

Brophy, J. E. "Classroom organization and management." *The Elementary School Journal* 83/4 (March 1983): 265–285.

Brophy, J. E. "Classroom management techniques." *Education and Urban Society* 18/2 (February 1986a): 182–194.

Brophy, J. E. "Teacher influences on student achievement." *American Psychologist* 4/10 (October 1986b): 1069–1077.

Brophy, J. E. "Synthesis of research on strategies for motivating students to learn." *Educational Leadership* 45/2 (October 1987): 40–48.

Brophy, J. E. "Research linking teacher behavior to student achievement: Potential implications for instruction of Chapter 1 students." *Educational Psychologist* 23/3 (Summer 1988b): 235–286 (ED 293 914).

Brophy, J. E., & Alleman, J. "A caveat: Curriculum integration isn't always a good idea." *Educational Leadership* 49/2 (October 1991): 66.

Brophy, J. E., & Good, T. L. "Teacher behavior and student achievement." In *Handbook of research on teaching*, 3rd ed., edited by M. C. Wittrock, 328–377. New York: Macmillan Publishing Co., 1986.

Brown, B. W., & Saks, D. H. "Measuring the effects of instructional time on student learning: Evidence from the Beginning Teacher Evaluation Study." *American Journal of Education* 94/4 (August 1986): 480–500.

Brown, S., McIntyre, D., & McAlpine, A. *The knowledge which underpins the craft of teaching.* Paper presented at the Annual Meeting of the American Educational Research Association, New Orleans, LA, April 1988 (ED 294 872).

Burns, R. B. "Mastery learning. Does it work?" *Educational Leadership* 37/2 (November 1979): 110–113.

Butler, J. A. *Homework.* Close-Up #1. Portland, OR: Northwest Regional Educational Laboratory, 1987.

Byra, M., & Coulon, S. C. "The effect of planning on the instructional behaviors of preservice teachers." *Journal of Teaching in Physical Education* 13/3 (January 1994): 123–139.

Calfee, R., & Brown, R. "Grouping students for instruction." In *Classroom management,* edited by D. L. Duke, 144–181. Chicago, IL: University of Chicago Press, 1979.

Callaway, R. *A study of teachers' planning.* Paper presented at the Annual Meeting of the American Educational Research Association, New Orleans, LA, April 1988 (ED 292 795).

Cameron, J., & Pierce, W. D. "Reinforcement, reward, and intrinsic motivation: A meta-analysis." *Review of Educational Research* 64/3 (Fall 1994): 363–423.

Cannella, G. S. "Praise and concrete rewards: Concerns for childhood education." *Childhood Education* 62/4 (March/April 1986): 297–301.

Chilcoat, G. W. "Instructional behaviors for clearer presentations in the classroom." *Instructional Science* 18/4 (December 1989): 289–314.

Ciardiello, A. V. "Teacher questioning and student interaction: An observation of three social studies classes." *Social Studies* 77/3 (May–June 1986): 119–122.

Cohen, E. C. "On the sociology of the classroom." In *The contributions of the social sciences to educational policy and practice, 1965–1986*, edited by J. Hannaway & M. E. Lockheed, 127–162. Berkeley, CA: McCutchan Publishing Corp., 1986.

Cohen, S. A. "Instructional alignment." In *International encyclopedia of education: Research and studies*, Vol. 5, 2nd ed., edited by T. Husen & T. N. Postlethwaite, 2852–2856. London: Pergamon Press, 1994.

Cohen, S. A., Hyman, J. S., Ashcroft, L., & Loveless, D. *Comparing effects of metacognition, learning styles, and human attributes with alignment*. Paper presented at the Annual Meeting of the American Educational Research Association, San Francisco, CA, 1989.

Cooper, H. "Synthesis of research on homework." *Educational Leadership* 47/3 (November 1989): 85–91.

Cooper, H. M., Findley, M., & Good, T. "Relations between student achievement and various indexes of teacher expectations." *Journal of Educational Psychology* 74/4 (August 1982): 577–579.

Cooper, H. M., & Good, T. L. *Pygmalion grows up: Studies in the expectation communication process*. New York: Longman Press, 1983.

Cooper, H. M., & Tom, D. Y. H. "Teacher expectation research: A review with implications for classroom instruction." *The Elementary School Journal* 85/1 (September 1984): 77–89.

Corno, L., & Snow, R. E. "Adapting teaching to individual differences among learners." In *Handbook of research on teaching*, 3rd ed., edited by M. C. Wittrock, 605–629. New York: Macmillan Publishing Co., 1986.

Costa, A. L., & Kallick, B. "Reassessing assessment." In *If minds matter: A foreword to the future*, Vol. 2, edited by A. Costa, J. Bellanca, & R. Fogarty. Palatine, IL: Skylight Publishing, Inc., 1992.

Cotton, K. *Classroom questioning*. Close-Up #5. Portland, OR: Northwest Regional Educational Laboratory, 1989a (ED 312 030).

Cotton, K. *Expectations and student outcomes*. Close Up #7. Portland, OR: Northwest Regional Educational Laboratory, 1989c.

Cotton, K. *Schoolwide and classroom discipline*. Close-Up #9. Portland, OR: Northwest Regional Educational Laboratory, 1990b.

Cotton, K. *Educating urban minority youth: Research on effective practices*. Topical Synthesis #4. Portland, OR: Northwest Regional Educational Laboratory, 1991b.

Cotton, K. *School–community collaboration to improve the quality of life for urban youth and their families*. Topical Synthesis #5. Portland, OR: Northwest Regional Educational Laboratory, 1992c.

Cotton, K., & Wikelund, K. R. *Parent involvement in education*. Close-Up #6. Portland, OR: Northwest Regional Educational Laboratory, 1989 (ED 312 030).

Crawford, J. "Instructional activities related to achievement gain in Chapter 1 classes." In *Effective programs for students at risk*, edited by R. E. Slavin, N. L. Karweit, & N. A. Madden, 264–290. Boston, MA: Allyn & Bacon, 1989.

Crawford, W. J., King, C. E., Brophy, J. E., & Evertson, C. M. *Error rates and question difficulty related to elementary children's learning*. Paper presented at the Annual Meeting of the American Educational Research Association, Washington, DC, April 1975 (ED 147 275).

Crump, W. D., Schlichter, C. L., & Palk, B. E. "Teaching HOTS in the middle and high school: A district-level initiative in developing higher order thinking skills." *Roeper Review* 10/4 (May 1988): 205–211.

Dalton, D. W., & Hannafin, M. J. "The effects of computer-assisted and traditional mastery methods on computation accuracy and attitudes." *Journal of Educational Research* 82/1 (September/October 1988): 27–33.

Darter, C. L., Jr., & Phelps, L. N. *The impact of the computer on the teaching of reading: A review of the literature*. Wichita Falls, TX: Midwestern State University, 1990 (ED 326 836).

Denham, C., & Lieberman, A., eds. *Time to learn: A review of the Beginning Teacher Evaluation Study*. Washington, DC: National Institute of Education, 1980

Dewalt, M. W., & Rodwell, F. G. "Effects of increased learning time in remedial math and science." *Spectrum* 6/1 (Winter 1988): 33–36.

Dillashaw, F. G., & Okey, J. R. "Effects of a modified mastery learning strategy on achievement, attitudes, and on-task behavior of high school chemistry students." *Journal of Research in Science Teaching* 20/3 (March 1983): 203–211.

DiPardo, A., & Freedman, S. W. "Peer response groups in the writing classroom: Theoretic foundations and new directions." *Review of Educational Research* 58/2 (Summer 1988): 119–149.

Doyle, W. "Classroom organization and management." In *Handbook of research on teaching*, 3rd ed., edited by M. C. Wittrock, 392–431. New York: Macmillan, 1986.

Druian, G., & Butler, J. A. *effective schooling practices and at-risk youth: What the research shows.* Topical Synthesis #1. Portland, OR: Northwest Regional Educational Laboratory, 1987 (ED 291 146).

Dunn, R. "Learning style: State of the science." *Theory Into Practice* 23/1 (Winter 1984): 10–19.

Edmonds, R. R. "Effective schools for the urban poor." *Educational Leadership* 37/1 (October 1979a): 15–24.

Edmonds, R. R. "Some schools work and more can." *Social Policy* 9 (1979b): 28–32.

Emmer, E. T., & Aussiker, A. "School and classroom discipline programs: How well do they work?" In *Strategies to reduce student misbehavior*, edited by O. C. Moles, 105–142. Washington, DC: Office of Educational Research and Improvement, U. S. Department of Education, 1989 (ED 311 608).

Emmer, E. T., & Evertson, C. M. *Effective management at the beginning of the school year in junior high classes*. Report No. 6107. Austin, TX: Research and Development Center for Teacher Education, University of Texas, 1980 (ED 241 499).

Emmer, E. T., & Evertson, C. M. "Synthesis of research on classroom management." *Educational Leadership* 38/4 (January 1981a): 342–347.

Emmer, E. T., & Evertson, C. M. *Teacher's manual for the Junior High Classroom Management Improvement Study*. Austin, TX: Research and Development Center for Teacher Education, University of Texas, 1981b.

Emmer, E. T., Evertson, C. M., & Anderson, L. "Effective management at the beginning of the school year." *Elementary School Journal* 80/5 (May 1980): 219–231.

Emmer, E. T., Sanford, J. P., Clements, B. S., & Martin, J. *Improving classroom management in junior high classrooms, an experimental investigation*. Austin, TX: Research and Development Center for Teacher Education, University of Texas, 1982 (ED 261 053).

Engman, L. R. "School effectiveness characteristics associated with Black student mathematics achievement." *Focus on Learning Problems in Mathematics* 11/4 (Fall 1989): 31–42.

Evertson, C. M. *Organizing and managing the elementary school classroom*. Austin, TX: Research and Development Center for Teacher Education, University of Texas, 1981 (ED 223 570).

Evertson, C. M. "Differences in instructional activities in higher and lower achieving junior high English and math classes." *Elementary School Journal* 82/4 (March 1982): 329–351.

Evertson, C. M. "Training teachers in classroom management: An experimental study in secondary school classrooms." *Journal of Educational Research* 79/1 (September/October 1985): 51–58.

Evertson, C. M. "Do teachers make a difference?" *Education and Urban Society* 18/2 (February 1986): 195–210.

Evertson, C. M. "Improving elementary classroom management: A school-based training program for beginning the year." *Journal of Educational Research* 83/2 (November/December 1989): 82–90.

Evertson, C. M., Anderson, C., & Anderson, L. "Relationship between classroom behavior and student outcomes in junior high mathematics and English classes." *American Elementary Research Journal* 17/1 (Spring 1980): 43–60.

Evertson, C. M., & Harris, A. L. "What we know about managing classrooms." *Educational Leadership* 49/7 (April 1992): 74–78.

Evertson, C. M., Weade, R., Green, J. L., & Crawford, J. *Effective classroom management and instruction: An exploration of models*. Washington, DC: National Institute of Education, 1985 (ED 271 423).

Fantuzzo, J. W., Riggio, R. E., Connelly, S., & Dimeff, L. A. "Effects of reciprocal peer tutoring on academic achievement and psychological adjustment: A component analysis." *Journal of Educational Psychology* 81/2 (June 1989): 173–177.

Fielding, L. G., & Pearson, P. D. "Reading comprehension: What works." *Educational Leadership* 51/5 (February 1994): 62–68.

Freseman, R. D. *Improving higher order thinking of middle school geography students by teaching skills directly*. Fort Lauderdale, FL: Nova University, 1990 (ED 320 842).

Friend, H. "The effect of science and mathematics integration on selected seventh grade students' attitudes toward and achievement in science." *School Science and Mathematics* 85/6 (October 1985): 453–461.

Fuchs, L., & Fuchs, D. "Effects of systematic formative evaluation: A meta-analysis." *Exceptional Children* 53/3 (November 1986): 199–208.

Fuchs, L., Fuchs, & Tindal, G. "Effects of mastery learning procedures on student achievement." *Journal of Educational Research* 79/5 (May/June 1986): 286–291.

Gall, M. D. "Synthesis of research on teachers' questioning." *Educational Leadership* 42/3 (November 1984): 40–47.

Gall, M. D., Gall, J. P., Jacobsen, D. R., & Bullock, T. L. *Tools for learning: A guide to teaching study skills*. Alexandria, VA: Association for Supervision and Curriculum Development, 1990 (ED 320 126).

Garcia, E. E. *An analysis of literacy enhancement for middle school Hispanic students through curriculum integration*. Paper presented at the Annual Meeting of the National Reading Conference, Miami, FL, November 1990 (ED 331 008).

Gersten, R., & Carnine, D. "Direct instruction in reading comprehension." *Educational Leadership* 43/7 (April 1986): 70–78.

Gersten, R., Carnine, D., & Zoref, L. "A multifaceted study of change in seven inner-city schools." *The Elementary School Journal* 86/3 (January 1986): 257–276.

Gettinger, M. "Student behaviors, teacher reinforcement, student ability, and learning." *Contemporary Educational Psychology* 8/4 (October 1983): 391–402.

Gettinger, M. "Achievement as a function of time spent in learning and time needed for learning." *American Educational Research Journal* 21/3 (Fall 1984): 617–628.

Gettinger, M. "Effects of maximizing time spent and minimizing time needed for learning on pupil achievement." *American Educational Research Journal* 26/1 (Spring 1989): 73–91.

Gettinger, M. "Methods of proactive classroom management." *School Psychology Review* 17/2 (1988): 227–242.

Glatthorn, A. A. *Secondary English classroom environments*. Greenville, NC: North Carolina State University and East Carolina University, 1989.

Glatthorn, A. A. "Teacher planning: A foundation for effective instruction." *NASSP Bulletin* 77/551 (March 1993): 1–7.

Gersten, R., Becker, W. D., Heiry, T. J., & White, W. A. T. "Entry IQ and yearly academic growth of children in direct instruction programs: A longitudinal study of low SES children." *Educational Evaluation and Policy Analysis* 6/2 (Summer 1984): 109–121.

Gersten, R., & Carnine, D. "Direct instruction in reading comprehension." *Educational Leadership* 43/7 (April 1986): 70–78.

Gettinger, M. "Effects of maximizing time spent and minimizing time needed for learning on pupil achievement." *American Educational Research Journal* 26/1 (Spring 1989): 73–91.

Gillingham, M. G., & Guthrie, J. T. "Relationships between CBI and research on teaching." *Contemporary Educational Psychology* 12/2 (April 1987): 189–199.

Glatthorn, A. A. *Secondary English classroom environments*. Greenville, NC: North Carolina State University and East Carolina University, 1989.

Gleason, M., Carnine, D., & Boriero, D. "Improving CAI effectiveness with attention to instructional design in teaching story problems to mildly handicapped students." *Journal of Special Education Technology* 10/3 (Spring 1990): 129-136.

Good, T. L. "Teacher effects." In *Making our schools more effective: Proceedings of three state conferences*. Columbia, MO: University of Missouri, 1984.

Good, T. L. "How teachers' expectations affect results." *American Education* 18/10 (December 1982): 25–32.

Good, T. L. "Two decades of research on teacher expectations: Findings and future directions." *Journal of Teacher Education* 38/4 (July/August 1987): 32–47.

Good, T. L., & Brophy, J. E. *Looking in classrooms*, 3rd ed. New York: Harper & Row, 1984.

Good, T. L., & Brophy, J. E. "School effects." In *Handbook of research on teaching*, 3rd ed., edited by M. C. Wittrock, 570–602. New York: Macmillan, 1986.

Good, T. L., & Grouws, D. A. "Teaching effects: A process-product study in fourth-grade mathematics classrooms." *Journal of Teacher Education* 28/3 (May/June 1977): 49–54.

Good, T. L., & Grouws, D. A. "The Missouri Mathematics Effectiveness Project: An experimental study in fourth-grade classrooms." *Journal of Educational Psychology* 71/3 (June 1979a): 355–362.

Good, T. L., & Grouws, D. A. "Teaching and mathematics learning." *Educational Leadership* 37/1 (October 1979b): 39–45.

Gottfried, A. E., & Gottfried, A. W. *Parents' reward strategies and children's academic intrinsic motivation and school performance*. Paper presented at the Biennial Meeting of the Society for Research in Child Development, Seattle, WA, April 1991 (ED 335 144).

Gottfredson, D. C., Gottfredson, G. D., & Hybl, L. G. "Managing adolescent behavior: A multiyear, multischool study." *American Educational Research Journal* 30/1 (Spring 1993): 179–215 (ED 333 549).

Greene, L. "Science-centered curriculum in elementary school." *Educational Leadership* 49/2 (October 1991): 42–46.

Griswold, P. A., Cotton, K. J., & Hansen, J. B. *Effective compensatory education sourcebook*, Vol. 1: *A review of effective educational practices*. Washington, DC: U. S. Department of Education, 1986 (ED 276 787).

Gursky, D. "A plan that works." *Teacher* 1/9 (June/July 1990): 46–54.

Guskey, T. R., & Gates, S. L. "Synthesis of research on the effects of mastery learning in elementary and secondary classrooms." *Educational Leadership* 43/8 (May 1986): 73–80.

Haller, E. P., Child, D. A., & Walberg, H. J. "Can comprehension be taught? A quantitative synthesis of 'metacognitive' studies." *Educational Researcher* 17/9 (December 1988): 5–8.

Hallinan, M. "Summary and implications." In *The social context of instruction: Group organization and group process*, edited by P. L. Peterson, L. C. Wilkinson, & M. Hallinan, 229–240. Orlando, FL: Academic Press, 1984.

Hansler, D. D. *Studies on the effectiveness of the cognition enhancement technique for teaching thinking skills*, 1985 (ED 266 432).

Hawkins, J. D., Doueck, H. J., & Lishner, D. M. "Changing teaching practices in mainstream classrooms to improve bonding and behavior of low achievers." *American Educational Research Journal* 25/1 (Spring 1988): 31–50.

Hawley, W. D., Rosenholtz, S. J., Goodstein, H., & Hasselbring, T. "Good schools: What research says about improving student achievement." *Peabody Journal of Education* 61/4 (Summer 1984): entire issue.

Helmke, A., & Schrader, F. W. "Successful student practice during seatwork: Efficient management and active supervision not enough." *Journal of Educational Research* 82/2 (November/December 1988): 70–75.

Henderson, A. *The evidence continues to grow: Parent involvement improves student achievement—An annotated bibliography*. Columbia, MD: National Committee for Citizens in Education, 1987 (ED 315 199).

Henderson, R. W., & Landesman, E. M. *Mathematics and middle school students of Mexican descent: The effects of thematically integrated instruction*. Research Report No. 5. Santa Cruz, CA: National Center for Research on Cultural Diversity and Second Language Learning, 1992 (ED 355 117).

Herrnstein, R. J., Nickerson, R. S., de Sanchez, M., & Swets, J. A. "Teaching thinking skills." *American Psychologist* 41/11 (November 1986): 1279–1289.

Honea, J. M., Jr. "Wait-time as an instructional variable: An influence on teacher and student." *The Clearing House* 56/4 (December 1982): 167–170.

Horton, J., & Ryba, K. "Assessing learning with Logo: A pilot study." *The Computing Teacher* 14/1 (1986): 24–28.

Hough, D. L. *A study of the effects of integrated curricula on young adolescent problem-solving ability*. Jefferson City, MO: Missouri Coordinating Board for Higher Education, 1994 (ED 373 051).

Howell, K. W., & McCollum-Gahley, J. "Monitoring instruction." *Teaching Exceptional Children* 19/1 (Fall 1986): 47–49.

Hoxmeier, K. A. *Questioning techniques for teachers: Teaching reading, thinking, and listening skills*. Paper presented at the Annual Meeting of the North Central Reading Association, South Bend, IN, October 1986 (ED 284 186).

Hudgins, B., & Edelman, S. "Teaching critical thinking skills to fourth and fifth graders through teacher-led small-group discussions." *Journal of Educational Research* 79/6 (July/August 1986): 333–342.

Johnson, G., Gersten, R., & Carnine, D. "Effects of instructional design variables on vocabulary acquisition of LD students: A study of computer-assisted instruction." *Journal of Learning Disabilities* 20/4 (April 1987): 206–213.

Johnson, L. C., Johnson, R. T., & Scott, L. "The effects of cooperative and individualized instruction on student attitudes and achievement." *Journal of School Psychology* 104 (1978): 207–216.

Johnston, J. D., Markle, G. C., & Haley-Oliphant, A. "What research says about questioning in the classroom." *Middle School Journal* 18/4 (August 1987): 29–33.

Johnson, L. C., Maruyama, G., Johnson, R., Nelson, D., & Skon, L. "Effects of cooperative, competitive, and individualistic goal structures on achievement: A meta-analysis." *Psychological Bulletin* 89 (1981): 47–62.

Kagan, D. M. "Evaluating a language arts program designed to teach higher level thinking skills." *Reading Improvement* 25/1 (Spring 1988): 29–33.

Kallison, J. M., Jr. "Effects of lesson organization on achievement." *American Educational Research Journal* 23/2 (Summer 1986): 337–347.

Karweit, N. "Time-on-task reconsidered: Synthesis of research on time and learning." *Educational Leadership* 41/8 (May 1984): 32–35.

Karweit, N. "Should we lengthen the school term?" *Educational Researcher* 14/6 (June/July 1985): 9–15.

Kastra, J., Tollefson, N., & Gilbert, E. "The effects of peer evaluation on attitude toward writing and writing fluency of ninth grade students." *Journal of Educational Research* 80/3 (January/February 1987): 168–172.

Kearns, J. *The impact of systematic feedback on student self-esteem*. Paper presented at the Annual Meeting of the American Educational Research Association, New Orleans, LA, April 1988 (ED 293 897).

Keneal, P. "Teacher expectations as predictors of academic success." *Journal of Social Psychology* 131/2 (April 1991): 305–306.

Kinzie, M. B., Sullivan, H. J., & Berdel, R. L. "Learner control and achievement in science computer-assisted instruction." *Journal of Educational Psychology* 80/3 (September 1988): 299–303.

Knorr, C. L. *A synthesis of homework research and related literature*. Paper presented to the Lehigh Chapter of Phi Delta Kappa, Bethlehem, PA: PDK, 1981 (ED 199 933).

Kooy, T. "The effect of graphic advance organizers on the math and science comprehension of high school special education students." *B.C. Journal of Special Education* 16/2 (1992): 101–111.

Kounin, J. S. *Discipline and group management in classrooms*. Huntington, NY: Robert E. Krieger Publishing Company, 1977

Kulik, J. A., & Kulik, C. C. *Computer-based instruction: What 200 evaluations say*. Paper presented at the Annual Convention of the Association for Educational Communications and Technology, Atlanta, GA, 1987 (ED 285 521).

Kulik, J. A., & Kulik, C. C. "Timing of feedback and verbal learning." *Review of Educational Research* 58/1 (Spring 1988): 79–97.

Ladewig, B. "The effective integration of basic competencies into an applied discipline." *Journal of Vocational Education Research* 12/1 (Winter 1987): 11–19.

Lake, K. *Integrated curriculum*. Close-Up #16. Portland, OR: Northwest Regional Educational Laboratory, May 1994.

Lazarowitz, R., Hertz, R. L., Baird, J. H., & Bowlden, V. "Academic achievement and on-task behavior of high school biology students instructed in a cooperative small investigative group." *Science Education* 72/4 (July 1988): 475–487.

Lee, V. E., & Smith, J. B. "Effects of school restructuring on the achievement and engagement of middle-grade students." *Sociology of Education* 66/3 (July 1993): 164–187.

Leinhardt, G., Weidman, C., & Hammond, K. M. "Introduction and integration of classroom routines by expert teachers." *Curriculum Inquiry* 17/2 (Summer 1987): 135–176.

Leithwood, K. A., & Montgomery, D. J. "The role of the elementary school principal in program improvement." *Review of Educational Research* 52/3 (Fall 1982): 309–339.

Leithwood, K. A., & Montgomery, D. J. "The role of the principal in school improvement." In *Research on Exemplary Schools*, edited by G. R. Austin & H. Garber, 155–177. Orlando, FL: Academic Press, 1985.

Leming, T. J. "In search of effective character education." *Educational Leadership* 51/3 (November 1993): 63–71.

Levine, D. "Successful approaches for improving academic achievement in inner-city elementary schools." *Phi Delta Kappan* 63/8 (April 1982): 523–526.

Levine, D. U., & Lezotte, L. W. *Unusually effective schools: A review and analysis of research and practice.* Madison, WI: The National Center for Effective Schools Research and Development, 1990 (ED 330 032).

Levine, D. U., & Stark, J. *Extended summary and conclusions: Institutional and organizational arrangements and processes for improving academic achievement at inner city elementary schools.* Kansas City, MO: University of Missouri – Kansas City School of Education, Center for the Study of Metropolitan Problems in Education, August 1981 (ED 221 636).

Levine, D. U., & Stark, J. "Instructional and organizational arrangements that improve achievement in inner city schools." *Educational Leadership* 40/3 (December 1982): 41–46.

Levitan, C. "The effects of enriching science by changing language arts from a literature base to a science literature base on below average 6th grade readers." *Journal of High School Science Research* 2/2 (September 1991): 20–25.

Lumpkins, B., Parker, F., & Hall, H. "Instructional equity for low achievers in elementary school mathematics." *Journal of Educational Research* 84/3 (January/February 1991): 135–139.

MacIver, D. "Meeting the needs of young adolescents: Advisory groups, interdisciplinary teaching teams, and school transition programs." *Phi Delta Kappan* 71/6 (February 1990): 458–465.

Madden, N. A., Slavin, R. E., Karweit, N. L., Dolan, L. J., & Wasik, B. A. "Success for All: Longitudinal effects of a restructuring program for inner-city elementary schools." *American Educational Research Journal* 30/1 (Spring 1993): 123–148.

Mansfield, B. "Students' perceptions of an integrated unit: A case study." *Social Studies* 80/4 (July/August 1989): 135–140.

Marshall, H. H., & Weinstein, R. S. *It's not how much brains you've got, it's how you use it: A comparison of classrooms expected to enhance or undermine students' self-evaluations.* Washington, DC: National Institute of Mental Health/Chicago, IL: Spencer Foundation, 1985 (ED 259 027).

Martinez, R. "Sparking interest in academics. Welding class helps students improve English, math grades." *Vocational Education Journal* 67/8 (November/December 1992), 34–37.

Matthews, D. B. "The effect of a thinking-skills program on the cognitive abilities of middle school students." *Clearing House* 62/5 (January 1989): 202–204.

Mayer, G. R. "A dropout prevention program for at-risk high school students: Emphasizing consulting to promote positive classroom climates." *Education and Treatment of Children* 16/2 (May 1993): 135–146.

McDevitt, T. M., Lennon, R., & Kopriva, R. J. "Adolescents' perceptions of mothers' and fathers' prosocial actions and empathic responses." *Youth and Society* 22/3 (March 1991): 387–409.

McGarity, J. R., Jr., & Butts, D. P. "The relationship among teacher classroom management behavior, student engagement, and student achievement of middle and high school science students of varying aptitude." *Journal of Research in Science Teaching* 21/1 (January 1984): 55–61.

McGinley, W. J., & Denner, P. R. *The use of semantic impressions as a previewing activity for providing clues to a story's episodic structure*. Paper presented at the Annual Meeting of the Northern Rocky Mountain Educational Research Association, Jackson, WY, October 1985 (ED 266 425).

Meckler, T. *Reading improvement using the health curriculum*. Paper presented at the Annual Meeting of the American Educational Research Association, San Francisco, CA, April 1992 (ED 254 836).

Medley, D. M. *Teacher competence and teacher effectiveness: A review of process-product research*. Washington, DC: American Association of Colleges for Teacher Education, 1978.

Medley, D. M. "The effectiveness of teachers." In *Research on teaching: Concepts, findings and interpretations*, edited by P. L. Peterson & H. Walberg, 11–27. Berkeley, CA: McCutchan Publishing Corp., 1979.

Metcalf, K. K., & Cruickshank, D. R. "Can teachers be trained to make clear presentations?" *Journal of Educational Research* 85/2 (November/December 1991): 107–116.

Mevarech, Z. R., & Rich, Y. "Effects of computer-assisted mathematics instruction on disadvantaged pupils' cognitive and affective development." *Journal of Educational Research* 79/1 (September/October 1985): 5–11.

Midgley, C., Feldlaufer, H., & Eccles, J. S. "Student/teacher relations and attitudes toward mathematics before and after the transition to junior high school." *Child Development* 60/4 (August 1989): 981–992.

Mills, R. S., & Grusec, J. E. "Cognitive, affective, and behavioral consequences of praising altruism." *Merrill-Palmer Quarterly* 35/3 (July 1989): 299–326.

Mitchell, F. *Bridging the communication gap between teacher and student: Composing assignments in the content areas*. Paper presented at the Annual Meeting of the National Council of Teachers of English, Los Angeles, CA, November 1987 (ED 289 178).

Morgan, M. "Reward-induced decrements and increments in intrinsic motivation." *Review of Educational Research* 54/1 (Spring 1984): 5–30.

Mortimore, P., & Sammons, P. "New evidence on effective elementary schools." *Educational Leadership* 45/1 (September 1987): 4–8.

Mortimore, P., Sammons, P., Stoll, L., Lewis, D., & Ecob, R. *School matters*. Berkeley, CA: University of California Press, 1988, 177.

Natriello, G. "The impact of evaluation processes on students." *Educational Psychologist* 22/3 (Summer 1987): 155–175.

Nickerson, R. S. "On improving thinking through instruction." In *Review of Research in Education, 15*, edited by E. Z. Rothkopf, 3–57. Washington, DC: American Educational Research Association, 1988.

Norris, S. P. "Synthesis of research on critical thinking." *Educational Leadership* 42/8 (May 1985): 40–45.

Paradise, L. V., & Block, C. "The relationship of teacher-student cognitive style to academic achievement." *Journal of Research and Development in Education* 17/4 (Summer 1984): 57–61.

Paredes, V., & Frazer, L. *School climate in the Austin Independent School District*. Austin, TX: Austin Independent School District, Office of Research and Evaluation, September 1992 (ED 353 677).

Paris, S. G., Oka, E. R., & DeBritto, A. M. "Beyond decoding: Synthesis of research on reading comprehension." *Educational Leadership* 41/2 (October 1983): 78–83.

Patriarca, L. A., & Kragt, D. M. "Teacher expectations and student achievement. The Ghost of Christmas Future." *Curriculum Review* 25/5-6 (May/June 1986): 48–50.

Pearson, P. D. *A context for instructional research on reading comprehension*. Champaign, IL: University of Illinois at Urbana-Champaign/Cambridge, MA: Bolt, Beranek, and Newman, Inc., 1982 (ED 215 307).

Pecukonis, E. V. "A cognitive/affective empathy training program as a function of ego development in aggressive adolescent females." *Adolescence* 25/97 (Spring 1990): 59–76.

Pogrow, S. "HOTS: A thinking skills program for at-risk students." *Principal* 67/4 (March 1988): 19–24.

Porter, A. C., & Brophy, J. "Synthesis of research on good teaching: Insights from the work of the Institute for Research on Teaching." *Educational Leadership* 45/8 (May 1988): 74–85.

Redfield, D. L., & Rousseau, E. W. "A meta-analysis of experimental research on teacher questioning behavior." *Review of Educational Research* 51/2 (Summer 1981): 237–245.

Render, G. F., Padilla, J. N. M., & Krank, H. M. "Assertive discipline: A critical review and analysis." *Teachers College Record* 90/4 (Summer 1989): 607–630.

Riding, R. J., & Powell, S. D. "The effect on reasoning, reading and number performance of computer-presented critical thinking activities in five-year-old children." *Educational Psychology* 7/1 (1987): 55–65.

Riley, J. P., II. "The effects of teachers' wait-time and knowledge comprehension questioning on science achievement." *Journal of Research in Science Teaching* 23/4 (1986): 335–342.

Ristow, R. S. "The teaching of thinking skills: Does it improve creativity?" *Gifted Child Today* 11/2 (March/April 1988): 44–46.

Robinson, I. S. *A program to incorporate high-order thinking skills into teaching and learning for Grades K–3*. Fort Lauderdale, FL: Nova University, 1987 (ED 284 689).

Rosenshine, B. "Recent research on teaching behaviors and student achievement." *Journal of Teacher Education* 27/1 (Spring 1976): 61–64.

Rosenshine, B. "Content, time and direct instruction." In *Research on teaching: Concepts, findings and implications*, edited by P. L. Peterson & H. J. Walberg, 28–56. Berkeley, CA: McCutchan Publishing Company, 1979.

Rosenshine, B. "Teaching functions in instructional programs." *Elementary School Journal* 83/4 (March 1983): 335–351.

Rosenshine, B., & Berliner, D. C. "Academic engaged time." *British Journal of Teacher Education* 4 (1978): 3–16 (ED 152 776).

Rosenshine, B., & Stevens, R. "Teaching functions." In *Handbook of research on teaching*, 3rd ed., edited by M. C. Wittrock, 376–391. New York: Macmillan, 1986.

Rosswork, S. "Goal-setting: The effects on an academic task with varying magnitudes of incentive." *Journal of Educational Psychology* 69/6 (December 1977): 710–715.

Rutter, M., Maughan, B., Mortimore, P., & Ouston, J. *Fifteen thousand hours: Secondary schools and their effects on children*. Cambridge, MA: Harvard University Press, 1979.

Sammons, P., Hillman, J., & Mortimore, P. *Key characteristics of effective schools: A review of school effectiveness research*. London: International School Effectiveness & Improvement Centre, University of London, November 1994.

Samson, G. E. "Effects of training in test-taking skills on achievement test performance: A quantitative synthesis." *Journal of Educational Research* 78/5 (May/June 1985): 261–266.

Samson, G. E., Strykowski, B., Weinstein, T., & Walberg, H. J. "The effects of teacher questioning levels on student achievement: A quantitative synthesis." *Journal of Educational Research* 80/5 (May/June 1987): 290–295.

Sanford, J. P., Emmer, E. T., & Clements, B. S. "Improving classroom management." *Educational Leadership* 40/7 (April 1983): 56–60.

Sanford, J. P., & Evertson, C. M. "Classroom management in a low SES junior high: Three case studies." *Journal of Teacher Education* 32/1 (January/February 1981): 34–38.

Saracho, O. N. "Young children's academic achievement as a function of their cognitive styles." *Journal of Research and Development in Education* 18/1 (Fall 1984): 44–50.

Saracho, O. N. "Teacher expectations of students' performance: A review of the research." *Early Child Development and Care* 76 (1991): 27–41.

Sarason, S. B. *The culture of the school and the problem of change*. Boston, MA: Allyn & Bacon, 1971.

Sattes, B. D. *Parent involvement: A review of the literature*. Charleston, WV: Appalachia Educational Laboratory, November 1985.

Scruggs, T. E., White, K. R., & Bennion, K. "Teaching test-taking skills to elementary-grade students: A meta-analysis." *The Elementary School Journal* 87/1 (September 1986): 69–82.

Seifert, E. H., & Beck, J. J., Jr. "Relationships between task time and learning gains in secondary schools." *Journal of Educational Research* 78/1 (September/October 1984): 5–10.

Shann, M. H. *Making schools more effective: Indicators for improvement*. Boston, MA: Boston University, School of Education, 1990 (ED 327 559).

Sindelar, P. T., Rosenberg, M. S., Wilson, R. J., & Bursuck, W. D. "The effects of group size and instructional method on the acquisition of mathematical concepts of fourth grade students." *Journal of Educational Research* 77/3 (January/February 1984): 178–183.

Slavin, R. E. "Cooperative learning." *Review of Educational Research* 50/2 (Summer 1980): 315–342.

Slavin, R. E. "Students motivating students to excel: Cooperative incentives, cooperative tasks, and student achievement." *The Elementary School Journal* 85/1 (September 1984): 53–63.

Slavin, R. E. "Ability grouping and student achievement in elementary schools: A best-evidence synthesis." *Review of Educational Research* 57/3 (Fall 1987a): 293–336.

Slavin, R. E. "Grouping for instruction: Equity and effectiveness." *Equity and Excellence* 23/1-2 (Spring 1987b): 31–36.

Slavin, R. E. "Cooperative learning and student achievement." *Educational Leadership* 46/2 (October 1988a): 31–33.

Slavin, R. E. "Synthesis of research on grouping in elementary and secondary schools." *Educational Leadership* 46/1 (September 1988b): 67–77.

Slavin, R. E. "Cooperative learning and student achievement." In *School and classroom organization*, edited by R.E. Slavin, 129–156. Hillsdale, NJ: Erlbaum, 1989a.

Slavin, R. E. "Research on cooperative learning: Consensus and controversy." *Educational Leadership* 47/4 (December/January 1989–90): 52–54.

Slavin, R. E. "Group rewards make groupwork work." *Educational Leadership* 48/5 (February 1991): 89–91.

Slavin, R. E. "Quality, appropriateness, incentive, and time: A model of instructional effectiveness." *International Journal of Educational Research* 21 (1994a): 141–157.

Slavin, R. E., Karweit, N. L., & Madden, N. A. *Effective programs for students at risk.* Boston, MA: Allyn & Bacon, 1989.

Slavin, R. E., Karweit, N. L., & Wasik, B. A., eds. *Preventing early school failure: Research, policy, and practice*. Boston, MA: Allyn & Bacon, 1994.

Slavin, R. E., & Madden, N. A. "Effective classroom programs for students at risk." In *Effective programs for students at risk*, by R. E. Slavin, N. L. Karweit, & N. A. Madden, 23–51. Boston, MA: Allyn & Bacon, 1989a.

Slavin, R. E., & Madden, N. A. "What works for students at risk: A research synthesis." *Educational Leadership* 46/5 (February 1989b): 4–13.

Smith, J. L., Johnson, H. A., & Rhodes, J. W. *Negotiation: Student–teacher collaborative decision making in an integrative curriculum*. Paper presented at the Annual Meeting of the American Educational Research Association, Atlanta, GA, April 1993 (ED 362 488).

Snapp, J. C., & Glover, J. A. "Advance organizers and study questions." *Journal of Educational Research* 83/5 (May/June 1990): 266–271.

Snyder, S., Bushur, L., Hoeksema, P., Olson, M., Clark, S., & Snyder, J. *The effect of instructional clarity and concept structure on student achievement and perception*. Paper presented at the Annual Meeting of the American Educational Research Association, Chicago, April 1991 (ED 331 809).

Solomon, D., Watson, M. S., Delucchi, K. L., Schaps, E., & Battistich, V. "Enhancing children's prosocial behavior in the classroom." *American Educational Research Journal* 25/4 (Winter 1988): 527–554.

Sorensen, A. G., & Hallinan, M. T. "Effects of ability grouping on growth in achievement." *American Educational Research Journal* 23/4 (Winter 1986): 519–542.

Stahl, S. A., & Clark, C. H. "The effects of participatory expectations in classroom discussion on the learning of science vocabulary." *American Educational Research Journal* 24/4 (Winter 1987): 541–555.

Stallings, J. A. "Allocated academic learning time revisited, or beyond time on task." *Educational Researcher* 9/11 (December 1980): 11–16.

Stallings, J. A. "Effective elementary classroom practices." In *Reaching for excellence: An effective schools sourcebook*. Washington, DC: National Institute of Education, May 1985a.

Stallings, J. A. "Program implementation and student achievement in a four-year Madeline Hunter follow-through project." *The Elementary School Journal* 87/2 (November 1986): 117–138.

Stein, M. K., Leinhardt, G., & Bickel, W. "Instructional issues for teaching students at risk." In *Effective programs for students at risk*, by R. E. Slavin, N. L. Karweit, & N. A. Madden, 145–194. Boston, MA: Allyn & Bacon, 1989.

Stennett, R. G. *Computer assisted instruction: A review of the reviews. Research Report 85-01*. London, Ontario: London Board of Education, Educational Research Services, 1985 (ED 260 687).

Sternberg, R. J., & Bhana, K. "Synthesis of research on the effectiveness of intellectual skills programs: Snake-oil remedies or miracle cures?" *Educational Leadership* 44/2 (October 1986): 60–67.

Stevens, B., ed. *School effectiveness: Eight variables that make a difference*. Lansing, MI: Michigan State Board of Education, 1985 (ED 257 218).

Stiggins, R. J. "Assessment literacy." *Educational Leadership* 72/7 (March 1991): 534–539

Streeter, B. B. "The effects of training experienced teachers in enthusiasm on students' attitudes toward reading." *Reading Psychology* 7/4 (1986): 249–259.

Strother, D. B. "Practical applications of research, classroom management." *Phi Delta Kappan* 66/10 (June 1985): 725–728.

Swift, J. N., & Gooding, C. R. "Interaction of wait-time, feedback and questioning instruction on middle school science teaching." *Journal of Research in Science Teaching* 20/8 (November 1983): 721–730.

Swift, J. N., Swift, P. R., & Gooding, C. T. *Two effective ways to implement wait time*. Paper presented at the Annual Meeting of the National Association for Research in Science Teaching, French Lick Springs, IN, April 1984 (ED 260 898).

Taylor, S. E. "The impact of an alternative high school program on students labeled 'deviant'." *Educational Research Quarterly* 11/1 (1986–87): 8–12.

Teddlie, C., Kirby, P. C., & Stringfield, S. "Effective versus ineffective schools: Observable differences in the classroom." *American Journal of Education* 97/3 (May 1989): 221–236.

Tenenbaum, G. "The effect of quality instruction on higher and lower mental processes and on the prediction of summative achievement." *Journal of Educational Research* 80/2 (1986): 105–114.

Tobin, K., & Capie, W. *The effects of teacher wait-time and questioning quality on middle school science achievement*. Paper presented at the Annual Meeting of the American Psychological Association, Montreal, September 1980 (ED 196 860).

Tobin, K., & Capie, W. *Wait-time and learning in science*. Burlington, NC: Carolina Biological Supply Co., 1981 (ED 221 353).

Tomic, W. "Teaching behavior and student learning outcomes in Dutch mathematics classrooms." *Journal of Educational Research* 82/6 (July/August 1989): 339–347.

Vars, G. *Interdisciplinary teaching in the middle grades: Why and how.* Columbus, OH: National Middle School Association, 1987

Venezky, R. L., & Winfield, L. F. "Schools that succeed beyond expectations in reading." *Studies in Education*. Newark, DE: University of Delaware, 1979 (ED 177 484).

Vincenzi, H., & Ayrer, J. G. "Determining effective schools." *Urban Education* 20/2 (July 1985): 123–132.

Vye, N. *The effects of anchored instruction for teaching social studies: Enhancing comprehension of setting information.* Paper presented at the Annual Meeting of the American Educational Research Association, Boston, MA, April 1990 (ED 317 984).

Walberg, H. J. "Synthesis of research on time and learning." *Educational Leadership* 45/6 (March 1988): 76–86.

Walberg, H. J., Paschal, R. A., & Weinstein, R. "Homework's powerful effects on learning." *Educational Leadership* 42/7 (April 1985): 76–79.

Wang, M. C., Haertel, G. D., & Walberg, H. J. "What helps students learn?" *Educational Leadership* 51/4 (December 1993–January 1994): 74–79.

Waxman, H., Wang, M. C., Anderson, K. A., & Walberg, H. J. "Synthesis of research on the effects of adaptive education." *Educational Leadership* 43/1 (September 1985): 26–29.

Webb, N. M. "A process-outcome analysis of learning in group and individual settings." *Educational Psychologist* 15/2 (Summer 1980): 69–83.

Weinstein, C. E., & Meyer, R. E. "The teaching of learning strategies." In *Handbook of research on teaching*, 3rd ed., edited by M. C. Wittrock, 315–327. New York: Macmillan, 1986.

Weinstein, C. E., Ridley, D. S., Dahl, T., & Weber, E. S. "Helping students develop strategies for effective learning." *Educational Leadership* 46/4 (December/January 1988–1989): 17–19.

Weinstein, R. S., & Marshall, H. H. *Ecology of students' achievement expectations. Executive summary.* Berkeley, CA: California University/Washington, DC: National Institute of Education, 1984 (ED 257 805).

Weade, R., & Evertson, C. M. "The construction of lessons in effective and less effective classrooms." *Teaching & Teacher Education* 4/3 (Summer 1988): 189–213.

Willett, L. *The efficacy of using the visual arts to teach math and reading concepts*. Paper presented at the Annual Meeting of the American Educational Research Association, San Francisco, CA, April 1992 (ED 348 171).

Williams, D. *A naturalistic study of unified studies: A holistic high school program.* Paper presented at the Annual Meeting of the American Educational Research Association, Chicago, IL, April 1991 (ED 333 552).

Winne, P. H. "Experiments relating teachers' use of higher cognitive questions to student achievement." *Review of Educational Research* 49/1 (Winter 1979): 13–50.

Woodward, J., Carnine, D., & Gersten, R. "Teaching problem solving though computer simulation." *American Educational Research Journal* 25/1 (Spring 1988): 72–86.

Woolfolk, A. E., & Brooks, D. M. "The influence of teachers' nonverbal behaviors on students' perceptions and performance." *The Elementary School Journal* 85/4 (March 1985): 513–528.

Wong, B. Y. L. "Self-questioning instructional research: A review." *Review of Educational Research* 55/2 (Summer 1985): 227–268.

Wyne, M. D., & Stuck, G. B. "Time-on-task and reading performance in underachieving children." *Journal of Reading Behavior* 11/2 (Summer 1979): 119–128.

REFERENCES

Anderson, J. R., Reder, L. M. & Simon, H. A. (1998). Radical constructivism and cognitive psychology. In D. Ravitch (Ed.), *Brookings Papers on Education Policy.* Washington DC: Brookings Institution Press.

Barton, P. E., Coley, R. J., & Weglinsky, H. (1998). *Order in the classroom: Violence, discipline, and student achievement*. Princeton, NJ: Policy Information Center, Educational Testing Service.

Brophy, J. & Good, T. L (1986). Teacher behavior and student achievement. In M. C. Wittrock (Ed.), *Handbook on research and teaching*. New York: Macmillan.

Bryk, A. S., Lee, V. E., & Holland, P. B. (1993). *Catholic schools and the common good.* Cambridge, MA: Harvard University Press.

Chubb, J. & Moe, T. M. (1990). *Politics, markets, and America's schools.* Washington, DC: The Brookings Institution.

Ehrenberg, R. G., & Brewer, D. J. (1994). Do school and teacher characteristics matter? Evidence from high school and beyond. *Economics of Education Review, 13*(1), 1–17.

Ferguson, R. F. (1991a). Paying for public education: New evidence on how and why money matters. *Harvard Journal on Legislation, 28*(1) (Winter), 465–498.

Ferguson, R. F. (1991b). Racial patterns in how school and teacher quality affect achievement and earnings. *Challenge: A Journal of Research on Black Men,* 2 (May), 1–35.

Ferguson, R. F. & Ladd, H. F. (1996). How and why money matters: An analysis of Alabama schools. In H. F. Ladd (Ed.), *Holding schools accountable. Performance-based reform in education* (pp. 265–298). Washington DC: The Brookings Institution.

Feistritzer, E. C. (2003). Alternative teacher certification: A state-by-state analysis 2003, Washington DC: National Center for Education Information.

Goldhaber D. D. & Brewer, D. J. (1999). In M. Kanstoroom and C. E. Finn Jr. (Ed.) *Better teachers, better schools* (pp. 83–102). Washington DC: The Thomas B. Fordham Foundation.

Klagholz, L. (2000). Growing better teachers in the Garden State. New Jersey's "Alternate Route" to teacher certification. Washington, DC: The Thomas B. Fordham Foundation.

Kwiatkowski, M. (1999). Debating alternative teacher certification: A trial by achievement. In M. Kanstoroom and C. E. Finn Jr. (Ed.) *Better teachers, better schools* (pp. 215–237). Washington DC: The Thomas B. Fordham Foundation.

Monk, D. H. (1994). Subject area preparation of secondary mathematics and science teachers and student achievement. *Economics of Education Review 13*(2), 125–145.

Murnane, R. J., Willett, J., & Levy, F. (1995). The growing importance of cognitive skills in wage determination. *Review of Economics and Statistics* 77 (May): 251–266.

Podgursky, M. & Ballou, D. (1997). *Teacher pay and teacher quality.* Kalamazoo: W.E. Upjohn.

Sanders, W. L., & Rivers, J. C. (1996). *Cumulative and residual effects of teachers on future student academic achievement.* Research progress report. Knoxville: University of Tennessee Value-Added Research and Assessment Center.

Wang, M. C., Haertel, G. D., & Walberg, H. J. (1993). "What helps students learn?" *Educational Leadership, 51*(4), 74–79.

CHAPTER 10

EVIDENCE-BASED INTERVENTIONS AND PRACTICES IN SCHOOL PSYCHOLOGY

The Scientific Basis of the Profession

Thomas R. Kratochwill

The purpose of this chapter is to provide an overview of the scientific basis of the profession of school psychology, with a specific focus on evidence-based prevention and intervention programs and practices. School psychology is an applied specialty, and as the name implies, school psychologists work primarily in school settings, although they are often employed in a number of diverse settings. Much has been written about the scientific basis of diagnostic, classification, and assessment practices of school psychology, but until recently less attention has been focused on the empirical agenda for prevention and intervention programs in graduate training and practice. Consideration of the scientific basis of school psychology interventions and practices is critically important inasmuch as some data suggest that schools are the largest provider of child mental

The Scientific Basis of Educational Productivity, 229–267

health services (Hoagwood, Burns, Kaiser, Ringeisen, & Schoenwald, 2001; Burns et al., 1995). Moreover, there is growing empirical evidence of a reciprocal relationship between academic problems and disabilities, on the one hand, and mental health problems and disorders, on the other. Thus, a scientific basis for school psychology prevention, intervention, and related practices seems essential to the promotion of student academic success and mental health.

Before reviewing issues posed by specific evidence-based interventions (EBIs), I provide an overview of some of the characteristics of the school psychology profession. Next, I briefly review the current work of the Task Force on Evidence-Based Interventions in School Psychology to set the stage for a discussion of graduate training and professional standards in school psychology. Finally, I examine strategies to promote the adoption of evidence-based practices in schools, as well as some barriers to the achievement of that goal.

THE PROFESSION OF SCHOOL PSYCHOLOGY

School psychologists are educated to provide a wide range of psychological and educational services. In comparison with child clinical and pediatric psychologists, school psychologists typically receive more education in classroom management and educational and systemic interventions related to broad educational practices in schools. Figure 10.1 documents the number of hours per week school psychologists currently spend—and the number of hours they would prefer to spend—in their different roles (Reschly, 2003). School psychology practice encompasses assessment, consultation, prevention and intervention, research and program evaluation, mental health services, and advocacy (National Association of School Psychologists, 2003). A more specific review of school psychology practice can be obtained in some of the basic textbooks of the field (as listed in Appendix A) and in the "blueprint" for training and practice by Ysseldyke et al. (1997).

Although school psychologists are primarily educated to work in public or private schools, some work in other service settings such as private practice, colleges and universities, community mental health centers, institutional/residential facilities, pediatric clinics and hospitals, the criminal justice system, and public agencies. According to recent survey data (Curtis, Hunley, Walker, & Baker, 1999; Curtis, Chesno Grier, Walker Abshier, Sutton, & Hunley, 2002), 70% of school psychologists are women and over 40 years of age, 45% work in suburban school districts, 30% work in urban school districts, and approximately 25% work in rural school districts. The number of school psychologists has increased dra-

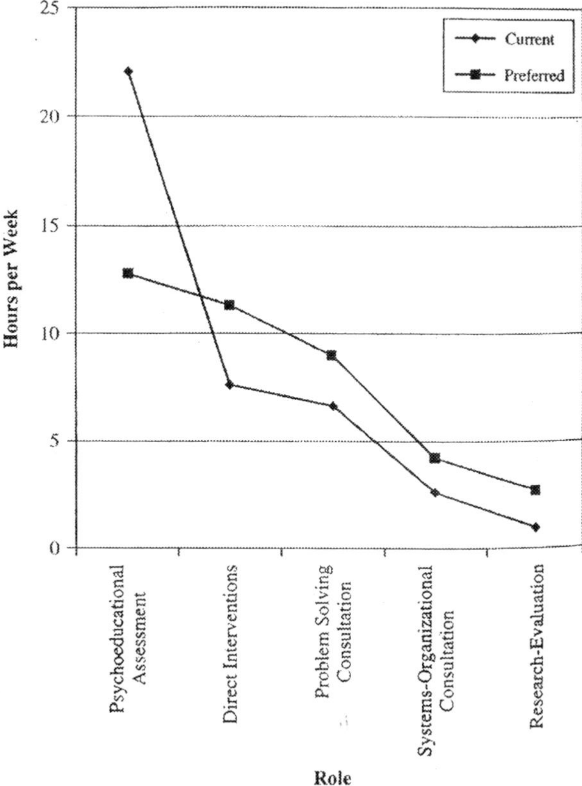

Source: Reschly (2003, Reprinted with permission).

Figure 10.1. Current and preferred hours per week in different roles.

matically since 1977 (see Figure 10.2). A recent membership survey by the National Association of School Psychologists (NASP) identified the ethnicity of school psychologists as 91% White/Caucasian.

School psychology is represented by two major national organizations: (a) Division 16 (School Psychology) of the American Psychological Association (APA) and (b) NASP. (Another organization called the Society for the Study of School Psychology [SSSP] is a research society and sponsors the *Journal of School Psychology*.) Both APA and NASP offer accreditation of graduate training programs. Programs accredited by APA lead to the doctoral degree; programs accredited by NASP typically offer specialist-level training but may offer doctoral training as well.

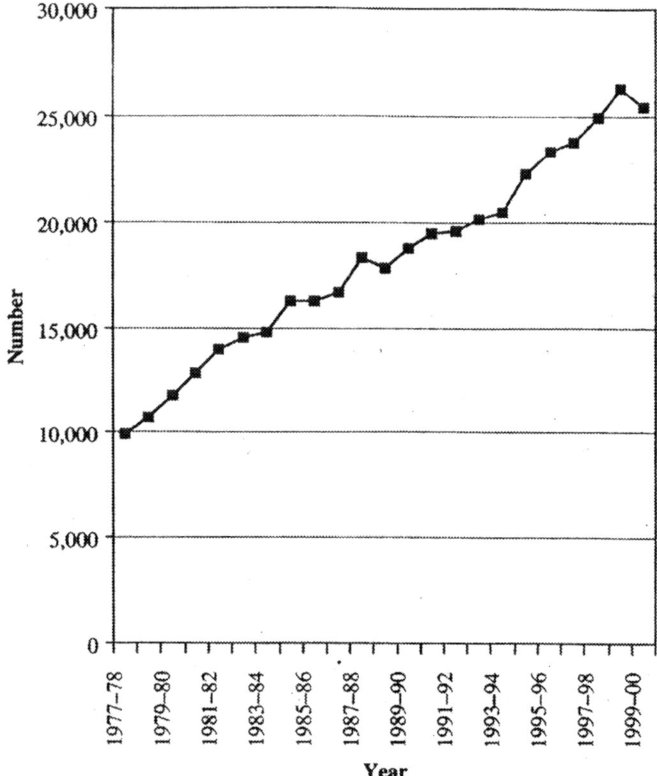

Source: U.S. Department of Education (1978-2001).

Figure 10.2. Growth of school psychology, 1977–1978 to 1998–1999.

The school psychology profession publishes a number of journals. Table 10.1 lists these journals and their circulation and citation rates. A new journal, *Applied School Psychology,* was launched in 2003. The NASP journal, *School Psychology Review,* has the largest circulation and citation rates (Reschly, 2003).

School psychologists who complete graduate training are typically certified or licensed by their state department of public instruction. If they complete a master's or educational specialist degree, they obtain an educational specialist certificate of advanced graduate standing or an advanced graduate studies certificate. Individuals completing the doctoral degree (e.g., the PhD or PsyD) are eligible for the same certificate from the state department of public instruction, which certifies school

Table 10.1. Citation Rates and Circulation of the Major School Psychology Journals

Title[a]	*First Volume*[b]	*Issues/Page Size Per Year*	*Estimated Circulation*[e]	*Number of Articles in 1998*	*1998 Total Citations*[f]
PITS	1964	6[c]	1,300	35	370
JPA	1983	4	500	15	190
JSP	1963	6[d]	1,500	25	338
SPQ	1986	4	2,500	21	220
SPR	1972	4	22,000	31	739

Notes: From *Journal Citation Reports* (www.isinet.com/products/evaltools/jcr/)
[a]*PITS* = *Psychology in the Schools*; *JPA* = *Journal of Psychoeducational Assessment*; *JSP* = *Journal of School Psychology*; *SPQ* = *School Psychology Quarterly*; and *SPR* = *School Psychology Review*.
[b]*First volume* refers to the first year the journal was published.
[c]*PITS* increased the number of issues per year from four to six with the 1999 volume.
[d]*JSP* increased the number of issues per volume from four to six with the 2001 volume.
[e]*Estimated circulation* is based on the *total paid and/or requested circulation* item in the U.S. Post Office from Statement of Ownership, Management, and Circulation published typically in either the first or last issue of each volume. Personal correspondence with the current editor was used to confirm this information.
[f]1998 total citations is the total number of times that an article from the journal was cited in 1998 in the journals included in the comprehensive *Social Science Citation Index* (1999).
Source: Reschly (2003, pp. 431–453, reproduced by permission).

psychologists for school practice. Individuals completing the doctoral degree are also eligible for licensing as psychologists if they meet state and/or national licensing criteria (e.g., those of the National Register of Health Service Providers in Psychology). Typically, specialist-level training involves 3 years of professional preparation or 60 hours of full-time training. Doctoral-level training is typically 5 years or more and requires completion of a dissertation and internship training. Full-time internship training occurs in both levels of graduate program training, and school psychologists must complete at least half the internship hours in a school setting. Graduate study in school psychology is offered through university departments of psychology and educational psychology and through interdisciplinary programs such as counseling psychology and special education. Some school psychology programs are offered in professional schools as well (e.g., Rutgers University).

EBIS AND ASSOCIATED PRACTICES IN SCHOOL PSYCHOLOGY

Following developments in evidence-based medicine, the profession of clinical psychology developed a task force to review "empirically validated" treatments for child and adult mental health problems. The first clinical psychology task force report, released in 1995, stimulated consid-

Table 10.2. Committees and Domains of the Task Force on Evidence-Based Interventions in School Psychology

Academic intervention programs
Comprehensive school health care
Conceptual and methodological issues
Evidence-based practice
Multicultural issues
Qualitative methods
School-based intervention programs for social behavior problems
School-based prevention programs
Schoolwide and classroom-based programs

erable interest in other psychology specialty areas in addressing what has often been called the EBI movement. The Task Force on Evidence-Based Interventions in School Psychology (hereafter the Task Force) was formed in 1999 and is currently cochaired by the author of this paper (for overviews, see Kratochwill & Stoiber, 2000, 2002; Kratochwill & Shernoff, 2003; Stoiber & Kratochwill, 2000). The Task Force is supported by APA Division 16 and SSSP and is endorsed by NASP. Table 10.2 provides an overview of the current organizational structure of the Task Force.

One of the first actions of the Task Force was to commission a committee to develop a procedural and coding manual for use in reviewing and documenting the research evidence for prevention and intervention programs. The development of such a coding system for evaluating prevention or intervention programs is critical to the project of establishing the scientific foundation of the profession (Kratochwill & Stoiber, 2002). The Task Force endorsed the idea that reviewing and documenting the evidence in support of interventions should be an ongoing, evolving activity and adopted the term *evidence-based* to describe interventions judged to have credible scientific support. The criteria and coding structure established in the *Procedural and Coding Manual for Review of Evidence-Based Interventions* (Task Force on Evidence-Based Interventions in School Psychology, 2003; hereafter the *Procedural and Coding Manual*) has important ramifications for the scientific basis of school psychology.

Recently, we reviewed the conceptual, philosophical, and methodological foundations of the *Procedural and Coding Manual* (see Kratochwill & Stoiber, 2002). In this review article, we addressed:

- Domains of prevention and intervention research;
- Key conceptual issues and potential areas of controversy related to the content and organization of the *Procedural and Coding Manual*;

- The rationale for the coding scheme adopted by the Task Force;
- The different approach taken by the APA Committee on Science and Practice in the *Procedural and Coding Manual for Identification of Evidence-Based Treatments* (Weisz & Hawley, 2001); and
- Ways in which the Task Force coding framework can be used to gain information on interventions as they are implemented in school psychology practice settings.

We also illustrated the application of the *Procedural and Coding Manual* to two investigations, one featuring a group design and the other a single-participant design.

Members of the Task Force Manual Subcommittee, as well as others outside the Task Force, were invited to offer their perspectives on our efforts, in recognition of the fact that the Task Force has not always achieved consensus among its members on the content and structure of the *Procedural and Coding Manual*. Reviews of the intervention literature using the *Procedural and Coding Manual* are beginning to appear in the school psychology journals listed in Table 10.1 (e.g., Lehr, Hansen, Sinclair, & Christenson, 2003; Prevatt & Kelly, 2003).

The work of the Task Force in identifying evidence-based prevention and intervention approaches is intended to narrow the gap between research and practice. This gap was described more than 15 years ago by Kazdin, Kratochwill, and VandenBos (1986). The research–practice gap in psychology and education has been attributed to infrequent and sporadic knowledge transfer that does not penetrate the day-to-day functions of practitioners in meaningful ways. The *Procedural and Coding Manual* has established guidelines for the field of school psychology that will be useful to both researchers and practitioners in evaluating and conducting intervention research.

THE SCIENTIFIC FOUNDATION OF THE PROFESSION: TRAINING AND PRACTICE IN EBIS

The scientific foundation of the school psychology profession can be evaluated, in part, by examining EBI practices in both graduate training programs and the practice of psychology in schools and other applied settings. In this section, I provide an overview of recent survey data on EBI practices in these two domains.

Training in Graduate Programs

The Task Force sponsored a survey of graduate programs in school psychology to determine what they are teaching about EBIs (Shernoff, Kratochwill, & Stoiber, 2003). The purpose of the study was to investigate the integration of EBI training in school psychology graduate programs and to understand any barriers to such training. The study addressed the following research questions:

1. What percentage of school psychology training directors are *familiar* with the EBIs included in the survey and endorse student exposure to those EBIs? In addition, how *important* are the EBIs to the training of school psychology graduate students?
2. What do training directors identify as the most serious *challenges* to providing training in EBIs?
3. What percentage of training directors report that programs teach the *criteria* developed by Divisions 12, 16, and 53 of the APA for evaluating the quality of intervention research, and how important are the criteria in evaluating the quality of intervention outcome studies?

Surveys were sent to 217 school psychology training directors listed in the *Directory of School Psychology Graduate Programs*[1] (Thomas, 1998). A total of 97 surveys were returned, representing a 44% return rate. Table 10.3 illustrates the demographic characteristics of the training programs surveyed. These data indicated that the most frequent degree offered was specialist (30%), followed by specialist and doctorate (17.5%), and master's (16.5%). The most common training philosophy embraced the scientist–practitioner model (43.3%); and behavioral/cognitive–behavioral theory (46.4%) was the most common theoretical orientation.

The first section of the survey included a list of interventions already identified as evidence-based by APA Division 12 (Society of Clinical Psychology) and APA Division 53 (Society of Clinical Child and Adolescent Psychology) and was developed to obtain responses to the first research question. In this study, EBIs were defined as interventions determined to be effective by highly regarded scientific methods. The list of interventions came from literature reviews and meta-analytic studies that identified "empirically supported" interventions for children with behavior problems and attention deficit hyperactivity disorder. These interventions were selected because of their particular relevance to the practice of school psychology. A brief explanation of the intervention and a citation of the major outcome studies associated with the intervention were also included on the survey. Three fictitious interventions were also included in the survey to detect acquiescence, social desirability, or the deliberate faking of responses.

For the actual ratings, two constructs guided the development of the first section of the survey. The first construct targeted training directors'

Table 10.3. Demographic Characteristics of Training Programs

Variable	*Frequency N*	*Percentage of Those Responding*
Degree(s) offered		
Master's (36, 48, or 60 hrs.)	16	16.5
Specialist	29	30
Doctorate	12	12.4
Master's + specialist	8	8.2
Master's + doctorate	11	11
Specialist + doctorate	17	17.5
Master's + specialist + doctorate	4	4.1
Accreditation status		
State dept. accreditation	17	17.5
NASP/NCATE	15	15.5
APA	3	3.1
State dept. accreditation + NASP/NCATE	32	33
State dept. accreditation + APA	2	2.1
NASP/NCATE + APA	5	5.2
State dept. accreditation + APA + NASP/NCATE	22	22.7
NCATE	1	1
Training philosophy		
Practitioner	16	16.5
Practitioner–scholar	9	9.3
Practitioner–scientist	21	21.6
Scholar–practitioner	2	2.1
Scientist–practitioner	42	43.3
Scientist–scholar–practitioner	2	2.1
Theorist–practitioner	1	1
Other	4	4.1
Theoretical approach		
Behavioral/cognitive behavioral	45	46.4
Eclectic	34	35
Ecological	8	8.2
Humanistic/interpersonal	2	2.1
Psychodynamic	3	3.1
Other	5	5.2
Specialty training offered[a]		
None	66	69
Clinical–school	2	2.1
Counseling–school	13	13.4
Counseling–clinical–school	6	6.2
Other	8	8.2

Note: NASP = National Association of School Psychologists; NCATE = National Council for Accreditation of Teacher Education; APA = American Psychological Association.
[a]Two programs lacked data for this variable.
Source: Shernoff, Kratochwill, and Stoiber (2003, pp. 467–583; copyright 2004 by Elsiver Science, Reprinted with permission).

familiarity with the interventions listed. Directors were instructed to mark *not familiar* if they had never heard of the intervention, *somewhat familiar* if they were familiar with the general techniques and principles of the intervention, and *familiar* if they were familiar with the intervention. The second construct targeted training directors' perceptions regarding student *exposure* to and experience with the EBIs listed on the survey. Thus, directors were asked to indicate the level of exposure students received for each intervention (i.e., *no exposure, exposure, experience, N/A*). The exposure ratings were based on a comprehensive model of training developed by the APA for approval of doctoral programs. *Exposure* was defined as learning about the intervention in a didactic seminar or through observation in an applied setting. *Experience* was defined as practicing the intervention in a case, practicum, or research project. If an intervention was not familiar, respondents marked N/A under "Level of Exposure" but still provided an importance rating based on the description of the intervention. Respondents rated the importance of the intervention to the training of school psychologists using a 4-point Likert scale, with response choices ranging from *not important* to *critical*. Respondents were also asked to indicate other EBIs that were taught in their program but not included in the survey. This procedure was used to avoid underestimating EBI training that occurs in school psychology programs and to capture interventions for which school psychology programs provide training that were not identified by APA Divisions 12 and 53 (e.g., academic interventions, prevention programs).

The second section of the survey, developed to obtain responses to the second research question, focused on identifying the challenges training programs face and the resources such programs need to include EBIs in their curriculum. Directors were asked to rate the seriousness of different challenges to providing training in EBIs, such as lack of time, financial constraints, lack of information about EBIs, the need for faculty training in EBIs, and faculty resistance to using or teaching EBIs. These challenges were selected based on a review of the literature related to EBI training. A 4-point Likert scale was used, with response choices ranging from *not a problem* to *serious*. Directors were also asked to note any additional challenges to providing EBI training that were not covered by the survey.

The third section of the survey addressed the criteria identified by APA Divisions 12, 16, and 53 as critical for evaluating the quality of intervention research and was developed to obtain responses to the third research question. Directors indicated which criteria were taught (i.e., *Yes* or *No*) and rated the importance of the criteria for evaluating the quality of intervention outcome studies (i.e., *not important* to *critical)*.

It should be noted that a high percentage of the directors (*M*% = 70) rated the fictitious EBIs as *not familiar* (range, 65% to 80%). In addition, a high percentage of the directors (*M*% = 82) rated students as receiving *no exposure* to those fictitious interventions (range, 81% to 86%). Low levels of familiarity with and exposure to these fictitious interventions increase confidence that acquiescence, social desirability, and the faking of responses were not sources of systematic error in this study. Directors who claimed familiarity with or student exposure to those fictitious interventions were excluded from the analyses.

Familiarity With EBIs

Table 10.4 presents the percentage of directors who indicated being familiar with each of the EBIs listed on the survey. The three most familiar interventions were Rational-Emotive Therapy (familiar to 76% of directors), Behavior Modification Across Home and School (familiar to 58% of directors), and Parent Training (familiar to 54% of directors).

Table 10.4 also documents that only 18% of directors were familiar with Time-Out Plus Signal Seat, only 17% were familiar with Multisystemic Therapy, and only 9% were familiar with the Delinquency Prevention Program. When averaging across all interventions, 29% of directors reported being *not familiar*, 30% reported being *somewhat familiar*, and 41% reported being *familiar* with the EBIs listed on the survey.

Exposure to and Experience With EBIs

With regard to exposure (i.e., learning about the intervention in didactic seminars or through observation in applied settings), Table 10.4 shows that, as reported by training directors, students were most often exposed to Anger Control Training With Stress Inoculation (reported by 63% of directors), Assertiveness Training (reported by 60% of directors), and Problem-Solving Skills Training (reported by 57% of directors). With regard to experience (i.e., practicing the intervention in a case, practicum, or research project), Table 10.4 documents that, as reported by training directors, school psychology graduate students received the most experience with two interventions, both titled Behavior Modification Across Home and School (reported by 40% and 35% of directors, respectively). On the other hand, small percentages of directors reported that graduate students received direct experience with the Videotape Modeling Parent Training Program (8%), Multisystemic Therapy (2%), and the Delinquency Prevention Program (1%). When averaging across all EBIs, 41% of directors reported that students received *no exposure*, 39% reported students received *exposure*, and 30% reported students received *experience* with the EBIs listed on the survey. As a whole, directors reported that EBI training occurred more frequently in the context of didactic

Table 10.4. Percentage of Training Directors Reporting Familiarity, Exposure, and Experience With EBIs

EBI	*Familiar*	*Exposure*	*Experience*
Rational-Emotive Therapy (Block, 1978)	76	55	25
Behavior Modification Across Home and School (Gittleman et al., 1980)	58	40	40
Parent Training Program (Patterson & Gullion, 1968)	54	54	23
Assertiveness Training (Huey & Rank, 1984)	53	60	12v
Behavior Modification Across Home and School (O'Leary et al., 1976)	52	36	35
Parent Training Program (Anastopoulos et al., 1993)	52	48	22
Problem-Solving Skills Training (Kazdin et al., 1987)	47	57	27
Helping the Non-Compliant Child (Peed et al., 1977)	43	42	14
Anger Control Training With Stress Inoculation (Feindler et al., 1984)	31	63	9
Parent–Child Interaction Therapy (Eyberg et al., 1995)	27	27	10
Videotape Modeling Parent Training Program (Webster-Stratton, 1994)	26	25	8
Anger Coping Therapy (Lochman et al., 1989)	26	27	12
Behavioral Parent Training (Pisterman et al., 1992)	23	34	11
Behavioral Parent Training Plus Self-Control Training (Horn et al., 1990)	23	34	11
Time-Out Plus Signal Seat (Hamilton & MacQuiddy, 1984)	18	25	10
Multisystemic Therapy (Henggeler et al., 1992)	17	27	2
Delinquency Prevention Program (Tremblay et al., 1995)	9	16	1

Note: Familiar = director's familiarity with the specific intervention referenced in the survey. Exposure = director's perceptions regarding student's level of exposure to the intervention through didactic seminar or observation in an applied setting. Experience = director's perceptions regarding student's experience practicing the EBI in a case, practicum, or research project.
Source: Shernoff, Kratochwill, and Stoiber (2003, pp. 467–483; copyright 2004 by Elsiver Science, Reprinted with permission).

course work or observation in an applied setting than it did through actual experience.

Additional Interventions Not Covered by the Survey

As noted earlier, training directors were given the opportunity to list EBIs that were taught in training programs but not covered by our survey. EBIs listed by directors included Skillstreaming the Adolescent: A Structured Learning Approach to Teaching Prosocial Skills (n = 6), Behavioral Consultation (n = 4), I Can Problem Solve: An Interpersonal Cognitive Problem-Solving Program (n = 4), behavior modification (n = 4), Aggression Replacement Training (n = 3), Defiant Children: A Clinician's Manual for Parent Training (n = 3), and academic interventions (n = 3).

Importance of EBIs

Respondents rated the importance of the EBIs to the training of school psychologists on a 4-point scale, with choices ranging from 1 (*not important*) to 4 (*critical*). Respondents rated all of the EBIs as either *somewhat important* or *important*. Behavior Modification Across Home and School received a high importance rating (M = 2.8, SD = .87), as did a similar behavioral intervention of the same title (M = 2.8, SD = .87) and Problem-Solving Skills Training (M = 2.8, SD = .72). The lowest importance ratings were received by Time-Out Plus Signal Seat (M = 2.1, SD = .84), Multisystemic Therapy (M = 2.1, SD = .75), and Parent–Child Interaction Therapy (M = 2.2, SD = .86).

Challenges to Providing Training in EBIs

Respondents rated the seriousness of different challenges to providing training in EBIs (i.e., lack of time, financial constraints, lack of information about EBIs, the need for faculty training in EBIs, and faculty resistance to using or teaching EBIs) on a 4-point scale (1 = *not a problem*, 2 = *small*, 3 = *moderate*, 4 = *serious*). Lack of time was rated the most serious challenge to EBI training (M = 3.0, SD = 1.0), followed by financial constraints (M = 2.7, SD = 1.0), need for faculty training (M = 2.4, SD = 1.0), and lack of information related to using or teaching EBIs (M = 2.2, SD = .95). Faculty resistance to using or teaching EBIs was rated as the least serious challenge (M = 1.7, SD = .91), and none of the mean challenge ratings fell in the serious range. Respondents were also given the opportunity to list challenges not covered by our survey. Several responses related to the nature of the current school psychology curriculum and perceptions that the curriculum is inflexible. For example, respondents rated "other required course work," "resistance to changing the curriculum," and "curriculum overly focused on assessment" as serious challenges. In addition, two directors in the sample viewed internship sites as responsible for students' acquisition of information and training on EBIs.

Criteria for Evaluating the Quality of Intervention Research

Overall, high percentages of directors (range, 75% to 100%) reported that students were taught to apply the criteria developed by APA Divisions 12, 16, and 53 when evaluating intervention outcome research. This finding suggests that, according to directors, school psychology training programs adequately cover these criteria. Criteria for which the lowest percentage of directors endorsed teaching students included "adherence to intervention manuals" (75%), "implementation fidelity" (81%), and "evaluating whether the intervention was more effective than a control or equivalent to an established intervention" (83%). Directors were also asked to rate the importance of the criteria developed by these professional organizations to evaluate the quality of intervention research, using a 4-point Likert scale with response choices ranging from 1 = *not important* to 4 = *critical.* All of the criteria were rated as falling between important and critical (see Table 10.5). Directors rated "strengths and weaknesses of the research design" as the most important criterion (M = 3.7, SD = .63), followed by "findings support the intervention" (M = 3.6, SD = .61) and "reliable baseline established" (M = 3.5, SD = .68). "Exter-

Table 10.5. Percentage of Training Directors Endorsing Teaching Each Criterion and Mean Importance Ratings of Each Criterion

Criterion	*Percentage*	*Mean Importance Ratings (SD)*
Findings support intervention	99	3.6 (.61)
Random assignment	99	3.4 (.68)
Statistical significance	99	3.4 (.73)
Strengths and weaknesses of research designs	98	3.7 (.63)
Strengths and weaknesses of comparison groups	98	3.3 (.71)
Importance of sample size, power, and control of Type I errors	98	3.4 (.70)
Replication	97	3.2 (.79)
Reliable baseline established	96	3.5 (.68)
Site or setting of implementation	94	3.1 (.79)
Clinical significance	93	3.5 (.68)
External validity	91	3.2 (.74)
Durability of intervention effects	87	3.1 (.74)
Intervention more effective than control or equivalent to an established intervention	83	3.4 (.67)
Implementation fidelity	81	3.2 (.76)
Adherence to intervention manuals	75	3.2 (.76)

Note: Respondents indicated whether the criterion was taught (i.e., *Yes* or *No*) and how important the criterion was to an evaluation of the quality of intervention research (i.e., 1 = *not important* to 4 = *critical*).

Source: Shernoff, Kratochwill, and Stoiber (2003, pp. 467–483; copyright 2004 by Elsiver Science, reprinted with permission).

nal validity" (M = 3.2, SD = .74), "replication of the intervention" (M = 3.2, SD = .79), and "site or setting of implementation" (M = 3.1, SD = .79) were rated as less important than the other criteria listed in the survey.

Overall View of EBIs

Training directors strongly endorsed the development and use of EBIs in the field of school psychology. For example, the development and use of EBIs was judged to be "good" or "very good" for the field of school psychology by 31% and 65% of the sample, respectively.

Implications and future directions

Results of the Shernoff et al. (2003) survey indicated:

- A relatively low percentage of school psychology graduate training directors were familiar with the EBIs included in the survey;
- Exposure to the EBIs occurred more frequently in course work then in practice experience;
- EBIs were rated as either somewhat important or important;
- Lack of time was rated as the most serious challenge to EBI training; and
- A high percentage of training directors reported that students were taught to apply the criteria developed by professional organizations in psychology and education when evaluating intervention outcome research.

As noted earlier, a number of interventions considered evidence-based by the training directors fell outside the EBIs incorporated in the survey. Some of these interventions, such as Skillstreaming the Adolescent and A Clinician's Manual for Parent Training, actually have a weak evidence base. It is unclear from the survey what criteria training directors invoked in determining these interventions to be evidence-based.

Currently, there is no formal requirement within school psychology training programs to mandate the teaching of EBIs. It is likely with the EBI movement within psychology and education that there will be a growing commitment to include scientifically supportable interventions in the curriculum. Moreover, a number of graduate training programs embrace a scientist–practitioner model (or a variant of that model, such as the scientist–scholar–practitioner model). These graduate programs are perhaps the most likely to embrace an evidence-based practice framework in future graduate training.

Evidence-Based Practices in Schools

Several recent surveys of evidence-based practices in schools do not paint a very positive picture. Ringwalt et al. (2002) assessed the prevalence of substance abuse curricula in U.S. public and private schools that include middle school grades. The respondents comprised the lead staff who taught substance abuse prevention in a representative sample of 1,905 public and private schools. Data were collected in 1999 through a self-administered survey. Ringwalt et al. found that 26.8% of the schools, including 34.6% of the public schools and 12.6% of the private schools, used at least 1 of the 10 effective curricula specified. Over two thirds of schools reported using more than one curriculum, and almost half reported using three or more. Results of the study suggest that many of our nation's middle schools continue to implement curricula that are either untested or ineffective.

Chafouleas, Weinstein, and Elinoff (2003) investigated school psychologists' use of research in practice through an examination of knowledge of effective interventions, actual use of effective interventions, and desire to use effective interventions. Barriers to the use of the intervention strategies were also explored. The authors found similar patterns across three intervention areas (cognitive behavioral strategies, social skills training, and teacher consultation). Specifically, skill and use were closely matched, and respondents indicated they would like to use the strategies with greater frequency. As in the Shernoff et al. study (2004), limited time was the top-rated barrier to the use of all intervention strategies. However, for cognitive behavior strategies and social skills training, training and the ability to adapt interventions to the school setting were significant factors in limiting use; lack of support was indicated as a significant barrier to the use of teacher consultation, suggesting some systemic support issues may be important.

We are currently conducting Task Force–sponsored surveys (a) to determine school psychologists' awareness of practice guidelines (White & Kratochwill, 2004) and (b) to examine practitioners' use of EBI manuals in their practice (Kumke & Kratochwill, 2004).

The White study investigated school psychologists' familiarity, use, and attitude towards treatment guidelines. Specifically, this study sought to (a) understand the unique challenges school psychologists face in implementing treatment guidelines, (b) determine school psychologists' general familiarity and confidence in existing treatment guidelines, and (c) uncover the contextual factors that affect school psychologists' use of and attitude towards treatment guidelines. Survey information was obtained from 151 practicing school psychologists affiliated with the National Association of School Psychologists. Results indicated that most of these practicing school psychologists were not very familiar with existing treatment guidelines relevant to the practice of school psychology, and rarely applied guideline recommendations to actual cases. Personal experience was found to have the most influence on practitioners' treatment decisions, whereas treatment guidelines, journal articles, and research syntheses had very little influence. However, respondents had a very positive attitude regarding the future development of treatment guidelines for school-based interventions. The vast majority of practitioners supported the development of treatment guidelines for school-based interventions regardless of their level of training, graduate training model, or theoretical orientation.

The Kumke study was designed to investigate the current use of EBIs and treatment manuals by practicing school psychologists using a two-part survey. Specifically, 184 practicing school psychologists responded to an initial survey that explored their use of EBIs and manuals. Information on whether, which ones, when, and how often EBIs and manuals are used was collected. Additionally, data were gathered on the decision-making process and variables that may have an effect on the familiarity and use of EBIs and manuals. Forty-seven self-selected practitioners of those surveyed were also sent an EBI treatment manual and an additional questionnaire to gain practitioner feedback on the product. Results indicated that even though practitioners have a very positive view of the EBI movement, they have limited familiarity with EBIs, have received limited training in EBIs during their graduate schooling, and rarely use them in their practices. Furthermore, although multiple criteria were found to be important to practitioners when making treatment decisions, client treatment acceptability and research support for the treatment were found to be the two most important. These findings suggest that the field of school psychology will continue to move toward embracing the EBI movement.

Professional Standards and Influences on Practice

To date, no formal requirements have made knowledge and use of EBIs and practice guidelines prerequisites of licensure and credentialing. The major professional groups involved in licensure and credentialing currently do not mandate this level of practice. Nor do national organizations in school psychology mandate training in EBIs as part of graduate program accreditation (e.g., APA, 1996; NASP, 2000).

A large number of textbooks are used within school psychology graduate programs, although there are no data specifically indicating which textbooks have been adopted. Appendix B lists some of the major intervention-focused textbooks, most of which have taken a strong scientific perspective in reviewing intervention techniques and practices. In addition, some of the books published by NASP promote the concept of "best practices" for use in both graduate education and practice. However, none of these books formally include EBI guidelines from the Task Force. The closest thing to criteria for evidence-based guidelines would be the *Procedural and Coding Manual*. This document has been shared with journal editors in the field of school psychology and with training program directors to facilitate knowledge of evidence-based criteria in selecting intervention programs.

STRATEGIES TO PROMOTE AND GUIDE THE USE OF EBIS IN SCHOOL PSYCHOLOGY PRACTICE

To implement future agendas of the Task Force, Kratochwill and Shernoff (2003) recently advanced the following five priority strategies for promoting evidence-based practices:

1. Develop a practice–research network in school psychology;
2. Promote an expanded methodology for evidence-based practice that takes into account EBIs in practice contexts;
3. Establish guidelines that school psychology practitioners can use in implementing and evaluating EBIs in practice;
4. Create professional development opportunities for practitioners, researchers, and trainers; and
5. Forge a partnership with other professional groups involved in the EBI movement.

The priority list is designed to move the EBI adoption agenda forward within the existing school context. These five priorities, although recommended specifically for the profession of school psychology, can be embraced by all professional groups involved in the EBI movement. The underlying purpose of the strategies is to establish a link between research and practice that will help us better understand the effectiveness of interventions and promote their adoption and sustainability.

The Practice–Research Network Concept

School psychology practitioners must be involved in the EBI research agenda. To date, they have not been involved except in the most limited manner: they have been told to implement EBIs. The practice–research concept refers to a group of practitioners engaged in the evaluation of clinical replication outcome research. The practice–research network is one strategy for facilitating practitioners' involvement in the research process and, most important, learning about the contextual variables that may affect the implementation of an intervention. In a practice–research network, practitioners are part of a research team and provide information to this team on a wide range of variables (e.g., evaluation procedures, intervention components, intervention integrity, cost of services, barriers to effective implementation, and adjustments needed to achieve successful implementation). Practitioners thus help build the evidence base related to implementing EBIs in school settings.

As a first step to accomplish the goal of developing a practice–research network in school psychology, the Task Force has invited school psychology practitioners to join the Task Force in organizing the testing of EBIs in practice settings. We also plan to spearhead efforts to evaluate EBIs in practice settings, which will likely require all of the following:

- *Local, state, regional, and possibly federal funding.* Although the Task Force cannot provide needed funds, it can act as a clearinghouse for funding information. In addition, Task Force members can develop relationships with various funding agencies to facilitate the process of securing funds.
- *Training.* The evaluation of EBIs in practice will entail competency-based training in EBIs, evaluation techniques, research methodologies, and the application of protocols for testing interventions in schools and other applied settings.
- *Assessment.* The evaluation of EBIs will further require the assessment of attitudes toward the adoption of evidence-based practices. Interventions to change negative attitudes toward adoption and sustainability of EBIs will need to be implemented.
- *Coding of interventions.* Coding interventions on qualitative practice criteria can provide a foundation for an expanded contextual knowledge base on EBIs. This activity is designed to strengthen the connection between practice and research and create more contextual information on interventions to inform practitioners' decisions about adopting and using EBIs.

Research Agendas on EBIs

The traditional method of promoting the adoption of scientific practices is to identify the best research methodology (typically, randomized controlled experiments) and then indicate which programs meet criteria of sound science standards. In recent years, intervention researchers have distinguished the concepts of effectiveness and efficacy. *Efficacy* is the standard for evaluating interventions in controlled research (true experiments), whereas *effectiveness* is the standard for evaluating interventions in a practice context (typically entailing relaxed standards of controlled experimentation). Efficacy studies are generally conducted in applied research facilities (although setting is not necessarily the primary defining characteristic) and researchers use well-designed and precise methodology (usually randomized controlled trials). Effectiveness studies, on the other hand, focus on the generalizability of the intervention to practice contexts.

Both efficacy and effectiveness studies are sorely needed by the psychology and education professions and should be promoted as part of our research agenda. To help conceptualize the research options that can be pursued, we can consider the framework advanced by Chorpita (2003), who grouped research designed to advance evidence-based practice into the following four types:

- *Type I: Efficacy studies.* As noted above, efficacy studies evaluate interventions in a controlled research context.
- *Type II: Transportability studies.* Transportability studies examine not only the degree to which intervention effects generalize from research to practice settings, but also the feasibility of implementing and gaining acceptance of EBIs in practice settings. Transportability research promotes evaluation of the various contextual factors—such as training requirements and resources, characteristics of the treatment provider, acceptability of treatments, cost and time efficiency, and administrative supports—that facilitate or constrain the effective transport of EBIs into practice settings.
- *Type III: Dissemination studies.* Dissemination studies use intervention agents that are part of the system of services (i.e., the school in our context). The intervention protocol would be deployed in the school and carried out by, for example, teachers or parents. Because Type III research involves a formal research protocol, researcher control and supervision may still have a significant impact on the intervention and its ultimate effectiveness.
- *Type IV: System evaluation studies.* To establish independence from the "investigator effect" present in dissemination studies, another type of research—system evaluation studies—can be undertaken. Such studies are typically implemented by the school system, with little involvement of a research team.

Forging a partnership between researchers and school practitioners will play a key role in facilitating these four types of research and in using the results to expand the knowledge base related to the successful integration of EBIs in educational settings. Our next steps in this scientific agenda will be to support the use of the four types of studies in our field and to take such research into account when coding intervention research using the Task Force (and other) coding criteria. As we grow in understanding what each type of research can contribute, it is likely that a marriage of these approaches will evolve. For example, Type I efficacy studies can help answer the question "Is the intervention effective?" in tightly controlled research trials, and Type II transportability research addresses the question "How does the intervention work in the real world, and who *can* and who *will* conduct the intervention, under what conditions, and to what effect?" Type III dissemination research will require an investment in collaboration with school professionals serving as intervention agents and will likely engage us in practice–research networks. Type IV system evaluation research will be much more difficult to conduct but will likely yield the very important information on interventions (vis-à-vis what school psychologists find when implementing interventions in practice). Type IV research is perhaps most likely to occur following implementation of an effective intervention or program as part of a Type II or Type III study. Traditionally, the *sustainability* of an intervention is investigated upon the withdrawal of investigator support, such as staff funding and research activities (e.g., materials, supervision). Thus, a logical extension of research could be to follow up on a Type II or Type III study with complete system adoption of the intervention program.

The four types of research have been presented in a developmental sequence beginning with Type I and ending in the Type IV study. Technically, different types of studies could be conducted in any order and provide useful information for the other types. For example, a program could be evaluated in Type IV research and lead to promising findings. The intervention could then be evaluated in a randomized trial to determine its efficacy.

It will become increasingly important for school psychology journal editors to consider these four types of studies for publication in our professional journals. It will also be important for researchers to articulate clearly the rationale for the particular focus of their studies. In this context, a variety of methodologies may be appropriate, depending on the type of study and development of scientific knowledge in the area. For example, Type I studies will typically involve traditional quantitative methodologies, whereas Type IV studies could involve formal qualitative case studies. As a profession, school psychology is in an excellent position to advance knowledge of effective interventions using this conceptual framework.

Practitioner Guidelines for Implementation and Evaluation of EBIs

Providing guidelines for implementation of EBIs may be a necessary but insufficient strategy for promoting the adoption of EBIs and associated practices. As suggested above, these guidelines can be enriched through a research partnership with practitioners. Kratochwill and Shernoff (2003) suggested that those implementing an intervention should consider such enhanced guidelines, including information related to the research process (e.g., the adoption feasibility, generalizability, and sustainability of the EBI). A protocol developed with funding from the MacArthur Foundation is currently being used to help acquire data on contextual factors related to the adoption and sustainability of evidence-based practices in community mental health settings. We hope to adapt this protocol to obtain information on EBIs in school settings (see Appendix C for an example of the adapted protocol for use in schools). The assumption is that these data can be added to the knowledge base of available information on an EBI to create an enhanced guideline for practice.

What would these enhanced guidelines look like? Enhanced guidelines would supplement intervention-specific guidance with principles common to all or most effective EBIs. For example, Nation et al. (2003) advanced general principles taken from effective interventions that can help practitioners select, modify, or create more effective prevention programs (see Table 10.6). Such enhanced guidelines can be designed specifically to educate trainers, graduate students, and practicing school psychologists in strategies that promote the use of EBIs, while at the same time addressing concerns about the perceived inflexibility of traditional manuals and practice guidelines associated with EBIs.

The following suggestions are advanced for the use of guidelines in implementing EBIs (Kratochwill & Stoiber, 2002):

1. *Focus on understanding basic principles of change.* A major assumption of the guidelines strategy is that all interventions involve some common features that can be generalized beyond the particular implementation. Basic principles of and strategies for achieving behavioral change must be taught and integrated into practice guidelines when recommending the use of EBIs.

Table 10.6. Definitions of the Principles of Effective Programs

Principle	*Definition*
Comprehensive	Programs are multicomponent interventions that address critical domains (e.g., family, peers, community) that influence the development and perpetuation of the behaviors to be prevented.
Varied teaching methods	Programs involve diverse teaching methods that focus on increasing awareness and understanding of the problem behaviors and on acquiring or enhancing skills.
Sufficient dosage	Programs provide enough intervention to produce the desired effects and provide follow-up as necessary to maintain effects.
Theory-driven	Programs have a theoretical justification, are based on accurate information, and are supported by empirical research.
Positive relationships	Programs provide exposure to adults and peers in a way that promotes strong relationships and supports positive outcomes.
Appropriately timed	Programs are initiated early enough to have an impact on the development of the problem behavior and are sensitive to the developmental needs of participants.
Socioculturally relevant	Programs are tailored to the community and cultural norms of the participants and make efforts to include the target group in program planning and implementation.
Outcome evaluation	Programs have clear goals and objectives and make an effort to systematically document their results relative to the goals.
Well-trained staff	Program staff support the program and are provided with training regarding the implementation of the intervention.

Source: Nation et al. (2003, pp. 449–456; copyright the American Psychological Association, reproduced with permission).

2. *Focus on understanding indications and contraindications of EBIs.* Practitioners and trainers considering an intervention that has been identified as evidence-based need guidelines for determining when the intervention is and is not likely to be effective. The determination that an intervention is evidence-based generally derives from a literature review that involves the use of meta-analysis. Meta-analysis can help identify the conditions under which the intervention may be questionable or even contraindicated in practice. For example, meta-analytic studies could help decision makers evaluate the feasibility of implementing an EBI that requires the training of parents and/or teachers as intervention agents.

3. *Focus on understanding the variability in intervention implementation.* Concerns about the variability in intervention implementation have focused primarily on the skill of school psychologists. However, as noted above, intervention agents are diverse, potentially including parents, teachers, counselors, administrators, and students' peers. Intervention outcomes are likely to be ineffective if the intervention agents receive inadequate training in the intervention techniques and consequently are unable to implement the intervention with integrity.
4. *Focus on teaching the basic principles of careful EBI selection.* Those responsible for selecting an intervention must have the knowledge and understanding to carefully match the target problem to an available EBI. Selection of an appropriate EBI requires an understanding of (a) the core psychological and educational processes involved in the particular problem or disorder, (b) pertinent risk and protective factors, and (c) the theoretical framework guiding the intervention. The procedures for evaluating the intervention should also be sensitive to the features of the problem that are likely to change as a function of the intervention.
5. *Focus on evaluation of EBIs in practice.* Kratochwill and Shernoff (2003) advocated evaluation of interventions in their practice contexts. No matter how much evidence is amassed for a particular EBI in Type I, II, III, and IV research, effective generalization of the intervention requires that it be evaluated under conditions of actual practice. An evaluation protocol is constructed during the development of the EBI and may even be represented in its manual or practice guidelines. Protocols for evaluating interventions in school and clinical settings have been developed and are recommended to facilitate the evaluation of EBIs.

Professional Development

Embracing the EBI movement requires a commitment to continuing professional development and self-evaluation in the long term. Such a commitment can be daunting in the face of the extraordinary growth in our knowledge base in psychology and education. Nevertheless, providing professional development to practitioners, researchers, and trainers in the identification, review, and dissemination of EBIs is a key part of the Task Force mission and must be an expanded agenda to embrace the scientific foundation of the movement. A large body of evidence shows that few practitioners—even those who have graduated from programs based on the scientist–practitioner model where one would expect greater commitment to scientific agenda—undertake research or, more important, can use research to inform their practice. Moreover, recent surveys have found that most graduate training programs in psychology and related internship sites do not teach EBIs to future clinical and school psychologists.

The ultimate goal of the Task Force is to disseminate findings that will be of use to the EBI movement. In line with this goal, the Task Force plans to offer educational and training opportunities to a number of constituencies. First, we hope to offer continuing education opportunities to individuals whose primary work is the practice of psychology in schools. Professional development opportunities related to EBIs could occur through presentations at state, regional, and national conferences and through dissemination of key information by professional organizations (e.g., the APA, NASP, and American Educational Research Association). Second, we hope to offer similar opportunities to researchers and scholars and will target similar professional and scientific groups (e.g., the SSSP) for disseminating information related to EBIs. Third, we hope to influence both faculty trainers and graduate students in our school psychology graduate education programs. To have a far-reaching impact, the knowledge base on EBIs must be integrated into course work in graduate training programs so that school psychology graduate students entering the workforce are trained in interventions that are effective. We are aware of some school psychology programs that have begun to offer course work on EBIs; other programs have established EBIs as an area of concentration (Shernoff et al., 2003). Dissemination efforts in graduate training programs would focus on use of the *Procedural and Coding Manual* in research courses and experiences. We have shared the *Procedural and Coding Manual* with training program directors to facilitate the integration of this knowledge base into graduate training. Dissemination of the results of EBI review efforts will begin through publications in journals and posting of reviews on the Task Force Website (www.sp-ebi.org). The next step will be for practitioners and trainers to use this information in their respective practices.

Graduate programs may provide at least two models for teaching EBIs. The first is competency-based training that would require students to master specific EBIs (this approach is similar that used by some programs to teach cognitive assessment measures). Competency-based training has traditionally been used in both assessment and consultation training. A second model for integrating content on EBIs into graduate training would require universities to encourage cross-disciplinary courses (e.g., courses offered jointly by departments of school, counseling, and clinical psychology) or interdisciplinary concentration courses on EBIs. Although this model could also be used with practitioners, it would require coordination of training institutes at state and national meetings.

Table 10.7. A Comparison of National Reviews of Programs

Name and Website of Review (Sponsoring Organization)	*Area of Interest*	*Designations or Ratings of Programs*
Blueprints for Violence Prevention (Office of Juvenile Justice and Delinquency Prevention) www.colorado.edu/cspv/blueprints/	School, family, and community programs whose strong, replicated evaluations suggest significant prevention effects on factors related to violence prevention	11 model and promising programs out of 600 considered
Exemplary and Promising Safe, Disciplined, and Drug-Free Schools Programs 2001 (U.S. Department of Education, Office of Safe and Drug-Free Schools) www.ed.gov/admins/lead/safety/exemplary01/exemplary01.pdf	School and community drug abuse and violence prevention and intervention programs	33 promising and 9 exemplary programs
Compendium of HIV Prevention Interventions With Evidence of Effectiveness (Centers for Disease Control and Prevention) www.cdc.gov/hiv/projects/rep/ compend.htm	Behavioral and social interventions related to HIV/AIDS prevention	24 selected as best state-of-the-science interventions (available as of June 30, 1998)
Making the Grade: A Guide to School Drug Prevention Programs (Drug Strategies) www.drugstrategies.org/pubs.html	Nationally available school-based drug abuse prevention programs	50 programs designated as very good, good, satisfactory, poor, very poor
Preventing Drug Use Among Children and Adolescents: A Research-Based Guide (The "Red Book") (National Institute on Drug Abuse) www.drugabuse.gov/pdf/prevention/RedBook.pdf	Substance abuse prevention programs that address 14 drug abuse prevention principles	10 research-based programs that addressed 14 principles of prevention (also funded by the National Institute on Drug Abuse)
Promising Practices Network www.promisingpractices.net/ programlist.asp	Broad prevention spectrum: health and safety, school readiness and success, drug abuse, teen pregnancy, violence, and family initiatives	44 promising and 20 proven programs

(Table continues)

Collaboration With Other Professional Groups

The number of professional groups that have embraced the EBI agenda with the intent of improving psychological and educational practice is growing rapidly. Table 10.7 presents an overview of some of the

Table 10.7. (Continued)

Name and Website of Review (Sponsoring Organization)	*Area of Interest*	*Designations or Ratings of Programs*
Safe and Sound: An Education Leader's Guide to Evidence-Based Social and Emotional Learning (SEL) Programs (Collaborative for Academic, Social, and Emotional Learning) (CASEL) www.CASEL.org	Multiyear programs to enhance social and emotional competence of students through skills-based instruction and establishment of supportive classroom environments	80 programs, including 22 "select," based on evidence of effectiveness, availability of professional development, five key social and emotional learning (SEL) skills; also rates availability of student assessment measures, support for schoolwide, family, and community involvement
Safe Schools, Safe Students: A Guide to Violence Prevention Strategies (Drug Strategies) www.drugstrategies.org/pubs.html	Nationally available school-based violence prevention programs	8 programs designated as very good, good, satisfactory, poor, very poor
SAMHSA Model Programs (Substance Abuse and Mental Health Services Administration) www.modelprograms.samhsa.gov	Prevention of substance abuse and other problem behaviors among youth	Searchable database of 44 programs designated as models with respect to substance abuse impacts or risk/protective factor impacts
Youth Violence: A Report of the Surgeon General (HHS) www.surgeongeneral.gov/library/youthviolence/report.html	Programs to prevent or reduce violent behaviors or associated risk factors among youth	28 programs designated as model or promising with respect to violence impacts or risk factor impacts

Source: Collaborative for Academic, Social, and Emotional Learning (2003).

major groups that are identifying evidence-based prevention and intervention programs for psychology and education. Fostering collaboration among our professional groups is essential; yet, collaboration has not yet occurred in a general and consistent manner.

Kratochwill and Shernoff (2003) proposed some activities to promote collaboration. First, a forum for dialogue should be created to give each group the opportunity to share its vision. The format of the forum would likely be some type of meeting with scheduled follow-up on the agenda crafted to sustain ongoing contact. Funding from federal and/or private foundations to establish national conferences seems advisable. On a positive note, members of the school psychology and APA Division 53 task forces on EBIs met with other scholars in the EBI and prevention communities in Chicago in September 2003. Called the Catalysis Conference, the meeting fostered new dialogue that will lay the basis for future collaborative writing and research.

Second, because each group involved in the EBI movement has established its own criteria for determining empirical support or designating an intervention as an EBI (e.g., the What Works Clearinghouse, the clinical and school psychology task forces), research comparing the various methods seems advisable. The basic question is whether the different coding systems yield similar results. Within clinical psychology, different coding systems generally do lead to the same conclusions about whether an intervention qualifies as evidence-based, but the coding systems compared are often hybrids of earlier systems. Coding across different professional groups may yield quite a different picture.

LOOKING AHEAD: BARRIERS AND PROMISING TRENDS

A major finding of the Shernoff et al. (2003) study of graduate training programs was the identification of lack of time as one the most serious obstacles to future training in EBIs. Incorporating EBIs into graduate training has many dimensions, however. It requires, for example, time to increase faculty skills in EBIs and to modify or supplement existing courses in the curriculum, and it is unclear which specific time requirements militate against or impede EBI training. In any event, if time is a major variable, more efficient methods of adding EBIs to existing course work and enhancing the skills of faculty must be found. It is one thing to include EBIs in the curriculum and quite another to ensure a high level of competency in related training and implementation. In this regard, it is important to consider field supervisors and other clinical faculty who are involved in direct supervision of school psychology graduate students when formulating competency-based training agendas.

The 3-year curriculum of specialist-level training represents another time constraint. Many doctoral-level programs, by contrast, have more options for incorporating EBIs and related practices in courses. In particular, doctoral programs typically include minor programs of study, which create the possibility of incorporating training in intervention domains. For example, the University of Wisconsin–Madison offers a minor in prevention science, which includes a number of intervention courses. In contrast, school psychology programs at the specialist level typically cannot exceed 60 semester credits; therefore, mechanisms need to be found to add EBIs and related practices to existing course work in specialist-level programs.

The good news from the Shernoff et al. study is that a high percentage of trainers and students appear to be knowledgeable about the criteria developed by APA Divisions 12, 16, and 53 for evaluating intervention outcome research. Increasingly, it will be important for graduate students to be exposed to the major coding systems from various task forces as well as from the What Works Clearinghouse (www.w-w-c.org/). Understanding these criteria will hopefully promote understanding and selection of appropriate EBIs once reviews of the literature are completed.

It is important to note that the Shernoff et al. study was based on interventions that had been established as evidence-based through criteria established by APA Divisions 12 and 53 in their task force on evidence-based treatments. Although these treatments are important, they are largely disorder-based and may not include typical interventions that school psychologists would routinely implement in school settings, such as academic interventions and large-scale mental health prevention programs at the universal, selected, and indicated levels (see Kratochwill & Stoiber, 2002). Thus, it will be important in the future to examine not only interventions and prevention programs identified as evidenced-based by the clinical psychology task forces, but also other interventions and programs with a strong educational and prevention focus. It will also be important for professional groups to disseminate information to school psychology trainers to help them select EBIs. Students who receive instruction in EBIs as part of their graduate training should generally master these programs within a competency-based framework (see Kratochwill & Shernoff, 2003). A competency-based model will ensure that students acquire the skills in a practice context, in the same way that they acquire skills in evidence-based diagnosis and assessment strategies.

Finally, a very promising direction in establishing EBIs in school settings is adoption of multiple levels of intervention programs in the system. Three-tiered systems of prevention (e.g., universal, selected, and indicated) will be especially promising as students can progress through a series of interventions prior to receiving traditional services such as special education (Osher, Dwyer, & Jackson, 2004; Walker & Shinn, 2002). Such systems of intervention raise concerns of their own such as the need for screening, progress monitoring to determine response to intervention and student outcomes, and major resources. Nevertheless, it will be critical to teach faculty and graduate students strategies for systemic change in schools so that such systems can be adopted. Such content will facilitate the adoption and sustainability of evidence-based practices and interventions.

ACKNOWLEDGMENT

The author expresses thanks to Karen O'Connell and Cathy Loeb for their assistance with this manuscript.

NOTE

1. This directory lists all school psychology programs, not just those approved by national associations.

APPENDIX A: LIST OF MAJOR SCHOOL PSYCHOLOGY INTRODUCTORY TEXTBOOKS

Fagan, T. K., & Wise, P. S. (1994). *School psychology: Past, present and future*. New York: Longman.

Gaughan, E., & Faherty, E. (Eds.). (1998). *School psychology: Prospective and retrospective views of the field*. New York: Lea R. Powell Institute for Children and Families at Alfred University.

Phillips, B. N. (1990). *School psychology at a turning point: Ensuring a bright future for the profession*. California: Jossey-Bass.

Thomas, A., & Grimes, J. (Eds.). (2002). *Best practices in school psychology IV* (Vols. 1–2). Bethesda, MD: National Association of School Psychologists.

Woody, R. H., LaVoie, J. C., & Epps, S. (1992). *School psychology: A developmental and social systems approach*. Needham Heights, MA: Allyn and Bacon.

APPENDIX B: LIST OF MAJOR INTERVENTION TEXTS USED IN SCHOOL PSYCHOLOGY GRADUATE TRAINING

Bergan, J. R., & Kratochwill, T. R. (1990). *Behavioral consultation and therapy*. New York: Plenum Press.

Brock, S. E., Lazarus, P. J., & Jimerson, S. R. (Eds.). (2002). *Best practice in school crisis prevention and intervention*. Bethesda, MD: National Association of School Psychologists.

Christophersen, E. R., & Mortweet, S. L. (2001). *Treatments that work with children: Empirically supported strategies for managing childhood problems*. Washington, DC: American Psychological Association.

Durlak, J. A. (1997). *Successful prevention programs for children and adolescents*. New York: Plenum Press.

Fine, M. J., & Carlson, C. (Eds.). (1992). *The handbook of family–school intervention: A systems perspective.* Needham Heights, MA: Allyn and Bacon.

Hibbs, E. D., & Jensen, P. S. (Eds.). (1996). *Psychosocial treatments for child and adolescent disorders: Empirically based strategies for clinical practice.* Washington, DC: American Psychological Association.

Kazdin, A. E., & Weisz, J. R. (2003). *Evidence-based psychotherapies for children and adolescents.* New York: Guilford Press.

Kratochwill, T. R., & Bergan, J. R. (1990). *Behavioral consultation in applied settings: An individual guide*. New York: Plenum Press.

Reynolds, C. R., & Gutkin, T. B. (1999). *The handbook of school psychology.* New York: John Wiley & Sons.

Sheridan, S. M., Kratochwill, T. R., & Bergan, J. R. (1996). *Conjoint behavioral consultation: A procedural manual.* New York: Plenum Press.

Shinn, M. R., Walker, H. M., & Stoner, G. (Eds.). (2002). *Interventions for academic and behavior problems II: Preventive and remedial approaches.* Bethesda, MD: National Association of School Psychologists.

Stoiber, K. C., & Kratochwill, T. K. (Eds.). (1998). *Handbook of group intervention for children and families.* Needham Heights, MA: Allyn and Bacon.

Thomas, A., & Grimes, J. (Eds.). (2002). *Best practices in school psychology IV* (Vols. 1–2). Bethesda, MD: National Association of School Psychologists.

APPENDIX C: EVIDENCE-BASED PRACTICES QUESTIONNAIRE

Name of school:

Name of interviewee:

Position: School Psychologist Director of Student Services
Other (specify)

Address of school site targeted:

Address of organization's main offices (if different):

A. Organization Information

1. In the past 5 years, have you implemented a new intervention, service, or model of service delivery?

   YES NO

2. If yes, what were the names of these new interventions, services, or models?

3. What prompted you to implement this program?

4. Was a public agency, such as a municipal, county, state, or federal department of education, mental health, health, child welfare, or juvenile justice involved in promoting this new intervention, service, or model?

   YES NO

5. **If yes to #4**, which public agency was it?

6. **If yes to #4**, in what ways was the public agency involved in promoting it? (e.g., new law mandated a new service; new agency head suggested program changes, etc.)

7. What were the major factors that made it possible for you to successfully implement the new intervention or service?

8. What were the major factors that made it difficult for you to implement the new service or intervention?

Please **rate the importance** of the following factors in the implementation of the new intervention or service in your school or other practice setting.

	Not Important						*Very Important*		
9. Description of the intervention or service that implied it is "evidence based" or "scientifically tested"	1	2	3	4	5	6	7	8	9
10. Leadership support from the administrator to whom psychological services report in your practical setting	1	2	3	4	5	6	7	8	9
11. Support for the intervention by particular individuals in your school or other practice setting who are respected by others in that setting	1	2	3	4	5	6	7	8	9
12. Support for the intervention by your state education agency or other relevant public authority	1	2	3	4	5	6	7	8	9
13. Support for the intervention by parents	1	2	3	4	5	6	7	8	9
14. Support for the intervention by advocacy or consumer groups in your county	1	2	3	4	5	6	7	8	9
15. Support for the intervention by psychologists, counselors, and other mental health professionals in your practice setting	1	2	3	4	5	6	7	8	9
16. Support for the intervention by teachers	1	2	3	4	5	6	7	8	9
17. Support for the intervention by the principal, superintendent, or other upper-level administrator in your practice setting	1	2	3	4	5	6	7	8	9
18. Support for the intervention by other agencies with which your school or other practice setting interacts	1	2	3	4	5	6	7	8	9
19. Support for the intervention by accreditation agencies or organizations	1	2	3	4	5	6	7	8	9
20. Financial benefits from adoption of the intervention	1	2	3	4	5	6	7	8	9

21. Fit or match between the needs of the children in your school or the other practice setting and the target population for this intervention	1	2	3	4	5	6	7	8	9
22. Fit or match of this intervention with the philosophy of your school or other practice setting	1	2	3	4	5	6	7	8	9
23. Fit or match of this intervention with the standard techniques or interventions already used by the staff of your school or other practice setting	1	2	3	4	5	6	7	8	9
24. Fit or match of the intervention with the supervision or consultation practices already in place	1	2	3	4	5	6	7	8	9
25. Fit or match of the intervention with the training, inservice, or continuing education practices already in place in your practice setting	1	2	3	4	5	6	7	8	9
26. Fit or match of it with the administrative training already in place	1	2	3	4	5	6	7	8	9
27. Level of administrative burden	1	2	3	4	5	6	7	8	9
28. Compatibility with existing equipment and technology	1	2	3	4	5	6	7	8	9
29. Political pressure	1	2	3	4	5	6	7	8	9

The following questions focus on intervention models for children or adolescents. Key features of these interventions are summarized on the attached fact sheets. We would like to get your thoughts about the factors that you believe would be important to consider before adopting either the xxxx intervention or the xxxx intervention or both, in your practice setting.

30. For what percentage of the students referred to you would this intervention be appropriate?

31. Given what you have just heard (read) about this intervention approach, what steps would you have to take in your school or other practice setting to prepare to implement this intervention?

32. Would staffing patterns have to change in your school or other practice setting to implement this intervention, such as number or qualifications of teachers, teacher aides, school psychologists, counselors, etc.? If yes, in what ways?

    YES NO

    If YES:

33. What type of supervision or consultation would be necessary for successful implementation of this intervention? How is this different from what currently exists in your school or other practice setting?
34. Would equipment or supplies not currently needed have to be purchased? If yes, what would you have to purchase?

    YES NO

    If YES:

35. Would you need to change your usual assessment procedures? If yes, in what ways?

    YES NO

    If YES:

36. Billing

    YES NO

37. Reimbursement

    YES NO

38. Sources of revenue

    YES NO

39. Would any personnel policies in your school or practice setting need to change in order to implement this intervention? If yes, in what ways?

    YES NO

    If YES:

40. Would approval have to be obtained from any regulatory or accreditation agency to implement this intervention?

    YES NO

    If YES:

Please rate the importance of the following factors for their impact on the successful adoption of a new intervention such as xxxx or xxxx in your school or other practice setting.

	Not Important								*Very Important*
41. Description of the intervention that implied it is "evidence-based" or "scientifically tested"	1	2	3	4	5	6	7	8	9
42. Leadership support from the administrator to whom psychological services reports in your practice setting	1	2	3	4	5	6	7	8	9
43. Support for the intervention by particular individuals in your school or other practice setting who are respected by others in that setting	1	2	3	4	5	6	7	8	9
44. Support for the intervention by your state education agency or other relevant public authority	1	2	3	4	5	6	7	8	9
45. Support for the intervention by parents	1	2	3	4	5	6	7	8	9
46. Support for the intervention by advocacy or consumer groups in your county	1	2	3	4	5	6	7	8	9
47. Support for the intervention by psychologists, counselors, and other mental health professionals in your practice setting	1	2	3	4	5	6	7	8	9
48. Support for the intervention by teachers	1	2	3	4	5	6	7	8	9
49. Support for the intervention by the principal, superintendent, or other upper-level administrator in your practice setting	1	2	3	4	5	6	7	8	9
50. Support for the intervention by other agencies with which your school or other practice setting interacts	1	2	3	4	5	6	7	8	9
51. Support for the intervention by accreditation agencies or organizations	1	2	3	4	5	6	7	8	9
52. Financial benefits from adoption of the intervention	1	2	3	4	5	6	7	8	9
53. Fit or match between the needs of the children in your school or other practice setting and the target population for this intervention	1	2	3	4	5	6	7	8	9
54. Fit or match of this intervention with the philosophy of your school or other practice setting	1	2	3	4	5	6	7	8	9
55. Fit or match of this intervention with the standard techniques already used by the staff of your school or other practice setting	1	2	3	4	5	6	7	8	9

56. Fit or match of the intervention with the supervision or consultation practices already in place	1	2	3	4	5	6	7	8	9
57. Fit or match of the intervention with the training, inservice, or continuing education practices already in place	1	2	3	4	5	6	7	8	9
58. Administrative training	1	2	3	4	5	6	7	8	9
59. Level of administrative burden	1	2	3	4	5	6	7	8	9
60. Compatibility with existing equipment and technology	1	2	3	4	5	6	7	8	9
61. Political pressure	1	2	3	4	5	6	7	8	9

REFERENCES

American Psychological Association. (1996). *Guidelines and principles for accreditation of programs in professional psychology*. Washington, DC: Author.

Anastopoulos, A. D., Shelton, T. L., DuPaul, G. J., & Guevremont, D. C. (1993). Parent training for attention-deficit hyperactivity disorder: Its impact on parent functioning. *Journal of Abnormal Child Psychology, 21*, 581–596.

Block, J. (1978). Effects of rationale-emotive mental health program on poorly achieving, disruptive high school students. *Journal of Counseling Psychology, 25*, 61–65.

Burns, B. J., Costello, E. J., Angold, A., Tweed, D., Stangl, D., Farmer, E. M. Z., et al. (1995). Children's mental health service use across service sectors. *Health Affairs, 14*, 147–159.

Chafouleaus, S. M., Weinstein, K. S., & Elinoff, M. J. (2003). *School psychologists' perspectives on the use of and barriers related to providing school-based mental health services.* Manuscript submitted for publication.

Chorpita, B. F. (2003). The frontier of evidence-based practice. In A. E. Kazdin & J. R. Weisz (Eds.), *Evidence-based psychotherapies for children and adolescents* (pp. 42–59). New York: Guilford Press.

Curtis, M. J., Chesno Grier, J. E., Walker Abshier, D., Sutton, N. T., & Hunley, S. (2002). School psychology: Turning the corner into the twenty-first century. *NASP Communique, 30*, 1.

Curtis, M. J., Hunley, S. A., Walker, K. J., & Baker, A. C. (1999). Demographic characteristics and professional practices in school psychology. *School Psychology Review, 28*, 104–116.

Eyberg, S. M., Boggs, S. R., & Algina, J. (1995). New developments in combined treatments of conduct disorders in aggressive children. *Psychopharmacology Bulletin, 31*, 83–91.

Feindler, E. L., Marriott, S. A., & Iwata, M. (1984). Group anger control training for junior high school delinquents. *Cognitive Therapy and Research, 8*, 299–311.

Gittleman, R., Abikoff, H., Pollack, E., Klein, D. F., Katz, S., & Mattes, J. (1980). A controlled trial of behavior modification and methylphenidate in hyperactive children. In C. K. Whalen & B. Henker (Eds.), *Hyperactive children: The social ecology of identification and treatment* (pp. 221–243). New York: Academic Press.

Hamilton, S. B., & MacQuiddy, S. L. (1984). Self-administered behavioral parent training: Enhancement of treatment efficacy using a time-out signal seat. *Journal of Clinical Child Psychology, 13*, 61–69.

Henggeler, S. W., Melton, G. B., & Smith, L. A. (1992). Family preservation using Multisystemic Therapy: An effective alternative to incarcerating serious juvenile offenders. *Journal of Consulting and Clinical Psychology, 60*, 953–961.

Hoagwood, K., Burns, B. J., Kiser, L., Ringeisen, H., & Schoenwald, S. K. (2001). Evidence-based practice in child and adolescent mental health services. *Psychiatric Services, 52*(9), 1179–1189. Retrieved February 24, 2004, from psychservices.psychiatryonline.org/cgi/reprint/52/9/1179.pdf

Horn, W. F., Ialongo, N., Greenberg, G., Packard, T., & Smith-Winberry, C. (1990). Additive effects of behavioral parent training and self-control therapy with attention deficit hyperactivity disordered children. *Journal of Clinical Child Psychology, 19*, 98–110.

Huey, W. C., & Rank, R, C. (1984). Effects of counselor and peer-led group assertiveness training on Black adolescent aggression. *Journal of Counseling Psychology, 31*, 95–98.

Kazdin, A. E., Esveldt-Dawson, D., French, N. H., & Unis, A. S. (1987). Effects of parent management training and problem-solving skills training combined in the treatment of antisocial child behavior. *Journal of the American Academy of Child and Adolescent Psychiatry, 26*, 416–424.

Kazdin, A. E., Kratochwill, T. R., & VandenBos, G. (1986). Beyond clinical trials: Generalizing from research to practice. *Professional Psychology: Research and Practice, 3*, 391–398.

Kratochwill, T. R., & Shernoff, E. (2003). Evidence-based practice: Promoting evidence-based interventions in school psychology. *School Psychology Quarterly, 18*, 389–408.

Kratochwill, T. R., & Stoiber, K. C. (2000). Empirically supported interventions and school psychology: Conceptual and practical issues: Part II. *School Psychology Quarterly, 15*, 233–253.

Kratochwill, T. R., & Stoiber, K. C. (2002). Evidence-based interventions in school psychology: Conceptual foundations of the procedural and coding manual of Division 16 and the Society for the Study of School Psychology Task Force. *School Psychology Quarterly, 17*, 341–389.

Kumke, P., & Kratochwill, T. R. (2004). Perceptions of the evidence-based intervention movement and use of evidence-based intervention manuals: A national survey of practicing school psychologists. Unpublished manuscript, University of Wisconsin–Madison.

Lehr, C. A., Hansen, A., Sinclair, M. F., & Christenson, S. L. (2003) Moving beyond dropout towards school completion: An integrative review of data-based interventions. *School Psychology Review, 32*, 342–364.

Lochman, J. E., Lampron, L. B., Gemmer, T. C., & Harris, S. R. (1989). Teacher consultation and cognitive-behavioral interventions with aggressive boys. *Psychology in the Schools, 26*, 138–145.

Nation, M., Crusto, C., Wandersman, A., Kumpfer, K. L., Seybolt, D., Morrissey-Kane, E., et al. (2003). What works in prevention: Principles of effective prevention programs. *American Psychologist, 58*, 449–456.

National Association of School Psychologists. (2003). *School psychology: A career that makes a difference.* Retrieved February 24, 2004, from www.naspcareer-center.org/students/intro_sp.html

O'Leary, K. D., Pelham, W. E., Rosenbaum, A., & Price, G. H. (1976). Behavioral treatment of hyperkinetic children: An experimental evaluation of its usefulness. *Clinical Pediatrics, 15*, 510–515.

Osher, D., Dwyer, K., & Jackson, S. (2004). *Safe, supportive and successful schools: Step by step*. Longmont, CO: Sopris West.

Patterson, G. R., & Gullion, M. E. (1968). *Living with children: New methods for parents and teachers*. Champaign, IL: Research Press.

Peed, S., Roberts, M., & Forehand, R. (1977). Evaluation of the effectiveness of a standardized parent training program in altering the interaction of mothers and their noncompliant children. *Behavior Modification, 1*, 323–350.

Pisterman, S., Firestone, P., McGrath, P., Goodman, J. T., Webster, I., Mallory, R., & Goffin, B. (1992). The role of parent training in treatment of preschoolers with ADHD. *American Journal of Orthopsychiatry, 62*, 397–408.

Prevatt, F., & Kelly, D. F. (2003). Dropping out of school: A review of intervention programs. *Journal of School Psychology, 41*, 377–395.

Reschly, D. J. (2003). School psychology. In W. M. Reynolds & G. E. Miller (Eds.), *Handbook of psychology*. Vol. 7, *Educational psychology* (pp. 431–453). New York: John Wiley & Sons.

Ringwalt, C. L., Ennett, S., Vincus, A., Thorne, J., Rohrbach, L. A., & Simmons-Rudolph, A. (2002). The prevalence of effective substance use prevention curricula in U.S. middle schools. *Prevention Science, 3*, 257–265.

Shernoff, E. S., Kratochwill, T. R., & Stoiber, K. C. (2003). Training in evidence-based interventions: What are school psychology programs teaching? *Journal of School Psychology, 41*, 467–483.

Stoiber, K. C., & Kratochwill, T. R. (2000). Empirically supported interventions and school psychology: Rationale and methodological issues: Part I. *School Psychology Quarterly, 15*, 75–105.

Task Force on Evidence-Based Interventions in School Psychology. (2003). *Procedural and coding manual for review of evidence-based interventions*. Retrieved February 6, 2004, from www.sp-ebi.org/_workingfiles/EBImanual1.pdf

Thomas, A. (1998). *Directory of school psychology graduate programs*. Bethesda, MD: National Association of School Psychologists.

Tremblay, R. E., Pagani-Kurtz, L., Masse, L. C., Vitaro, F., & Pihl, R. O. (1995). A bimodal preventive intervention for disruptive kindergarten boys: Its impact through mid-adolescence. *Journal of Consulting and Clinical Psychology, 63*, 560–568.

Walker, H. M. & Shinn, M. R. (2002). Structuring school-based interventions to achieve integrated primary, secondary, and tertiary prevention goals for safe and effective schools. In Shinn, M. R., Walker, H. M., & Stoner, G. (Eds.), *Interventions for academic and behavior problems II: Preventive and remedial approaches* (pp. 1–25). Bethesda, MD: National Association of School Psychologists.

Webster-Stratton, C. (1994). Advancing videotape parent training: A comparison study. *Journal of Consulting and Clinical Psychology, 62*, 583–593.

Weisz, J. R., & Hawley, K. M. (2001). *Procedural and coding manual for identification of beneficial treatments* (Draft #4). Washington, DC: American Psychological Association, Society for Clinical Psychology Division 12 Committee on Science and Practice.

White, J., & Kratochwill, T. R. (2004). School psychologists' use and awareness of treatment guidelines: Present and future. Unpublished manuscript, University of Wisconsin–Madison.

Ysseldyke, J., Dawson, P., Lehr, C., Reschly, D., Reynolds, M., & Telzrow, C. (1997). *School psychology: A blueprint for training and practice II*. Bethesda, MD: National Association of School Psychologists.

CHAPTER 11

THE INSTITUTE OF EDUCATION SCIENCES' WHAT WORKS CLEARINGHOUSE

Robert Boruch and Rebecca Herman

In the United States, whenever science has made remarkable advances, the government has, at times, formed new organizations to recognize, foster, and support the science. The creation of the National Institutes of Health, the National Science Foundation, and the National Aeronautics and Space Administration are cases in point. The Institute of Education Sciences (IES), created under the Education Sciences Reform Act of 2002, is a new case in point. Its promise is as substantial as that of its older siblings.

The What Works Clearinghouse, an IES initiative, was designed to provide educators, policymakers, researchers, and the public with a central and trusted source of scientific evidence on what works in education (see http://whatworks.ed.gov).

The WWC is not designed to endorse particular interventions. Rather its focus is on reviewing and summarizing the evidence pertaining to the effects of interventions, notably evidence that permits causal inferences. Nor does the WWC conduct randomized trials or quasi-experiments. Rather, part of the mission is to assure that all reports on such studies in a

The Scientific Basis of Educational Productivity, 269–282

WWC topic area are identified and screened for dependability of the evidence.

In what follows, we outline the main features of the What Works Clearinghouse as of August 2005. Because the effort is evolving, and changes are made when we see opportunity for improvement, readers are encouraged to consult the WWC website—http://whatworks.ed.gov—for up-to-date information.

THE WHAT WORKS CLEARINGHOUSE AND EMBODIMENTS OF SCIENCE

The WWC embodies science in at least three ways. The first concerns the WWC's attention to unbiased estimation of an intervention's effect. As a practical matter, this means the WWC puts randomized trials at a high priority, a status these studies have had since the 1950s in medicine, and in employment, training, and welfare research since the 1970s.

Randomized trials produce fair comparisons because, at the outset, the children, or families, or schools, etc. who are involved in one intervention do not differ systematically from those who are involved in another intervention that is purported to be more effective.

The WWC's focus on unbiased estimates does not preclude estimates based on quasi-experiments. But the WWC recognizes that the results of quasi-experiments are frequently more equivocal than those based on randomized trials because sources of bias cannot always be identified, much less estimated (Duncan et al., 2004; Boruch, 1997). The WWC's emphasis on randomized trials accords with the IES emphasis on higher quality evidence about what works, especially randomized trials (U.S. Department of Education, 2003a, 2003b).

The second embodiment lies in science's emphasis on cumulation of knowledge. As a practical matter, the WWC will exploit state-of-the-art methods developed over the past 20 years in the science of systematic reviews. The aims are to search literatures so as to produce an unbiased assembly of studies, screen them on the basis of the trustworthiness of the scientific evidence they have produced, and analyze and synthesize the information so as to properly understand and communicate the results (see, for example, Lipsey & Wilson, 2001).

For education research in the United States, the WWC's approach to instantiating reliance on scientific evidence is unique. There is similar interest in counties other than the United States. The WWC may also help to inform their efforts as others may inform the WWC's development. For instance, the Organization for Economic Cooperation and Development's reviews of education in Mexico and the United Kingdom point out the value of scientific research as a basis for informing policy and practice. The World Bank's Operations Evaluation Department Biennial Conference in 2003 focused substantially for the first time on randomized trials in education and elsewhere. In the United Kingdom, the Cabinet Office, Treasury Department, and Home Office are putting resources into controlled trials. The Cabinet Office is investing in systematic reviews and in at least one organization to produce them.

Both the Cochrane Collaboration in health care and the Campbell Collaboration in the social, criminological, and education sectors are international. Their cross-discipline efforts will advance higher standards of evidence in the review of studies, and ultimately in their production. The WWC builds on these international initiatives also, and expects that these other initiatives will capitalize on the WWC's work. The WWC also builds on earlier efforts in the United States that transcended political squabbles and that depended on the interest of teachers, administrators, and researchers in learning what works, notably Herman et al. (1999).

The third way that the IES's What Works Clearinghouse embodies scientific standards is through the use of transparent decision rules and protocols, developed under the guidance of substantive and methodological experts. The What Works Clearinghouse's Technical Advisory Group (TAG) contributed to the development of study review standards, and TAG members help resolve technical issues as they arise. The WWC's reliance on peer review is basic to vetting the quality of the research in the sciences. The review production system relies on explicit, consistent protocols, coding guides, and technical guidance, and the work of expert teams, led by principal investigators who are themselves experts in the areas under review.

ASSUMPTIONS AND PROSPECTS

The success of the Institute for Education Sciences' What Works Clearinghouse depends on some things that are in the WWC's control and some that are not. The prospects, for instance, depend partly on the public appetite for good evidence on what works. The No Child Left Behind Act attaches high value to scientific evidence. But if interest in good evidence evaporates, governmental support for producing good evidence might then decline.

Because the WWC reviews field studies rather than executing them, the WWC also has no direct control over the production of high-quality research on the effects of interventions, especially randomized trials. If the supply of such studies is cut short, the WWC mission might have to change. The WWC can and does, of course, encourage production indirectly, by recognizing the value of randomized trials and what appear to be good quasi-experiments, and enhancing their visibility in its standards for reviewing the research.

The prospects for success depend heavily on resources, especially people, for the production of reviews. The intellectual resources include research and development over the last 20 years, on which the What Works Clearinghouse depends to develop, operationalize, and apply explicit standards of evidence and uniform, structured reporting. These include published work on standards of evidence and reporting on individual studies in the health sector, such as the CONSORT (Consolidated Standards of Reporting Trials) statement (Altman et al., 2001), and advances in the state of the art in the social, behavioral, and education sectors on producing fair estimates of an intervention's effect (Boruch, 1997; Mosteller & Boruch, 2002; Sherman, 2003).

The resources include procedures, methodological advances in meta-analysis and reviews, and standards that have been developed for assessing assemblies of studies and reporting systematic reviews of studies in health care (Mohrer et al., 1999) and in the social, behavioral, and educational sectors (Cooper, 1998; Halvorsen, 1994). They also build on precedents such as Herman et al. (1999) in education and Chalmers (2003) in health care, among others. We discuss other resources later.

OPERATING PRINCIPLES

Assuring the quality of evidence is the first of the WWC's operating principles, represented partly in the WWC's focus on scientific excellence. This focus is embodied in the standards developed for assessing evidence such as the Design and Implementation Assessment Device described below. A second operating principle requires the WWC to be procedurally and organizationally efficient. Identifying dependable studies from the morass is demanding and complicated, but it requires efficiency to serve the public interest. Because the WWC is exploring new terrain, a willingness and capacity to improve is a third operating principle. Emphasizing accessibility and transparency in organization and procedures, in identifying and explaining the evidential standards, and in efforts to improve constitutes a fourth operating principle under the contract.

The WWC's credibility depends on these principles, of course. But as an ancient Latin aphorism puts it, being virginal is not sufficient. One must also appear virginal. Independence in the sense of anonymous peer review, for example, is a theme that is instantiated in the WWC operations. A Technical Advisory Group provides counsel and recommendations on the major scientific products of the Clearinghouse.

Science asks to be surpassed and outdated. Consequently, the WWC is attentive to the need for course correction as the knowledge base changes. Course corrections depend on everyone who contributes to WWC, include people in the IES, sibling organizations such as the Cochrane Collaboration in health and the Campbell Collaboration in the social sectors, and others who contribute to the effort.

CONTEMPORARY HISTORY

The WWC's aims and operating principles, described above, were made explicit in a competitive contract that the IES awarded to a joint venture of Campbell Collaboration (C2) and the American Institutes for Research (AIR). C2, a young organization, had been the locus for an unprecedented international effort to develop systematic reviews of the effects of interventions in social welfare, crime and justice, and education. AIR, created in 1950, had been the source of a major review of school reform models that revealed an alarming absence of scientific evidence on the effects of such reforms (Herman et al., 1999), among other products.

During 2002, the WWC's Technical Advisory Group (TAG) was assembled. The prospective members' knowledgeability about scientific evidence, including randomized trials and measurement, and the production of systematic reviews of evidence was crucial to their invitation to serve.

During 2001–2004, in a process of incremental and often demanding improvement, tools and standards for assessing quality of evidence were developed.

During 2004, the WWC undertook a pilot phase to test the application of WWC standards in the review area of Middle-School Math Curricula. The pilot effort revealed major challenges in the sense of designing detailed reporting structures that give WWC users, including practioners and researchers, what they need to know about each study. The WWC website and WWC operations underwent at least three major changes and many smaller modifications to shape the WWC's presentation of review results.

THE WWC'S ORGANIZATION AND PEOPLE

The IES's What Works Clearinghouse depends on different organizations to achieve its aims. The people in the Campbell Collaboration and the American Institutes for Research, the prime joint contractors, work with subcontractors—Duke University, Caliber Associates, Aspen Systems, the University of Pennsylvania, Mathematica Policy Research, Inc., and the Council for Excellence in Government—as well as with IES.

Under federal law, the IES Director, Grover (Russ) Whitehurst, has a 6-year term of office. This term, of course, is longer than that of the President of the United States. The relevant section of the law was framed partly to enhance the IES's ability to operationalize a coherent scientific research agenda and to reduce the IES's vulnerability to episodic nonscientific influences on the research agenda.

The What Works Clearinghouse's Technical Advisory Group (TAG) was formed to assure expert counsel on standards of evidence from different social, behavioral, and educational sciences. As of 2005, its members include the TAG Chair Larry Hedges, Andrew Porter (Educational Leadership and Policy, Vanderbilt), Jesse Berlin (Biostatistics, University of Pennsylvania), Will Shadish (Social Sciences, Humanities, and Arts, University of California, Merced), Betsy Becker (Education Research, Michigan State University), David Francis (Psychology, University of Texas), Mark Lipsey (Public Policy, Vanderbilt), Cecilia Rouse (Economics, Princeton), Douglas Carnine (Education, University of Oregon), David Myers (Sociology, Mathematica Policy Research), David Rindskopf (Psychology, CUNY), Thomas Cook (Sociology and Social Policy, Northwestern), and Robert Linn (Education, University of Colorado).

THE WWC'S PRODUCTS

The WWC's reviews of research, at two levels of reporting, are the most important tangible products. The WWC's standards of evidence developed and used in the reviews are a deeper level of product. The WWC's Evaluator Register, another product, is designed to assure that capacity for generating higher quality evidence can be fostered and exploited well. The use of the reviews by policymakers, researchers, and practitioners is itself an important ultimate product of the effort.

Two Levels of WWC Reports

The WWC's appraisal of the original study's dependability is based on standards that were developed by the WWC with guidance from the Technical Advisory Group (TAG). These standards depend in turn on standards of evidence in statistics, the social sciences, and medicine—such as CONSORT (Altman et al., 2001).

The first level of WWC reporting capitalizes on multiple studies on the same intervention. Operationally, this involves analyzing an assembly of studies that concern the same intervention, so as to produce a WWC Intervention Report. The WWC Intervention Report describes the intervention, the studies that were reviewed to understand the intervention's effects, and the dependability of the evidence for drawing conclusions.

At this writing, the second level involves production of the WWC Topic Area Report. In such a report, all interventions on a given topic, such as Beginning Reading, are considered, and all studies done on each intervention are reviewed. A WWC Topic Area Report on Beginning Reading interventions, for instance, might then cover all relevant programs, curricula, instructional practices, and policies. It covers all WWC Intervention Reports that fall in the ambit of the topic. The resulting evidence is evaluated and summarized.

To go from the most general to the specific, WWC Topic Area Reports will cover different interventions that are supposed to affect similar outcome variables in specified target populations. WWC Intervention Reports focus on individual interventions—such as a specific curriculum. During 2003–2004, an additional level of reporting was explored. This "study report" summarized the strengths, weaknesses, and findings of a single study. This level of reporting was terminated; too much effort was required and too little benefit given to potential users. Instead, an appendix in each intervention report contains capsule descriptions of each study which meets standards for that intervention. The structured abstracts of such studies, of the sort being considered by the new ERIC, or being done with low resources by the Campbell Collaboration, may suffice for specialized consumers.

Standards of Evidence as a WWC Product

A major theme underlying all standards enunciated by the What Works Clearinghouse is that one must be able to make causal inferences about what works, what does not work, and what harms. As a practical matter, this means that all standards for Intervention Reports and Topic Area Reports pay attention to randomized trials and to certain types of quasi-experimental trials, and to the important differences in dependability of randomized trials as opposed to some forms of quasi-experiments.

Operationally, this theme means that randomized trials get top priority. They are more dependable in making a causal inference about what works than quasi-experiments. Operationally, this also means that quasi-experiments have a lower priority, and are designated as meeting a lower standard of scientific evidence in any reports produced by the WWC. Randomized trials with no serious problems in design or execution are rated as "Meets Evidence Standards." Quasi-experiments that (1) match on pretests (or a proxy) and other appropriate matching variables or (2) covary on these measures are designated as "Meets Evidence Standards with Reservations." The language "reservations" is to remind readers that a quasi-experiment cannot provide the assurance of unbiased estimates of difference that a randomized trial can. The WWC also looks at regression discontinuity studies (which is a quasi-experimental design with especially strong causal validity) and single subject studies which meet qualifying criteria.

In addition to this primary focus on causal validity, the WWC standards screen out studies for other reasons. WWC, for example, encounters reports at times that do not contain basic statistical information such as variance within groups being compared. A study which does not provide enough information to compute—and verify—study authors' reported findings would be screened out. The WWC does use a uniform query to request the missing information from study authors in such cases so as to assure reviewers have all pertinent information.

Beyond the broad rating, WWC reviewers also examine and describe certain features of studies to provide at least minimum assurance that the study can be interpreted properly and reviewed accurately and uniformly across topics and interventions. These features include descriptions of the intervention, outcome measures, study settings, subgroups tested, and analysis statistics.

The WWC's efforts to develop standards must confront the fact that we do not know the answers to some questions, and that we must be attentive to the accretion of empirical evidence that could help address such questions. Consider, for instance, a randomized trial in which children or families attrite from one arm of the trial at a 5% rate and in the second arm at a 20% rate. Is this potentially serious difference important enough to incorporate into a standard that directs attention to internal validity of a trial? Does it depend on a recruitment process and context? Of course, it may do so. And how do we take into account the continuously accumulating evidence on attrition rates from well-conducted trials, and then make judgments about the dependability of the evidence at hand. And how do we incorporate this into a standard? WWC is working on such issues and how to take new evidence into account.

The standards underwent repeated scrutiny and modification during 2002–2003, based on the WWC's Technical Advisory Group, public comments, and comparisons to related standards in the medical arena (Valentine & Cooper 2003). The earliest version, called the Design and Implementation Assessment Device (DIAD), was eventually put aside because of its complexity. Many seasoned researchers could not understand it. The more transparent standards are given on the WWC website. The standards and technical guidance are periodically updated on the WWC website. The WWC is developing an archive of technical issues confronted in WWC reviews, their resolution, and application of the resolution in WWC review standards. Readers are encouraged to see the site for the most recent version.

WWC Evaluator Register

In 2005, the WWC launched an Evaluator Registry that provides information about people and organizations that have the capacity to produce high-quality evidence on the effects of educational interventions. Entries to the register are based on submissions made by the people and organizations that provide information on their performance—for instance, in designing and executing trials and in having the products of their research and evaluations published in peer-reviewed scientific venues.

Information about who and what organizations produce high-quality research is potentially important to school districts or publishing firms, for instance, that do not themselves have the capacity to generate evidence that meets high standards. At the national level, it is also essential to understanding the resources that are available and how those resources might be leveraged or enhanced to build more capacity to generate better evidence.

THE INTENDED CONSUMERS AND THEIR USE OF WWC PRODUCTS

The WWC aims to assure that its products are used, by policy people, practitioners, researchers, and others. The WWC understands that getting research used is no easy task. In the medical research arena, for instance, it takes 5 to 10 years for a tested innovation to be incorporated into practice. In the education arena, the results of Tennessee's class size trials were not recognized, much less used, by many policy people for over 5 years. The WWC would like to foster a brisker pace.

Potential users of high-quality research, of course, must be aware of the research. To build the awareness, WWC has been industrious in presenting its work at national educational and research conferences and related venues. These have routinely included national meetings of the American Educational Research Association and the Council of Great City Schools, and conferences convened by the National Academy of Sciences and the Coalition for Evidence-Based Policy.

Building the awareness included presentations at education organizations such as the American Federal of Teachers' QUEST Conference that serves teaches and principals such as the American Association of School Principals. And it included presentations at international meetings of the

Campbell Collaboration. During 2002–2003, this included meetings of the IES regional laboratories, the National Council of Teaches of Mathematics, and the Region III Conferences in Oklahoma. The venues for the presentations, dates, and presenters are continuously updated and entered on the WWC website at http://whatworks.ed.gov.

Because WWC depends on advances in the state of the art in conducting studies, and attempts to advance the state of the art in reviewing them, researchers are part of the target. One of the aims is to vet ideas and products in peer-reviewed scientific forums. Consequently, papers covering some WWC activities have been developed for peer-reviewed journals such as the Annals of the American Academy of Political and Social Sciences (Turner et al., 2003) and books (Valentine & Cooper, 2003).

Media is important, given the WWC's interest in people such as teachers, parents, and policymakers learning about the WWC's intent, processes, and products. A media tool kit has been developed and put up on the WWC's website, and contact people and substantial detail are given on the site. Some of this has been covered often in the press and trade journals such as Education Week.

Attracting attention to websites and assuring repeat visits can be a fiercely competitive enterprise. The WWC's website has undergone at least three major changes in the years since its creation, and continues in its effort to improve. Nonetheless, it must confront the fact that there are hundreds, if not thousands, of websites that purport to tell "what works" on topics ranging from astrology to zoo keeping, and that the phrase is also common in sites that purport to provide evidence about education practice and policy. Because the site is part of a network of IES-related sites, we are a bit more optimistic than we might otherwise be about the attention the site will receive.

THE WWC TOPICS AND WORKFLOW

The WWC's production process differs somewhat for each kind of WWC report because each type has a different function. Nonetheless, WWC aims to be as attentive to quality and as transparent as possible. Most important, the workflow includes quality control at repeated definable points.

At the first stage of the WWC's workflow, people submit their opinions about what topics, interventions, or studies ought to be reviewed by the WWC. The people who make submissions include anybody—parents, teachers, executives in publishing houses, researchers, or other individuals or organizations who have an interest in discerning what works or who might benefit or suffer from a WWC review or what works.

The candidate topics are nominated in professorial forums to which WWC contributes, and through the WWC's website. An internal electronic registry of nominations has been set up.

The WWC's choice of a particular topic for review depends on (a) the relevance of the topic to current education policy and practice, (b) the topic's probable importance in decisions about what interventions can be adopted, and (c) the level of evidence available. These are complex interrelated criteria. Reaching decisions has involved assuring that different prospective users of information weigh in on the information they want: policymakers, practitioners, and researchers. The choices of topics in the short term are published on the WWC website so that people can comment on them (quality control of a sort) and understand the expected products (transparency). As of August 2005, the topics for review include Elementary-School Math, Middle-School Math, Dropout Prevention, Adult Literacy, Character Education, Beginning Reading, English Language Learning, and Early Childhood Education.

A WWC review on an intervention area begins with an exquisitely detailed protocol that defines the intervention and inclusionary criteria, the target population including high-risk subpopulations, the outcome variables that are pertinent, and the study designs that are eligible or ineligible for a WWC review of any kind. The protocol's ingredients are to be summarized on the WWC website, partly to assure quality and transparency. The WWC's process for generating a review in a particular intervention area continues with worldwide web literature searches, which do not suffice, and full-text readings of published and unpublished reports. Outcome studies that depended solely on testimonials or simple correlations are eliminated at the outset. Randomized trials and high-end quasi-experiments on relevant interventions were admitted to candidacy for WWC review.

Once the studies are identified, the coding process depends on double coding certain characteristics of each study, beginning with basic categorical distinction between randomized trials and quasi-experimental designs such as regression-discontinuity. For each category of study, characteristics that influence internal validity are identified. For instance, a randomized trial that has large difference in the attrition rate between intervention arms could be downgraded to quasi-experimental status absent other information that speaks to the biases that attrition engenders. Some of the ingredients of the standards, such as the questions on attrition, are critical in making judgments about the study.

Characteristics of studies are double coded by two independent coders to assure that coding reliability can be estimated. Differences of opinion in coding are adjudicated by a principal investigator and a project coordinator. Principal investigators provide substantive expertise to teams that do the coding and guide decisions that depend on the particular topic being examined. Some people might expect that adjudication issues are few and take little time. That has not been the case. Adjudicating ambiguities in a report from a peer-reviewed journal can easily take hours. Because standards of reporting research in journals have changed, and because the WWC may cover up to 20 years of preceding research in a review area, the number of adjudicated cases can be large.

Results of coding are linked to information that appears in the study and justifies the particular code. The guidelines for collecting study sample details during the coding process are based partly on the CONSORT statement about reporting on randomized trials (Altman et al., 2001).

Because combining studies in an Intervention Report requires substantive expertise, the principal investigators and the relevant WWC review team are engaged early in the report's production. This includes the protocol stage, of course. More important, it involves their quality control over and provision of guidance in combining the assembly of studies and in analysis of results. The body of the Intervention Report summarizes Study Reports and explains how they were uncovered and why they are dependable sources of information or not. The Intervention Reports' conclusions—including key findings, their generalizability, and gaps in the evidence—are reviewed independently by the WWC Steering Committee, members of the independent WWC Technical Advisory Group, and anonymous peer reviewers.

CONCLUDING REMARKS

The Institute of Education Sciences' What Works Clearinghouse is unprecedented in its focus on the quality of evidence that is generated about the effects of education interventions and its focus on scientific standards in making judgments about evidence quality. It is also unprecedented, in education, for operationalizing standards that are as public and transparent as possible. It is unprecedented in having to create an organization, processes and procedures, and teams of people that are essential in developing reviews.

Despite lack of precedent, the IES's Clearinghouse depends on experience and advances in building scientific knowledge. This includes work over the last 3 decades on randomized trials so as to produce unbiased estimates of the relative effects of interventions. It includes scientific work over roughly the same period—in health care, criminology, and welfare, as well as education—to understand how to summarize the results of studies uniformly and against clear standards.

The aims are high and the products important. In identifying what works, the Clearinghouse will help us, as a fine aphorism suggests, to "Test all things and hold fast to that which is good."

ACKNOWLEDGMENT

The What Works Clearinghouse is funded through a contract from the U.S. Department of Education Institute of Education Sciences to the Campbell Collaboration–American Institutes for Research, a Joint Venture. This report is about the facts on the Clearinghouse. The personal views expressed in this paper do not necessarily agree with the views of the Department, nor do they necessarily disagree.

REFERENCES

Altman, D. G., Schulz, K. F., Moher, D., Egger, M., Davidoff, F., Elbourne, D., et al. (2001). The revised CONSORT Statement for Reporting Randomized Trials. *Annals of Internal Medicine, 134*(8), 663–694.

Boruch, R.F. (1997). *Randomized experiments for planning and evaluation: A practical guide*. Thousand Oaks, CA: Sage.

Chalmers, I. (2003) Trying to do more good than harm: The role of rigorous, transparent, up-to-date evaluations. *Annals of the American Academy of Political and Social Sciences*, 589, 22–40.

Cooper, H. (1998). *Synthesizing research: A guide for literature reviews*. Thousand Oaks, CA: Sage.

Duncan, G. J., Magnuson, K. A., Ludwig, J. (2004). The endogeneity problem in developmental studies. *Research in Human Development, 1*(1&2), 59–80.

Halvorsen, K. T. (1994). The reporting format. In H. Cooper & L. Hedges (Eds.), *Handbook of research synthesis* (pp. 425–438). New York: Sage.

Herman, R., Aladjem, D., McMahon, P., Masem, E., Mulligan, I., O'Malley, A., et al. (1999). *An educators' guide to schoolwide reform*. Washington, DC: American Institutes for Research.

Lipsey, M.W., & Wilson, D.B. (2001). Practical meta-analysis. Thousand Oaks, CA: Sage.

Moher, D., Cook, D. J., Eastwood, S., Olkin, I., Rennie, D., & Stroup, D.T. (1999). *Improving the quality of reports of meta-analyses of randomised controlled trials: The QUORUM Statement. Lancet, 354*(27), 1896–1900.

Mosteller, F., & Boruch, R. (2002). *Evidence matters: Randomized trials in educational research*. Washington, DC: Brookings Institution Press.

Sherman, L. W. (Ed.). (2003). Misleading evidence and evidence-led policy: Making social science more experimental. *Annals of the American Academy of Political and Social Science, 589*(1), 6–19.

Turner, H., Boruch, R., Petrosino, A., Lavenberg, J., de Moya, D., & Rothstein, H. (2003). Populating an international web-based randomized trials register in the social, behavioral, criminological, and education sciences. *Annals of the American Academy of Political and Social Sciences, 589*(1), 203–223.

Valentine, J., & Cooper, H. (2003). *What Works Clearinghouse Study Design and Implementation Assessment Device (Version 1.0)*. Washington, DC: U.S. Department of Education.

U. S. Department of Education, Institute of Education Sciences (2003a). *Random assignment in program valuation and intervention research: Questions and answers*. Washington DC: Author.

U. S. Department of Education, Institute of Education Sciences (2003b). *Identifying and implementing educational practices supported by rigorous evidence: A user friendly guide*. Washington DC: Author.

CHAPTER 12

CONCLUSIONS AND RECOMMENDATIONS

Herbert J. Walberg and Rena F. Subotnik

The conferees met seven times to set forth conclusions and recommendations based on the preliminary, precirculated versions of the chapters and the participants' own expertise and experience. Smaller work groups met several times to formulate consensual recommendations to present at the last plenary session of the conference. Not every participant agreed on every point, but several points gained consensus. This concluding chapter summarizes the largely agreed-upon recommendations as well as dissenting views. We have felt free to consolidate duplicative recommendations from the separate small group notes, reorganize the material, use our own words, and explain points that might seem overly terse outside the conference deliberations.

QUALITY OF RESEARCH

The standards of education research should be raised, and researchers should better address important questions of education policy and practice. Randomized, control-group experiments are most definitive in probing causal assertions, which should serve as one of the bases of K–12

The Scientific Basis of Educational Productivity, 283–290

education practice and policy along with costs and other practical considerations. Other forms of research, however, can supplement and complement randomized experiments. Compared with randomized experiments, these other forms of research have some distinctive advantages and disadvantages worth enumerating and considering.

1. *Quasi-experiments*: These designs use preconstituted groups and are usually much less expensive and easier to do than experiments because they do not require arbitrarily reassigning students to groups. For this reason, quasi-experiments may also enable investigators to make their findings more generally applicable by studying different kinds of students in a great variety of school conditions. Quasi-experiments may also be more realistic because, by their nature, experiments are contrived and may lead to Hawthorne or "hothouse" effects. But quasi-experiments may be less causally definitive than randomized experiments because the groups may differ substantially in various known and unknown ways before the study starts.

2. *Formative research*: Engineering and garage experimentation, as in the case of the first Apple computer, follow a rich tradition of pragmatism that remains vibrant today. The Wright brothers did not use randomized experiments leading up to the first human flight. As they tinkered with various wing configurations and other plane variations, they gradually added improvements as they gained information from failures as well as successes.

Similarly, behaviorists have long carried out rigorous research on one individual at a time and have shown sharp differences in behavior between alternating experimental control periods. With this design, large and obvious effects make statistical inferences unnecessary. Particularly in the development of computer-based instruction programs, such "formative research" rather than experiments is in order. But these programs may require later experimentation, independent of the developers, to establish their efficacy.

3. *Observations*: Observations can lead to fruitful hypotheses for testing in experiments and other research designs. Reflecting a long-lived precedent in science, "outlier studies" of exceptionally high- or low-performing individuals, organizations, or even countries may prove particularly fruitful. For example, the famous 1983 report *A Nation at Risk* stimulated interest in Japanese schools, which produce high achievement at comparatively low costs. The report's background papers and subsequent research on Japanese schools revealed features that explained their productivity: intensive maternal support of their children's studies; a school year of 240 days in contrast to the usual 180 in the United States; a nationwide curriculum; competitive examinations for admission to mid-

dle schools, high schools, and colleges; the prevalence of private tutoring schools; and knowledgeable teachers.

Observations of experiments themselves may also be fruitful, particularly for investigating whether or not programs have been well or poorly implemented. Perhaps, for example, a new practice or policy was poorly applied or even remained largely unapplied, which might account for no differences among experimental and control groups. Even well-demonstrated practices may require observation to monitor how well they are being used. But observational research usually cannot stand on its own in making causal inferences. Aside from possible observer bias, observations are costly and, therefore, limited in number and generalizability.

4. *Regression analysis*: Economists and policy analysts have a long tradition of inferring causality from analyses of nonexperimental data, which they use partly because they cannot, for example, randomly change currency values and tax policies. They can, however, include and test rival hypotheses in regression equations to test their validity.

Still, analyses done by economists and policy analysts may depend heavily on theories and assumptions that lack evidence and consensus. For this reason, these analysts increasingly turn to experimentation when policy questions are sufficiently important, such as in welfare reform and job training. They can also make use of "natural experiments," such as in the case of oversubscribing students lotteried in and out of charter schools and voucher programs.

5. *Cost effectiveness*: Even statistically "significant" programs may have such small effects, high costs, or implementation difficulties that they make a poor choice for continuation and expansion. A "decision tree" may be helpful in making explicit such considerations when coming to major decisions. Thus, the size of policy, program, and practice effects should be weighed against but not necessarily dominated by costs, including training and other requirements. Chosen programs should be both efficient and effective.

6. *Consumer research*: Several conferees held that, because educators and clients may not be well informed about risks and outcomes, their opinions should not be designated as rigorous or even relevant. Still, many human contacts in free societies involve voluntary transactions determined by lay opinions and partial knowledge. Thus, in evaluating charter schools, investigators, policymakers, parents, and others might greatly value information about both achievement effects and parental satisfaction.

7. *Synthesis research*: In education, a single study should rarely be the sole basis for conclusions, recommendations, and decisions. For this reason, the What Works Clearinghouse holds great promise for meta-ana-

lyzing many high-quality studies to come to relatively definitive findings, particularly about the size and consistency of achievement effects. Summaries and critical reviews of studies are also valuable, particularly if they can reasonably conclude that findings from a variety of studies in several of the categories already mentioned lead to the same conclusion. Actually, a substantial corpus of such extant research is ready for such syntheses, both for application to K–12 education and as a basis for future research.

A single investigation may combine two or more of these methods. Observations, for example, may illuminate experiments; cost data may be simultaneously gathered to inform decision making. In addition, programs of sequential research may efficiently yield great benefits. Syntheses, for instance, may suggest hypotheses that lead to formative studies of an idea, followed by an experiment to test its field efficacy in ideal circumstances, followed by consumer research and quasi-experiments to probe its attractiveness to users and its effectiveness for various students in a variety of circumstances.

RESEARCH QUESTIONS

Before collecting data, some questions are generally applicable to many areas of education research:

1. What is the problem? What is the nature of the problem? How severe is it? What is the context of the problem?
2. Who thinks so? Why? Have they thought comprehensively about the problem?
3. What considerations may have been omitted or slighted?
4. How does the problem affect service delivery and outcomes?
5. What are the exceptions to the problem? Do they suggest solutions? What do professional judgments suggest?
6. What does extant research indicate? How well? What are the gaps in knowledge?
7. What are the most promising solutions to be investigated?

These questions can be even more important than the choice of methodology and rigor of investigations: better an approximate answer to the right question than a precise answer to the wrong question. Clear questions, moreover, can lead to clear conclusions, and the means of investigation should be guided by the questions asked and the body of extant knowledge available.

QUESTION ORIGINS

Questions might originate with policymakers, educators, or investigators. Motivated by the problems and questions of educators, for example, educational psychologists derive principles from psychology and help apply them to educational practice. This is a tricky and difficult business: we all seem cursed by insufficient time, and psychologists and educators (and undoubtedly others) do not ordinarily read each other's literatures and may not even speak to one another. The field of psychology is splintered; hence, educational psychologists themselves pursue such narrow specializations as measurement, motivation, and instruction. Similar to other academics, educational psychologists may tend to know more and more about less and less.

The following personal anecdote illustrates the problem even within a single organization. A former secretary of education asked Walberg to investigate the possible relation of policy and research in the U.S. Department of Education. Interviews with the assistant secretaries, the staff, and the research division of the National Institute of Education and of the division heads of elementary secondary, higher, special, and bilingual education revealed little correspondence between the research questions being pursued and the questions policymakers were asking. What should be done about this disconnect?

POSSIBLE RESEARCH–POLICY–PRACTICE LINKS

Professional organizations that include more than 2.5 million members do or potentially can reduce the research gap. They include the two very large teachers unions as well as such member groups as the National Association of Secondary School Principals, the Education Commission of the States, the Association for Supervision and Curriculum Development, the American Psychological Association, and Educational Leaders Council. In addition to local, state, and national conferences, these organizations publish books, magazines, and pamphlets, and disseminate research and ideas. The U.S. and state departments of education and larger school districts make research information available. The American Legislative Exchange Council, the Brookings Institution, the Hoover Institution, and the Heartland Institute carry out and make available policy research, with Congress and state legislators as their intended audience.

Yet the gap remains and, in some instances, educators and their organizations have promoted policies and practices based on inadequate and nonindependent research. What can be done? What new and provocative ideas should be considered?

Education policy analysts sometimes look to the medical model. Although it took centuries to accomplish, physicians are educated not only in evidence-based procedures but also in their evidentiary basis. Increasingly, physicians can draw upon broad meta-analyses of many studies conducted throughout the world. For problems for which they are unfamiliar, they can make use of such publications as the *Merck Manual* and more specialized handbooks on diagnosis and treatment.

In medicine, multiple randomized experiments with placebos and other features help enable confident causal inferences. When experiments cannot be performed, physicians and public health officials can found practice and policy on the work of biostatisticians and epidemiologists who carry out statistically controlled studies, as in econometric research. Physicians and hospitals can be sued for malpractice or violating the evidence-based standards of practice. Increasingly, various consumer organizations rate hospitals and physicians. Medicine is increasingly incentivized and sanctioned.

Still, medicine is different from education in many ways, including medicine's longevity as a scientific field, the size of research funding, and the constraints faced. In addition, pharmaceutical firms sponsor medical research, which may not be entirely independent and objective, especially when researchers work for or own firms. Holding up medicine as the model for education argues by analogy rather than evidence of success. Skepticism and open-mindedness seem in order.

Even so, it seems reasonable for undergraduate majors in education, similar to medical students, to know not only about research conclusions but also how evidence is gathered and analyzed; they should become critical consumers of research. Graduate programs might foster completion of small studies and the critical syntheses of research on a given topic. One working group of conferees went so far as to say that teacher tenure and merit raises should be granted partly on syntheses and successful applications of research.

Another provocative and possibly useful analogy is the behavior of business firms and markets. The problem in education is "disseminating" research. The problem for firms is retaining proprietary trade secrets. Firms are driven by market competition and conduct formative research and market surveys; they try to favorably "brand" their products and services.

The federal No Child Left Behind Act and state legislation lead to the closing of failing schools and opening up competition to charter schools and other forms of privatization. Under such régimes, for-profit educational management organizations such as Edison Schools carry out substantial formative and experimental research on the effectiveness of their methods. They are more likely than conventional public schools to carry out market research and "brand" their offerings. Such research may create tighter links between research and practices than those used in public schools. Again, open-mindedness and skepticism are in order.

KNOW THAT, KNOW HOW, CAN DO

To increase knowledge utilization, investigators and educators must somehow collaborate or at least communicate. A 1960s answer was dubbed "action research," a strategy in which educators themselves simultaneously did research and put it into practice. Perhaps because of the difficulty of doing two things well and the increasing division of labor in modern societies, action research fizzled and was characterized as being neither action nor research.

In view of the continuing difficulties of research collaboration, the mid-Atlantic Laboratory for Student Success, one of the conference sponsors, adopted at its inception the motto "Know That, Know How, Can Do." It is intended to suggest the acquisition and knowledge of evidenced-based principles; the general knowledge of putting them in practice; and, distinctively, how practical educators can suit them to their own purposes, students, and conditions.

The conference itself exemplifies the motto's application. Eminent scholars from around the country write authoritative "Know That" chapters summarizing the principles from an area of research, in the present case methods of research themselves. They meet together with parents, educators, leaders of Washington-area organizations, and federal agencies to discuss "Know How" or how the principles can be generally used as well as "Can Do" or how the principles can best be suited to the educators' particular students, purposes, needs, and circumstances.

All three sets of conference ideas are shared, first, in a promptly published pamphlet-sized publication called *The LSS Review* and on the Internet. Later, taking into consideration discussion of policy leaders' and educators' concerns and insights, the authors revise their educator-informed "Know That" chapters for the published book, and further conferences take place led by one or more of the original conferees and geared even more to educators and policymakers informed by "Know That" but focused more on "Know How" and "Can Do."

Thus, the conference on which the book is based benefited greatly from the precirculated conference papers. The small-group discussions among investigators and educators yielded insights for both. A much larger group benefited from the quickly distributed *LSS Review*, which summarized the papers. And, as a result of the conference deliberations, the authors improved their papers that constitute the chapters in this book. We hope readers may find in them insights for helping to enlarge the scientific basis of educational productivity.

ABOUT THE CONTRIBUTORS

ABOUT THE EDITORS

Rena F. Subotnik began her position as director of the Center for Psychology in Schools and Education at the American Psychological Association (APA) in January 2002. Before coming to the APA, Subotnik was a professor of education at Hunter College, where she coordinated the secondary education program and served as research and curriculum liaison to the Hunter College laboratory schools (grades pre-K–12). In 1997–1998, Subotnik was an APA Congressional fellow in child policy with U.S. Senator Jeff Bingaman, a member of the Senate Health, Education, Labor and Pensions committee. Her fellowship assignment involved drafting and promoting legislation related to teacher quality, which passed as a component of Title II of the Higher Education Act in 1998. Since the fellowship, Subotnik has been actively involved in the community of scholars and practitioners concerned about federal policy related to teacher education. Subotnik has been awarded grants from the McDonnell Foundation, Institute for Education Sciences, Jack Kent Cooke Foundation, Camille and Henry Dreyfus Foundation, National Science Foundation, U.S. Department of Education Javits Program, and Spencer Foundation.

Herbert J. Walberg is university scholar and emeritus research professor of education and psychology at the University of Illinois at Chicago (UIC) and a principal investigator and long-time collaborator with the Laboratory of Student Success at Temple University. He is also distinguished visiting fellow (1999–2005) at Stanford University Hoover Institution, where he serves on the Koret Task Force on K–12 Education. He also serves on several charitable and educational boards. Holding a PhD from the University of Chicago and formerly an assistant professor at Harvard University, he has written and edited more than 75 books and has written about 425 articles on educational effectiveness, exceptional accomplishments, and related topics. Among Walberg's latest books are the *International Encyclopedia of Educational Evaluation*, *Psychology and Educational Practice*, and *New Directions for Teaching Practice and Research*. Elected fellow of the American Association for the Advancement of Science, American Psychological Association, and the Royal Statistical Society, Walberg is also a fellow and vice president of the International Academy of Education, headquartered in Brussels, Belgium. For the academy, he edits a booklet series on effective educational practices. For the U.S. Department of Education and the National Science Foundation, Walberg carried out comparative research in Japanese and American schools. For the U.S. Department of State and the White House, he organized a radio series and book about American education that was distributed in 74 countries. Walberg chaired the Scientific Advisory Group for the Paris-based Organization for Economic Cooperation and Development project on international educational indicators. He also advised UNESCO and the government officials of Australia, Israel, Italy, Japan, Sweden, and the United Kingdom on education policy and practice. Walberg served on the National Assessment Governing Board. He is a board member of the Chicago Charter School Foundation, which governs the largest public charter school in the United States, with more than 6,000 largely poor and minority students on nine campuses.

ABOUT THE CHAPTER AUTHORS

Robert F. Boruch is University Trustee Chair Professor, Graduate School of Education and the Statistics Department Wharton School; codirector, Center for Research and Evaluation of Social Policy; and codirector, Policy Research, Evaluation, and Measurement Program at the University of Pennsylvania. He earned his PhD in psychology from Iowa State University. Before coming to the University of Pennsylvania in 1989, Boruch was a member of Northwestern University's faculty. He serves on the board of trustees for the W.T. Grant Foundation; the board of directors for the American Institutes for Research; and advisory committees for the U.S. Department of Education, U.S. General Accounting Office, and other federal agencies. He is a fellow of the American Academy of Arts and Sciences and the American Statistical Association. Boruch's research involves determining the severity and scope of social and educational problems, implementing programs and policies, and estimating the effects and effectiveness of interventions. He contributes to work on randomized trials in education and training, welfare reform, health services, housing, and crime and justice, with a particular interest in the assessment or improvement of programs sponsored by federal governments in the United States and abroad and by private foundations. Current projects include the Third International Science and Mathematics Study; International Campbell Collaboration on Systematic Reviews; place-based randomized field experiments; and record systems, survey systems, field trials, and their linkage.

Diane F. Halpern is a professor of psychology and director of the Berger Institute for Work, Family, and Children at Claremont McKenna College. She has won many awards for her teaching and research, including the 2002 Outstanding Professor Award from the Western Psychological Association, 1999 American Psychological Foundation Award for Distinguished Teaching, 1996 Distinguished Career Award for Contributions to Education given by the American Psychological Association (APA), California State University's State-Wide Outstanding Professor Award, Outstanding Alumna Award from the University of Cincinnati, Silver Medal Award from the Council for the Advancement and Support of Education, Wang Family Excellence Award, and G. Stanley Hall Lecture Award from the APA. She is the author of several books, including *Thought and Knowledge: An Introduction to Critical Thinking* (4th ed., 2003), *Thinking Critically About Critical Thinking* (with Heidi Riggio, 2003), and *From Work–Family Balance to Work–Family Interaction: Changing the Metaphor* (2004; coedited with Susan Murphy). Halpern has served as president of the Western Psychological Association, Society for the Teaching of Psychology, and Division of General Psychology of the APA. She cochaired the Education Work Group of the American Psychological Society with Milton Hakel. She recently chaired a conference on "Applying the Science of Learning to the University and Beyond: Cognitive, Social, and Motivational Factors," which was funded by the Spencer Foundation and Marshall-Reynolds Trust. She presented the outcomes from the conference to the White House Office of Science and Technology and the Science Committee of the U.S. House of Representatives. Halpern was the 2004 president of the APA.

Rebecca Herman holds an MA and PhD in sociology from Johns Hopkins University. She is a principal research scientist at American Institutes for Research in Washington, DC, specializes in evaluating, designing, and conducting research on educational improvement, setting standards for the quality of educational research, and reviewing research based on those standards. As the project director for the What Works Clearinghouse (WWC), she is responsible for the U.S. Department of Education's flagship project to set standards for educational research and use those standards to identify effective educational programs, practices, and approaches. She was also project director of the *Educators' Guide to Schoolwide Reform*, which provided a critical look at the research and implementation of the most prominent and promising comprehensive school reform efforts in this country and developed standards for the quality of research on comprehensive school reform. She also conducts original research on comprehensive school reform and other strategies for improving K–12 education. She is principal investigator of the National Longitudinal Evaluation of Comprehensive School Reform (NLECSR), a large-scale quantitative and qualitative study of the effects of national school improvement efforts and the single largest federal investment in studying whole-school reform efforts and their impact on student achievement.

Michael L. Kamil is a professor in the Stanford School of Education, where he is a member of the Psychological Studies in Education Committee and on the faculty of the Learning, Design, and Technology Program. He has been a principal investigator for the Laboratory for Student Success at the Temple University Center for Research in Human Development and Education for almost 5 years. He is an accomplished researcher who has published a vast amount of work in the field of reading instruction, literacy, and technology use in reading. He is well versed in research methods and policy and their implications for education. He has been editor of *Reading Research Quarterly*, *Journal of Reading Behavior*, and *The Yearbook of The National Reading Conference*. He currently serves on the editorial advisory boards for all of the major reading research journals including *the Journal of Educational Psychology*. He was the lead editor for the *Handbook of Reading Research*, Vol. III and is the managing editor for Vol. IV. He was a member of the National Reading Panel and the RAND Corporation Reading Study Group, and currently is a member of the National Literacy Panel, synthesizing research reading on language minority students. He is Chair of the Planning Committee for the 2009 National Assessment of Educational Progress. Kamil is a member of numerous research, professional, and educational organizations, including the American Psychological Association, the American Educational Research Association, the International Reading Association and the National Reading Conference.

Thomas R. Kratochwill received his PhD in educational psychology from the University of Wisconsin–Madison in 1973 with a specialization in school psychology. He joined the faculty at the University of Arizona in 1973 in the Department of Educational Psychology. In 1983, he returned to the University of Wisconsin–Madison to direct the school psychology program and the Psychoeducational Clinic. He currently serves director of the Educational and Psychological Training Center, an interdisciplinary unit for clinical and research training for counseling psychology, rehabilitation psychology and special education, and school psychology. Currently, he is codirector of the Child and Adolescent Mental Health and Education Resource Center. Kratochwill has been an active researcher and contributor to the scientific psychological literature in a number of areas. He is the author of more than 150 journal articles, book chapters, and monographs. He has written or edited 25 books and has made more than 100 presentations at professional meetings. Kratochwill's research has received recognition from national and state organizations. In 1977, he received the Lightner Witner Award from Division 16 of the American Psychological Association (APA). He received the Outstanding Research Contributions Award from the Arizona State Psychological Association in 1981, and an award for Outstanding Contributions to the Advancement of Scientific Knowledge in Psychology from the Wisconsin Psychological Association in 1995. He was the recipient of the Senior Scientist Award from Division 16 of the APA in 1995 and the Jack Bardon Distinguished Achievement Award in 2005. In 1995, the Wisconsin Psychological Association selected his research for its Margaret Bernauer Psychology Research Award and, in 1996 and 2001, the APA Division 16 journal *School Psychology Quarterly* selected one of his articles as best research of the year. He received the Distinguished Service Award from the School of Education at the University of Wisconsin–Madison. He has been associate editor of *Behavior Therapy, The Journal of Applied Behavior Analysis*, and *School Psychology Review* as well as a guest editor of *Behavioral Assessment*. He was selected as the founding editor of the APA Division 16 journal *School Psychology Quarterly* from 1984 to 1992. He is coeditor of the special section of *School Psychology Quarterly* devoted to evidence-based intervention research. He is also past president of the Society for the Study of School Psychology and cochair of the Task Force on Evidence-Based Interventions in School Psychology.

T.V. Joe Layng cofounded Headsprout and serves as senior scientist, where he led the scientific team that developed Headsprout's patented Generative Learning Technology. This technology forms the basis of the company's Headsprout Early Reading program, for which Layng was the chief architect. From 1991 to 1996, Layng was the director of the Academic Support Center and then dean of Public Agency and Special Training Programs at Malcolm X College in Chicago. While there, Layng founded the Personalized Curriculum Institute (PCI), which rapidly equips underprepared students with the skills needed for college success, and worked with the Chicago Public Schools and the Chicago White Sox Charities to bring research-based instruction to Chicago's schools. Layng has more than 25 years of experience in the experimental analysis of behavior and the learning sciences in a wide variety of settings, both laboratory and applied. He earned a PhD in behavioral science (biopsychology) from the University of Chicago, where he performed basic research and developed some of the key elements upon which the Headsprout Generative Learning Technology is based. Layng is a frequently sought-after speaker and has published on a wide variety of research, conceptual, clinical, and social topics.

Kathleen Madigan serves as president of the American Board for the Certification of Teacher Excellence. The American Board is dedicated to increasing the number of highly qualified teachers available to schools across the country through the Passport to Teaching certification program. The American Board is also developing the Master Teacher certification, which will recognize teachers of proven effectiveness. As vice president for Instruction and Behavior at Advantage Schools, a company that specialized in charter school management and direct instruction, Madigan was responsible for shaping and implementing the curriculum, behavior management, and staff development at 16 charter schools. Madigan has also been an assistant dean of education at the University of Oregon, where her duties included work as a liaison from the university to the state's Teacher Standards and Practice Commission as well as oversight for graduate education programs. Madigan has been a regular and special education classroom teacher, principal, college professor, curriculum coordinator, and research project director. She is experienced in the field of neurological health care and administration. As regional vice president for Learning Services Corp., Madigan managed a post-acute traumatic brain injury rehabilitation center and conducted research in memory and learning. Before that, she directed an adult psychiatric program with direct responsibility for supervision of medical and clinical staff. Regarded as an expert in effective instruction and behavior management, she has conducted more than 400 workshops to improve schoolwide, individual teacher, and leadership practices throughout the United States and Canada. Madigan's recent accomplishments include an appointment by Governor Paul Cellucci of Massachusetts to serve on a five-person Education Management Audit Council, which operates as the independent oversight board for educational accountability in the state.

Susan J. Paik is an associate professor at Claremont Graduate University in the School of Educational Studies. Her research interests include urban and international studies, K–12 educational productivity, family–school partnerships, minority talent development and learning, and research methods. She has participated in education projects in Africa, Asia, Central America, Europe, and the United States, where she founded and directed a character-development program for inner-city youth. Paik has presented her work at the annual meetings of the American Educational Research Association (AERA), Oxford University in England, University of Cape Town in South Africa, University of Bologna in Italy, and University of Oviedo in Spain, and professional meetings in South America, Australia, Germany, and the United States. She has been a fellow of the National Institute of Mental Health and the Center for Urban Educational Research and Development, and has received prestigious awards, grants (i.e., AERA), and scholarships, including the Teaching Incentive Award, Chancellor's Award, and Early Outreach Award for her dedication to inner-city youth, and was designated as a Young Scholar by the Koret K–12 Task Force at Stanford University. Paik has written numerous publications, including "Educational Productivity in South Korea and the United States," a research monograph published by the *International Journal of Educational Research*. She is the editor of *Advancing Educational Productivity: Policy Implications from National Databases*. She is also a coauthor of a booklet called *Effective Educational Practices*, which has been translated and disseminated to almost 200 countries by UNESCO Publications, and she is presently working on a book on minority youth, families, and schooling.

Elizabeth S. Pang received her BA in English from the University of Oxford, England. She has an MA and PhD in Educational Linguistics from Stanford University. While at Stanford, she was a research assistant to the National Reading Panel synthesizing research on the education and professional development of reading teachers. Among her publications on reading and literacy are studies of children's comprehension of hypertext, teacher professional development, bilingual reading development, and use of technology in teacher education. She coauthored a monograph on effective reading instruction for the International Bureau of Education of the United Nations Educational, Scientific and Cultural Organization (UNESCO). She was an English teacher and curriculum developer in Singapore and has worked extensively with literacy teachers. Her research examines the cross-linguistic transfer of reading skills in bilingual children. She is currently Assistant Director of Languages and Literature at the Ministry of Education in Singapore.

Robert J. Sternberg is now dean of arts and sciences at Tufts University, and a principal investigator at the Laboratory for Student Success at Temple University. He was the 2003 president of the American Psychological Association. Before moving to Tufts, he was IBM Professor of Psychology and Education and director of the Center for the Psychology of Abilities, Competencies, and Expertise at Yale University. Sternberg received his BA summa cum laude, Phi Beta Kappa, from Yale University in 1972 and his PhD from Stanford University in 1975. He also holds honorary doctorates from five European universities. Sternberg is the author of more than 1,000 articles, chapters, and books, and has received more than $20 million in grants and contracts for his research. The central focus of his research is intelligence, creativity, and wisdom, and he also has studied love and close relationships as well as hate. His research has been conducted on five different continents. Sternberg has won many awards for his work and is most well known for his theory of successful intelligence, investment theory of creativity (developed with Todd Lubart), theory of thinking styles as mental self-government, balance theory of wisdom, triangular theory of love, and theory of love as a story.

Greg Stikeleather is president and CEO and a cofounder of Headsprout, a learning sciences company. He and was previously a managing director at Sofinnova Ventures. Over the prior decade, Stikeleather successfully led, as CEO, two venture-backed, high-tech companies: Aha! Software and Portola Communications. Both companies produced successful technology and products and were acquired by Microsoft and Netscape, respectively. Headsprout brings Stikeleather back to his learning science and education roots. Stikeleather was trained in the learning sciences with a graduate degree in experimental psychology from Northeastern University and a BS, summa cum laude, in behavior analysis from Western Michigan University. He was a member of one of the first groups of American behavioral scientists to visit and study the political and social processes of mainland China. While at Northeastern University, Stikeleather collaborated with Murray Sidman and others in the early groundbreaking basic research on stimulus equivalence, or how humans come to form classes of equivalent meanings. Stikeleather focused on how carefully analyzed program sequences could affect such relations. In the early 1980s, Stikeleather applied his learning science training as an instructional and user interface designer for Apple Computer, where he developed and ran the first usability testing laboratory. Stikeleather assisted Apple in meeting its goal to get novice users up and going in 20 minutes or less using Apple's first graphical user interface.

Lisa Towne is a senior program officer in the Center for Education at the National Research Council (NRC) and adjunct instructor of statistics at the Johns Hopkins University Institute for Policy Studies. Her work at the NRC has focused on the nature of education research and its implications for evidence-based education policy. Towne was coeditor of a series the National Academies Press (NAP) publications, including *Scientific Research in Education* and *Advancing Scientific Research in Education*. She has presented findings from these reports at several national conferences and events, including giving congressional testimony at a 2002 hearing on the reauthorization of the U.S. Office of Educational Research and Improvement. Prior to joining the NRC, Towne was the assistant director for Social and Behavioral Sciences in the White House Office Of Science and Technology Policy, where she coordinated interagency research efforts in education and child health and provided guidance on the research evidence associated with policy proposals. Towne was also a presidential management fellow and social science analyst in the U.S. Department of Education's Planning and Evaluation Service, where she specialized in standards-based reform and public school choice programs. At Caliber Associates, a consulting firm in Virginia, she has conducted evaluation work for such federal agencies as the Head Start Bureau, the Office of Juvenile Justice and Delinquency Prevention, and the Department of Defense Education Activity. Towne has also been an adjunct instructor of quantitative methods at the Georgetown Public Policy Institute, where she received the GPPI Outstanding Faculty Member award in 2001. She has an MPP from Georgetown University and a BS in mathematics from the University of Vermont.

Janet S. Twyman, is the vice president of instructional development at Headsprout, where she significantly contributed to the development of Headsprout's Generative Learning Technology and led the effort to build that technology into a highly effective beginning reading program. Twyman developed the research methods and systems that led to Headsprout's groundbreaking scientific formative evaluation model of program development, coordinating all elements of instructional design, scripting, graphic creation, animation, sound engineering, story development and writing, software engineering, and usability testing within the research model. Twyman was formerly the executive director of the Fred S. Keller School, a model early childhood center, and an adjunct associate professor at Columbia University Teachers College. Twyman is a longtime advocate and investigator of research-based instruction and systems design. While at the Keller School and Columbia University, she conducted research and taught courses focusing on effective instruction, technology and education, teacher development, and systems approaches to effective education. She has published experimental studies with a particular emphasis on the verbal behavior of children and on topics of broader conceptual interest. She is a board member of several schools and organizations and is currently a member of the Executive Council of the Association for Behavior Analysis. In addition, she oversees the association's graduate program accreditation processes. Twyman earned her PhD from Columbia University Teachers College. She holds certification as an elementary and special education teacher and as a principal/school administrator.

Printed in the United States
62157LVS00002B/30

9 781593 114497